MYTHS and FACTS

A GUIDE TO THE
Arab-Israeli Conflict

By *Mitchell G. Bard*

American-**I**sraeli **C**ooperative **E**nterprise (AICE)

2810 Blaine Dr.
Chevy Chase, MD 20815

http://www.JewishVirtualLibrary.org

ISBN 0-9712945-4-2

Printed in the United States of America

American Israeli Cooperative Enterprise (AICE)
2810 Blaine Dr.
Chevy Chase, MD 20815
Tel. 301-565-3918
Fax. 301-587-9056
Email. mgbard@aol.com
http://www.JewishVirtualLibrary.org

Other studies available from AICE (all are now available on our web site)**:**

■ **Partners for Change:** How U.S.-Israel Cooperation Can Benefit America
■ **Learning Together:** Israeli Innovations In Education That Could Benefit Americans
■ **Breakthrough Dividend:** Israeli Innovations In Biotechnology That Could Benefit Americans
■ **Experience Counts:** Innovative Programs For The Elderly In Israel That Can Benefit Americans
■ **Building Bridges:** Lessons For America From Novel Israeli Approaches To Promote Coexistence
■ **Good Medicine:** Israeli Innovations In Health Care That Could Benefit Americans
■ **Rewriting History in Textbooks**
■ **On One Foot:** A Middle East guide for the perplexed or How to respond on your way to class, when your best friend joins an anti-Israel protest
■ **TENURED OR TENUOUS:** Defining the Role of Faculty in Supporting Israel on Campus

Production, new cover art and maps by North Market Street Graphics
Original Book Logo Design, Cover concept, Typography, Map Illustration: *Danakama / Nick Moscovitz / NYC*

Table of Contents

Preface

"The great enemy of truth is very often not the lie—deliberate, contrived and dishonest—but the myth—persistent, persuasive and repeated."

—President John F. Kennedy*

I am often asked to name the most prevalent myth about the Middle East. The answer is the suggestion, in one form or another, that Israelis do not want peace.

No one craves peace more desperately than Israelis, who have lived through seven wars and an ongoing campaign of terror for nearly six decades. This is why, as this book discusses, Israel has repeatedly sought compromises, often at great risk, that would bring an end to the conflict.

Each time a new peace initiative is launched, our hopes are raised that we will not need to publish another edition of *Myths and Facts,* which was first printed more than 40 years ago. We remain optimistic that Israel's neighbors will accept a Jewish state in their midst. In the meantime, old myths, including ancient blood libels, continue to be recycled and new calumnies promulgated. These must not be allowed to go unanswered.

Myths and Facts pulls no punches when it comes to addressing Israel's responsibility for events and policies that tarnish its image. Friends of Israel do not try to whitewash the truth, but they do try to put events in proper context. That is also our goal. When friends criticize Israel, it is because they want the country to be better. Israel's detractors do not have that goal; they are only interested in delegitimizing the country, placing a wedge between Israel and its allies, and working toward its destruction.

This new edition covers the basics of the history of the conflict and offers documented facts to respond to the most common myths. To learn more, visit our **Jewish Virtual Library (www.JewishVirtualLibrary. org),** where we continually update the online edition of *Myths,* archive material we could not fit in the book, and present key original documents. AICE is also pleased to offer Spanish, German, Portuguese, Russian, French, Swedish and Hebrew translations online. In addition, we have a listserv for weekly myths/facts and other periodic updates. To sign up, visit the News section of the Library.

*President John F. Kennedy, Commencement Address at Yale University, (June 11, 1962).

I would like to acknowledge the contributions of the distinguished group of past editors: Sheila Segal, Wolf Blitzer, Alan Tigay, Moshe Decter, M.J. Rosenberg, Jeff Rubin, Eric Rozenman, Lenny Davis and Joel Himelfarb. I would also like to thank Rafi Danziger, Rebecca Weiner, Isaac Wolf, David Shyovitz, Alden Oreck, Elihai Braun, Sarah Szymkowicz, Avi Hein, Joanna Sloame, Stephanie Persin, Ariel Scheib, and David Krusch for their invaluable assistance in the AICE editions.

AICE is especially grateful to the sponsors of this edition: the Harry and Jeanette Weinberg Foundation, and Evelyn and Dr. Shmuel Katz from Bal-Harbour Florida, who contributed in loving memory of the AUSCH and KATZ family members O.B.M. H.Y.D. who perished during the Holocaust in Europe. May their greatness be an inspiration to all people of good will.

"Facts are stubborn things," observed John Adams, "and whatever may be our wishes, our inclinations, or the dictates of our passion, they cannot alter the state of facts and evidence." The following pages lay out the stubborn facts about the Arab-Israeli conflict. They are the best weapons we have to insure that truth triumphs over myth.

Mitchell G. Bard
January 2006

1. Israel's Roots

MYTH

"The Jews have no claim to the land they call Israel."

FACT

A common misperception is that all the Jews were forced into the Diaspora by the Romans after the destruction of the Second Temple in Jerusalem in the year 70 C.E. and then, 1,800 years later, suddenly returned to Palestine demanding their country back. In reality, the Jewish people have maintained ties to their historic homeland for more than 3,700 years.

The Jewish people base their claim to the Land of Israel on at least four premises: 1) the Jewish people settled and developed the land; 2) the international community granted political sovereignty in Palestine to the Jewish people; 3) the territory was captured in defensive wars and 4) God promised the land to the patriarch Abraham.

Even after the destruction of the Second Temple in Jerusalem, and the beginning of the exile, Jewish life in the Land of Israel continued and often flourished. Large communities were reestablished in Jerusalem and Tiberias by the ninth century. In the 11th century, Jewish communities grew in Rafah, Gaza, Ashkelon, Jaffa and Caesarea. The Crusaders massacred many Jews during the 12th century, but the community rebounded in the next two centuries as large numbers of rabbis and Jewish pilgrims immigrated to Jerusalem and the Galilee. Prominent rabbis established communities in Safed, Jerusalem and elsewhere during the next 300 years.

By the early 19th century—years before the birth of the modern Zionist movement—more than 10,000 Jews lived throughout what is today Israel.[1] The 78 years of nation-building, beginning in 1870, culminated in the reestablishment of the Jewish State.

Israel's international "birth certificate" was validated by the promise of the Bible; uninterrupted Jewish settlement from the time of Joshua onward; the Balfour Declaration of 1917; the League of Nations Mandate, which incorporated the Balfour Declaration; the United Nations partition resolution of 1947; Israel's admission to the UN in 1949; the recognition of Israel by most other states; and, most of all, the society created by Israel's people in decades of thriving, dynamic national existence.

"Nobody does Israel any service by proclaiming its 'right to exist.'

Israel's right to exist, like that of the United States, Saudi Arabia and 152 other states, is axiomatic and unreserved. Israel's legitimacy is not suspended in midair awaiting acknowledgement. . . .

There is certainly no other state, big or small, young or old, that would consider mere recognition of its 'right to exist' a favor, or a negotiable concession."

—Abba Eban[2]

MYTH

"Palestine was always an Arab country."

FACT

The term "Palestine" is believed to be derived from the Philistines, an Aegean people who, in the 12th Century B.C.E.*, settled along the Mediterranean coastal plain of what are now Israel and the Gaza Strip. In the second century C.E., after crushing the last Jewish revolt, the Romans first applied the name *Palaestina* to Judea (the southern portion of what is now called the West Bank) in an attempt to minimize Jewish identification with the land of Israel. The Arabic word *"Filastin"* is derived from this Latin name.[3]

The Hebrews entered the Land of Israel about 1300 B.C.E., living under a tribal confederation until being united under the first monarch, King Saul. The second king, David, established Jerusalem as the capital around 1000 B.C.E. David's son, Solomon, built the Temple soon thereafter and consolidated the military, administrative and religious functions of the kingdom. The nation was divided under Solomon's son, with the northern kingdom (Israel) lasting until 722 B.C.E., when the Assyrians destroyed it, and the southern kingdom (Judah) surviving until the Babylonian conquest in 586 B.C.E. The Jewish people enjoyed brief periods of sovereignty afterward before most Jews were finally driven from their homeland in 135 C.E.

Jewish independence in the Land of Israel lasted for more than 400 years. This is much longer than Americans have enjoyed independence in what has become known as the United States.[4] In fact, if not for foreign conquerors, Israel would be more than 3,000 years old today.

Palestine was never an exclusively Arab country, although Arabic gradually became the language of most of the population after the Muslim invasions of the seventh century. No independent Arab or Palestinian

---

*We use B.C.E. (Before the Common Era) and C.E. (Common Era), because they are neutral terms for the periods traditionally labeled B.C. (Before Christ) and A.D. (Anno Domini—"Year of the Lord").

state ever existed in Palestine. When the distinguished Arab-American historian, Princeton University Prof. Philip Hitti, testified against partition before the Anglo-American Committee in 1946, he said: "There is no such thing as 'Palestine' in history, absolutely not."[5]

Prior to partition, Palestinian Arabs did not view themselves as having a separate identity. When the First Congress of Muslim-Christian Associations met in Jerusalem in February 1919 to choose Palestinian representatives for the Paris Peace Conference, the following resolution was adopted:

> We consider Palestine as part of Arab Syria, as it has never been separated from it at any time. We are connected with it by national, religious, linguistic, natural, economic and geographical bonds.[6]

In 1937, a local Arab leader, Auni Bey Abdul-Hadi, told the Peel Commission, which ultimately suggested the partition of Palestine: "There is no such country [as Palestine]! 'Palestine' is a term the Zionists invented! There is no Palestine in the Bible. Our country was for centuries part of Syria."[7]

The representative of the Arab Higher Committee to the United Nations submitted a statement to the General Assembly in May 1947 that said, "Palestine was part of the Province of Syria" and that, "politically, the Arabs of Palestine were not independent in the sense of forming a separate political entity." A few years later, Ahmed Shuqeiri, later the chairman of the PLO, told the Security Council: "It is common knowledge that Palestine is nothing but southern Syria."[8]

Palestinian Arab nationalism is largely a post-World War I phenomenon that did not become a significant political movement until after the 1967 Six-Day War and Israel's capture of the West Bank.

MYTH

"The Palestinians are descendants of the Canaanites and were in Palestine long before the Jews."

FACT

Palestinian claims to be related to the Canaanites are a recent phenomenon and contrary to historical evidence. The Canaanites disappeared from the face of the earth three millennia ago, and no one knows if any of their descendants survived or, if they did, who they would be.

Sherif Hussein, the guardian of the Islamic Holy Places in Arabia, said the Palestinians' ancestors had only been in the area for 1,000 years.[9] Even the Palestinians themselves have acknowledged their association with the region came long after the Jews. In testimony before the Anglo-American Committee in 1946, for example, they claimed a connection to Palestine of more than 1,000 years, dating back no further than the conquest of Muhammad's followers in the 7th century.[10] And that claim is also dubious. Over the last 2,000 years, there have been massive invasions (e.g., the Crusades) that killed off most of the local people, migrations, the plague, and other manmade or natural disasters. The entire local population was replaced many times over. During the British mandate alone, more than 100,000 Arabs emigrated from neighboring countries and are today considered Palestinians.

By contrast, no serious historian questions the more than 3,000-year-old Jewish connection to the Land of Israel, or the modern Jewish people's relation to the ancient Hebrews.

MYTH

"The Balfour Declaration did not give Jews a right to a homeland in Palestine."

FACT

In 1917, Britain issued the Balfour Declaration:

> His Majesty's Government views with favor the establishment in Palestine of a national home for the Jewish people, and will use their best endeavors to facilitate the achievement of this object, it being clearly understood that nothing shall be done which may prejudice the civil and religious rights of existing non-Jewish communities in Palestine or the rights and political status enjoyed by Jews in any other country.

The Mandate for Palestine included the Balfour Declaration. It specifically referred to "the historical connections of the Jewish people with Palestine" and to the moral validity of "reconstituting their National Home in that country." The term *"reconstituting"* shows recognition of the fact that Palestine had been the Jews' home. Furthermore, the British were instructed to "use their best endeavors to facilitate" Jewish immigration, to encourage settlement on the land and to "secure" the Jewish National Home. The word "Arab" does not appear in the Mandatory award.[11]

The Mandate was formalized by the 52 governments at the League of Nations on July 24, 1922.

MYTH

"The 'traditional position' of the Arabs in Palestine was jeopardized by Jewish settlement."

FACT

For many centuries, Palestine was a sparsely populated, poorly cultivated and widely-neglected expanse of eroded hills, sandy deserts and malarial marshes. As late as 1880, the American consul in Jerusalem reported the area was continuing its historic decline. "The population and wealth of Palestine has not increased during the last forty years," he said.[12]

The Report of the Palestine Royal Commission quotes an account of the Maritime Plain in 1913:

> The road leading from Gaza to the north was only a summer track suitable for transport by camels and carts...no orange groves, orchards or vineyards were to be seen until one reached [the Jewish village of] Yabna [Yavne]....Houses were all of mud. No windows were anywhere to be seen.... The ploughs used were of wood.... The yields were very poor.... The sanitary conditions in the village were horrible. Schools did not exist.... The western part, towards the sea, was almost a desert.... The villages in this area were few and thinly populated. Many ruins of villages were scattered over the area, as owing to the prevalence of malaria, many villages were deserted by their inhabitants.[13]

Surprisingly, many people who were not sympathetic to the Zionist cause believed the Jews would improve the condition of Palestinian Arabs. For example, Dawood Barakat, editor of the Egyptian paper *Al-Ahram,* wrote: "It is absolutely necessary that an entente be made between the Zionists and Arabs, because the war of words can only do evil. The Zionists are necessary for the country: The money which they will bring, their knowledge and intelligence, and the industriousness which characterizes them will contribute without doubt to the regeneration of the country."[14]

Even a leading Arab nationalist believed the return of the Jews to their homeland would help resuscitate the country. According to Sherif Hussein, the guardian of the Islamic Holy Places in Arabia:

> The resources of the country are still virgin soil and will be developed by the Jewish immigrants. One of the most amazing things until recent times was that the Palestinian used to leave his country, wandering over the high seas in every direction. His native soil could not retain a hold on him, though his ancestors had lived on it for 1000 years. At the same time we have seen the Jews from foreign countries streaming to Palestine from Russia, Germany, Austria, Spain, America. The cause of causes could not escape those who had a gift of deeper insight. They knew that the country was for its original sons (*abna 'ihilasliyin*), for all their differences, a sacred and beloved homeland. The return of these exiles (*jaliya*) to their homeland will prove materially and spiritually [to be] an experimental school for their brethren who are with them in

the fields, factories, trades and in all things connected with toil and labor.[15]

As Hussein foresaw, the regeneration of Palestine, and the growth of its population, came only after Jews returned in massive numbers.

Mark Twain, who visited Palestine in 1867, described it as "... [a] desolate country whose soil is rich enough, but is given over wholly to weeds—a silent mournful expanse.... A desolation is here that not even imagination can grace with the pomp of life and action.... We never saw a human being on the whole route.... There was hardly a tree or a shrub anywhere. Even the olive and the cactus, those fast friends of the worthless soil, had almost deserted the country."[16]

MYTH

"Zionism is racism."

FACT

In 1975, the UN General Assembly adopted a resolution slandering Zionism by equating it with racism. Zionism is the national liberation movement of the Jewish people, which holds that Jews, like any other nation, are entitled to a homeland.

History has demonstrated the need to ensure Jewish security through a national homeland. Zionism recognizes that Jewishness is defined by shared origin, religion, culture and history. The realization of the Zionist dream is exemplified by more than five million Jews, from more than 100 countries, who are Israeli citizens.

Israel's Law of Return grants automatic citizenship to Jews, but non-Jews are also eligible to become citizens under naturalization procedures similar to those in other countries. More than one million Muslim and Christian Arabs, Druze, Baha'is, Circassians and other ethnic groups also are represented in Israel's population. The presence in Israel of thousands of dark-skinned Jews from Ethiopia, Yemen and India is the best refutation of the calumny against Zionism. In a series of historic airlifts, labeled Moses (1984), Joshua (1985) and Solomon (1991), Israel rescued more than 20,000 members of the ancient Ethiopian Jewish community.

Zionism does not discriminate against anyone. Israel's open and democratic character, and its scrupulous protection of the religious and political rights of Christians and Muslims, rebut the charge of exclusivity. Moreover, anyone—Jew or non-Jew, Israeli, American, or Saudi, black, white, yellow or purple—can be a Zionist.

Writing after "Operation Moses" was revealed, William Safire noted:

"...For the first time in history, thousands of black people are being brought to a country not in chains but in dignity, not as slaves but as citizens." [17]

By contrast, the Arab states define citizenship strictly by native parentage. It is almost impossible to become a naturalized citizen in many Arab states, especially Algeria, Saudi Arabia and Kuwait. Several Arab nations have laws that facilitate the naturalization of foreign Arabs, with the specific exception of Palestinians. Jordan, on the other hand, instituted its own "law of return" in 1954, according citizenship to all former residents of Palestine, except for Jews.[18]

To single out Jewish self-determination for condemnation is itself a form of racism. When approached by a student at Harvard in 1968 who attacked Zionism, Martin Luther King responded: "When people criticize Zionists, they mean Jews. You're talking anti-Semitism." [19]

The 1975 UN resolution was part of the Soviet-Arab Cold War anti-Israel campaign. Almost all the former non-Arab supporters of the resolution have apologized and changed their positions. When the General Assembly voted to repeal the resolution in 1991, only some Arab and Muslim states, as well as Cuba, North Korea and Vietnam were opposed.

MYTH

"The delegates of the UN World Conference Against Racism agreed that Zionism is racism."

FACT

In 2001, Arab nations again were seeking to delegitimize Israel by trying to equate Zionism with racism at the UN World Conference Against Racism in Durban, South Africa. The United States joined Israel in boycotting the conference when it became clear that rather than focus on the evils of racism, anti-Semitism and xenophobia that were supposed to be the subject of the event, the conference had turned into a forum for bashing Israel.

The United States withdrew its delegation "to send a signal to the freedom loving nations of the world that we will not stand by if the world tries to describe Zionism as racism. That is as wrong as wrong can be." White House Press Secretary Ari Fleisher added "the President is proud to stand by Israel and by the Jewish community and send a signal that no group around the world will meet with international acceptance and respect if its purpose is to equate Zionism with racism." [20]

MYTH

"The Zionists could have chosen another country besides Palestine."

FACT

In the late 19th century, the rise of religious and racist anti-Semitism led to a resurgence of pogroms in Russia and Eastern Europe, shattering promises of equality and tolerance. This stimulated Jewish immigration to Palestine from Europe.

Simultaneously, a wave of Jews immigrated to Palestine from Yemen, Morocco, Iraq and Turkey. These Jews were unaware of Theodor Herzl's political Zionism or of European pogroms. They were motivated by the centuries-old dream of the "Return to Zion" and a fear of intolerance. Upon hearing that the gates of Palestine were open, they braved the hardships of travel and went to the Land of Israel.

The Zionist ideal of a return to Israel has profound religious roots. Many Jewish prayers speak of Jerusalem, Zion and the Land of Israel. The injunction not to forget Jerusalem, the site of the Temple, is a major tenet of Judaism. The Hebrew language, the Torah, laws in the Talmud, the Jewish calendar and Jewish holidays and festivals all originated in Israel and revolve around its seasons and conditions. Jews pray toward Jerusalem and recite the words "next year in Jerusalem" every Passover. Jewish religion, culture and history make clear that it is only in the land of Israel that the Jewish commonwealth can be built.

In 1897, Jewish leaders formally organized the Zionist political movement, calling for the restoration of the Jewish national home in Palestine, where Jews could find sanctuary and self-determination, and work for the renascence of their civilization and culture.

MYTH

"Herzl himself proposed Uganda as the Jewish state as an alternative to Palestine."

FACT

Theodor Herzl sought support from the great powers for the creation of a Jewish homeland. He turned to Great Britain, and met with Joseph Chamberlain, the British colonial secretary and others. The British agreed, in principle, to Jewish settlement in East Africa.

At the Sixth Zionist Congress at Basle on August 26, 1903, Herzl proposed the British Uganda Program as a *temporary emergency refuge* for Jews in Russia in immediate danger. While Herzl made it clear that this program would not affect the ultimate aim of Zionism, a Jewish entity in the Land of Israel, the proposal aroused a storm at the Congress and nearly led to a split in the Zionist movement. The Uganda Program, which never had much support, was formally rejected by the Zionist movement at the Seventh Zionist Congress in 1905.

MYTH

"All Arabs opposed the Balfour Declaration, seeing it as a betrayal of their rights."

FACT

Emir Faisal, son of Sherif Hussein, the leader of the Arab revolt against the Turks, signed an agreement with Chaim Weizmann and other Zionist leaders during the 1919 Paris Peace Conference. It acknowledged the "racial kinship and ancient bonds existing between the Arabs and the Jewish people" and concluded that "the surest means of working out the consummation of their national aspirations is through the closest possible collaboration in the development of the Arab states and Palestine." Furthermore, the agreement looked to the fulfillment of the Balfour Declaration and called for all necessary measures "... to encourage and stimulate immigration of Jews into Palestine on a large scale, and as quickly as possible to settle Jewish immigrants upon the land through closer settlement and intensive cultivation of the soil."[21]

Faisal had conditioned his acceptance of the Balfour Declaration on the fulfillment of British wartime promises of independence to the Arabs. These were not kept.

Critics dismiss the Weizmann-Faisal agreement because it was never enacted; however, the fact that the leader of the Arab nationalist movement and the Zionist movement could reach an understanding is significant because it demonstrated that Jewish and Arab aspirations were not necessarily mutually exclusive.

MYTH

"The Zionists were colonialist tools of Western imperialism."

FACT

"Colonialism means living by exploiting others," Yehoshofat Harkabi has written. "But what could be further from colonialism than the idealism of city-dwelling Jews who strive to become farmers and laborers and to live by their own work?"[22]

Moreover, as British historian Paul Johnson noted, Zionists were hardly tools of imperialists given the powers' general opposition to their cause. "Everywhere in the West, the foreign offices, defense ministries and big business were against the Zionists."[23]

Emir Faisal also saw the Zionist movement as a companion to the Arab nationalist movement, fighting against imperialism, as he explained in a letter to Harvard law professor and future Supreme Court Justice Felix Frankfurter on March 3, 1919, one day after Chaim Weizmann presented the Zionist case to the Paris conference. Faisal wrote:

> The Arabs, especially the educated among us, look with deepest sympathy on the Zionist movement.... We will wish the Jews a hearty welcome home.... We are working together for a re-formed and revised Near East and our two movements complete one another. *The Jewish movement is nationalist and not imperialist.* And there is room in Syria for us both. Indeed, I think that neither can be a real success without the other (emphasis added).[24]

In the 1940s, the Jewish underground movements waged an *anticolonial* war against the British. The Arabs, meanwhile, were concerned primarily with fighting the Jews rather than expelling the British imperialists.

"Our settlers do not come here as do the colonists from the Occident to have natives do their work for them; they themselves set their shoulders to the plow and they spend their strength and their blood to make the land fruitful. But it is not only for ourselves that we desire its fertility. The Jewish farmers have begun to teach their brothers, the Arab farmers, to cultivate the land more intensively; we desire to teach them further: together with them we want to cultivate the land to 'serve' it, as the Hebrew has it. The more fertile this soil becomes, the more space there will be for us and for them. We have no desire to dispossess them: we want to live with them. We do not want to dominate them: we want to serve with them...."

—Martin Buber[25]

MYTH

"The British promised the Arabs independence in Palestine in the Hussein-MacMahon Correspondence."

FACT

The central figure in the Arab nationalist movement at the time of World War I was Hussein ibn 'Ali, who was appointed by the Turkish Committee of Union and Progress to the position of Sherif of Mecca in 1908. As Sherif, Hussein was responsible for the custody of Islam's shrines in the Hejaz and, consequently, was recognized as one of the Muslims' spiritual leaders.

In July 1915, Hussein sent a letter to Sir Henry MacMahon, the High Commissioner for Egypt, informing him of the terms for Arab participation in the war against the Turks.

The letters between Hussein and MacMahon that followed outlined the areas that Britain was prepared to cede to the Arabs. The Hussein-MacMahon correspondence conspicuously fails to mention Palestine. The British argued the omission had been intentional, thereby justifying their refusal to grant the Arabs independence in Palestine after the war.[26] MacMahon explained:

> I feel it my duty to state, and I do so definitely and emphatically, that it was not intended by me in giving this pledge to King Hussein to include Palestine in the area in which Arab independence was promised. I also had every reason to believe at the time that the fact that Palestine was not included in my pledge was well understood by King Hussein.[27]

Nevertheless, the Arabs held then, as now, that the letters constituted a promise of independence for the Arabs.

MYTH

"Israeli policies cause anti-Semitism."

FACT

Anti-Semitism has existed for centuries, well before the rise of the modern State of Israel. Rather than Israel being the cause of anti-Semitism, it is more likely that the distorted media coverage of Israeli policies is reinforcing latent anti-Semitic views.

As writer Leon Wieseltier observed, "The notion that all Jews are responsible for whatever any Jews do is not a Zionist notion. It is an anti-Semitic notion." Wieseltier adds that attacks on Jews in Europe have nothing whatsoever to do with Israel. To blame Jews for anti-Semitism is similar to saying blacks are responsible for racism.

Many Jews may disagree with policies of a particular Israeli government, but this does not mean that Israel is bad for the Jews. As Wieseltier noted, "Israel is not bad for the Jews of Russia, who may need a haven; or for the Jews of Argentina, who may need a haven; or for any Jews who may need a haven."[28]

"Israel is the only state in the world today, and the Jews the only people in the world today, that are the object of a standing set of threats from governmental, religious, and terrorist bodies seeking their destruction. And what is most disturbing is the silence, the indifference, and sometimes even the indulgence, in the face of such genocidal anti-Semitism."

—Canadian Minister of Justice and Attorney General Irwin Cotler[29]

MYTH

"Supporters of Israel only criticize Arabs and never Israelis."

FACT

Israel is not perfect. Even the most committed friends of Israel acknowledge that the government sometimes makes mistakes, and that it has not solved all the problems in its society. Supporters of Israel may not emphasize these faults, however, because there is no shortage of groups and individuals who are willing to do nothing but focus on Israel's imperfections. The public usually has much less access to Israel's side of the story of its conflict with the Arabs, or the positive aspects of its society.

Israelis themselves are their own harshest critics. If you want to read criticism of Israeli behavior, you do not need to seek out anti-Israel sources, you can pick up any Israeli newspaper and find no shortage of news and commentary critical of government policy. The rest of the world's media provides constant attention to Israel, and the coverage is far more likely to be unfavorable than complimentary.

Notes

1. Dan Bahat, ed. *Twenty Centuries of Jewish Life in the Holy Land,* (Jerusalem: The Israel Economist, 1976), pp. 61–63.
2. *New York Times,* (November 18, 1981).
3. Yehoshua Porath, *The Emergence of the Palestinian-Arab National Movement, 1918-1929,* (London: Frank Cass, 1974), p. 4.
4. Max Dimont, *Jews, God and History,* (NY: Signet, 1962), pp. 49–53.
5. Moshe Kohn, "The Arabs' 'Lie' of the Land," *Jerusalem Post,* (October 18, 1991).
6. Yehoshua Porath, *Palestinian Arab National Movement: From Riots to Rebellion: 1929-1939,* vol. 2, (London: Frank Cass and Co., Ltd., 1977), pp. 81–82.
7. Moshe Kohn, "The Arabs' 'Lie' of the Land," *Jerusalem Post,* (October 18, 1991).
8. Avner Yaniv, *PLO,* (Jerusalem: Israel Universities Study Group of Middle Eastern Affairs, August 1974), p. 5.
9. *Al-Qibla,* (March 23, 1918), quoted in Samuel Katz, *Battleground-Fact and Fantasy in Palestine,* (NY: Bantam Books, 1977), p. 128.
10. British Government, Report of the Anglo-American Committee of Enquiry, 1946, Part VI, (April 20, 1946).
11. Howard Sachar, *A History of Israel: From the Rise of Zionism to Our Time,* (NY: Alfred A. Knopf, 1979), p. 129.

12. Ben Halpern, *The Idea of a Jewish State*, (MA: Harvard University Press, 1969), p. 108.
13. Palestine Royal Commission Report, p. 233.
14. Neville Mandel, "Attempts at an Arab-Zionist Entente: 1913–1914," *Middle Eastern Studies,* (April 1965), p. 243.
15. *Al-Qibla,* (March 23, 1918), quoted in Samuel Katz, *Battleground-Fact and Fantasy in Palestine,* (NY: Bantam Books, 1977), p. 128.
16. Mark Twain, *The Innocents Abroad,* (London, 1881).
17. *New York Times,* (January 7, 1985).
18. Jordanian Nationality Law, Article 3(3) of Law No. 6 of 1954, Official Gazette, No. 1171, February 16, 1954.
19. Seymour Martin Lipset, "The Socialism of Fools-The Left, the Jews and Israel," *Encounter,* (December 1969), p. 24.
20. White House briefing regarding U.S. threat to boycott the UN Conference on racism, (July 27, 2001).
21. Chaim Weizmann, *Trial and Error,* (NY: Schocken Books, 1966), pp. 246–247; Howard Sachar, *A History of Israel: From the Rise of Zionism to Our Time,* (NY: Alfred A. Knopf, 1979), p. 121.
22. Yehoshofat Harkabi, *Palestinians and Israel,* (Jerusalem: Keter, 1974), p. 6.
23. Paul Johnson, *Modern Times: The World from the Twenties to the Nineties,* (NY: Harper & Row, 1983), p. 485.
24. Samuel Katz, *Battleground-Fact and Fantasy in Palestine,* (NY: Bantam Books, 1977), p. 55.
25. From an open letter from Martin Buber to Mahatma Gandhi in 1939, quoted in Arthur Hertzberg, *The Zionist Idea,* (PA: Jewish Publications Society, 1997), p. 464.
26. George Kirk, *A Short History of the Middle East,* (NY: Frederick Praeger Publishers, 1964), p. 314.
27. *London Times,* (July 23, 1937).
28. Leon Wieseltier, "Israel, Palestine, and the Return of the Binational Fantasy," *The New Republic,* (October 24, 2003).
29. *Jerusalem Post,* (February 5, 2004).

2. The Mandatory Period

MYTH

*"The British helped the Jews displace the
native Arab population of Palestine."*

FACT

Herbert Samuel, a British Jew who served as the first High Commissioner
of Palestine, placed restrictions on Jewish immigration "in the 'interests
of the present population' and the 'absorptive capacity' of the country."[1]
The influx of Jewish settlers was said to be forcing the Arab fellahin (native peasants) from their land. This was at a time when less than a million
people lived in an area that now supports more than 10 million.

The British actually limited the absorptive capacity of Palestine by
partitioning the country.

In 1921, Colonial Secretary Winston Churchill severed nearly four-
fifths of Palestine—some 35,000 square miles—to create a brand new
Arab entity, Transjordan. As a consolation prize for the Hejaz and Arabia
(which are both now Saudi Arabia) going to the Saud family, Churchill
rewarded Sherif Hussein's son Abdullah for his contribution to the war
against Turkey by installing him as Transjordan's emir.

The British went further and placed restrictions on Jewish land purchases in what remained of Palestine, contradicting the provision of the
Mandate (Article 6) stating that "the Administration of Palestine . . . shall
encourage, in cooperation with the Jewish Agency . . . close settlement
by Jews on the land, including State lands and waste lands not acquired
for public purposes." By 1949, the British had allotted 87,500 acres (47
percent) of the 187,500 acres of cultivable land to Arabs and only 4,250
acres (2 percent) to Jews.[2]

Ultimately, the British admitted the argument about the absorptive capacity of the country was specious. The Peel Commission said: "The heavy
immigration in the years 1933-36 would seem to show that the Jews have
been able to enlarge the absorptive capacity of the country for Jews."[3]

MYTH

*"The British allowed Jews to flood Palestine while
Arab immigration was tightly controlled."*

FACT

The British response to Jewish immigration set a precedent of appeasing
the Arabs, which was followed for the duration of the Mandate. The Brit-

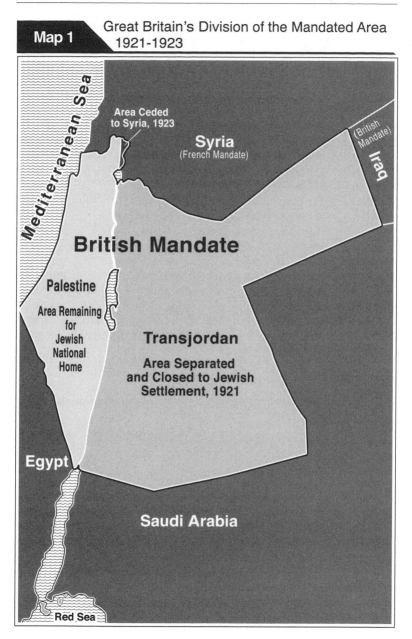

Map 1 — Great Britain's Division of the Mandated Area 1921-1923

Area Ceded
to Syria, 1923

Syria
(French Mandate)

(British Mandate)

Iraq

Mediterranean Sea

British Mandate

Palestine

Area Remaining
for
Jewish
National
Home

Transjordan

**Area Separated
and Closed to Jewish
Settlement, 1921**

Egypt

Saudi Arabia

Red Sea

ish placed restrictions on Jewish immigration while allowing Arabs to enter the country freely. Apparently, London did not feel that a flood of Arab immigrants would affect the country's absorptive capacity. During World War I, the Jewish population in Palestine declined because of the war, famine, disease and expulsion by the Turks. In 1915, approximately 83,000 Jews lived in Palestine among 590,000 Muslim and Christian Arabs. According to the 1922 census, the Jewish population was 84,000, while the Arabs numbered 643,000.[4] Thus, the Arab population grew exponentially while that of the Jews stagnated.

In the mid-1920s, Jewish immigration to Palestine increased primarily because of anti-Jewish economic legislation in Poland and Washington's imposition of restrictive quotas.[5]

The record number of immigrants in 1935 (see table) was a response to the growing persecution of Jews in Nazi Germany. The British administration considered this number too large, however, so the Jewish Agency was informed that less than one-third of the quota it asked for would be approved in 1936.[6]

The British gave in further to Arab demands by announcing in the 1939 White Paper that an independent Arab state would be created within 10 years, and that Jewish immigration was to be limited to 75,000 for the next five years, after which it was to cease altogether. It also forbade land sales to Jews in 95 percent of the territory of Palestine. The Arabs, nevertheless, rejected the proposal.

Jewish Immigrants to Palestine[7]

Year	Number	Year	Number
1919	1,806	1931	4,075
1920	8,223	1932	12,533
1921	8,294	1933	37,337
1922	8,685	1934	45,267
1923	8,175	1935	66,472
1924	13,892	1936	29,595
1925	34,386	1937	10,629
1926	13,855	1938	14,675
1927	3,034	1939	31,195
1928	2,178	1940	10,643
1929	5,249	1941	4,592
1930	4,944		

By contrast, throughout the Mandatory period, Arab immigration was unrestricted. In 1930, the Hope Simpson Commission, sent from London to investigate the 1929 Arab riots, said the British practice of ignoring the uncontrolled illegal Arab immigration from Egypt, Transjordan and Syria had the effect of displacing the prospective *Jewish* immigrants.[8]

The British Governor of the Sinai from 1922–36 observed: "This illegal immigration was not only going on from the Sinai, but also from Transjordan and Syria, and it is very difficult to make a case out for the misery of the Arabs if at the same time their compatriots from adjoining states could not be kept from going in to share that misery."[9]

The Peel Commission reported in 1937 that the "shortfall of land is . . . due less to the amount of land acquired by Jews than to the increase in the Arab population."[10]

MYTH

"The British changed their policy after World War II to allow the survivors of the Holocaust to settle in Palestine."

FACT

The gates of Palestine remained closed for the duration of the war, stranding hundreds of thousands of Jews in Europe, many of whom became victims of Hitler's "Final Solution." After the war, the British refused to allow the survivors of the Nazi nightmare to find sanctuary in Palestine. On June 6, 1946, President Truman urged the British government to relieve the suffering of the Jews confined to displaced persons camps in Europe by immediately accepting 100,000 Jewish immigrants. Britain's Foreign Minister, Ernest Bevin, replied sarcastically that the United States wanted displaced Jews to immigrate to Palestine "because they did not want too many of them in New York."[11]

Some Jews reached Palestine, many by way of dilapidated ships that members of the Jewish resistance organizations used to smuggle them in. Between August 1945 and the establishment of the State of Israel in May 1948, 65 "illegal" immigrant ships, carrying 69,878 people, arrived from European shores. In August 1946, however, the British began to intern those they caught in camps in Cyprus. Approximately 50,000 people were detained in the camps, 28,000 of whom were still imprisoned when Israel declared independence.[12]

MYTH

"As the Jewish population in Palestine grew, the plight of the Palestinian Arabs worsened."

FACT

The Jewish population increased by 470,000 between World War I and World War II, while the non-Jewish population rose by 588,000.[13] In fact, the permanent Arab population increased 120 percent between 1922 and 1947.[14]

This rapid growth was a result of several factors. One was immigration from neighboring states—constituting 37 percent of the total immigration to pre-state Israel—by Arabs who wanted to take advantage of the higher standard of living the Jews had made possible.[15] The Arab population also grew because of the improved living conditions created by the Jews as they drained malarial swamps and brought improved sanitation and health care to the region. Thus, for example, the Muslim infant mortality rate fell from 201 per thousand in 1925 to 94 per thousand in 1945, and life expectancy rose from 37 years in 1926 to 49 in 1943.[16]

The Arab population increased the most in cities where large Jewish populations had created new economic opportunities. From 1922–1947, the non-Jewish population increased 290 percent in Haifa, 131 percent in Jerusalem and 158 percent in Jaffa. The growth in Arab towns was more modest: 42 percent in Nablus, 78 percent in Jenin and 37 percent in Bethlehem.[17]

MYTH

"Jews stole Arab land."

FACT

Despite the growth in their population, the Arabs continued to assert they were being displaced. The truth is that from the beginning of World War I, part of Palestine's land was owned by absentee landlords who lived in Cairo, Damascus and Beirut. About 80 percent of the Palestinian Arabs were debt-ridden peasants, semi-nomads and Bedouins.[18]

Jews actually went out of their way to avoid purchasing land in areas where Arabs might be displaced. They sought land that was largely uncultivated, swampy, cheap and, most important, without tenants. In 1920, David Ben-Gurion expressed his concern about the Arab *fellahin,* whom he viewed as "the most important asset of the native population." Ben-Gurion said "under no circumstances must we touch land belonging to *fellahs* or worked by them." He advocated helping liberate them from their oppressors. "Only if a *fellah* leaves his place of settlement," Ben-Gurion added, "should we offer to buy his land, at an appropriate price."[19]

It was only after the Jews had bought all of the available uncultivated land that they began to purchase cultivated land. Many Arabs were willing to sell because of the migration to coastal towns and because they needed money to invest in the citrus industry.[20]

When John Hope Simpson arrived in Palestine in May 1930, he observed: "They [Jews] paid high prices for the land, and in addition they paid to certain of the occupants of those lands a considerable amount of money which they were not legally bound to pay."[21]

In 1931, Lewis French conducted a survey of landlessness and eventually offered new plots to any Arabs who had been "dispossessed." British officials received more than 3,000 applications, of which 80 percent were ruled invalid by the Government's legal adviser because the applicants were not landless Arabs. This left only about 600 landless Arabs, 100 of whom accepted the Government land offer.[22]

In April 1936, a new outbreak of Arab attacks on Jews was instigated by a Syrian guerrilla named Fawzi al-Qawukji, the commander of the Arab Liberation Army. By November, when the British finally sent a new commission headed by Lord Peel to investigate, 89 Jews had been killed and more than 300 wounded.[23]

The Peel Commission's report found that Arab complaints about Jewish land acquisition were baseless. It pointed out that "much of the land now carrying orange groves was sand dunes or swamp and uncultivated when it was purchased. . . . there was at the time of the earlier sales little evidence that the owners possessed either the resources or training needed to develop the land."[24] Moreover, the Commission found the shortage was "due less to the amount of land acquired by Jews than to the increase in the Arab population." The report concluded that the presence of Jews in Palestine, along with the work of the British Administration, had resulted in higher wages, an improved standard of living and ample employment opportunities.[25]

In his memoirs, Transjordan's King Abdullah wrote:

> It is made quite clear to all, both by the map drawn up by the Simpson Commission and by another compiled by the Peel Commission, that *the Arabs are as prodigal in selling their land as they are in useless wailing and weeping* (emphasis in the original).[26]

Even at the height of the Arab revolt in 1938, the British High Commissioner to Palestine believed the Arab landowners were complaining about sales to Jews to drive up prices for lands they wished to sell. Many Arab landowners had been so terrorized by Arab rebels they decided to leave Palestine and sell their property to the Jews.[27]

The Jews were paying exorbitant prices to wealthy landowners for small tracts of arid land. "In 1944, Jews paid between $1,000 and $1,100 per acre in Palestine, mostly for arid or semiarid land; in the same year, rich black soil in Iowa was selling for about $110 per acre."[28]

By 1947, Jewish holdings in Palestine amounted to about 463,000 acres. Approximately 45,000 of these acres were acquired from the Mandatory Government; 30,000 were bought from various churches and 387,500 were purchased from Arabs. Analyses of land purchases from 1880 to 1948 show that 73 percent of Jewish plots were purchased from large landowners, not poor *fellahin.*[29] Those who sold land included the mayors of Gaza, Jerusalem and Jaffa. As'ad el-Shuqeiri, a Muslim religious scholar and father of PLO chairman Ahmed Shuqeiri, took Jewish money for his land. Even King Abdullah leased land to the Jews. In fact, many leaders of the Arab nationalist movement, including members of the Muslim Supreme Council, sold land to Jews.[30]

MYTH

"The British helped the Palestinians to live peacefully with the Jews."

FACT

In 1921, Haj Amin el-Husseini first began to organize *fedayeen* ("one who sacrifices himself") to terrorize Jews. Haj Amin hoped to duplicate the success of Kemal Atatürk in Turkey by driving the Jews out of Palestine just as Kemal had driven the invading Greeks from his country.[31] Arab radicals were able to gain influence because the British Administration was unwilling to take effective action against them until they finally revolted against British rule.

Colonel Richard Meinertzhagen, former head of British military intelligence in Cairo, and later Chief Political Officer for Palestine and Syria, wrote in his diary that British officials "incline towards the exclusion of Zionism in Palestine." In fact, the British encouraged the Palestinians to attack the Jews. According to Meinertzhagen, Col. Waters-Taylor (financial adviser to the Military Administration in Palestine 1919–23) met with Haj Amin a few days before Easter, in 1920, and told him "he had a great opportunity at Easter to show the world . . . that Zionism was unpopular not only with the Palestine Administration but in Whitehall, and if disturbances of sufficient violence occurred in Jerusalem at Easter, both General Bols [Chief Administrator in Palestine, 1919–20] and General Allenby [Commander of Egyptian Force, 1917–19, then High Commissioner of Egypt] would advocate the abandonment of the Jewish Home. Waters-Taylor explained that freedom could only be attained through violence."[32]

Haj Amin took the Colonel's advice and instigated a riot. The British withdrew their troops and the Jewish police from Jerusalem, allowing the Arab mob to attack Jews and loot their shops. Because of Haj Amin's overt role in instigating the pogrom, the British decided to arrest him. Haj Amin escaped, however, and was sentenced to 10 years imprisonment in absentia.

A year later, some British Arabists convinced High Commissioner Herbert Samuel to pardon Haj Amin and to appoint him Mufti. By contrast, Vladimir Jabotinsky and several of his followers, who had formed a Jewish defense organization during the unrest, were sentenced to 15 years' imprisonment.[33]

Samuel met with Haj Amin on April 11, 1921, and was assured "that the influences of his family and himself would be devoted to tranquility." Three weeks later, riots in Jaffa and elsewhere left 43 Jews dead.[34]

Haj Amin consolidated his power and took control of all Muslim religious funds in Palestine. He used his authority to gain control over the mosques, the schools and the courts. No Arab could reach an influential position without being loyal to the Mufti. His power was so absolute "no Muslim in Palestine could be born or die without being beholden to Haj Amin."[35] The Mufti's henchmen also insured he would have no opposition by systematically killing Palestinians from rival clans who were discussing cooperation with the Jews.

As the spokesman for Palestinian Arabs, Haj Amin did not ask that Britain grant them independence. On the contrary, in a letter to Churchill in 1921, he demanded that Palestine be reunited with Syria and Transjordan.[36]

The Arabs found rioting to be an effective political tool because of the lax British attitude and response toward violence against Jews. In handling each riot, the British did everything in their power to prevent Jews from protecting themselves, but made little or no effort to prevent the Arabs from attacking them. After each outbreak, a British commission of inquiry would try to establish the cause of the violence. The conclusion was always the same: the Arabs were afraid of being displaced by Jews. To stop the rioting, the commissions would recommend that restrictions be placed on Jewish immigration. Thus, the Arabs came to recognize that they could always stop the influx of Jews by staging a riot.

This cycle began after a series of riots in May 1921. After failing to protect the Jewish community from Arab mobs, the British appointed the Haycraft Commission to investigate the cause of the violence. Although the panel concluded the Arabs had been the aggressors, it rationalized the cause of the attack: "The fundamental cause of the riots was a feeling among the Arabs of discontent with, and hostility to, the Jews, due to political and economic causes, and connected with Jewish immigration, and with their conception of Zionist policy...."[37] One consequence of the violence was the institution of a temporary ban on Jewish immigration.

The Arab fear of being "displaced" or "dominated" was used as an excuse for their merciless attacks on peaceful Jewish settlers. Note, too, that these riots were not inspired by nationalistic fervor—nationalists would have rebelled against their British overlords—they were motivated by racial strife and misunderstanding.

In 1929, Arab provocateurs succeeded in convincing the masses that the Jews had designs on the Temple Mount (a tactic that would be repeated on numerous occasions, the most recent of which was in

2000 after the visit of Ariel Sharon). A Jewish religious observance at the Western Wall, which forms a part of the Temple Mount, served as a catalyst for rioting by Arabs against Jews that spilled out of Jerusalem into other villages and towns, including Safed and Hebron.

Again, the British Administration made no effort to prevent the violence and, after it began, the British did nothing to protect the Jewish population. After six days of mayhem, the British finally brought troops in to quell the disturbance. By this time, virtually the entire Jewish population of Hebron had fled or been killed. In all, 133 Jews were killed and 399 wounded in the pogroms.[38]

After the riots were over, the British ordered an investigation, which resulted in the Passfield White Paper. It said the "immigration, land purchase and settlement policies of the Zionist Organization were already, or were likely to become, prejudicial to Arab interests. It understood the Mandatory's obligation to the non-Jewish community to mean that Palestine's resources must be primarily reserved for the growing Arab economy...."[39] This, of course, meant it was necessary to place restrictions not only on Jewish immigration but on land purchases.

MYTH

"The Mufti was not anti-Semitic."

FACT

In 1941, Haj Amin al-Husseini fled to Germany and met with Adolf Hitler, Heinrich Himmler, Joachim Von Ribbentrop and other Nazi leaders. He wanted to persuade them to extend the Nazis' anti-Jewish program to the Arab world.

The Mufti sent Hitler 15 drafts of declarations he wanted Germany and Italy to make concerning the Middle East. One called on the two countries to declare the illegality of the Jewish home in Palestine. Furthermore, "they accord to Palestine and to other Arab countries the right to solve the problem of the Jewish elements in Palestine and other Arab countries, in accordance with the interest of the Arabs and, by the same method, that the question is now being settled in the Axis countries."[40]

In November 1941, the Mufti met with Hitler, who told him the Jews were his foremost enemy. The Nazi dictator rebuffed the Mufti's requests for a declaration in support of the Arabs, however, telling him the time was not right. The Mufti offered Hitler his "thanks for the sympathy which he had always shown for the Arab and especially Palestinian cause, and to which he had given clear expression in his public speeches.... The Arabs were Germany's natural friends because they had the same enemies as had Germany, namely.... the Jews...." Hitler replied:

Germany stood for uncompromising war against the Jews. That naturally included active opposition to the Jewish national home in Palestine.... Germany would furnish positive and practical aid to the Arabs involved in the same struggle.... Germany's objective [is] ... solely the destruction of the Jewish element residing in the Arab sphere.... In that hour the Mufti would be the most authoritative spokesman for the Arab world. The Mufti thanked Hitler profusely.[41]

In 1945, Yugoslavia sought to indict the Mufti as a war criminal for his role in recruiting 20,000 Muslim volunteers for the SS, who participated in the killing of Jews in Croatia and Hungary. He escaped from French detention in 1946, however, and continued his fight against the Jews from Cairo and later Beirut.

MYTH

"The Irgun bombed the King David Hotel as part of a terror campaign against civilians."

FACT

The King David Hotel was the site of the British military command and the British Criminal Investigation Division. The Irgun chose it as a target after British troops invaded the Jewish Agency on June 29, 1946, and confiscated large quantities of documents. At about the same time, more than 2,500 Jews from all over Palestine were placed under arrest. The information about Jewish Agency operations, including intelligence activities in Arab countries, was taken to the King David Hotel.

A week later, news of a massacre of 40 Jews in a pogrom in Poland reminded the Jews of Palestine how Britain's restrictive immigration policy had condemned thousands to death.

Irgun leader Menachem Begin stressed his desire to avoid civilian casualties. In fact, the plan was to warn the British so they would evacuate the building before it was blown up. Three telephone calls were placed, one to the hotel, another to the French Consulate, and a third to the *Palestine Post,* warning that explosives in the King David Hotel would soon be detonated.

On July 22, 1946, the calls were made. The call into the hotel was apparently received and ignored. Begin quotes one British official who supposedly refused to evacuate the building, saying: "We don't take orders from the Jews."[42] As a result, when the bombs exploded, the casualty toll was high: a total of 91 killed and 45 injured. Among the casualties were 15 Jews. Few people in the hotel proper were injured by the blast.[43]

In contrast to Arab attacks against Jews, which were widely hailed by Arab leaders as heroic actions, the Jewish National Council denounced the bombing of the King David.[44]

For decades the British denied they had been warned. In 1979, however, a member of the British Parliament introduced evidence that the Irgun had indeed issued the warning. He offered the testimony of a British officer who heard other officers in the King David Hotel bar joking about a Zionist threat to the headquarters. The officer who overheard the conversation immediately left the hotel and survived.[45]

Notes

1. Aharon Cohen, *Israel and the Arab World*, (NY: Funk and Wagnalls, 1970), p. 172; Howard Sachar, *A History of Israel: From the Rise of Zionism to Our Time*, (NY: Alfred A. Knopf, 1979), p. 146.
2. Moshe Auman, "Land Ownership in Palestine 1880-1948," in Michael Curtis, et al., *The Palestinians*, (NJ: Transaction Books, 1975), p. 25.
3. *Palestine Royal Commission Report* (the Peel Report), (London: 1937), p. 300. [Henceforth Palestine Royal Commission Report].
4. Arieh Avneri, *The Claim of Dispossession*, (Tel Aviv: Hidekel Press, 1984), p. 28; Yehoshua Porath, *The Emergence of the Palestinian-Arab National Movement, 1918-1929*, (London: Frank Cass, 1974), pp. 17-18.
5. Porath (1974), p. 18.
6. Cohen, p. 53.
7. Yehoshua Porath, *Palestinian Arab National Movement: From Riots to Rebellion: 1929-1939*, vol. 2, (London: Frank Cass and Co., Ltd., 1977), pp. 17-18, 39.
8. John Hope Simpson, *Palestine: Report on Immigration, Land Settlement and Development*, (London, 1930), p. 126.
9. *Palestine Royal Commission Report*, p. 291.
10. *Palestine Royal Commission Report*, p. 242.
11. George Lenczowski, *American Presidents and the Middle East*, (NC: Duke University Press, 1990), p. 23.
12. Cohen p. 174.
13. Dov Friedlander and Calvin Goldscheider, *The Population of Israel*, (NY: Columbia Press, 1979), p. 30.
14. Avneri, p. 254.
15. Curtis, p. 38.
16. Avneri, pp. 264; Cohen p. 60.
17. Avneri, pp. 254-55.
18. Moshe Aumann, *Land Ownership in Palestine 1880-1948*, (Jerusalem: Academic Committee on the Middle East, 1976), p. 5.
19. Shabtai Teveth, *Ben-Gurion and the Palestinian Arabs: From Peace to War*, (London: Oxford University Press, 1985), p. 32.
20. Porath, pp. 80, 84.
21. Hope Simpson Report, p. 51.
22. Avneri, pp. 149-158; Cohen, p. 37; based on the Report on Agricultural Development and Land Settlement in Palestine by Lewis French, (December 1931, Supplementary Report, April 1932) and material submitted to the Palestine Royal Commission.
23. Netanel Lorch, *One Long War*, (Jerusalem: Keter, 1976), p. 27; Sachar, p. 201.
24. Palestine Royal Commission Report (1937), p. 242.
25. Palestine Royal Commission (1937), pp. 241-242.

26. King Abdallah, *My Memoirs Completed,* (London, Longman Group, Ltd., 1978), pp. 88–89.
27. Porath (77), pp. 86–87.
28. Aumann, p. 13.
29. Abraham Granott, *The Land System in Palestine,* (London, Eyre and Spottiswoode, 1952), p. 278.
30. Avneri, pp. 179–180, 224–225, 232–234; Porath (77), pp. 72–73.
31. Jon Kimche, *There Could Have Been Peace: The Untold Story of Why We Failed With Palestine and Again With Israel,* (England: Dial Press, 1973), p. 189.
32. Richard Meinertzhagen, *Middle East Diary 1917-1956,* (London: The Cresset Press, 1959), pp. 49, 82, 97.
33. Samuel Katz, *Battleground-Fact and Fantasy in Palestine,* (NY: Bantam Books, 1977), pp. 63–65; Howard Sachar, *A History of Israel: From the Rise of Zionism to Our Time,* (NY: Alfred A. Knopf, 1979), p. 97.
34. Paul Johnson, *Modern Times: The World from the Twenties to the Nineties,* (NY: Harper & Row, 1983), p. 438.
35. Larry Collins and Dominique Lapierre, *O Jerusalem!,* (NY: Simon and Schuster, 1972), p. 52.
36. Kimche, p. 211.
37. Ben Halpern, *The Idea of a Jewish State,* (MA: Harvard University Press, 1969), p. 323.
38. Sachar, p. 174.
39. Halpern, p. 201.
40. "Grand Mufti Plotted To Do Away With All Jews In Mideast," *Response,* (Fall 1991), pp. 2–3.
41. Record of the Conversation Between the Fuhrer and the Grand Mufti of Jerusalem on November 28, 1941, in the Presence of Reich Foreign Minister and Minister Grobba in Berlin, *Documents on German Foreign Policy, 1918-1945,* Series D, Vol. XIII, London, 1964, p. 881ff in Walter Lacquer and Barry Rubin, *The Israel-Arab Reader,* (NY: Penguin Books, 2001), pp. 51–55.
42. Menachem Begin, *The Revolt,* (NY: Nash Publishing, 1977), p. 224.
43. J. Bowyer Bell, *Terror Out Of Zion,* (NY: St. Martin's Press), p. 172.
44. Anne Sinai and I. Robert Sinai, *Israel and the Arabs: Prelude to the Jewish State,* (NY: Facts on File, 1972), p. 83.
45. Benjamin Netanyahu, ed., "International Terrorism: Challenge And Response," Proceedings of the Jerusalem Conference on International Terrorism, July 25, 1979, (Jerusalem: The Jonathan Institute, 1980), p. 45.

3. Partition

MYTH

"The United Nations unjustly partitioned Palestine."

FACT

As World War II ended, the magnitude of the Holocaust became known. This accelerated demands for a resolution to the question of Palestine so the survivors of Hitler's "Final Solution" might find sanctuary in a homeland of their own.

The British tried to work out an agreement acceptable to both Arabs and Jews, but their insistence on the former's approval guaranteed failure because the Arabs would not make any concessions. The British subsequently turned the issue over to the UN in February 1947.

The UN established a Special Commission on Palestine (UNSCOP) to devise a solution. Delegates from 11 nations* went to the area and found what had long been apparent: The conflicting national aspirations of Jews and Arabs could not be reconciled.

The contrasting attitudes of the two groups "could not fail to give the impression that the Jews were imbued with the sense of right and were prepared to plead their case before any unbiased tribunal, while the Arabs felt unsure of the justice of their cause, or were afraid to bow to the judgment of the nations."[1]

When they returned, the delegates of seven nations—Canada, Czechoslovakia, Guatemala, The Netherlands, Peru, Sweden and Uruguay—recommended the establishment of two separate states, Jewish and Arab, to be joined by economic union, with Jerusalem an internationalized enclave. Three nations—India, Iran and Yugoslavia—recommended a unitary state with Arab and Jewish provinces. Australia abstained.

The Jews of Palestine were not satisfied with the small territory allotted to them by the Commission, nor were they happy that Jerusalem was severed from the Jewish State; nevertheless, they welcomed the compromise. The Arabs rejected UNSCOP's recommendations.

The *ad hoc* committee of the UN General Assembly rejected the Arab demand for a unitary Arab state. The majority recommendation for partition was subsequently adopted 33-13 with 10 abstentions on November 29, 1947.[2]

---

*Australia, Canada, Czechoslovakia, Guatemala, India, Iran, the Netherlands, Peru, Sweden, Uruguay and Yugoslavia.

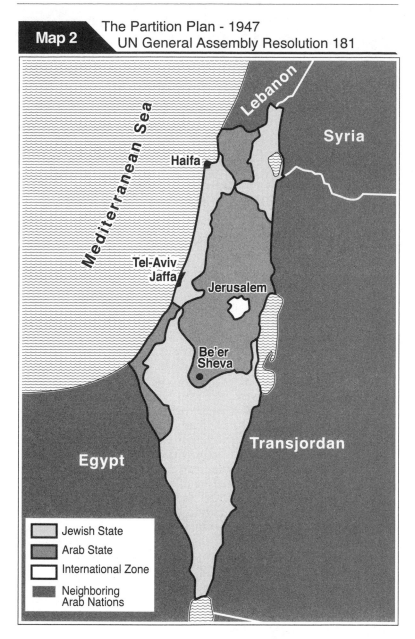

Map 2

The Partition Plan - 1947
UN General Assembly Resolution 181

Lebanon

Syria

Mediterranean Sea

Haifa

Tel-Aviv
Jaffa

Jerusalem

Be'er
Sheva

Transjordan

Egypt

Jewish State

Arab State

International Zone

Neighboring
Arab Nations

"It is hard to see how the Arab world, still less the Arabs of Palestine, will suffer from what is mere recognition of accomplished fact—the presence in Palestine of a compact, well organized, and virtually autonomous Jewish community."

—*London Times* **editorial**[3]

MYTH

"The partition plan gave the Jews most of the land, and all of the cultivable area."

FACT

The partition plan took on a checkerboard appearance largely because Jewish towns and villages were spread throughout Palestine. This did not complicate the plan as much as the fact that the high living standards in Jewish cities and towns had attracted large Arab populations, which insured that any partition would result in a Jewish state that included a substantial Arab population. Recognizing the need to allow for additional Jewish settlement, the majority proposal allotted the Jews land in the northern part of the country, the Galilee, and the large, arid Negev desert in the south. The remainder was to form the Arab state.

These boundaries were based solely on demographics. The borders of the Jewish State were arranged with no consideration of security; hence, the new state's frontiers were virtually indefensible. Overall, the Jewish State was to be comprised of roughly 5,500 square miles, and the population was to be 538,000 Jews and 397,000 Arabs. Approximately 92,000 Arabs lived in Tiberias, Safed, Haifa and Bet Shean, and another 40,000 were Bedouins, most of whom were living in the desert. The remainder of the Arab population was spread throughout the Jewish state.

The Arab State was to be 4,500 square miles with a population of 804,000 Arabs and 10,000 Jews.[4] Critics claim the UN gave the Jews fertile land while the Arabs were allotted hilly, arid land. To the contrary, approximately 60 percent of the Jewish state was to be the desert in the Negev while the Arabs occupied most of the agricultural land.[5]

Further complicating the situation was the UN majority's insistence that Jerusalem remain apart from both states and be administered as an international zone. This arrangement left more than 100,000 Jews in Jerusalem isolated from their country and circumscribed by the Arab state.

According to British statistics, more than 70 percent of the land in what would become Israel was not owned by Arab farmers, it belonged to the mandatory government. Those lands reverted to Israeli control after the departure of the British. Nearly 9 percent of the land was owned by Jews and about 3 percent by Arabs who became citizens of Israel. That means only about 18 percent belonged to Arabs who left the country before and after the Arab invasion of Israel.[6]

MYTH

"Israel usurped all of Palestine in 1948."

FACT

Nearly 80 percent of what was the historic land of Palestine and the Jewish National Home, as defined by the League of Nations, was severed by the British in 1921 and allocated to what became Transjordan. Jewish settlement there was barred. The UN partitioned the remaining 20-odd percent of Palestine into two states. With Jordan's annexation of the West Bank in 1950, and Egypt's control of Gaza, Arabs controlled more than 80 percent of the territory of the Mandate, while the Jewish State held a bare 17.5 percent.[7]

MYTH

"The Palestinian Arabs were never offered a state and therefore have been denied the right to self-determination."

FACT

The Peel Commission in 1937 concluded the only logical solution to resolving the contradictory aspirations of the Jews and Arabs was to partition Palestine into separate Jewish and Arab states. The Arabs rejected the plan because it forced them to accept the creation of a Jewish state, and required some Palestinians to live under "Jewish domination." The Zionists opposed the Peel Plan's boundaries because they would have been confined to little more than a ghetto of 1,900 out of the 10,310 square miles remaining in Palestine. Nevertheless, the Zionists decided to negotiate with the British, while the Arabs refused to consider any compromises.

In 1939, the British White Paper called for the establishment of an Arab state in Palestine within 10 years, and for limiting Jewish immigration to no more than 75,000 over the following five years. Afterward, no one would be allowed in without the consent of the Arab population. Though the Arabs had been granted a concession on Jewish immigration, and been offered independence—the goal of Arab nationalists—they repudiated the White Paper.

With partition, the Palestinians were given a state and the opportunity for self-determination. This too was rejected.

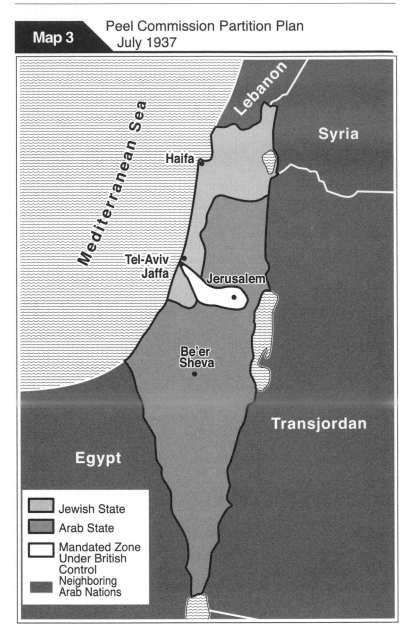

Map 3 — Peel Commission Partition Plan, July 1937

Legend:
- Jewish State
- Arab State
- Mandated Zone Under British Control
- Neighboring Arab Nations

MYTH

"The majority of the population in Palestine was Arab; therefore, a unitary Arab state should have been created."

FACT

At the time of the 1947 partition resolution, the Arabs did have a majority in western Palestine as a whole—1.2 million Arabs versus 600,000 Jews.[8] But the Jews were a majority *in the area allotted to them* by the resolution, and in Jerusalem.

The Jews never had a chance of reaching a majority in the country given the restrictive immigration policy of the British. By contrast, Palestine's Arab population, which had been declining prior to the Mandate in 1922, grew exponentially because Arabs from all the surrounding countries were free to come—and thousands did—to take advantage of the rapid economic development and improved health conditions stimulated by Zionist settlement.

The decision to partition Palestine was not determined solely by demographics; it was based on the conclusion that the territorial claims of Jews and Arabs were irreconcilable, and that the most logical compromise was the creation of two states. Ironically, that same year, 1947, the Arab members of the United Nations supported the partition of the Indian sub-continent and the creation of the new, predominantly Muslim state of Pakistan.

MYTH

"The Arabs were prepared to compromise to avoid bloodshed."

FACT

As the partition vote approached, it became clear little hope existed for a political solution to a problem that transcended politics: the Arabs' unwillingness to accept a Jewish state in Palestine and the refusal of the Zionists to settle for anything less. The implacability of the Arabs was evident when Jewish Agency representatives David Horowitz and Abba Eban made a last-ditch effort to reach a compromise in a meeting with Arab League Secretary Azzam Pasha on September 16, 1947. Pasha told them bluntly:

> The Arab world is not in a compromising mood. It's likely, Mr. Horowitz, that your plan is rational and logical, but the fate of nations is not decided by rational logic. Nations never concede; they fight. You won't get anything by peaceful means or compromise. You can, perhaps, get something, but only by the force of your arms. We shall try to defeat you. I am not sure we'll succeed, but we'll try. We were able to drive out the Crusad-

ers, but on the other hand we lost Spain and Persia. It may be that we shall lose Palestine. But it's too late to talk of peaceful solutions.[9]

Notes

1. Aharon Cohen, *Israel and the Arab World,* (Boston: Beacon Press, 1976), pp. 369-370.

2. Voting in *favor* of partition: Australia, Belgium, Bolivia, Brazil, Byelorussian SSR, Canada, Costa Rica, Czechoslovakia, Denmark, Dominican Republic, Ecuador, France, Guatemala, Haiti, Iceland, Liberia, Luxembourg, Netherlands, New Zealand, Nicaragua, Norway, Panama, Paraguay, Peru, Philippines, Poland, Sweden, Ukrainian SSR, Union of South Africa, USSR, USA, Uruguay, Venezuela.

   Voting against partition: Afghanistan, Cuba, Egypt, Greece, India, Iran, Iraq, Lebanon, Pakistan, Saudi Arabia, Syria, Turkey, Yemen.

   Abstained: Argentina, Chile, China, Columbia, El Salvador, Ethiopia, Honduras, Mexico, UK, Yugoslavia. *Yearbook of the United Nations, 1947-48,* (NY: United Nations, 1949), pp. 246-47.

3. *London Times,* (December 1, 1947).

4. Howard Sachar, *A History of Israel: From the Rise of Zionism to Our Time,* (NY: Alfred A. Knopf, 1998), p. 292.

5. Cohen, p. 238.

6. Moshe Aumann, "Land Ownership in Palestine, 1880-1948," in Michael Curtis, et al., *The Palestinians,* (NJ: Transaction Books, 1975), p. 29, quoting p. 257 of the Government of Palestine, Survey of Palestine.

7. Historic Palestine comprised what is today Jordan (approximately 35,640 square miles), Israel (8,019 square miles), Gaza (139 square miles) and the West Bank (2,263 square miles).

8. Arieh Avneri, *The Claim of Dispossession,* (NJ: Transaction Books, 1984), p. 252.

9. David Horowitz, *State in the Making,* (NY: Alfred A. Knopf, 1953), p. 233.

4. The War of 1948

MYTH

"The Jews started the first war with the Arabs."

FACT

The chairman of the Arab Higher Committee said the Arabs would "fight for every inch of their country."[1] Two days later, the holy men of Al-Azhar University in Cairo called on the Muslim world to proclaim a *jihad* (holy war) against the Jews.[2] Jamal Husseini, the Arab Higher Committee's spokesman, had told the UN prior to the partition vote the Arabs would drench "the soil of our beloved country with the last drop of our blood...."[3]

Husseini's prediction began to come true almost immediately after the UN adopted the partition resolution on November 29, 1947. The Arabs declared a protest strike and instigated riots that claimed the lives of 62 Jews and 32 Arabs. Violence continued to escalate through the end of the year.[4]

The first large-scale assaults began on January 9, 1948, when approximately 1,000 Arabs attacked Jewish communities in northern Palestine. By February, the British said so many Arabs had infiltrated they lacked the forces to run them back.[5] In fact, the British turned over bases and arms to Arab irregulars and the Arab Legion.

In the first phase of the war, lasting from November 29, 1947, until April 1, 1948, the Palestinian Arabs took the offensive, with help from volunteers from neighboring countries. The Jews suffered severe casualties and passage along most of their major roadways was disrupted.

On April 26, 1948, Transjordan's King Abdullah said:

> [A]ll our efforts to find a peaceful solution to the Palestine problem have failed. The only way left for us is war. I will have the pleasure and honor to save Palestine.[6]

On May 4, 1948, the Arab Legion attacked Kfar Etzion. The defenders drove them back, but the Legion returned a week later. After two days, the ill-equipped and outnumbered settlers were overwhelmed. Many defenders were massacred after they had surrendered.[7] This was prior to the invasion by the regular Arab armies that followed Israel's declaration of independence.

The UN blamed the Arabs for the violence. The UN Palestine Commission, which was never permitted by the Arabs or British to go to

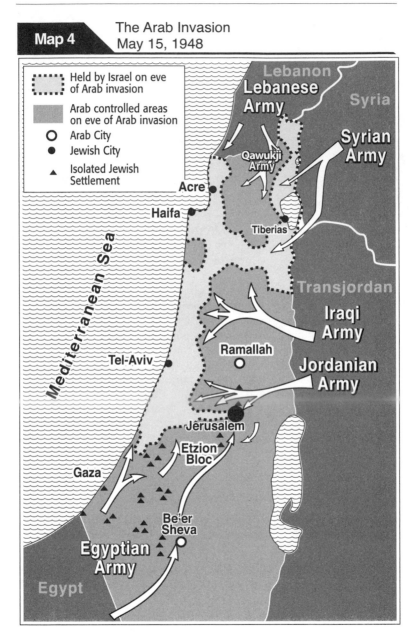

Map 4 The Arab Invasion
May 15, 1948

Palestine to implement the resolution, reported to the Security Council on February 16, 1948, that powerful Arab interests, both inside and outside Palestine, are defying the resolution of the General Assembly and are engaged in a deliberate effort to alter by force the settlement envisaged therein.[8]

The Arabs were blunt in taking responsibility for starting the war. Jamal Husseini told the Security Council on April 16, 1948:

> The representative of the Jewish Agency told us yesterday that they were not the attackers, that the Arabs had begun the fighting. We did not deny this. We told the whole world that we were going to fight.[9]

The British commander of Jordan's Arab Legion, John Bagot Glubb admitted:

> Early in January, the first detachments of the Arab Liberation Army began to infiltrate into Palestine from Syria. Some came through Jordan and even through Amman...They were in reality to strike the first blow in the ruin of the Arabs of Palestine.[10]

Despite the disadvantages in numbers, organization and weapons, the Jews began to take the initiative in the weeks from April 1 until the declaration of independence on May 14. The Haganah captured several major towns including Tiberias and Haifa, and temporarily opened the road to Jerusalem.

The partition resolution was never suspended or rescinded. Thus, Israel, the Jewish State in Palestine, was born on May 14, as the British finally left the country. Five Arab armies (Egypt, Syria, Transjordan, Lebanon and Iraq) immediately invaded Israel. Their intentions were declared by Azzam Pasha, Secretary-General of the Arab League: "This will be a war of extermination and a momentous massacre which will be spoken of like the Mongolian massacres and the Crusades."[11]

MYTH

"The United States was the only nation that criticized the Arab attack on Israel."

FACT

The United States, the Soviet Union and most other states recognized Israel soon after it declared independence on May 14, 1948, and immediately indicted the Arabs for their aggression. The United States urged a resolution charging the Arabs with breach of the peace.

Soviet delegate Andrei Gromyko told the Security Council, May 29, 1948:

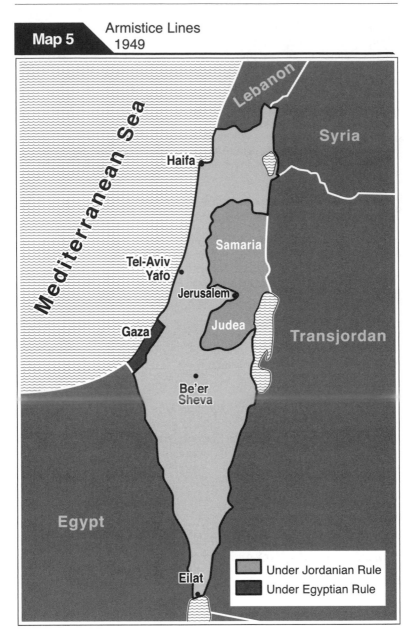

Map 5 Armistice Lines 1949

Mediterranean Sea

Lebanon

Syria

Haifa

Samaria

Tel-Aviv Yafo

Jerusalem

Judea

Gaza

Transjordan

Be'er Sheva

Egypt

Eilat

Under Jordanian Rule
Under Egyptian Rule

This is not the first time that the Arab states, which organized the invasion of Palestine, have ignored a decision of the Security Council or of the General Assembly. The USSR delegation deems it essential that the council should state its opinion more clearly and more firmly with regard to this attitude of the Arab states toward decisions of the Security Council.[12]

On July 15, the Security Council threatened to cite the Arab governments for aggression under the UN Charter. By this time, the Israel Defense Forces (IDF) had succeeded in stopping the Arab offensive and the initial phase of the fighting ended.

MYTH

"The West's support of Israel allowed the Jews to conquer Palestine."

FACT

The Jews won their war of independence with minimal help from the West. In fact, they won despite efforts to undermine their military strength.

Although the United States vigorously supported the partition resolution, the State Department did not want to provide the Jews with the means to defend themselves. "Otherwise," Undersecretary of State Robert Lovett argued, "the Arabs might use arms of U.S. origin against Jews, or Jews might use them against Arabs."[13] Consequently, on December 5, 1947, the U.S. imposed an arms embargo on the region.

Many in the State Department saw the embargo as yet another means of obstructing partition. President Truman nevertheless went along with it hoping it would be a means of averting bloodshed. This was naive given Britain's rejection of Lovett's request to suspend weapons shipments to the Arabs and subsequent agreements to provide additional arms to Iraq and Transjordan.[14]

The Arabs had no difficulty obtaining all the arms they needed. In fact, Jordan's Arab Legion was armed and trained by the British, and led by a British officer. At the end of 1948, and beginning of 1949, British RAF planes flew with Egyptian squadrons over the Israel-Egypt border. On January 7, 1949, Israeli planes shot down four of the British aircraft.[15]

The Jews, on the other hand, were forced to smuggle weapons, principally from Czechoslovakia. When Israel declared its independence in May 1948, the army did not have a single cannon or tank. Its air force consisted of nine obsolete planes. Although the Haganah had 60,000 trained fighters, only 18,900 were fully mobilized, armed and prepared for war.[16] On the eve of the war, chief of operations Yigael Yadin told David Ben-Gurion: "The best we can tell you is that we have a 50-50 chance."[17]

The Arab war to destroy Israel failed. Indeed, because of their aggression, the Arabs wound up with less territory than they would have had if they had accepted partition.

The cost to Israel, however, was enormous. "Many of its most productive fields lay gutted and mined. Its citrus groves, for decades the basis of the Yishuv's [Jewish community] economy, were largely destroyed."[18] Military expenditures totaled approximately $500 million. Worse yet, 6,373 Israelis were killed, nearly one percent of the Jewish population of 650,000.

Had the West enforced the partition resolution or given the Jews the capacity to defend themselves, many lives might have been saved.

The Arab countries signed armistice agreements with Israel in 1949, starting with Egypt (Feb. 24), followed by Lebanon (March 23), Jordan (April 3) and Syria (July 20). Iraq was the only country that did not sign an agreement with Israel, choosing instead to withdraw its troops and hand over its sector to Jordan's Arab Legion. None of the Arab states would negotiate a peace agreement.

MYTH

"The Arab economic boycott of Israel was imposed after the 1948 war."

FACT

The Arab boycott was formally declared by the newly formed Arab League Council on December 2, 1945: "Jewish products and manufactured goods shall be considered undesirable to the Arab countries." All Arab "institutions, organizations, merchants, commission agents and individuals" were called upon "to refuse to deal in, distribute, or consume Zionist products or manufactured goods."[19] As is evident in this declaration, the terms "Jewish" and "Zionist" were used synonymously. Thus, even before the establishment of Israel, the Arab states had declared an economic boycott against the Jews of Palestine.

The boycott, as it evolved after 1948, is divided into three components. The primary boycott prohibits direct trade between Israel and the Arab nations. The secondary boycott is directed at companies that do business with Israel. The tertiary boycott involves the blacklisting of firms that trade with other companies that do business with Israel.[20]

The objective of the boycott has been to isolate Israel from its neighbors and the international community, and deny it trade that might be used to augment its military and economic strength. While undoubtedly isolating Israel and separating the Jewish State from its most natural markets, the boycott failed to undermine Israel's economy to the degree intended.

In 1977, Congress prohibited U.S. companies from cooperating with the Arab boycott. When President Carter signed the law, he said the "issue goes to the very heart of free trade among nations" and that it was designed to "end the divisive effects on American life of foreign boycotts aimed at Jewish members of our society."[21]

The boycott has gradually crumbled and few countries outside the Middle East comply with it. The primary boycott—prohibiting direct relations between Arab countries and Israel—cracked when nations such as Qatar, Oman and Morocco negotiated deals with Israel. Other countries, such as Saudi Arabia, have pledged to end their economic boycott to meet the requirement for membership in the World Trade Organization.[22] Still, the boycott remains technically in force.[23]

Notes

1. *New York Times,* (December 1, 1947).
2. *Facts on File Yearbook,* (NY: Facts on File, Inc., 1948), p. 48.
3. J.C. Hurewitz, *The Struggle For Palestine,* (NY: Shocken Books, 1976), p. 308.
4. *Facts on File 1948,* p. 231.
5. *Facts on File 1947,* p. 231.
6. Howard Sachar, *A History of Israel: From the Rise of Zionism to Our Time,* (NY: Alfred A. Knopf, 1979), p. 322.
7. Netanel Lorch, *One Long War,* (Jerusalem: Keter Books, 1976), p. 47; Ralph Patai, ed., *Encyclopedia of Zionism and Israel,* (NY: McGraw Hill, 1971), pp. 307-308.
8. Security Council Official Records, Special Supplement, (1948), p. 20.
9. Security Council Official Records, S/Agenda/58, (April 16, 1948), p. 19.
10. John Bagot Glubb, *A Soldier with the Arabs,* (London: Staughton and Hodder, 1957), p. 79.
11. Isi Leibler, *The Case For Israel,* (Australia: The Globe Press, 1972), p. 15.
12. Security Council Official Records, SA/Agenda/77, (May 29, 1948), p. 2.
13. *Foreign Relations of the United States 1947,* (DC: GPO, 1948), p. 1249. [Henceforth FRUS].
14. Mitchell Bard, *The Water's Edge And Beyond,* (NJ: Transaction Books, 1991), pp. 171-175; *FRUS,* pp. 537-39; Robert Silverberg, *If I Forget Thee O Jerusalem: American Jews and the State of Israel,* (NY: William Morrow and Co., Inc., 1970), pp. 366, 370; Shlomo Slonim, "The 1948 American Embargo on Arms to Palestine," *Political Science Quarterly,* (Fall 1979), p. 500.
15. Sachar, p. 345.
16. Larry Collins and Dominique Lapierre, *O Jerusalem!,* (NY: Simon and Schuster, 1972), p. 352.
17. Golda Meir, *My Life,* (NY: Dell, 1975), pp. 213, 222, 224.
18. Sachar, p. 452.
19. Terence Prittie and Walter Nelson, *The Economic War Against The Jews,* (London: Corgi Books, 1977), p. 1; Dan Chill, *The Arab Boycott of Israel,* (NY: Praeger, 1976), p. 1.
20. Prittie and Nelson, pp. 47-48; Sol Stern, "On and Off the Arabs' List," *The New Republic,* (March 27, 1976), p. 9; Kennan Teslik, *Congress, the Executive Branch and Special Interests,* (CT: Greenwood Press, 1982), p. 11.
21. Bard, pp. 91-115.
22. "Israel nod let Saudis into WTO," Jewish Telegraphic Agency, (November 11, 2005).
23. *Jerusalem Post,* (June 25, 2002).

5. The 1956 War

MYTH

"Arab governments were prepared to accept Israel after the 1948 war."

FACT

In the fall of 1948, the UN Security Council called on Israel and the Arab states to negotiate armistice agreements. Thanks to UN mediator Ralph Bunche's insistence on direct bilateral talks between Israel and each Arab state, armistice agreements between Israel and Egypt, Jordan, Lebanon and Syria were concluded by the summer of 1949. Iraq, which had also fought against Israel, refused to follow suit.

Meanwhile, on December 11, 1948, the General Assembly adopted a resolution calling on the parties to negotiate peace and creating a Palestine Conciliation Commission (PCC), which consisted of the United States, France and Turkey. All Arab delegations voted against it.

After 1949, the Arabs insisted that Israel accept the borders in the 1947 partition resolution and repatriate the Palestinian refugees before they would negotiate an end to the war they had initiated. This was a novel approach that they would use after subsequent defeats: the doctrine of the limited-liability war. Under this theory, aggressors may reject a compromise settlement and gamble on war to win everything in the comfortable knowledge that, even if they fail, they may insist on reinstating the status quo ante.

MYTH

"Israel's military strike in 1956 was unprovoked."

FACT

Egypt had maintained its state of belligerency with Israel after the armistice agreement was signed. The first manifestation of this was the closing of the Suez Canal to Israeli shipping. On August 9, 1949, the UN Mixed Armistice Commission upheld Israel's complaint that Egypt was illegally blocking the canal. UN negotiator Ralph Bunche declared: "There should be free movement for legitimate shipping and no vestiges of the wartime blockade should be allowed to remain, as they are inconsistent with both the letter and the spirit of the armistice agreements."[1]

On September 1, 1951, the Security Council ordered Egypt to open the Canal to Israeli shipping. Egypt refused to comply.

The Egyptian Foreign Minister, Muhammad Salah al-Din, said early in 1954 that "The Arab people will not be embarrassed to declare: We shall not be satisfied except by the final obliteration of Israel from the map of the Middle East."[2]

In 1955, Egyptian President Gamal Abdel Nasser began to import arms from the Soviet Bloc to build his arsenal for the confrontation with Israel. In the short-term, however, he employed a new tactic to prosecute Egypt's war with Israel. He announced it on August 31, 1955:

> Egypt has decided to dispatch her heroes, the disciples of Pharaoh and the sons of Islam and they will cleanse the land of Palestine.... There will be no peace on Israel's border because we demand vengeance, and vengeance is Israel's death.[3]

These "heroes" were Arab terrorists, or *fedayeen,* trained and equipped by Egyptian intelligence to engage in hostile action on the border, and to infiltrate Israel to commit acts of sabotage and murder. The *fedayeen* operated mainly from bases in Jordan, so that Jordan would bear the brunt of Israel's retaliation, which inevitably followed. The terrorist attacks violated the armistice agreement provision that prohibited the initiation of hostilities by paramilitary forces; nevertheless, it was Israel that was condemned by the UN Security Council for its counterattacks.

The escalation continued with the Egyptian blockade of Israel's shipping lane in the Straits of Tiran, and Nasser's nationalization of the Suez Canal in July 1956. On October 14, Nasser made clear his intent:

> I am not solely fighting against Israel itself. My task is to deliver the Arab world from destruction through Israel's intrigue, which has its roots abroad. Our hatred is very strong. There is no sense in talking about peace with Israel. There is not even the smallest place for negotiations.[4]

Less than two weeks later, on October 25, Egypt signed a tripartite agreement with Syria and Jordan placing Nasser in command of all three armies.

The blockade of the Suez Canal and Gulf of Aqaba to Israeli shipping, combined with the increased *fedayeen* attacks and the bellicosity of Arab statements, prompted Israel, with the backing of Britain and France, to attack Egypt on October 29, 1956. The Israeli attack on Egypt was successful, with Israeli forces capturing the Gaza Strip, much of the Sinai and Sharm al-Sheikh. A total of 231 Israeli soldiers died in the fighting.

Israeli Ambassador to the UN Abba Eban explained the provocations to the Security Council on October 30:

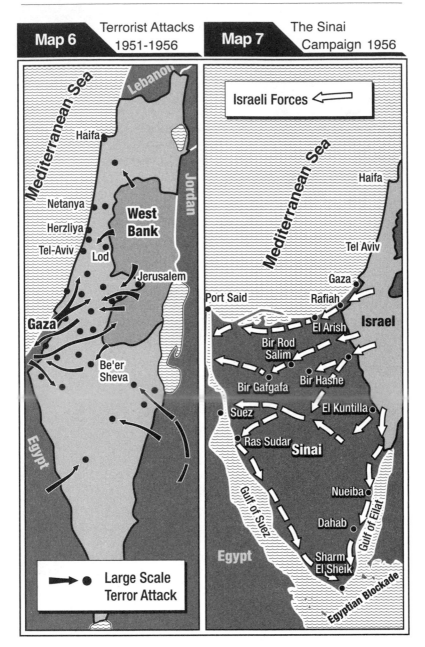

Map 6 — Terrorist Attacks 1951-1956

Map 7 — The Sinai Campaign 1956

During the six years during which this belligerency has operated in violation of the Armistice Agreement there have occurred 1,843 cases of armed robbery and theft, 1,339 cases of armed clashes with Egyptian armed forces, 435 cases of incursion from Egyptian controlled territory, 172 cases of sabotage perpetrated by Egyptian military units and *fedayeen* in Israel. As a result of these actions of Egyptian hostility within Israel, 364 Israelis were wounded and 101 killed. In 1956 alone, as a result of this aspect of Egyptian aggression, 28 Israelis were killed and 127 wounded.[5]

One reason these raids were so intolerable for Israel was that the country had chosen to create a relatively small standing army and to rely primarily on reserves in the event of war. This meant that Israel had a small force to fight in an emergency, that threats provoking the mobilization of reserves could virtually paralyze the country, and that an enemy's initial thrust would have to be withstood long enough to complete the mobilization.

MYTH

"The United States' blind support for Israel was apparent during the Suez War."

FACT

President Eisenhower was upset by the fact that Israel, France and Great Britain had secretly planned the campaign to evict Egypt from the Suez Canal. Israel's failure to inform the United States of its intentions, combined with ignoring American entreaties not to go to war, sparked tensions between the countries. The United States subsequently joined the Soviet Union (ironically, just after the Soviets invaded Hungary) in a campaign to force Israel to withdraw. This included a threat to discontinue all U.S. assistance, UN sanctions and expulsion from the UN.

U.S. pressure resulted in an Israeli withdrawal from the areas it conquered without obtaining any concessions from the Egyptians. This sowed the seeds of the 1967 war.

One reason Israel did give in to Eisenhower was the assurance he gave to Prime Minister David Ben-Gurion. Before evacuating Sharm al-Sheikh, the strategic point guarding the Straits of Tiran, Israel elicited a promise that the United States would maintain the freedom of navigation in the waterway.[6] In addition, Washington sponsored a UN resolution creating the United Nations Emergency Force (UNEF) to supervise the territories vacated by the Israeli forces.

Notes

1. Eliezer Ereli, "The Bat Galim Case Before the Security Council," *Middle Eastern Affairs,* (April 1955), pp. 108-9.
2. *Al-Misri,* (April 12, 1954).
3. *Middle Eastern Affairs,* (December 1956), p. 461.
4. *Middle Eastern Affairs,* (December 1956), p. 460.
5. *Security Council Official Records,* S/3706, (October 30, 1956), p. 14.
6. Janice Gross Stein and Raymond Tanter, *Rational Decision Making: Israel's Security Choices,* (OH: Ohio State University, 1976), p. 163.

6. The 1967 Six-Day War

MYTH

"Arab governments recognized Israel after the Suez War."

FACT

Israel consistently expressed a desire to negotiate with its neighbors. In an address to the UN General Assembly on October 10, 1960, Foreign Minister Golda Meir challenged Arab leaders to meet with Prime Minister David Ben-Gurion to negotiate a peace settlement. Egyptian President Nasser answered on October 15, saying that Israel was trying to deceive the world, and reiterating that his country would never recognize the Jewish State.[1]

The Arabs were equally adamant in their refusal to negotiate a separate settlement for the refugees. Nasser made clear that solving the refugee issue was not his concern. "The danger of Israel," he said, "lies in the very existence of Israel as it is in the present and in what she represents."[2]

Meanwhile, Syria used the Golan Heights, which tower 3,000 feet above the Galilee, to shell Israeli farms and villages. Syria's attacks grew more frequent in 1965 and 1966, while Nasser's rhetoric became increasingly bellicose: "We shall not enter Palestine with its soil covered in sand," he said on March 8, 1965. "We shall enter it with its soil saturated in blood."[3]

Again, a few months later, Nasser expressed the Arabs' aspiration: ". . . the full restoration of the rights of the Palestinian people. In other words, we aim at the destruction of the State of Israel. The immediate aim: perfection of Arab military might. The national aim: the eradication of Israel."[4]

MYTH

"Israel's military strike in 1967 was unprovoked."

FACT

A combination of bellicose Arab rhetoric, threatening behavior and, ultimately, an act of war left Israel no choice but preemptive action. To do this successfully, Israel needed the element of surprise. Had it waited for an Arab invasion, Israel would have been at a potentially catastrophic disadvantage.

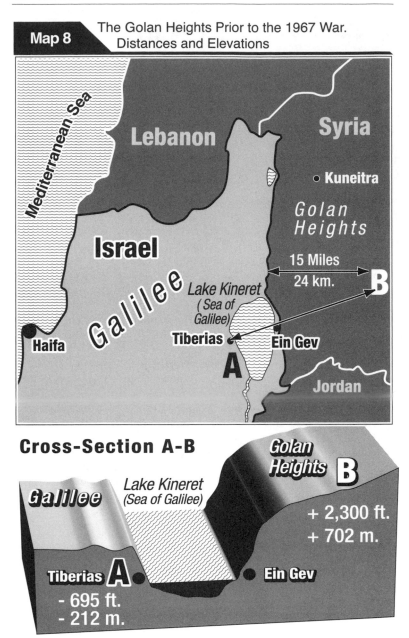

Map 8 The Golan Heights Prior to the 1967 War. Distances and Elevations

Mediterranean Sea

Lebanon

Syria

• Kuneitra

Golan Heights

Israel

15 Miles
24 km.

B

Lake Kineret
(*Sea of Galilee*)

Galilee

Tiberias •

Ein Gev

Haifa

A

Jordan

Cross-Section A-B

Galilee

Lake Kineret
(Sea of Galilee)

Golan Heights **B**

+ 2,300 ft.
+ 702 m.

Tiberias **A**

Ein Gev

- 695 ft.
- 212 m.

While Nasser continued to make speeches threatening war, Arab terrorist attacks grew more frequent. In 1965, 35 raids were conducted against Israel. In 1966, the number increased to 41. In just the first four months of 1967, 37 attacks were launched.[5]

Meanwhile, Syria's attacks on Israeli kibbutzim from the Golan Heights provoked a retaliatory strike on April 7, 1967, during which Israeli planes shot down six Syrian MiGs. Shortly thereafter, the Soviet Union—which had been providing military and economic aid to both Syria and Egypt—gave Damascus information alleging a massive Israeli military buildup in preparation for an attack. Despite Israeli denials, Syria decided to invoke its defense treaty with Egypt.

On May 15, Israel's Independence Day, Egyptian troops began moving into the Sinai and massing near the Israeli border. By May 18, Syrian troops were prepared for battle along the Golan Heights.

Nasser ordered the UN Emergency Force, stationed in the Sinai since 1956, to withdraw on May 16. Without bringing the matter to the attention of the General Assembly, as his predecessor had promised, Secretary-General U Thant complied with the demand. After the withdrawal of the UNEF, the Voice of the Arabs proclaimed (May 18, 1967):

> As of today, there no longer exists an international emergency force to protect Israel. We shall exercise patience no more. We shall not complain any more to the UN about Israel. The sole method we shall apply against Israel is total war, which will result in the extermination of Zionist existence.[6]

An enthusiastic echo was heard on May 20 from Syrian Defense Minister Hafez Assad:

> Our forces are now entirely ready not only to repulse the aggression, but to initiate the act of liberation itself, and to explode the Zionist presence in the Arab homeland. The Syrian army, with its finger on the trigger, is united. . . . I, as a military man, believe that the time has come to enter into a battle of annihilation.[7]

On May 22, Egypt closed the Straits of Tiran to all Israeli shipping and all ships bound for Eilat. This blockade cut off Israel's only supply route with Asia and stopped the flow of oil from its main supplier, Iran. President Johnson declared the blockade illegal and tried, unsuccessfully, to organize an international flotilla to test it.

Nasser was fully aware of the pressure he was exerting to force Israel's hand. The day after the blockade was set up, he said defiantly: "The Jews threaten to make war. I reply: Welcome! We are ready for war."[8]

Nasser challenged Israel to fight almost daily. "Our basic objective will be the destruction of Israel. The Arab people want to fight," he said on May 27.[9] The following day, he added: "We will not accept any . . . coexistence with Israel . . . Today the issue is not the establishment of peace between the Arab states and Israel. . . . The war with Israel is in effect since 1948."[10]

King Hussein of Jordan signed a defense pact with Egypt on May 30. Nasser then announced:

> The armies of Egypt, Jordan, Syria and Lebanon are poised on the borders of Israel . . . to face the challenge, while standing behind us are the armies of Iraq, Algeria, Kuwait, Sudan and the whole Arab nation. This act will astound the world. Today they will know that the Arabs are arranged for battle, the critical hour has arrived. We have reached the stage of serious action and not declarations.[11]

President Abdur Rahman Aref of Iraq joined in the war of words: "The existence of Israel is an error which must be rectified. This is our opportunity to wipe out the ignominy which has been with us since 1948. Our goal is clear—to wipe Israel off the map."[12] On June 4, Iraq joined the military alliance with Egypt, Jordan and Syria.

The Arab rhetoric was matched by the mobilization of Arab forces. Approximately 250,000 troops (nearly half in Sinai), more than 2,000 tanks and 700 aircraft ringed Israel.[13]

By this time, Israeli forces had been on alert for three weeks. The country could not remain fully mobilized indefinitely, nor could it allow its sea lane through the Gulf of Aqaba to be interdicted. Israel's best option was to strike first. On June 5, the order was given to attack Egypt.

MYTH

"Nasser had the right to close the Straits of Tiran to Israeli shipping."

FACT

In 1956, the United States gave Israel assurances that it recognized the Jewish State's right of access to the Straits of Tiran. In 1957, at the UN, 17 maritime powers declared that Israel had a right to transit the Strait. Moreover, the blockade violated the Convention on the Territorial Sea and Contiguous Zone, which was adopted by the UN Conference on the Law of the Sea on April 27, 1958.[14]

The closure of the Strait of Tiran was the casus belli in 1967. Israel's attack was a reaction to this Egyptian first strike. President Johnson acknowledged as much after the war (June 19, 1967):

> If a single act of folly was more responsible for this explosion than any other it was the arbitrary and dangerous announced decision that the Strait of Tiran would be closed. The right of innocent maritime passage must be preserved for all nations.[15]

Map 9 Israel Before June 1967

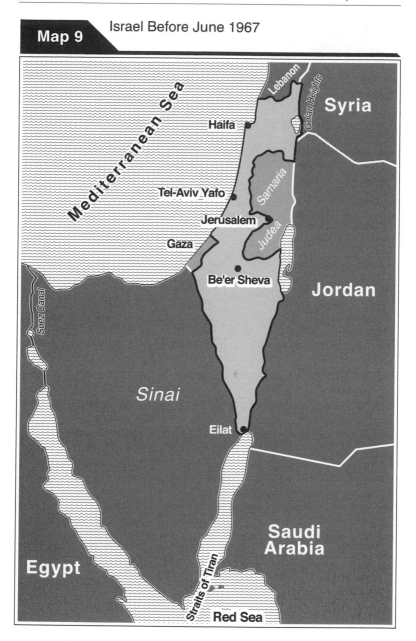

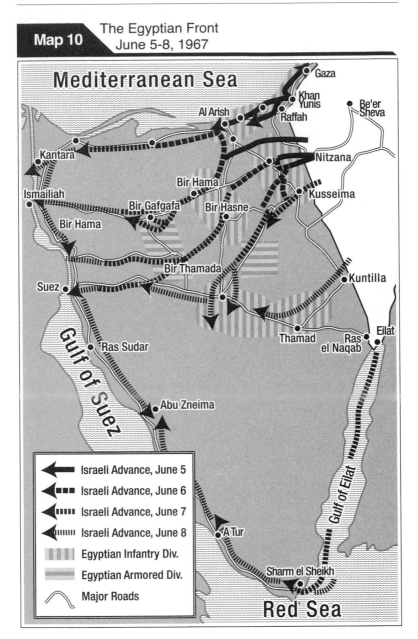

Map 10 The Egyptian Front June 5-8, 1967

MYTH

"The United States helped Israel defeat the Arabs in six days."

FACT

The United States tried to prevent the war through negotiations, but it could not persuade Nasser or the other Arab states to cease their belligerent statements and actions. Still, right before the war, President Johnson warned: "Israel will not be alone unless it decides to go alone."[16] Then, when the war began, the State Department announced: "Our position is neutral in thought, word and deed."[17]

Moreover, while the Arabs were falsely accusing the United States of airlifting supplies to Israel, Johnson imposed an arms embargo on the region (France, Israel's other main arms supplier, also embargoed arms to Israel).

By contrast, the Soviets were supplying massive amounts of arms to the Arabs. Simultaneously, the armies of Kuwait, Algeria, Saudi Arabia and Iraq were contributing troops and arms to the Egyptian, Syrian and Jordanian fronts.[18]

MYTH

"Israel attacked Jordan to capture Jerusalem."

FACT

Prime Minister Levi Eshkol sent a message to King Hussein saying Israel would not attack Jordan unless he initiated hostilities. When Jordanian radar picked up a cluster of planes flying from Egypt to Israel, and the Egyptians convinced Hussein the planes were theirs, he ordered the shelling of West Jerusalem. It turned out the planes were Israel's, and were returning from destroying the Egyptian air force on the ground.

Had Jordan not attacked, the status of Jerusalem would not have changed during the course of the war. Once the city came under fire, however, Israel needed to defend it, and, in doing so, took the opportunity to unify its capital once and for all.

MYTH

"Israel did not have to shoot first."

FACT

After just six days of fighting, Israeli forces broke through the enemy lines and were in a position to march on Cairo, Damascus and Amman. A ceasefire was invoked on June 10.

Map 11 The Battle for Jerusalem
June 5-7, 1967

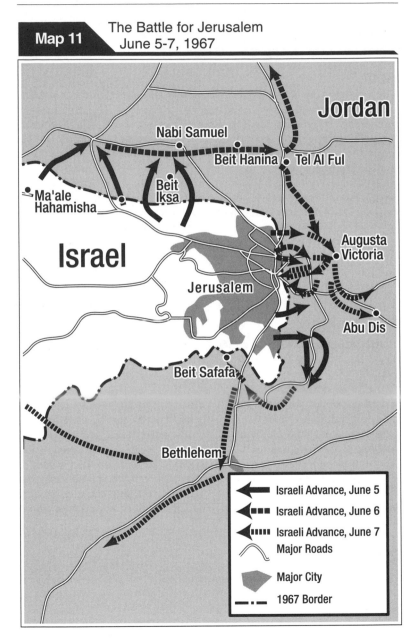

Jordan

Nabi Samuel

Beit Hanina Tel Al Ful

Ma'ale
Hahamisha

Beit
Iksa

Israel

Augusta
Victoria

Jerusalem

Abu Dis

Beit Safafa

Bethlehem

⬅	Israeli Advance, June 5
◀▪▪▪	Israeli Advance, June 6
◀▪▪▪▪	Israeli Advance, June 7
⌒	Major Roads
◆	Major City
▪—▪—	1967 Border

The victory came at a very high cost. In storming the Golan Heights, Israel suffered 115 dead—roughly the number of Americans killed during Operation Desert Storm. Altogether, Israel lost twice as many men—777 dead and 2,586 wounded—in proportion to her total population as the U.S. lost in eight years of fighting in Vietnam.[19] Also, despite the incredible success of the air campaign, the Israeli Air Force lost 46 of its 200 fighters.[20] Had Israel waited for the Arabs to strike first, as it did in 1973, and not taken preemptive action, the cost would certainly have been much higher and victory could not have been assured.

MYTH

"Israel had no intention of negotiating over the future of the territories it captured."

FACT

By the end of the war, Israel had captured enough territory to more than triple the size of the area it controlled, from 8,000 to 26,000 square miles. The victory enabled Israel to unify Jerusalem. Israeli forces had also captured the Sinai, the Golan Heights, the Gaza Strip and the West Bank.

Israel's leaders expected to negotiate a peace agreement with their neighbors and, almost immediately after the war, expressed their willingness to negotiate a return of at least some of the territories. Israel subsequently returned all of the Sinai to Egypt, territory claimed by Jordan was returned to the Hashemite Kingdom, and all of the Gaza Strip and more than 40 percent of the West Bank were given to the Palestinians to establish the Palestinian Authority.

To date, approximately 94 percent of the territories won in the defensive war have been given by Israel to its Arab neighbors. This demonstrates Israel's willingness to make territorial compromises.

MYTH

"Israel expelled peaceful Arab villagers from the West Bank and prevented them from returning after the war."

FACT

After Jordan launched its attack on June 5, approximately 325,000 Palestinians living in the West Bank fled.[21] These were Jordanian citizens who moved from one part of what they considered their country to another, primarily to avoid being caught in the cross fire of a war.

A Palestinian refugee who was an administrator in a UNRWA camp in Jericho said Arab politicians had spread rumors in the camp. "They said all the young people would be killed. People heard on the radio

Map 12 Cease-Fire Lines After the Six-Day War 1967

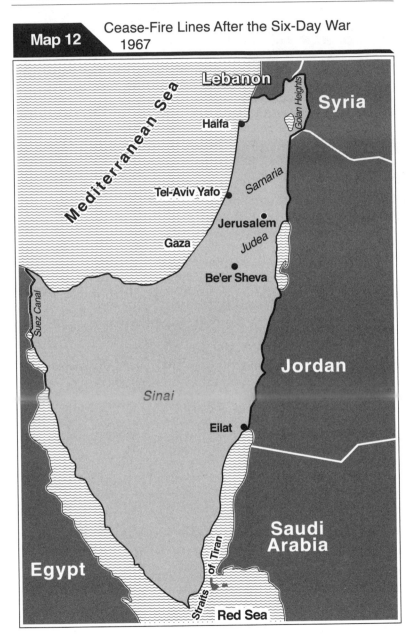

that this is not the end, only the beginning, so they think maybe it will be a long war and they want to be in Jordan."[22]

Some Palestinians who left preferred to live in an Arab state rather than under Israeli military rule. Members of various PLO factions fled to avoid capture by the Israelis. Nils-Göran Gussing, the person appointed by the UN Secretary-General to investigate the situation, found that many Arabs also feared they would no longer be able to receive money from family members working abroad.[23]

Israeli forces ordered a handful of Palestinians to move for "strategic and security reasons." In some cases, they were allowed to return in a few days, in others Israel offered to help them resettle elsewhere.[24]

Israel now ruled more than three-quarters of a million Palestinians— most of whom were hostile to the government. Nevertheless, more than 9,000 Palestinian families were reunited in 1967. Ultimately, more than 60,000 Palestinians were allowed to return.[25]

After the Six-Day War ended, President Johnson announced his view of what was required next to end the conflict:

"Certainly, troops must be withdrawn; but there must also be recognized rights of national life, progress in solving the refugee problem, freedom of innocent maritime passage, limitation of the arms race and respect for political independence and territorial integrity."[26]

MYTH

"Israel deliberately attacked the USS Liberty."

FACT

The Israeli attack on the *USS Liberty* was a grievous error, largely attributable to the confusion of war. Ten official United States investigations and three Israeli inquiries have all conclusively established the attack was a tragic mistake.

On June 8, 1967, the fourth day of the Six-Day War, the Israeli high command received reports that Israeli troops in El Arish were being fired upon from the sea, presumably by an Egyptian vessel. The United States had earlier announced at the UN that it had no naval forces within hundreds of miles of the front; however, the *USS Liberty,* an American intelligence ship assigned to monitor the fighting, had sailed into the area. Following a series of United States communication failures, whereby messages directing the ship not to approach within 100 miles were not received by the *Liberty,* the ship moved within 14 miles of the Sinai coast. The Israelis mistakenly thought this was the ship shelling their soldiers and directed war planes and torpedo boats to attack the ship. Thirty-four members of the *Liberty's* crew were killed and 171 were wounded.

Tapes of the radio transmissions made prior, during and after the attack do not contain any statement suggesting the pilots saw a U.S. flag on the ship. During the raid, a pilot specifically says, "there is no flag on her!" The recordings also indicate that once the pilots became concerned about the identity of the ship, by virtue of reading its hull number, they terminated the attack and they were given an order to leave the area.[27] Critics claimed the Israeli tape was doctored, but the National Security Agency of the United States released formerly top secret transcripts in July 2003 that confirmed the Israeli version.

Numerous mistakes were made by both the United States and Israel. For example, the *Liberty* was first reported—incorrectly, as it turned out—to be cruising at 30 knots (it was later recalculated to be 28 knots). Under Israeli (and U.S.) naval doctrine at the time, a ship proceeding at that speed was presumed to be a warship. The sea was calm and the U.S. Navy Court of Inquiry found that the Liberty's flag was very likely drooped and not discernible; moreover, members of the crew, including the Captain, Commander William McGonagle, testified that the flag was knocked down after the first or second assault.

According to Israeli Chief of Staff Yitzhak Rabin's memoirs, there were standing orders to attack any unidentified vessel near the shore.[28] The day fighting began, Israel had asked that American ships be removed from its coast or that it be notified of the precise location of U.S. vessels.[29] The Sixth Fleet was moved because President Johnson feared being drawn into a confrontation with the Soviet Union. He also ordered that no aircraft be sent near Sinai.

A CIA report on the incident issued June 13, 1967, also found that an overzealous pilot could mistake the *Liberty* for an Egyptian ship, the *El Quseir.* After the air raid, Israeli torpedo boats identified the *Liberty* as an Egyptian naval vessel. When the *Liberty* began shooting at the Israelis, they responded with the torpedo attack, which killed 28 of the sailors.

Initially, the Israelis were terrified that they had attacked a *Soviet* ship and might have provoked the Soviets to join the fighting.[30] Once the Israelis were sure what had happened, they reported the incident to the U.S. Embassy in Tel Aviv and offered to provide a helicopter for the Americans to fly out to the ship and to help evacuate the injured and salvage the ship. The offer was accepted and a U.S. naval attaché was flown to the *Liberty.*

The Israelis were "obviously shocked" by the error they made in attacking the ship, according to the U.S. Ambassador in Tel Aviv. In fact, according to a secret report on the 1967 war, the immediate concern was that the Arabs might see the proximity of the *Liberty* to the conflict as evidence of U.S.-Israel collusion.[31]

A U.S. spy plane was sent to the area as soon as the NSA learned of the attack on the *Liberty* and recorded the conversations of two Israeli Air Force helicopter pilots, which took place between 2:30 and 3:37 p.m. on June 8. The orders radioed to the pilots by their supervisor at the Hatzor base instructing them to search for Egyptian survivors from the "Egyptian warship" that had just been bombed were also recorded by the NSA. "Pay attention. The ship is now identified as Egyptian," the pilots were informed. Nine minutes later, Hatzor told the pilots the ship was believed to be an Egyptian cargo ship. At 3:07, the pilots were first told the ship might not be Egyptian and were instructed to search for survivors and inform the base immediately the nationality of the first person they rescued. It was not until 3:12 that one of the pilots reported that he saw an American flag flying over the ship at which point he was instructed to verify if it was indeed a U.S. vessel.[32]

In October 2003, the first Israeli pilot to reach the ship broke his 36-year silence on the attack. Brig.-Gen. Yiftah Spector said he had been told an Egyptian ship was off the Gaza coast. "This ship positively did not have any symbol or flag that I could see. What I was concerned with was that it was not one of ours. I looked for the symbol of our navy, which was a large white cross on its deck. This was not there, so it wasn't one of ours." The *Jerusalem Post* obtained a recording of Spector's radio transmission in which he said, "I can't identify it, but in any case it's a military ship."[33]

Many of the survivors of the *Liberty* remain bitter, and are convinced the attack was deliberate. None of Israel's accusers, however, can explain why Israel would deliberately attack an American ship at a time when the United States was Israel's only friend and supporter in the world. Confusion in a long line of communications, which occurred in a tense atmosphere on both the American and Israeli sides is a more probable explanation.

Accidents caused by "friendly fire" are common in wartime. In 1988, the U.S. Navy mistakenly downed an Iranian passenger plane, killing 290 civilians. During the Gulf War, 35 of the 148 Americans who died in battle were killed by "friendly fire." In April 1994, two U.S. Black Hawk helicopters with large U.S. flags painted on each side were shot down by U.S. Air Force F-15s on a clear day in the "no fly" zone of Iraq, killing 26 people. In April 2002, an American F-16 dropped a bomb that killed four Canadian soldiers in Afghanistan. In fact, the day before the *Liberty* was attacked, Israeli pilots accidentally bombed one of their own armored columns.[34]

Retired Admiral, Shlomo Erell, who was Chief of the Navy in Israel in June 1967, told the Associated Press (June 5, 1977): "No one would ever have dreamt that an American ship would be there. Even the United States didn't know where its ship was. We were advised by the proper authorities that there was no American ship within 100 miles."

Secretary of Defense Robert McNamara told Congress on July 26, 1967: "It was the conclusion of the investigatory body, headed by an admiral of the Navy in whom we have great confidence, that the attack was not intentional." Twenty years later, he repeated his belief that the attack was a mistake, telling a caller on the "Larry King Show" that he had seen nothing in the 20 years since to change his mind that there had been no "coverup."[35]

In January 2004, the State Department held a conference on the *Liberty* incident and also released new documents, including CIA memos dated June 13 and June 21, 1967, which say that Israel did not know it was striking an American vessel. The historian for the National Security Agency, David Hatch, said the available evidence "strongly suggested" Israel did not know it was attacking a U.S. ship. Two former U.S. officials, Ernest Castle, the United States Naval Attaché at the U.S. Embassy in Tel Aviv in June 1967, who received the first report of the attack from Israel, and John Hadden, then CIA Chief of Station in Tel Aviv, also agreed with the assessment that the attack on the *Liberty* was a mistake.[36]

Israel apologized for the tragedy and paid nearly $13 million in humanitarian reparations to the United States and to the families of the victims in amounts established by the U.S. State Department. The matter was officially closed between the two governments by an exchange of diplomatic notes on December 17, 1987.

Notes

1. *Encyclopedia Americana Annual 1961*, (NY: Americana Corporation, 1961), p. 387.
2. Speech by Nasser to the United Arab Republic National Assembly, March 26, 1964, quoted in Yehoshafat Harkabi, *Arab Attitudes To Israel*, (Jerusalem: Keter Publishing House, 1972), p. 27.
3. Howard Sachar, *A History of Israel: From the Rise of Zionism to Our Time*, (NY: Alfred A. Knopf, 1979), p. 616.
4. Samuel Katz, *Battleground-Fact and Fantasy in Palestine*, (NY: Bantam Books, 1985), pp. 10-11, 185.
5. Netanel Lorch, *One Long War*, (Jerusalem: Keter, 1976), p. 110.
6. Isi Leibler, *The Case For Israel*, (Australia: The Globe Press, 1972), p. 60.
7. Ibid.
8. Abba Eban, *Abba Eban*, (NY: Random House, 1977 p. 330.
9. Leibler, p. 60.
10. Leibler, p. 18.
11. Leibler, p. 60.
12. Leibler, p. 18.
13. Chaim Herzog, *The Arab-Israeli Wars*, (NY: Random House, 1982), p. 149.
14. *United Nations Conference on the Law of the Sea*, (Geneva: UN Publications 1958), pp. 132-134.
15. Yehuda Lukacs, *Documents on the Israeli-Palestinian Conflict 1967-1983*, (NY: Cambridge University Press, 1984), pp. 17-18; Eban, p. 358.
16. Lyndon B. Johnson, *The Vantage Point: Perspectives of the Presidency 1963-1969*, (NY: Holt, Rinehart and Winston, 1971), p. 293.
17. Associated Press, (June 5, 1967).

18. Sachar, p. 629.
19. Katz, p. 3.
20. *Jerusalem Post,* (April 23, 1999).
21. *Encyclopedia Americana Annual 1968,* p. 366.
22. George Gruen, "The Refugees of Arab-Israeli Conflict," (NY: American Jewish Committee, March 1969), p. 5.
23. Gruen, p. 5.
24. Gruen, p. 4.
25. *Encyclopedia Americana Annual 1968,* p. 366.
26. Lyndon B. Johnson, *Public Papers of the President,* (DC: GPO 1968), p. 683.
27. Hirsh Goodman, "Messrs. Errors and No Facts," *Jerusalem Report,* (November 21, 1991); Arieh O'Sullivan, "Exclusive: Liberty attack tapes revealed," *Jerusalem Post,* (June 3, 2004).
28. For the most comprehensive analysis, see A. Jay Cristol, *The Liberty Incident,* (Washington, D.C.: Brassey's Inc., 2002); Yitzhak Rabin, *The Rabin Memoirs,* (CA: University of California Press, 1996), pp. 108–109.
29. Rabin, p. 110.
30. Dan Kurzman, *Soldier of Peace: The Life of Yitzhak Rabin,* (NY: HarperCollins, 1998), pp. 224–227; Rabin, p. 108–109.
31. "United States Policy and Diplomacy in the Middle East Crisis, May 15–June 10, 1967," declassified secret document, Lyndon Johnson Presidential Library, pp. 143–144.
32. Nathan Guttman, "Memos show Liberty attack was an error," *Ha'aretz,* (July 9, 2003).
33. "Pilot who bombed 'Liberty' talks to Post," *Jerusalem Post,* (October 10, 2003).
34. Hirsh Goodman and Ze'ev Schiff, "The Attack on the *Liberty,*" *Atlantic Monthly,* (September 1984).
35. *"The Larry King Show"* (radio), (February 5, 1987).
36. *Jerusalem Post,* (January 13, 2004); *Washington Times,* (January 13, 2004).

7. The War of Attrition, 1967–1970

MYTH

"The Palestinians were willing to negotiate a settlement after the Six-Day War."

FACT

The Arab League created the Palestine Liberation Organization (PLO) in Cairo in 1964 as a weapon against Israel. Until the Six-Day War, the PLO engaged in terrorist attacks that contributed to the momentum toward conflict. Neither the PLO nor any other Palestinian groups campaigned for Jordan or Egypt to create an independent Palestinian state in the West Bank and Gaza. The focus of Palestinian activism was on the destruction of Israel.

After the Arab states were defeated in 1967, the Palestinians did not alter their basic objective. With one million Arabs coming under Israeli rule, some Palestinians believed the prospect for waging a popular war of liberation had grown. Toward that end, Yasser Arafat instigated a campaign of terror from the West Bank. During September–December 1967, 61 attacks were launched, most against civilian targets such as factories, movie theaters and private homes.[1]

Israeli security forces gradually became more effective in thwarting terrorist plans inside Israel and the territories. Consequently, the PLO began to pursue a different strategy—attacking Jews and Israeli targets abroad. In early 1968, the first of many aircraft was hijacked by Palestinian terrorists.

MYTH

"After the 1967 war, Israel refused to negotiate a settlement with the Arabs."

FACT

After its victory in the Six-Day War, Israel hoped the Arab states would enter peace negotiations. Israel signaled to the Arab states its willingness to relinquish virtually all the territories it acquired in exchange for peace. As Moshe Dayan put it, Jerusalem was waiting only for a telephone call from Arab leaders to start negotiations.[2]

But these hopes were dashed in August 1967 when Arab leaders meeting in Khartoum adopted a formula of three noes: "no peace with Israel, no negotiations with Israel, no recognition of Israel. . . ."[3]

As former Israeli President Chaim Herzog wrote: "Israel's belief that the war had come to an end and that peace would now reign along the borders was soon dispelled. Three weeks after the conclusion of hostilities, the first major incident occurred on the Suez Canal."[4]

MYTH

"According to Security Council Resolution 242, Israel's acquisition of territory through the 1967 war is 'inadmissible.' "

FACT

On November 22, 1967, the UN Security Council unanimously adopted Resolution 242, establishing the principles that were to guide the negotiations for an Arab-Israeli peace settlement. This resolution was a tortuously negotiated compromise between competing proposals.

The first point addressed by the resolution is the "inadmissibility of the acquisition of territory by war." Some people take this to mean that Israel is required to withdraw from all the territories it captured. On the contrary, the reference clearly applies only to an offensive war. If not, the resolution would provide an incentive for aggression. If one country attacks another, and the defender repels the attack and acquires territory in the process, the former interpretation would require the defender to return all the land it took. Thus, aggressors would have little to lose because they would be insured against the main consequence of defeat.

"This is the first war in history which has ended with the victors suing for peace and the vanquished calling for unconditional surrender."

—Abba Eban[5]

The ultimate goal of 242, as expressed in paragraph 3, is the achievement of a "peaceful and accepted settlement." This means a negotiated agreement based on the resolution's principles rather than one imposed upon the parties. This is also the implication of Resolution 338, according to Arthur Goldberg, the American ambassador who led the delegation to the UN in 1967.[6] That resolution, adopted after the 1973 war, called for negotiations between the parties to start immediately and concurrently with the ceasefire.

MYTH

"Resolution 242 requires Israel to return to its pre-1967 boundaries."

FACT

The most controversial clause in Resolution 242 is the call for the "Withdrawal of Israeli armed forces from territories occupied in the recent conflict." This is linked to the second unambiguous clause calling for "termination of all claims or states of belligerency" and the recognition that "every State in the area" has the "right to live in peace within secure and recognized boundaries free from threats or acts of force."

The resolution does not make Israeli withdrawal a prerequisite for Arab action. Moreover, it does not specify how much territory Israel is required to give up. The Security Council did not say Israel must withdraw from "all the" territories occupied after the Six-Day War. This was quite deliberate. The Soviet delegate wanted the inclusion of those words and said that their exclusion meant "that part of these territories can remain in Israeli hands." The Arab states pushed for the word "all" to be included, but this was rejected. They nevertheless asserted that they would read the resolution as if it included the word "all." Lord Caradon, the British Ambassador who drafted the approved resolution, declared after the vote: "It is only the resolution that will bind us, and we regard its wording as clear."[7]

This literal interpretation, without the implied "all," was repeatedly declared to be the correct one by those involved in drafting the resolution. On October 29, 1969, for example, the British Foreign Secretary told the House of Commons the withdrawal envisaged by the resolution would not be from "all the territories."[8] When asked to explain the British position later, Lord Caradon said: "It would have been wrong to demand that Israel return to its positions of June 4, 1967, because those positions were undesirable and artificial."[9]

Similarly, U.S. Ambassador Arthur Goldberg explained: "The notable omissions—which were not accidental—in regard to withdrawal are the words 'the' or 'all' and 'the June 5, 1967 lines' . . . the resolution speaks of withdrawal from occupied territories without defining the extent of withdrawal."[10]

The resolutions clearly call on the Arab states to make peace with Israel. The principal condition is that Israel withdraw from "territories occupied" in 1967. Since Israel withdrew from approximately 94 percent of the territories when it gave up the Sinai, the Gaza Strip and portions of West Bank, it has already partially, if not wholly, fulfilled its obligation under 242.

The Arab states also objected to the call for "secure and recognized boundaries" because they feared this implied negotiations with Israel. The Arab League explicitly ruled this out at Khartoum in August 1967, when it proclaimed the three "noes." Goldberg explained that this phrase was specifically included because the parties were expected to make "territorial adjustments in their peace settlement encompassing less than a complete withdrawal of Israeli forces from occupied territories, inasmuch as Israel's prior frontiers had proved to be notably insecure."

The question, then, is whether Israel has to give up any additional territory. Now that peace agreements have been signed with Egypt and Jordan, and Israel has withdrawn to the international border with Lebanon, the only remaining territorial disputes are with the Palestinians (who are not even mentioned in 242) and Syria.

The dispute with Syria is over the Golan Heights. Israel has repeatedly expressed a willingness to negotiate a compromise in exchange for peace; however, Syria has refused to consider even a limited peace treaty unless Israel first agrees to a complete withdrawal. Under 242, Israel has no obligation to withdraw from any part of the Golan in the absence of a peace accord with Syria.

Meanwhile, other Arab states—such as Saudi Arabia, Lebanon, and Libya—continue to maintain a state of war with Israel, or have refused to grant Israel diplomatic recognition, even though they have no territorial disputes with Israel. These states have nevertheless conditioned their relations (at least rhetorically) on an Israeli withdrawal to the pre-1967 borders.

Although ignored by most analysts, Resolution 242 does have other provisions. One requirement is that freedom of navigation be guaranteed. This clause was included because a principal cause of the 1967 war was Egypt's blockade of the Strait of Tiran.

MYTH

"Resolution 242 recognizes a Palestinian right to self-determination."

FACT

The Palestinians are not mentioned anywhere in Resolution 242. They are only alluded to in the second clause of the second article of 242, which calls for "a just settlement of the refugee problem." Nowhere does it require that Palestinians be given any political rights or territory.

MYTH

"The Arab states and the PLO accepted Resolution 242 whereas Israel rejected it."

FACT

The Arab states have traditionally said they accepted 242 as defined by them, that is, as requiring Israel's total, unconditional withdrawal from the disputed territories.

In a statement to the General Assembly on October 15, 1968, the PLO rejected Resolution 242, insisting "the implementation of said resolution will lead to the loss of every hope for the establishment of peace and security in Palestine and the Middle East region." By contrast, Ambassador Abba Eban expressed Israel's position to the Security Council on May 1, 1968: "My government has indicated its acceptance of the Security Council resolution for the promotion of agreement on the establishment of a just and lasting peace. I am also authorized to reaffirm that we are willing to seek agreement with each Arab State on all matters included in that resolution."

It took nearly a quarter century, but the PLO finally agreed that Resolutions 242 and 338 should be the basis for negotiations with Israel when it signed the Declaration of Principles in September 1993.

MYTH

"Israel was responsible for the War of Attrition."

FACT

Egypt's President Gamal Nasser thought that because most of Israel's army consisted of reserves, it could not withstand a lengthy war of attrition. He believed Israel would be unable to endure the economic burden, and the constant casualties would undermine Israeli morale. To pursue this strategy of slowly weakening Israel, Nasser ordered attacks on Israel that were calibrated so that they would not provoke an all-out Israeli war in response.

As early as July 1, 1967, Egypt began shelling Israeli positions near the Suez Canal. On October 21, 1967, Egypt sank the Israeli destroyer *Eilat,* killing 47. A few months later, Egyptian artillery began to shell Israeli positions along the Suez Canal and Israeli military patrols were ambushed. This bloody War of Attrition, as it became known, lasted three years. The Israeli death toll between June 15, 1967, and August 8, 1970 (when a cease-fire was declared), was 1,424 soldiers and more than 100 civilians. Another 2,000 soldiers and 700 civilians were wounded.[11]

MYTH

"Egypt terminated the War of Attrition and offered peace to Israel, only to have Jerusalem spurn these initiatives."

FACT

In the summer of 1970, the United States persuaded Israel and Egypt to accept a cease-fire. This cease-fire was designed to lead to negotiations under UN auspices. Israel declared that it would accept the principle of withdrawal from territories it had captured.

But on August 7, the Soviets and Egyptians deployed sophisticated ground-to-air SAM-2 and SAM-3 missiles in the restricted 32-mile-deep zone along the west bank of the Suez Canal. This was a clear violation of the cease-fire agreement, which barred the introduction or construction of any military installations in this area.

Time magazine observed that U.S. reconnaissance "showed that the 36 SAM-2 missiles sneaked into the cease-fire zone constitute only the first line of the most massive anti-aircraft system ever created."[12]

Defense Department satellite photos demonstrated conclusively that 63 SAM-2 sites were installed in a 78-mile band between the cities of Ismailia and Suez. Three years later, these missiles provided air coverage for Egypt's surprise attack against Israel.[13]

Despite the Egyptian violations, the UN-sponsored talks resumed—additional evidence that Israel was anxious to make progress toward peace. The talks were swiftly short-circuited, however, by UN Special Envoy Gunnar Jarring, when he accepted the Egyptian interpretation of Resolution 242 and called for Israel's total withdrawal to the pre-June 5, 1967, demarcation lines.

On that basis, Egypt expressed its willingness "to enter into a peace agreement with Israel" in a February 20, 1971, letter to Jarring. But this seeming moderation masked an unchanging Egyptian irredentism and unwillingness to accept a real peace, as shown by the letter's sweeping reservations and preconditions.

The crucial sentences about a "peace agreement with Israel" were neither published nor broadcast in Egypt. Moreover, Egypt refused to enter direct talks. Israel attempted to at least transform the struggling Jarring mission into indirect talks by addressing all letters not to Jarring, but to the Egyptian government. Egypt refused to accept them.

Just after the letter to Jarring, Anwar Sadat, Egypt's new president, addressed the Palestine National Council (PNC) meeting in Cairo. He promised support to the PLO "until victory" and declared that Egypt would not accept Resolution 242.[14]

Five days after Sadat suggested he was ready to make peace with Israel, Mohammed Heikal, a Sadat confidant and editor of the semi-official *Al-Ahram,* wrote:

> Arab policy at this stage has but two objectives. The first, the elimination of the traces of the 1967 aggression through an Israeli withdrawal from all the territories it occupied that year. The second objective is the elimination of the traces of the 1948 aggression, by the means of the elimination of the State of Israel itself. This is, however, as yet an abstract, undefined objective, and some of us have erred in commencing the latter step before the former.[15]

MYTH

"Israel's rejection of Egyptian peace initiatives led to the Yom Kippur War."

FACT

With the collapse of the Jarring mission, the United States undertook a new initiative. It proposed an Israeli-Egyptian interim agreement, calling for Israel's partial withdrawal from the Suez Canal and the opening of that waterway.

Israel was willing to enter negotiations without preconditions, but Sadat demanded that Israel agree, as part of an interim agreement, to withdraw ultimately to the old 1967 lines. In effect, Sadat was seeking an advance guarantee of the outcome of "negotiations." This was unacceptable to Israel and suggested that Sadat was not genuinely interested in peace.

Notes

1. Netanel Lorch, *One Long War,* (Jerusalem: Keter, 1976), pp. 139–146.
2. Walter Lacquer, *The Road to War,* (London: Weidenfeld and Nicolson, 1968), p. 297.
3. Yehuda Lukacs, *Documents on the Israeli-Palestinian Conflict 1967-1983,* (NY: Cambridge University Press, 1984), p. 213.
4. Chaim Herzog, *The Arab-Israeli Wars,* (NY: Random House, 1982), p. 195.
5. Abba Eban, *Abba Eban,* (NY: Random House, 1977), p. 446.
6. *Jerusalem Post,* (May 28, 1984).
7. Prosper Weil, "Territorial Settlement in the Resolution of November 22, 1967," in John Moore, ed., *The Arab-Israeli Conflict,* (NJ: Princeton University Press, 1974), p. 321.
8. Eban, p. 452.
9. *Beirut Daily Star,* (June 12, 1974).
10. Speech to AIPAC Policy Conference, (May 8, 1973).
11. Some historians consider the starting date of the War of Attrition in 1968 or 1969. We are using Chaim Herzog's time frame. Chaim Herzog, *The Arab-Israeli Wars,* (NY: Random House, 1984), pp. 195-221; Nadav Safran, *Israel The Embattled Ally,* (MA: Harvard University Press, 1981), p. 266.
12. *Time,* (September 14, 1970).
13. John Pimlott, *The Middle East Conflicts From 1945 to the Present,* (NY: Crescent Books, 1983), p. 99.
14. Radio Cairo, (February 27, 1971).
15. *Al-Ahram,* (February 25, 1971).

8. The 1973 War

MYTH

"Israel was responsible for the 1973 war."

FACT

On October 6, 1973—Yom Kippur, the holiest day in the Jewish calendar—Egypt and Syria opened a coordinated surprise attack against Israel. The equivalent of the total forces of NATO in Europe was mobilized on Israel's borders.[1] On the Golan Heights, approximately 180 Israeli tanks faced an onslaught of 1,400 Syrian tanks. Along the Suez Canal, fewer than 500 Israeli defenders were attacked by 80,000 Egyptians.

Thrown onto the defensive during the first two days of fighting, Israel mobilized its reserves and eventually repulsed the invaders and carried the war deep into Syria and Egypt. The Arab states were swiftly resupplied by sea and air from the Soviet Union, which rejected United States efforts to work toward an immediate ceasefire. As a result, the United States belatedly began its own airlift to Israel. Two weeks later, Egypt was saved from a disastrous defeat by the UN Security Council, which had failed to act while the tide was in the Arabs' favor.

The Soviet Union showed no interest in initiating peacemaking efforts while it looked like the Arabs might win. The same was true for UN Secretary-General Kurt Waldheim.

On October 22, the Security Council adopted Resolution 338 calling for "all parties to the present fighting to cease all firing and terminate all military activity immediately." The vote came on the day that Israeli forces cut off and isolated the Egyptian Third Army and were in a position to destroy it.[2]

Despite the Israel Defense Forces' ultimate success on the battlefield, the war was considered a diplomatic and military failure. A total of 2,688 Israeli soldiers were killed.

MYTH

"Anwar Sadat agreed to U.S. peace proposals and did not seek war."

FACT

In 1971, Egyptian President Anwar Sadat raised the possibility of signing an agreement with Israel, provided that all the disputed territories were

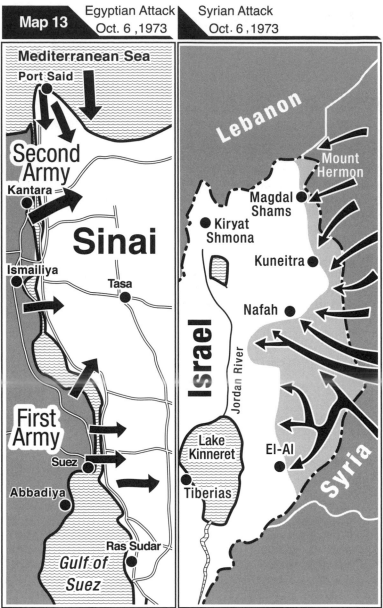

Map 13   Egyptian Attack Oct. 6 ,1973   Syrian Attack Oct. 6 ,1973

returned by Israel. No progress toward peace was made, however, so, the following year, Sadat said war was inevitable and he was prepared to sacrifice one million soldiers in the showdown with Israel.[3] His threat did not materialize that year.

Throughout 1972, and for much of 1973, Sadat threatened war unless the United States forced Israel to accept his interpretation of Resolution 242—total Israeli withdrawal from territories taken in 1967.

Simultaneously, the Egyptian leader carried on a diplomatic offensive among European and African states to win support for his cause. He appealed to the Soviets to bring pressure on the United States and to provide Egypt with more offensive weapons to cross the Suez Canal. The Soviet Union was more interested in maintaining the appearance of détente with the United States than in confrontation in the Middle East; therefore, it rejected Sadat's demands. Sadat's response was to abruptly expel approximately 20,000 Soviet advisers from Egypt.

In an April 1973 interview, Sadat again warned he would renew the war with Israel.[4] But it was the same threat he had made in 1971 and 1972, and most observers remained skeptical.

The United States agreed with Israel's view that Egypt should engage in direct negotiations. The U.S.-sponsored truce was three-years-old and Secretary of State Henry Kissinger had opened a new dialogue for peace at the UN. Almost everyone was confident the prospect of a new war was remote.

Sadat reacted acidly to Kissinger's initiative:

> The United States is still under Zionist pressure. The glasses the United States is wearing on its eyes are entirely Zionist glasses, completely blind to everything except what Israel wants. We do not accept this.[5]

"All countries should wage war against the Zionists, who are there to destroy all human organizations and to destroy civilization and the work which good people are trying to do."

—King Faisal of Saudi Arabia[6]

MYTH

"Egypt and Syria were the only Arab states involved in the 1973 war."

FACT

At least nine Arab states, including four non-Middle Eastern nations, actively aided the Egyptian-Syrian war effort.

A few months before the Yom Kippur War, Iraq transferred a squadron of Hunter jets to Egypt. During the war, an Iraqi division of some 18,000 men and several hundred tanks was deployed in the central Golan and participated in the October 16 attack against Israeli positions.[7] Iraqi MiGs began operating over the Golan Heights as early as October 8, the third day of the war.

Besides serving as financial underwriters, Saudi Arabia and Kuwait committed men to battle. A Saudi brigade of approximately 3,000 troops was dispatched to Syria, where it participated in fighting along the approaches to Damascus. Also, violating Paris's ban on the transfer of French-made weapons, Libya sent Mirage fighters to Egypt (from 1971-1973, Libyan President Muammar Qaddafi gave Cairo more than $1 billion in aid to rearm Egypt and to pay the Soviets for weapons delivered).[8]

Other North African countries responded to Arab and Soviet calls to aid the frontline states. Algeria sent three aircraft squadrons of fighters and bombers, an armored brigade and 150 tanks. Approximately 1,000-2,000 Tunisian soldiers were positioned in the Nile Delta. The Sudan stationed 3,500 troops in southern Egypt, and Morocco sent three brigades to the front lines, including 2,500 men to Syria.

Lebanese radar units were used by Syrian air defense forces. Lebanon also allowed Palestinian terrorists to shell Israeli civilian settlements from its territory. Palestinians fought on the Southern Front with the Egyptians and Kuwaitis.[9]

The least enthusiastic participant in the October fighting was probably Jordan's King Hussein, who apparently had been kept uninformed of Egyptian and Syrian war plans. But Hussein did send two of his best units to Syria. This force took positions in the southern sector, defending the main Amman-Damascus route and attacking Israeli positions along the Kuneitra-Sassa road on October 16. Three Jordanian artillery batteries also participated in the assault, carried out by nearly 100 tanks.[10]

Notes

1. Chaim Herzog, *The Arab-Israeli Wars,* (NY: Random House, 1984), p. 230.
2. Herzog, p. 280.
3. Howard Sachar, *A History of Israel: From the Rise of Zionism to Our Time,* (NY: Alfred A. Knopf, 1979), p. 747.
4. *Newsweek,* (April 9, 1973).
5. Radio Cairo, (September 28, 1973).
6. *Beirut Daily Star,* (November 17, 1972).
7. Trevor Dupuy, *Elusive Victory: The Arab-Israeli Wars, 1947-1974,* (NY: Harper & Row, 1978), p. 462.
8. Dupuy, p. 376; Herzog, p. 278; Nadav Safran, *Israel The Embattled Ally,* (MA: Harvard University Press, 1981), p. 499.
9. Herzog, p. 278, 285, 293; Dupuy, 534.
10. Herzog, p. 300.

9. Boundaries

MYTH

"The creation of Israel in 1948 changed political and border arrangements between independent states that had existed for centuries."

FACT

The boundaries of Middle East countries were arbitrarily fixed by the Western powers after Turkey was defeated in World War I and the French and British mandates were set up. The areas allotted to Israel under the UN partition plan had all been under the control of the Ottomans, who had ruled Palestine from 1517 until 1917.

When Turkey was defeated in World War I, the French took over the area now known as Lebanon and Syria. The British assumed control of Palestine and Iraq. In 1926, the borders were redrawn and Lebanon was separated from Syria.

Britain installed the Emir Faisal, who had been deposed by the French in Syria, as ruler of the new kingdom of Iraq. In 1922, the British created the emirate of Transjordan, which incorporated all of Palestine east of the Jordan River. This was done so that the Emir Abdullah, whose family had been defeated in tribal warfare in the Arabian peninsula, would have a Kingdom to rule. None of the countries that border Israel became independent until the Twentieth Century. Many other Arab nations became independent after Israel.[1]

MYTH

"Israel has been an expansionist state since its creation."

FACT

Israel's boundaries were determined by the United Nations when it adopted the partition resolution in 1947. In a series of defensive wars, Israel captured additional territory. On numerous occasions, Israel has withdrawn from these areas.

As part of the 1974 disengagement agreement, Israel returned territories captured in the 1967 and 1973 wars to Syria.

Under the terms of the 1979 Israeli-Egyptian peace treaty, Israel withdrew from the Sinai peninsula for the third time. It had already withdrawn from large parts of the desert area it captured in its War of

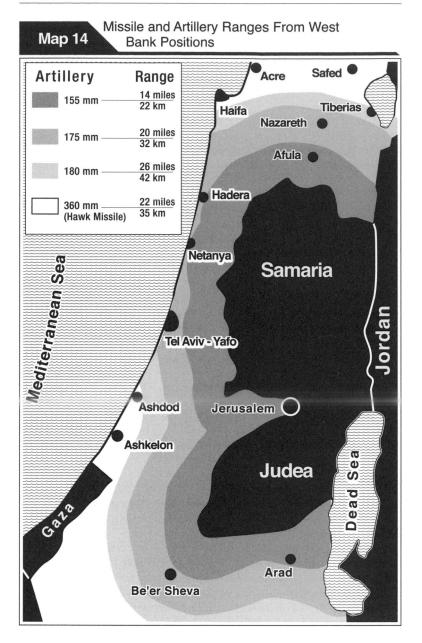

Map 14 — Missile and Artillery Ranges From West Bank Positions

Artillery		Range
	155 mm	14 miles / 22 km
	175 mm	20 miles / 32 km
	180 mm	26 miles / 42 km
	360 mm (Hawk Missile)	22 miles / 35 km

Independence. After capturing the entire Sinai in the 1956 Suez conflict, Israel relinquished the peninsula to Egypt a year later. In September 1983, Israel withdrew from large areas of Lebanon to positions south of the Awali River. In 1985, it completed its withdrawal from Lebanon, except for a narrow security zone just north of the Israeli border. That too was abandoned, unilaterally, in 2000.

After signing peace agreements with the Palestinians, and a treaty with Jordan, Israel agreed to withdraw from most of the territory in the West Bank captured from Jordan in 1967. A small area was returned to Jordan, and more than 40 percent was ceded to the Palestinian Authority. The agreement with the Palestinians also involved Israel's withdrawal in 1994 from most of the Gaza Strip, which had been captured from Egypt in 1973.

Israeli Prime Minister Ehud Barak offered to withdraw from 97 percent of the West Bank and 100 percent of the Gaza Strip in a final settlement. In addition, Prime Minister Yitzhak Rabin and his successors offered to withdraw from virtually all of the Golan Heights in exchange for peace with Syria.

In August 2005, all Israeli troops and civilians were evacuated from the Gaza Strip and the territory was turned over to the control of the Palestinian Authority. In addition, four communities in Northern Samaria that covered an area larger than the entire Gaza Strip were also evacuated as part of the disengagement plan. As a result, Israel has now withdrawn from approximately 94 percent of the territory it captured in 1967.

Negotiations continue regarding the final disposition of the remaining 6 percent (about 1,600 square miles) of the disputed territories in Israel's possession. Israel's willingness to make territorial concessions in exchange for security proves its goal is peace, not expansion.

MYTH

"The West Bank is part of Jordan."

FACT

The West Bank was never legally part of Jordan. Under the UN's 1947 partition plan—which the Jews accepted and the Arabs rejected—it was to have been part of an independent Arab state in western Palestine. But the Jordanian army invaded and occupied it during the 1948 war. In 1950, Jordan annexed the West Bank. Only two governments—Great Britain and Pakistan—formally recognized the Jordanian takeover. The rest of the world, including the United States, never did.

MYTH

"Israel seized the Golan Heights in a war of aggression."

FACT

Between 1948 and 1967, Syria controlled the Golan Heights and used it as a military stronghold from which its troops randomly sniped at Israeli civilians in the Hula Valley below, forcing children living on kibbutzim to sleep in bomb shelters. In addition, many roads in northern Israel could be crossed only after being cleared by mine-detection vehicles. In late 1966, a youth was blown to pieces by a mine while playing soccer near the Lebanon border. In some cases, attacks were carried out by Yasser Arafat's Fatah, which Syria allowed to operate from its territory.[2]

Israel repeatedly, and unsuccessfully, protested the Syrian bombardments to the UN Mixed Armistice Commission, which was charged with enforcing the cease-fire. For example, Israel went to the UN in October 1966 to demand a halt to the Fatah attacks. The response from Damascus was defiant. "It is not our duty to stop them, but to encourage and strengthen them," the Syrian ambassador responded.[3]

Nothing was done to stop Syria's aggression. A mild Security Council resolution expressing "regret" for such incidents was vetoed by the Soviet Union. Meanwhile, Israel was condemned by the UN when it retaliated. "As far as the Security Council was officially concerned," historian Netanel Lorch wrote, "there was an open season for killing Israelis on their own territory."[4]

After the Six-Day War began, the Syrian air force attempted to bomb oil refineries in Haifa. While Israel was fighting in the Sinai and West Bank, Syrian artillery bombarded Israeli forces in the eastern Galilee, and armored units fired on villages in the Hula Valley below the Golan Heights.

On June 9, 1967, Israel moved against Syrian forces on the Golan. By late afternoon, June 10, Israel was in complete control of the plateau. Israel's seizure of the strategic heights occurred only after 19 years of provocation from Syria, and after unsuccessful efforts to get the international community to act against the aggressors.

MYTH

"The Golan has no strategic significance for Israel."

FACT

Syria—deterred by an IDF presence within artillery range of Damascus—has kept the Golan quiet since 1974. But during this time, Syria has provided a haven and supported numerous terrorist groups that attack Israel from Lebanon and other countries. These include the Democratic

Map 15

The Golan Heights Ridge Line

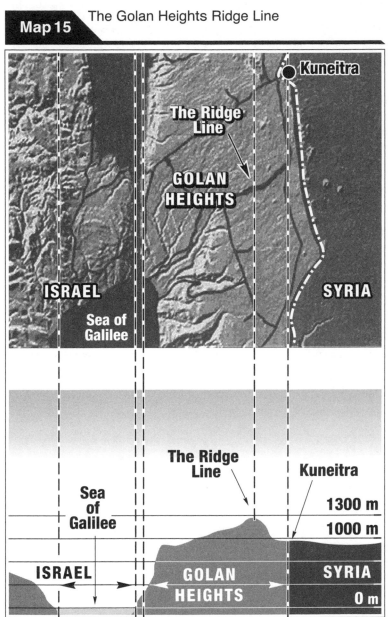

Front for the Liberation of Palestine (DFLP), the Popular Front for the Liberation of Palestine (PFLP), Hizballah and the Popular Front for the Liberation of Palestine-General Command (PFLP-GC). In addition, Syria still deploys hundreds of thousands of troops—as much as 75 percent of its army—on the Israeli front near the Heights.

From the western Golan, it is only about 60 miles—without major terrain obstacles—to Haifa and Acre, Israel's industrial heartland. The Golan—rising from 400 to 1700 feet in the western section bordering on pre-1967 Israel—overlooks the Hula Valley, Israel's richest agricultural area. In the hands of a friendly neighbor, the escarpment has little military importance. If controlled by a hostile country, however, the Golan has the potential to again become a strategic nightmare for Israel.

Before the Six-Day War, when Israeli agricultural settlements in the Galilee came under fire from the Golan, Israel's options for countering the Syrian attacks were constrained by the geography of the Heights. "Counterbattery fires were limited by the lack of observation from the Huleh Valley; air attacks were degraded by well-dug-in Syrian positions with strong overhead cover, and a ground attack against the positions . . . would require major forces with the attendant risks of heavy casualties and severe political repercussions," U.S. Army Col. (Ret.) Irving Heymont observed.[5]

For Israel, relinquishing the Golan to a hostile Syria without adequate security arrangements could jeopardize its early-warning system against surprise attack. Israel has built radar systems on Mt. Hermon, the highest point in the region. If Israel withdrew from the Golan and had to relocate these facilities to the lowlands of the Galilee, they would lose much of their strategic effectiveness.

MYTH

"Israel refuses to compromise on the Golan Heights while Syria has been willing to trade peace for land."

FACT

Under Hafez Assad, Syria's position was consistent: Israel must completely withdraw from the entire Golan Heights before he would entertain any discussion of what Syria might do in return. He never expressed any willingness to make peace with Israel if he received the entire Golan or any part of it.

Israel has been equally adamant that it would not give up any territory without knowing what Syria was prepared to concede. Israel's willingness to trade some or all of the Golan is dependent on Syria's agreement to normalize relations and to sign an agreement that would bring about an end to the state of war Syria says exists between them.

The topographical concerns associated with withdrawing from the Golan Heights could be offset by demilitarization, but Israel needs to have a defensible border from which the nation can be defended with minimum losses. The deeper the demilitarization, and the better the early warning, the more flexible Israel can be regarding that border.

In addition to military security, Israelis seek the normalization of relations between the two countries. At a minimum, ties with Syria should be on a par with those Israel has with Egypt; ideally, they would be closer to the type of peace Israel enjoys with Jordan. This means going beyond a bare minimum of an exchange of ambassadors and flight links and creating an environment whereby Israelis and Syrians will feel comfortable visiting each other's country, engaging in trade and pursuing other forms of cooperation typical of friendly nations.

In the meantime, substantial opposition exists within Israel to withdrawing from the Golan Heights. The expectation of many is that public opinion will shift if and when the Syrians sign an agreement and take measures, such as reigning in Hizballah attacks on Israel from southern Lebanon, that demonstrate a genuine interest in peace. President Hafez Assad died in June 2000, and there have not been any negotiations with Assad's son and successor, Bashar, who has not indicated any shift in Syria's position on the Golan. Absent dramatic changes in Syria's attitude toward Israel, the Jewish State's security will depend on its retention of military control over the Golan Heights.

> *"From a strictly military point of view, Israel would require the retention of some captured territory in order to provide militarily defensible borders."*
>
> **—Memorandum for the Secretary of Defense from the Joint Chiefs of Staff, June 29, 1967**

MYTH

"Israel illegally annexed the Golan Heights in 1981, contravening international law and UN Resolution 242."

FACT

On December 14, 1981, the Knesset voted to annex the Golan Heights. The statute extended Israeli civilian law and administration to the residents of the Golan, replacing the military authority that had ruled the

Map 16 Relative Size of the Golan Heights

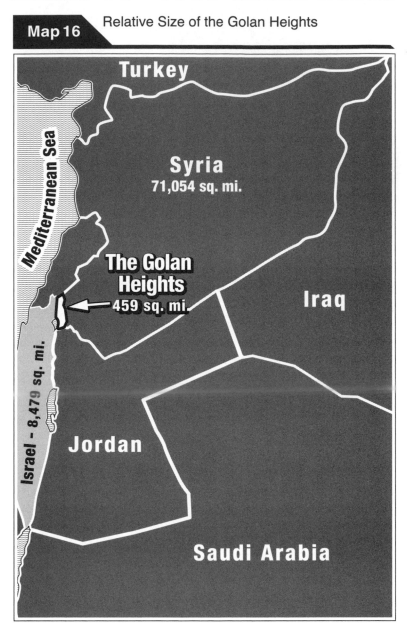

Turkey

Mediterranean Sea

Syria
71,054 sq. mi.

The Golan
Heights
459 sq. mi.

Iraq

Israel – 8,479 sq. mi.

Jordan

Saudi Arabia

area since 1967. The law does not foreclose the option of negotiations on a final settlement of the status of the territory.

Following the Knesset's approval of the law, Professor Julius Stone of Hastings College of the Law wrote:"There is no rule of international law which requires a lawful military occupant, in this situation, to wait forever before [making] control and government of the territory permanent. . . . Many international lawyers have wondered, indeed, at the patience which led Israel to wait as long as she did."[6]

"It is impossible to defend Jerusalem unless you hold the high ground. . . . An aircraft that takes off from an airport in Amman is going to be over Jerusalem in two-and-a-half minutes, so it's utterly impossible for me to defend the whole country unless I hold that land."

—Lieutenant General (Ret.) Thomas Kelly, director of operations for the Joint Chiefs of Staff during the Gulf War[7]

MYTH

"Israel can withdraw from the West Bank with little more difficulty than was the case in Sinai."

FACT

Several pages of Israel's peace treaty with Egypt are devoted to security arrangements. For example, Article III of the treaty's annex concerns the areas where reconnaissance flights are permitted, and Article V allows the establishment of early-warning systems in specific zones.

The security guarantees, which were required to give Israel the confidence to withdraw, were only possible because the Sinai was demilitarized. They provide Israel a large buffer zone of more than 100 miles of sparsely populated desert. Today, the Egyptian border is 60 miles from Tel Aviv and 70 from Jerusalem, the nearest major Israeli cities.

The situation in the territories is entirely different. More than two million Arabs live in the West Bank, many in crowded cities and refugee camps. Most of them are located close to Israeli cities such as Tel Aviv and Jerusalem. The infiltration in recent years of terrorists from the Palestinian Authority, who have committed horrific acts such as suicide bombings, illustrate the danger.

Despite the risks, Israel has withdrawn from more than 40 percent of the West Bank since Oslo. In past negotiations, Israel has offered to give up 97 percent of it in return for a final settlement with the Palestinians. Israel will not, however, return to the pre-1967 borders as demanded by the Palestinians and the Arab states.

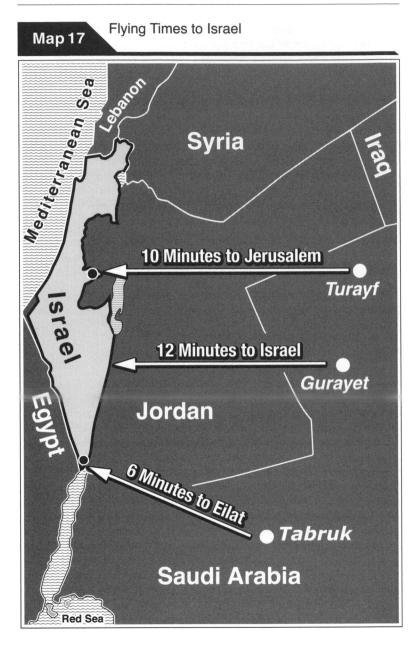

Map 17 — Flying Times to Israel

MYTH

"Israel's demands for defensible borders are unrealistic in an era of ballistic missiles and long-range bombers."

FACT

History shows that aerial attacks have never defeated a nation. Countries are only conquered by troops occupying land. One example of this was Iraq's invasion of Kuwait, in which the latter nation was overrun and occupied in a matter of hours. Though the multinational force bombed Iraq for close to six weeks, Kuwait was not liberated until the Allied troops marched into that country in the war's final days. Defensible borders are those that would prevent or impede such a ground assault.

Israel's return to its pre-1967 borders, which the Arab states want to reimpose, would sorely tempt potential aggressors to launch attacks on the Jewish State—as they did routinely before 1967. Israel would lose the extensive system of early-warning radars it has set up in the hills of Judea and Samaria. Were a hostile neighbor then to seize control of these mountains, its army could split Israel in two: From there, it is only about 15 miles—without any major geographic obstacles—to the Mediterranean.

At their narrowest point, these 1967 lines are within 9 miles of the Israeli coast, 11 miles from Tel Aviv, 10 from Beersheba, 21 from Haifa and one foot from Jerusalem.

To defend Jerusalem, the U.S. Joint Chiefs concluded in a 1967 report to the Secretary of Defense, Israel would need to have its border "positioned to the east of the city."[8] Control over the Jordan River Valley is also critical to Israeli security because it "forms a natural security barrier between Israel and Jordan, and effectively acts as an anti-tank ditch," military analyst Anthony Cordesman noted. "This defensive line sharply increases the amount of time Israel has to mobilize and its ability to ensure control over the West Bank in the event of a war." He added that sacrificing control over the routes up to the heights above the West Bank makes it more difficult for the IDF to deploy and increases the risk of Jordanian, Syrian, or Palestinian forces deploying on the heights.[9]

Even in the era of ballistic missiles, strategic depth matters. The Jaffee Center for Strategic Studies, an Israeli think tank considered dovish, concluded: "Early-warning stations and the deployment of surface-to-air missile batteries can provide the time needed to sound an air-raid alert, and warn the population to take shelter from a missile attack. They might even allow enemy missiles to be intercepted in mid-flight. . . . As long as such missiles are armed with conventional warheads, they may cause painful losses and damage, but they cannot decide the outcome of a war."[10]

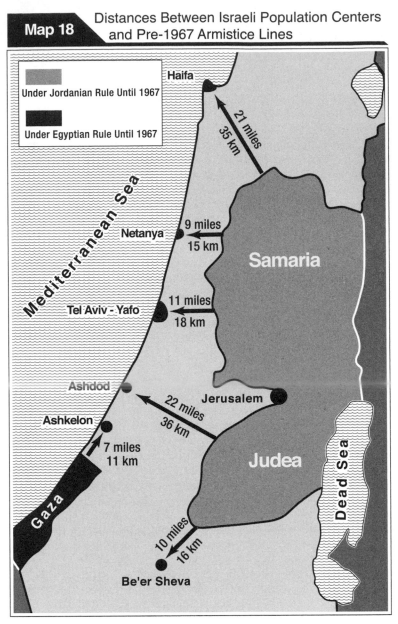

Map 18

Distances Between Israeli Population Centers and Pre-1967 Armistice Lines

Under Jordanian Rule Until 1967

Under Egyptian Rule Until 1967

Haifa

21 miles
35 km

Mediterranean Sea

Netanya

9 miles
15 km

Samaria

Tel Aviv - Yafo

11 miles
18 km

Ashdod

Jerusalem

22 miles
36 km

Ashkelon

7 miles
11 km

Judea

Dead Sea

Gaza

10 miles
16 km

Be'er Sheva

MYTH

"Israel 'occupies' the West Bank."

FACT

In politics words matter and, unfortunately, the misuse of words applying to the Arab-Israeli conflict has shaped perceptions to Israel's disadvantage. As in the case of the term "West Bank," the word "occupation" has been hijacked by those who wish to paint Israel in the harshest possible light. It also gives apologists a way to try to explain away terrorism as "resistance to occupation," as if the women and children killed by suicide bombers in buses, pizzerias, and shopping malls were responsible for the plight of the Arabs.

Given the negative connotation of an "occupier," it is not surprising that Arab spokespersons use the word, or some variation, as many times as possible when interviewed by the press. The more accurate description of the territories in Judea and Samaria, however, is "disputed" territories.

> *"For a Texan, a first visit to Israel is an eye-opener. At the narrowest point, it's only 8 miles from the Mediterranean to the old Armistice line: That's less than from the top to the bottom of Dallas-Ft. Worth Airport. The whole of pre-1967 Israel is only about six times the size of the King Ranch near Corpus Christi."*
>
> **—President George W. Bush**[11]

In fact, most other disputed territories around the world are not referred to as being occupied by the party that controls them. This is true, for example, of the hotly contested region of Kashmir.[12]

Occupation typically refers to foreign control of an area that was under the previous sovereignty of another state. In the case of the West Bank, there was no legitimate sovereign because the territory had been illegally occupied by Jordan from 1948 to 1967. Only two countries—Britain and Pakistan—recognized Jordan's action. The Palestinians never demanded an end to Jordanian occupation and the creation of a Palestinian state.

It is also important to distinguish the acquisition of territory in a war of conquest as opposed to a war of self-defense. A nation that attacks another and then retains the territory it conquers is an occupier. One that gains territory in the course of defending itself is not in the same category. And this is the situation with Israel, which specifically told King Hussein that if Jordan stayed out of the 1967 war, Israel would not fight against him. Hussein ignored the warning and attacked Israel.

While fending off the assault and driving out the invading Jordanian troops, Israel came to control the West Bank.

By rejecting Arab demands that Israel be required to withdraw from all the territories won in 1967, the UN Security Council, in Resolution 242, acknowledged that Israel was entitled to claim at least part of these lands for new defensible borders.

Since Oslo, the case for tagging Israel as an occupying power has been further weakened by the fact that Israel transferred virtually all civilian authority to the Palestinian Authority. Israel retained the power to control its own external security and that of its citizens, but 98 percent of the Palestinian population in the West Bank and Gaza came under the PA's authority. The extent to which Israel has been forced to maintain a military presence in the territories has been governed by the Palestinians' unwillingness to end violence against Israel. The best way to end the dispute over the territories is for the Palestinians to fulfill their obligations under the road map, reform the Palestinian Authority, stop the terror and negotiate a final settlement.

Notes

1. Egypt didn't achieve independence until 1922; Lebanon, 1946; Jordan, 1946; and Syria, 1946. Many of the Gulf states became independent after Israel: Kuwait, 1961; Bahrain, 1970; the United Arab Emirates, 1971; and Qatar, 1971.
2. Netanel Lorch, *One Long War,* (Jerusalem: Keter, 1976), pp. 106–110.
3. Anne Sinai and Allen Pollack, *The Syrian Arab Republic,* (NY: American Academic Association for Peace in the Middle East, 1976), p. 117.
4. Lorch, p. 111.
5. Sinai and Pollack, pp. 130–31.
6. *Near East Report,* (January 29, 1982).
7. *Jerusalem Post,* (November 7, 1991).
8. Memorandum for the Secretary of Defense, June 29, 1967, cited in Michael Widlanski, *Can Israel Survive a Palestinian State?,* (Jerusalem: Institute for Advanced Strategic and Political Studies, 1990), p. 148.
9. Anthony Cordesman, "Escalating to Nowhere: The Israeli-Palestinian War—Fighting and Failed Peace Efforts," (DC: CSIS, August 22, 2003).
10. *Israel's Options for Peace,* (Tel Aviv: The Jaffee Center for Strategic Studies, 1989), pp. 171–72.
11. Speech to the American Jewish Committee, (May 3, 2001).
12. U.S. Department of State, Consular Information Sheet: India, (February 22, 2002).

10. Israel and Lebanon

MYTH

"The PLO posed no threat to Israel and was observing a cease-fire when Israel attacked Lebanon."

FACT

The PLO repeatedly violated the July 1981 cease-fire agreement. By June 1982, when the IDF went into Lebanon, the PLO had made life in northern Israel intolerable. The PLO staged 270 terrorist actions in Israel, the West Bank and Gaza, and along the Lebanese and Jordanian borders. Twenty-nine Israelis died, and more than 300 were injured in the attacks.[1] The frequency of attacks in the Galilee forced thousands of residents to flee their homes or to spend large amounts of time in bomb shelters.

A force of some 15-18,000 PLO members was encamped in scores of locations in Lebanon. About 5,000-6,000 were foreign mercenaries, coming from such countries as Libya, Iraq, India, Sri Lanka, Chad and Mozambique.[2] The PLO had an arsenal that included mortars, Katyusha rockets, and an extensive anti-aircraft network. Israel later discovered enough light arms and other weapons in Lebanon to equip five brigades.[3] The PLO also brought hundreds of T-34 tanks into the area.[4] Syria, which permitted Lebanon to become a haven for the PLO and other terrorist groups, brought surface-to-air missiles into that country, creating yet another danger for Israel.

Israeli strikes and commando raids were unable to stem the growth of this PLO army. Israel was not prepared to wait for more deadly attacks to be launched against its civilian population before acting against the terrorists.

After Israel launched one assault on June 4-5, 1982, the PLO responded with a massive artillery and mortar attack on the Israeli population of the Galilee. On June 6, the IDF moved into Lebanon to drive out the terrorists.

Former Secretary of State Henry Kissinger defended the Israeli operation:"No sovereign state can tolerate indefinitely the buildup along its borders of a military force dedicated to its destruction and implementing its objectives by periodic shellings and raids."[5]

MYTH

"The PLO treated the Lebanese with dignity and respect."

FACT

For Arab residents of south Lebanon, PLO rule was a nightmare. After the PLO was expelled from Jordan by King Hussein in 1970, many of its cadres went to Lebanon. The PLO seized whole areas of the country, where it brutalized the population and usurped Lebanese government authority.

On October 14, 1976, Lebanese Ambassador Edward Ghorra told the UN General Assembly the PLO was bringing ruin upon his country: "Palestinian elements belonging to various splinter organizations resorted to kidnapping Lebanese, and sometimes foreigners, holding them prisoners, questioning them, and even sometimes killing them."[6]

Countless Lebanese told harrowing tales of rape, mutilation and murders committed by PLO forces. The PLO "killed people and threw their corpses in the courtyards. Some of them were mutilated and their limbs were cut off. We did not go out for fear that we might end up like them," said two Arab women from Sidon. "We did not dare go to the beach, because they molested us, weapons in hand." The women spoke of an incident, which occurred shortly before the Israeli invasion, in which PLO men raped and murdered a woman, dumping her body near a famous statue. A picture of the victim's mangled corpse had been printed in a local newspaper.[7]

New York Times correspondent David Shipler visited Damour, a Christian village near Beirut, which had been occupied by the PLO since 1976, when Palestinians and Lebanese leftists sacked the city and massacred hundreds of its inhabitants. The PLO, Shipler wrote, had turned the town into a military base, "using its churches as strongholds and armories."[8]

When the IDF drove the PLO out of Damour in June 1982, Prime Minister Menachem Begin announced that the town's Christian residents could come home and rebuild. Returning villagers found their former homes littered with spray-painted Palestinian nationalist slogans, Fatah literature and posters of Yasser Arafat. They told Shipler how happy they were that Israel had liberated them.[9]

MYTH

"Israel was responsible for the massacre of thousands of Palestinian refugees at Sabra and Shatila."

FACT

The Lebanese Christian Phalangist militia was responsible for the massacres that occurred at the two Beirut-area refugee camps on September

16-17, 1982. Israeli troops allowed the Phalangists to enter Sabra and Shatila to root out terrorist cells believed located there. It had been estimated that there may have been up to 200 armed men in the camps working out of the countless bunkers built by the PLO over the years, and stocked with generous reserves of ammunition.[10]

When Israeli soldiers ordered the Phalangists out, they found hundreds dead (estimates range from 460 according to the Lebanese police, to 700-800 calculated by Israeli intelligence). The dead, according to the Lebanese account, included 35 women and children. The rest were men: Palestinians, Lebanese, Pakistanis, Iranians, Syrians and Algerians.[11] The killings were perpetrated to avenge the murders of Lebanese President Bashir Gemayel and 25 of his followers, killed in a bomb attack earlier that week.[12]

Israel had allowed the Phalange to enter the camps as part of a plan to transfer authority to the Lebanese, and accepted responsibility for that decision. The Kahan Commission of Inquiry, formed by the Israeli government in response to public outrage and grief, found that Israel was indirectly responsible for not anticipating the possibility of Phalangist violence. Defense Minister Ariel Sharon subsequently resigned and the Army Chief of Staff, Gen. Raful Eitan, was dismissed.

The Kahan Commission, declared former Secretary of State Henry Kissinger, was "a great tribute to Israeli democracy.... There are very few governments in the world that one can imagine making such a public investigation of such a difficult and shameful episode."[13]

Ironically, while 300,000 Israelis protested the killings, little or no reaction occurred in the Arab world. Outside the Middle East, a major international outcry against Israel erupted over the massacres. The Phalangists, who perpetrated the crime, were spared the brunt of the condemnations for it.

By contrast, few voices were raised in May 1985, when Muslim militiamen attacked the Shatila and Burj-el Barajneh Palestinian refugee camps. According to UN officials, 635 were killed and 2,500 wounded. During a two-year battle between the Syrian-backed Shiite Amal militia and the PLO, more than 2,000 people, including many civilians, were reportedly killed. No outcry was directed at the PLO or the Syrians and their allies over the slaughter. International reaction was also muted in October 1990 when Syrian forces overran Christian-controlled areas of Lebanon. In the eight-hour clash, 700 Christians were killed—the worst single battle of Lebanon's Civil War.[14] These killings came on top of an estimated 95,000 deaths that had occurred during the civil war in Lebanon from 1975-1982.[15]

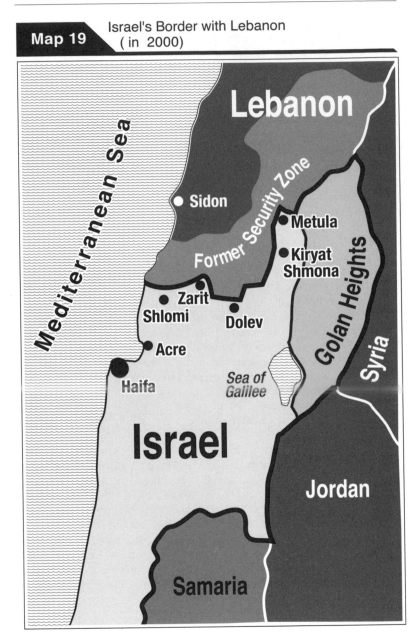

Map 19 Israel's Border with Lebanon
(in 2000)

MYTH

"Israel still has not satisfied the UN's demand to withdraw completely from Lebanon because of its illegal occupation of Shebaa Farms."

FACT

Despite the UN ruling that Israel completed its withdrawal from southern Lebanon,[16] Hizballah and the Lebanese government insist that Israel still holds Lebanese territory in eastern Mount Dov, a 100-square-mile, largely uninhabited patch called Shebaa Farms. This claim provides Hizballah with a pretext to continue its activities against Israel. Thus, after kidnapping three Israeli soldiers in that area, it announced that they were captured on Lebanese soil.

Israel, which has built a series of observation posts on strategic hilltops in the area, maintains that the land was captured from Syria; nevertheless, the Syrians have supported Hizballah's claim. The controversy benefits each of the Arab parties, according to the *Washington Post.* "For Syria, it means Hizballah can still be used to keep the Israelis off balance; for Lebanon, it provides a way to apply pressure over issues, like the return of Lebanese prisoners still held in Israeli jails. For Hizballah, it is a reason to keep its militia armed and active, providing a ready new goal for a resistance movement that otherwise had nothing left to resist."[17]

In January 2005, the UN Security Council condemned the violence along the Israel-Lebanon border and reasserted that the Lebanese claim to the Shebaa Farms area is "not compatible with Security Council resolutions" affirming that Israel completely withdrew from Lebanon.

"If they go from Shebaa, we will not stop fighting them. Our goal is to liberate the 1948 borders of Palestine ... [Jews] can go back to Germany or wherever they came from."

—Hizballah spokesperson Hassan Ezzedin[18]

MYTH

"Syria has been a force for stability and good in Lebanon."

FACT

Damascus has a long and bloody history of intervention in Lebanon, and has made no secret of its hope to make its weaker neighbor part of Syria. Since the creation of contemporary Lebanon in 1920, "most Syrians have never accepted modern Lebanon as a sovereign and independent state."[19] The outbreak of the Lebanese Civil War in 1975 gave Damascus the opportunity to act on its belief that Lebanon and Syria are one.

In 1976, Syria intervened in the Lebanese civil war on behalf of Lebanese Christians. By 1978, Damascus had switched sides, and was supporting a leftist coalition of Palestinians, Druze and Muslims against the Christians. Eventually, Syrian troops occupied two-thirds of Lebanon. Syria's deployment of surface-to-air missile batteries in Lebanon, and its policy of allowing the PLO and other terrorist groups to attack Israel from there, helped trigger the 1982 Lebanon War.[20]

During the first week of Israel's "Operation Peace for Galilee," in June 1982, Syrian troops engaged in battles with Israeli forces. The Israelis destroyed or damaged 18 of the 19 Syrian missile batteries and, in one day, shot down 29 Syrian MiG fighters without the loss of a single plane. Syria and Israel carefully avoided confrontations for the remainder of the war.

Nevertheless, Syria found other ways to hurt Israel. In 1982, Syrian agents murdered President-elect Bashir Gemayel, who wanted peace with Israel. Two years later, Syria forced President Amin Gemayel, Bashir's brother, to renege on a peace treaty he signed with Israel a year earlier.[21]

Syria's activities were aimed not only at Israel, but also at the West. In April 1983, Hizballah terrorists, operating from Syrian-controlled territory, bombed the U.S. embassy in Beirut, killing 49 and wounding 120. Six months later, Hizballah terrorists drove two trucks carrying explosives into the U.S. Marine and French military barracks near Beirut, killing 241 Americans and 56 French soldiers.

In 1985, Hizballah operatives began kidnapping Westerners off the streets of Beirut and other Lebanese cities. From the beginning, it was clear the Syrians and their Iranian collaborators could order the release of the Western hostages at any time. For example, when a Frenchman was kidnapped in August 1991, the Syrians demanded that he be freed. Within days, he was. Most of the hostages were held in the Bekaa Valley or the suburbs of Beirut. Both areas were controlled by Syria.

From 1985–88, Amal Shiite militiamen, closely aligned with Syria, killed hundreds of Palestinian civilians in attacks on refugee camps.

In October 1990, with the West's attention focused on Kuwait, Syrian troops stormed the Beirut stronghold of Christian insurgent Gen. Michel Aoun. Besides battle deaths, approximately 700 people were massacred.[22] With that blitzkrieg, Damascus wiped out the only remaining threat to its hegemony in Lebanon.

On May 22, 1991, Lebanese President Elias Hrawi signed a treaty with Syrian President Hafez Assad that said Syria would ensure Lebanon's "sovereignty and independence," even though Damascus was allowed to keep its occupation army in that country. A hint of Syria's real intentions came earlier when Defense Minister Mustafa predicted that unity would be achieved between the two countries "soon, or at least in our generation."[23]

After signing the treaty, Syria kept a tight grip on Lebanon and ruthlessly suppressed challenges to its domination. The situation changed dramatically, however, after Syria was suspected of playing a role in the assassination of former Lebanese Prime Minister Rafik Hariri on February 14, 2005. The UN adopted a resolution calling for the withdrawal of non-Lebanese forces and an investigation into the killing. Syria subsequently removed its remaining troops from Lebanon, but still exerts a great deal of influence through "political patronage and behind-the-scenes alliances."[24]

MYTH

"Syria intervened in Lebanon only because it was asked to do so by the Arab League."

FACT

Syria moved troops into Lebanon before receiving the Arab League's approval. Damascus intervened in April 1976 after Lebanese Druze warlord Kemal Jumblatt refused Syrian President Hafez Assad's demand for a cease-fire in the war. Jumblatt's refusal to stop his forces' attacks upon Lebanese Christians gave Assad the pretext he needed to intervene.

In June 1976, the Arab League Secretariat convened a meeting at which Syria, Libya, Saudi Arabia and the Sudan agreed to send troops to "enforce peace." Assad sent more Syrian troops into the country, while the others sent only token forces.[25] The Arab League's "endorsement," in short, constituted nothing more than the recognition of a fait accompli.

Notes

1. Jillian Becker, *The PLO,* (London: Weidenfeld and Nicolson, 1984), p. 205.
2. Becker, pp. 202, 209.
3. *Jerusalem Post,* (June 28, 1982).
4. Quoted in Raphael Israeli, ed., *PLO in Lebanon,* (London: Weidenfeld and Nicolson, 1983), p. 7.
5. *Washington Post,* (June 16, 1982).
6. Israeli, p. 259. See also *New York Times,* (October 15, 1976); Official Records of the General Assembly, Thirty-first Session, Plenary Meetings, 32nd meeting.
7. Interview with Israel Television, (July 23, 1982).
8. *New York Times,* (June 21, 1982).
9. *New York Times,* (June 21, 1982).
10. Zeev Schiff and Ehud Yaari, *Israel's Lebanon War,* (NY: Simon and Schuster, 1984), p. 70.
11. Becker, p. 212.
12. Schiff and Yaari, p. 257.
13. *Washington Post,* (February 8, 1983).

14. *New York Times,* (October 19, 1990).
15. Becker, p. 212.
16. "Security Council Endorses Secretary-General's Conclusion on Israeli Withdrawal from Lebanon as of 16 June," UN Press Release, (June 18, 2000).
17. *Washington Post,* (January 30, 2001).
18. *New Yorker,* (October 14, 2002).
19. Daniel Pipes, *Damascus Courts The West,* (DC: The Washington Institute for Near East Policy, 1991), p. 26.
20. Becker, pp. 204-205.
21. Patrick Seale, *Asad,* (Berkeley: University of California Press, 1988), p. 417.
22. Pipes, p. 27.
23. *al-Hayat,* (May 9, 1991).
24. "Q & A: Syria and Lebanon," BBC News, (April 25, 2005).
25. Becker, p. 131.

11. The Gulf Wars

MYTH

"The 1991 Gulf War was fought for Israel."

FACT

Prior to President George Bush's announcement of Operation Desert Storm, critics of Israel were claiming the Jewish State and its supporters were pushing Washington to start a war with Iraq to eliminate it as a military threat. President Bush made the U.S. position clear, however, in his speech on August 2, 1990, saying that the United States has "long-standing vital interests" in the Persian Gulf. Moreover, Iraq's "naked aggression" violated the UN charter. The President expressed concern for other small nations in the area as well as American citizens living or working in the region. "I view a fundamental responsibility of my Presidency [as being] to protect American citizens."[1]

Over the course of the Gulf crisis, the President and other top Administration officials made clear that U.S. interests—primarily oil supplies—were threatened by the Iraqi invasion of Kuwait.

Most Americans agreed with the President's decision to go to war. For example, the *Washington Post*/ABC News Poll on January 16, 1991, found that 76 percent of Americans approved of the U.S. going to war with Iraq and 22 percent disapproved.[2]

It is true that Israel viewed Iraq as a serious threat to its security given its leadership of the rejectionist camp. Israeli concerns proved justified after the war began and Iraq fired 39 Scud missiles at its civilian population centers.

Israel has never asked American troops to fight its battles. Although Israeli forces were prepared to participate in the Gulf War, they did not because the United States asked them not to. Even after the provocation of the Scud missile attacks, Israel assented to U.S. appeals not to respond.

MYTH

"Israel's low profile in the Gulf War proved it has no strategic value to the United States."

FACT

Israel was never expected to play a major role in hostilities in the Gulf. American officials knew the Arabs would not allow Israel to help defend them; they also knew U.S. troops would have to intervene because the Gulf states could not protect themselves.

Israel's posture reflected a deliberate political decision in response to American requests. Nevertheless, it did aid the United States' successful campaign to roll back Iraq's aggression. For example:

- By warning that it would take military measures if any Iraqi troops entered Jordan, Israel, in effect, guaranteed its neighbor's territorial integrity against Iraqi aggression.

- The United States benefited from the use of Israeli-made Have Nap air-launched missiles on its B52 bombers. The Navy, meanwhile, used Israeli Pioneer pilotless drones for reconnaissance in the Gulf.

- Israel provided mine plows that were used to clear paths for allied forces through Iraqi minefields.

- Mobile bridges flown directly from Israel to Saudi Arabia were employed by the U.S. Marine Corps.

- Israeli recommendations, based upon system performance observations, led to several software changes that made the Patriot a more capable missile defense system.

- Israel Aircraft Industries developed conformal fuel tanks that enhanced the range of F-15 aircraft used in the Gulf.

- An Israeli-produced targeting system was used to increase the Cobra helicopter's night-fighting capabilities.

- Israel manufactured the canister for the highly successful Tomahawk missile.

- Night-vision goggles used by U.S. forces were supplied by Israel.

- A low-altitude warning system produced and developed in Israel was utilized on Blackhawk helicopters.

- Israel offered the United States the use of military and hospital facilities. U.S. ships utilized Haifa port shipyard maintenance and support on their way to the Gulf.

- Israel destroyed Iraq's nuclear reactor in 1981. Consequently, U.S. troops did not face a nuclear-armed Iraq.

MYTH

"Israel benefited from the 1991 Gulf War without paying any price."

FACT

It is true that Israel benefited from the destruction of Iraq's military capability by the United States-led coalition, but the cost was enormous. Even before hostilities broke out, Israel had to revise its defense budget to maintain its forces at a heightened state of alert. The Iraqi missile attacks justified Israel's prudence in keeping its air force flying round the clock. The war required the defense budget to be increased by more than $500 million. Another $100 million boost was needed for civil defense.

The damage caused by the 39 Iraqi Scud missiles that landed in Tel Aviv and Haifa was extensive. Approximately 3,300 apartments and other buildings were affected in the greater Tel Aviv area. Some 1,150 people who were evacuated had to be housed at a dozen hotels at a cost of $20,000 per night.

Beyond the direct costs of military preparedness and damage to property, the Israeli economy was also hurt by the inability of many Israelis to work under the emergency conditions. The economy functioned at no more than 75 percent of normal capacity during the war, resulting in a net loss to the country of $3.2 billion.[3]

The biggest cost was in human lives. A total of 74 people died as a consequence of Scud attacks. Two died in direct hits, four from suffocation in gas masks and the rest from heart attacks.[4]

A UN committee dealing with reparation claims against Iraq approved more than $31 million to be paid to Israeli businesses and individuals. The 1999 decision stemmed from a 1992 Security Council decision calling on Iraq to compensate victims of the Gulf War.[5] In 2001, the United Nations Compensation Commission awarded $74 million to Israel for the costs it incurred from Iraqi Scud missile attacks. The Commission rejected most of the $1 billion that Israel had requested.[6]

MYTH

"Iraq was never a threat to Israel."

FACT

Iraqi President Saddam Hussein was a leader of the rejectionist Arab states and one of the most belligerent foes of Israel. On April 2, 1990, Saddam's rhetoric became more threatening: "I swear to God we will let our fire eat half of Israel if it tries to wage anything against Iraq." Saddam said his nation's chemical weapons capability was matched only by that of the United States and the Soviet Union, and that he would annihilate anyone who threatened Iraq with an atomic bomb by the "double chemical."[7]

Several days later, Saddam said that war with Israel would not end until all Israeli-held territory was restored to Arab hands. He added that Iraq could launch chemical weapons at Israel from several different sites.[8] The Iraqi leader also made the alarming disclosure that his commanders had the freedom to launch attacks against Israel without consulting the high command if Israel attacked Iraq. The head of the Iraqi Air Force subsequently said he had orders to strike Israel if the Jewish State launched a raid against Iraq or any other Arab country.[9]

On June 18, 1990, Saddam told an Islamic Conference meeting in Baghdad: "We will strike at [the Israelis] with all the arms in our possession if they attack Iraq or the Arabs." He declared "Palestine has been stolen," and exhorted the Arab world to "recover the usurped rights in Palestine and free Jerusalem from Zionist captivity."[10]

Saddam's threat came in the wake of revelations that Britain and the United States foiled an attempt to smuggle American-made "krytron" nuclear triggers to Iraq.[11] Britain's MI6 intelligence service prepared a secret assessment three years earlier that Hussein had ordered an all-out effort to develop nuclear weapons.[12] After Saddam used chemical weapons against his own Kurdish population in Halabja in 1988, few people doubted his willingness to use nuclear weapons against Jews in Israel if he had the opportunity.

In April 1990, British customs officers found tubes about to be loaded onto an Iraqi-chartered ship that were believed to be part of a giant cannon that would enable Baghdad to lob nuclear or chemical missiles into Israel or Iran.[13] Iraq denied it was building a "supergun," but, after the war, it was learned that Iraq had built such a weapon.[14]

Iraq emerged from its war with Iran with one of the largest and best-equipped military forces in the world. In fact, Iraq had one million battle-tested troops, more than 700 combat aircraft, 6,000 tanks, ballistic missiles and chemical weapons. Although the U.S. and its allies won a quick victory, the magnitude of Hussein's arsenal only became clear after the war when UN investigators found evidence of a vast program to build chemical and nuclear weapons.[15]

Iraq also served as a base for several terrorist groups that menaced Israel, including the PLO and Abu Nidal's Fatah Revolutionary Council.

After the Iraqi invasion of Kuwait, Saddam Hussein consistently threatened to strike Israel if his country was attacked. If the U.S. moves against Iraq, he said in December 1990, "then Tel Aviv will receive the next attack, whether or not Israel takes part."[16] At a press conference, following his January 9, 1991, meeting with Secretary of State James Baker, Iraqi Foreign Minister Tariq Aziz was asked if the war starts, would Iraq attack Israel. He replied bluntly: "Yes. Absolutely, yes."[17]

Ultimately, Saddam carried out his threat.

MYTH

"Saddam Hussein was never interested in acquiring nuclear weapons."

FACT

In 1981, Israel became convinced Iraq was approaching the capability to produce a nuclear weapon. To preempt the building of a weapon they believed would undoubtedly be directed against them, the Israelis launched a surprise attack that destroyed the Osirak nuclear complex. At the time, Israel was widely criticized. On June 19, the UN Security Council unanimously condemned the raid. Critics minimized the importance of Iraq's nuclear program, claiming that because Baghdad had signed the Nuclear Non-Proliferation Treaty and permitted its facilities to be inspected, Israeli fears were baseless.

It was not until after Iraq invaded Kuwait that U.S. officials began to acknowledge publicly that Baghdad was developing nuclear weapons and that it was far closer to reaching its goal than previously thought. Again, many critics argued the Administration was only seeking a justification for a war with Iraq.

Months later, after allied forces had announced the destruction of Iraq's nuclear facilities, UN inspectors found Saddam's program to develop weapons was far more extensive than even the Israelis believed. Analysts had thought Iraq was incapable of enriching uranium for bombs, but Saddam's researchers used several methods (including one thought to be obsolete) that may have made it possible for Iraq to build at least one bomb.

"Leaders of Israel's peace movement expressed their disgust for the PLO's actions. One would need a gas mask to overcome the "toxic, repulsive stench" of the PLO's attitude toward Saddam Hussein, Yossi Sarid said.[18] *Another activist, Yaron London, wrote in an open letter to the Palestinians in the territories: "This week you proved to me for many years I was a great fool. When you ask once again for my support for your 'legitimate rights,' you will discover that your shouts of encouragement to Saddam have clogged my ears."*[19]

MYTH

"The PLO was neutral in the 1991 Gulf War."

FACT

The PLO, Libya and Iraq were the only members who opposed an Arab League resolution calling for an Iraqi withdrawal from Kuwait. The intifada leadership congratulated Saddam Hussein and described the invasion of Kuwait as the first step toward the "liberation of Palestine."[20]

In Jenin, on August 12, 1,000 Palestinians marched, shouting: "Saddam, you hero, attack Israel with chemical weapons."[21]

According to some sources, the PLO played an active role in facilitating Iraq's conquest of Kuwait. The logistical planning for the Iraqi invasion was at least partially based on intelligence supplied by PLO officials and supporters based in Kuwait.[22]

When the U.S. began massing troops in Saudi Arabia, Arafat called this a "new crusade" that "forebodes the gravest dangers and disasters for our Arab and Islamic nation." He also made clear his position on the conflict: "We can only be in the trench hostile to Zionism and its imperialist allies who are today mobilizing their tanks, planes, and all their advanced and sophisticated war machine against our Arab nation."[23]

Once the war began, the PLO Executive Committee reaffirmed its support for Iraq: "The Palestinian people stand firmly by Iraq's side." The following day, Arafat sent a message to Saddam hailing Iraq's struggle against "American dictatorship" and describing Iraq as "the defender of the Arab nation, of Muslims and of free men everywhere."[24]

Arafat's enthusiasm for Hussein was undaunted by the outcome of the war. "I would like to take this opportunity to renew to your excellency the great pride that we take in the ties of fraternity and common destiny binding us," he said in November 1991. "Let us work together until we achieve victory and regain liberated Jerusalem."[25]

MYTH

"American Jews goaded the United States to go to war against Iraq in 2003 to help Israel."

FACT

Some opponents of the U.S.-led war against Iraq in 2003 claimed that American Jews somehow were responsible for persuading President George W. Bush to launch the military campaign on Israel's behalf. In fact, President Bush decided that Iraq posed a threat to the United States because it was believed to possess weapons of mass destruction and was pursuing a nuclear capability that could have been used directly against Americans or could have been transferred to terrorists who would use them against U.S. targets. The removal of Saddam Hussein was also designed to eliminate one of the principal sponsors of terrorism.

The war in Iraq liberated the Iraqi people from one of the world's most oppressive regimes. Even in the Arab world, where many people objected to the U.S. action, no Arab leader rose to Saddam Hussein's defense.

It is true that Israel will benefit from the elimination of a regime that launched 39 missiles against it in 1991, paid Palestinians to encourage them to attack Israelis, and led a coalition of Arab states committed to Israel's destruction. It is also true, however, that many Arab states benefited from the removal of Saddam Hussein, in particular, Saudi Arabia and Kuwait. This is why these nations allowed Allied forces to use their countries as bases for operations.

As for the role of American Jews, it is important to remember that Jews comprise less than three percent of the U.S. population and were hardly the most vocal advocates of the war. On the contrary, the Jewish community had divisions similar to those in the country as a whole, and most major Jewish organizations avoided taking any position on the war. Meanwhile, public opinion polls showed that a significant majority of all Americans initially supported the President's policy toward Iraq.

Some critics have suggested that prominent Jewish officials in the Bush Administration pushed for the war; however, only a handful of officials in the Administration were Jewish, and not one of the President's top advisers at the time—the Secretary of Defense, Secretary of State, Vice President, or National Security Adviser—was Jewish.

The suggestion that American Jews are more loyal to Israel than to the United States, or that they have undue influence on U.S. Middle East policy, is an example of anti-Semitism. Unfortunately, some critics of the war on Iraq chose the age-old approach of blaming the Jews for a policy they disagreed with rather than addressing the substantive arguments in the debate.

Notes

1. *Washington Post,* (August 3, 1990).
2. *Washington Post,* (January 17, 1991).
3. *Near East Report,* (February 4, 1991).
4. *Jerusalem Post,* (January 17, 1992).
5. Jewish Telegraphic Agency, (April 14, 1999).
6. Jewish Telegraphic Agency, (June 21, 2001).
7. Reuters, (April 2, 1990).
8. Reuters, (April 18, 1990).
9. UPI, (April 22, 1990).
10. Baghdad Domestic Service, (June 18, 1990).
11. *Washington Post,* (March 29, 1990).
12. Washington Times, (April 3, 1990).
13. Reuters, (April 17, 1990).
14. *Washington Post,* (August 14, 1991).
15. *Washington Post,* (August 8, 1991).
16. Reuters, (December 26, 1990).
17. Transcript of January 9, 1991, press conference.
18. *Haaretz,* (August 17, 1990).
19. *Yediot Aharonot,* (August 1990).
20. *Mideast Mirror,* (August 6, 1990).
21. Associated Press, (August 12, 1990).
22. *Jerusalem Post,* (August 8, 1990).
23. *Sawt al-Sha'b,* (September 4, 1990).
24. Agence France-Presse, (February 26, 1991).
25. Baghdad Republic of Iraq Radio Network, (November 16, 1991).

12. The United Nations

MYTH

"The United Nations plays a constructive role in Middle East affairs. Its record of fairness and balance makes it an ideal forum for settling the Arab-Israeli dispute."

FACT

Starting in the mid-1970s, an Arab-Soviet-Third World bloc joined to form what amounted to a pro-Palestinian lobby at the United Nations. This was particularly true in the General Assembly where these countries—nearly all dictatorships or autocracies—frequently voted together to pass resolutions attacking Israel and supporting the PLO.

In 1975, at the instigation of the Arab states and the Soviet Bloc, the Assembly approved Resolution 3379, which slandered Zionism by branding it a form of racism. U.S. Ambassador Daniel Moynihan called the resolution an "obscene act." Israeli Ambassador Chaim Herzog told his fellow delegates the resolution was "based on hatred, falsehood and arrogance." Hitler, he declared, would have felt at home listening to the UN debate on the measure.[1]

On December 16, 1991, the General Assembly voted 111-25 (with 13 abstentions and 17 delegations absent or not voting) to repeal Resolution 3379. No Arab country voted for repeal. The PLO denounced the vote and the U.S. role.

Israel is the object of more investigative committees, special representatives and rapporteurs than any other state in the UN system. The special representative of the Director-General of UNESCO visited Israel 51 times during 27 years of activity. A "Special Mission" has been sent by the Director-General of the ILO to Israel and the territories every year for the past 17 years.

The Commission on Human Rights routinely adopts disproportionate resolutions concerning Israel. Of all condemnations of this agency, 26 percent refer to Israel alone, while rogue states such as Syria and Libya are never criticized.[2]

In September 2003, the UN held a two-day International Conference of Civil Society in Support of the Palestinian People with the theme "End the Occupation!" During the event, the Palestinian observer to the UN, Nasser al-Kidwa, said that "violence in self-defense in the occupied Palestinian territories is not terrorism."[3] This was just one of many such conferences held under UN auspices over the years.

Even when Israel is not directly involved in an issue, UN officials find ways to interject their biases against the Jewish State. For example, in April 2004, the UN envoy to Iraq, Lakhdar Brahimi, called Israel's policies "the great poison in the region." The remark reflected a lack of professionalism and impartiality expected of representatives of the organization.[4]

In March 2005, the Security Council issued an unprecedented condemnation of a suicide bombing in Tel Aviv carried out by Islamic Jihad. Unlike Israeli actions that provoke resolutions, the Security Council issued only a "policy statement" urging the Palestinian Authority to "take immediate, credible steps to find those responsible for this terrorist attack" and bring them to justice. It also encouraged "further and sustained action to prevent other acts of terror." The statement required the consent of all 15 members of the Security Council. The one Arab member, Algeria, signed on after a reference to Islamic Jihad was deleted.[5]

In August 2005, just as Israel was prepared to implement its disengagement from the Gaza Strip, the Palestinian Authority produced materials to celebrate the Israeli withdrawal. These included banners that read, "Gaza Today. The West Bank and Jerusalem Tomorrow." News agencies reported that the banners were produced with funds from the UN Development Program and were printed with the UNDP's logo.[6]

While the Arab-Israeli peace process that was launched in Madrid in 1991 is structured on the basis of direct negotiations between the parties, the UN constantly undercuts this principle. The General Assembly routinely adopts resolutions that attempt to impose solutions on critical issues such as Jerusalem, the Golan Heights and settlements. Ironically, UN Security Council Resolutions 242 and 338 proposed the bilateral negotiations that are consistently undermined by the General Assembly resolutions.

Thus, the record to date indicates the UN has not played a useful role in resolving the Arab-Israeli conflict.

"What takes place in the Security Council more closely resembles a mugging than either a political debate or an effort at problem-solving."

—former UN Ambassador Jeane Kirkpatrick[7]

MYTH

"The Palestinians have been denied a voice at the UN."

FACT

Besides the support the Palestinians have received from the Arab and Islamic world, and most other UN members, the Palestinians have been afforded special treatment at the UN since 1975. That year, the General Assembly awarded permanent representative status to the PLO and the UN established the "Committee on the Inalienable Rights of the Palestinian People." The panel became, in effect, part of the PLO propaganda apparatus, issuing stamps, organizing meetings, and preparing films and draft resolutions in support of Palestinian "rights."

In 1976, the committee recommended "full implementation of the inalienable rights of the Palestinian people, including their return to the Israeli part of Palestine." It also recommended that November 29—the day the UN voted to partition Palestine in 1947—be declared an "International Day of Solidarity with the Palestinian People." Since then, it has been observed at the UN with anti-Israel speeches, films and exhibits.

In 1988, the PLO's status was upgraded when the General Assembly designated the PLO as "Palestine." Ten years later, the General Assembly voted to give the Palestinians a unique status as a non-voting member of the 185 member Assembly. The vote in favor was overwhelming, 124 in favor and 4 against with 10 abstentions. The countries opposing the resolution were Israel, the United States, Micronesia and the Marshall Islands.

Palestinian representatives can now raise the issue of the peace process in the General Assembly, cosponsor draft resolutions on Middle East peace and have the right of reply. They still do not have voting power and cannot put forward candidates for UN bodies such as the Security Council.

MYTH

"Israel enjoys the same rights as any other member of the United Nations."

FACT

Without membership in a regional group, Israel could not sit on the Security Council or other key UN bodies. For 40 years, Israel was the only UN member excluded from a regional group. Geographically, it belongs in the Asian Group; however, the Arab states have barred its membership.

A breakthrough in Israel's exclusion from UN bodies occurred in 2000, when Israel was given temporary membership in the Western European and Others (WEOG) regional group. The WEOG is the only regional group that is geopolitical rather than purely geographical. WEOG's 27 members—the West European states, Australia, Canada, New Zealand and the United States—share a Western-Democratic common denominator. This historic step opened the door to Israeli participation in the Security Council. Israel formally applied for membership to the Council in 2005, but the next seat will not be available until 2019.

Israel's position within the UN improved further in February 2003 when Israel was elected to serve on the UN General Assembly Working Group on Disarmament, its first committee posting since 1961 (after 1961, the UN split the membership into regional groups and that was when Israel became isolated). An Israeli representative was elected as one of the group's three vice-chairmen and received votes from Iran and several Arab states. On the other hand, during the same month, an Israeli candidate was defeated for a position on the UN Committee on the Rights of the Child. The year before Israeli candidates also lost votes for positions on the UN Human Rights Committee, the UN Committee on the Elimination of Discrimination Against Women, and the UN Racial Discrimination Committee.[8]

Israel's standing at the UN improved significantly in 2005 starting with the election in July of Israel's Ambassador to the UN, Dan Giller-man, as one of 20 vice presidents who set the agenda for the next General Assembly session. Shortly thereafter, Israel was tapped to serve as deputy chair of the UN Disarmament Commission (UNDC), a General Assembly sub-committee that serves as an advisory body on disarmament issues. In October 2005, an Israeli representative was chosen for the first time to serve as a member of the UNESCO World Heritage Committee.

MYTH

"The United Nations and its affiliate institutions are critical of Israeli policies, but never attack Jews or engage in anti-Semitic rhetoric."

FACT

The UN has condemned virtually every conceivable form of racism. It has established programs to combat racism and its multiple facets—including xenophobia—but had consistently refused to do the same against anti-Semitism. It was only on November 24, 1998, more than 50 years after the UN's founding, that the word "anti-Semitism" was first mentioned in a UN resolution, appearing near the end of GA Res. A/53/623, "Elimination of Racism and Racial Discrimination."[9]

Since the early 1970s, the UN itself has become permeated with anti-Semitic and anti-Zionist sentiment. The following examples illustrate how ugly the atmosphere has become:

■ "Is it not the Jews who are exploiting the American people and trying to debase them?"—Libyan UN Representative Ali Treiki.[10]

■ "The Talmud says that if a Jew does not drink every year the blood of a non-Jewish man, he will be damned for eternity."—Saudi Arabian delegate Marouf al-Dawalibi before the 1984 UN Human Rights Commission conference on religious tolerance.[11] A similar remark was made by the Syrian Ambassador who insisted at a 1991 meeting that Jews killed Christian children to use their blood to make matzos.[12]

■ On March 11, 1997, the Palestinian representative to the UN Human Rights Commission claimed the Israeli government had injected 300 Palestinian children with the HIV virus. Despite the efforts of Israel, the United States and others, this blood libel remains on the UN record.[13]

■ In July 2005, Jean Ziegler, the UN Special Rapporteur on the Right to Food, called the Gaza Strip "an immense concentration camp" and compared Israelis to Nazis. A year earlier (May 28, 2004), Ziegler sent on official UN stationery a demand that the Caterpillar company boycott Israel.[14]

In 2003, the first resolution explicitly condemning anti-Semitism was offered in the General Assembly, but its sponsor, Ireland, later withdrew it due to lack of support.

There is ample justification for the conclusion of Professor Anne Bayefsky of York University, Canada, writing of the UN Human Rights system: "It is the tool of those who would make Israel the archetypal human rights violator in the world today. It is a breeding ground for anti-Semitism. It is a sanctuary for moral relativists. In short, it is a scandal." [15]

MYTH

"The Arab states approved the 1991 repeal of the resolution libeling Zionism."

FACT

The repeal vote was marred by the fact that 13 of the 19 Arab countries—including those engaged in negotiations with Israel—Syria, Lebanon and Jordan—voted to retain the resolution, as did Saudi Arabia. Six, including Egypt—which lobbied against repeal—were absent.

The Arabs "voted once again to impugn the very birthright of the Jewish State," the *New York Times* noted. "That even now most Arab states cling to a demeaning and vicious doctrine mars an otherwise belated triumph for sense and conscience."[16]

MYTH

"Even if the General Assembly is biased, the Security Council has always been balanced in its treatment of the Middle East."

FACT

A careful analysis of the Security Council's actions on the Middle East shows it has been little better than the General Assembly in its treatment of Israel.

Candidates for the Security Council are proposed by regional blocs. In the Middle East, this means the Arab League and its allies are usually included. Israel, which joined the UN in 1949, has never been elected to the Security Council whereas at least 16 Arab League members have. Syria, a nation on the U.S. list of countries that sponsor terrorism, began a two-year term as a member of the Security Council in 2002 and served as president of the body in June 2002.

Debates on Israel abound, and the Security Council has repeatedly condemned the Jewish State, but not once has it unequivocally criticized an Arab terror attack. Emergency special sessions of the General Assembly are rare. No such session has ever been convened with respect to the Chinese occupation of Tibet, the Indonesian occupation of East Timor, the slaughters in Rwanda, the disappearances in Zaire or the horrors of Bosnia. For nearly two decades, these sessions have been called primarily to condemn Israel.

MYTH

"The United States always supports Israel and vetoes critical resolutions."

FACT

Many people believe the United States can always be relied upon to support Israel with its veto in the UN Security Council. The historical record, however, shows that the U.S. has often opposed Israel in the Council.

The United States did not cast its first veto until 1972, on a Syrian-Lebanese complaint against Israel. From 1967-72, the U.S. supported or abstained on 24 resolutions, most critical of Israel. From 1973-2004, the Security Council adopted approximately 100 resolutions on the Middle East, again, most critical of Israel. The U.S. vetoed a total of 40 resolutions and, hence, supported the Council's criticism of Israel by its vote of support, or by abstaining, roughly 60 percent of the time.[17]

In July 2002, the United States shifted its policy and announced that it would veto any Security Council resolution on the Middle East that did not condemn Palestinian terror and name Hamas, Islamic Jihad and the Al-Aksa Martyrs Brigade as the groups responsible for the attacks. The U.S. also said that resolutions must note that any Israeli withdrawal is linked to the security situation, and that both parties must be called upon to pursue a negotiated settlement.[18] The Arabs can still get around the United States by taking issues to the General Assembly, where non-binding resolutions pass by majority vote, and support for almost any anti-Israel resolution is assured.

MYTH

"America's Arab allies routinely support U.S. positions at the UN."

FACT

In 2004, Jordan was the Arab nation that voted with the United States most often, and that was on only 30 percent of the resolutions. The other Arab countries, including allies Saudi Arabia, Kuwait and Egypt, voted against the United States 80 percent of the time or more. As a group, in 2004, the Arab states voted *against* the United States on just under 80 percent of the resolutions. By contrast, Israel has consistently been America's top UN ally. Israel voted with the U.S. 100 percent of the time in 2004, outpacing the support levels of major U.S. allies such as Great Britain, France and Canada by more than 30 percent.[19]

> *"The UN has the image of a world organization based on universal principles of justice and equality. In reality, when the chips are down, it is nothing other than the executive committee of the Third World dictatorships."*
>
> **—former UN Ambassador Jeane Kirkpatrick[20]**

MYTH

"Israel's failure to implement UN resolutions is a violation of international law."

FACT

UN resolutions are documents issued by political bodies and need to be interpreted in light of the constitution of those bodies. They represent the political viewpoints of those who support them rather than embodying any particular legal rules or principles. Resolutions can have moral and political force when they are perceived as expressing the agreed view of the international community, or the views of leading, powerful and respected nations.

The UN Charter (Articles 10 and 14) specifically empowers the General Assembly to make only nonbinding "recommendations." Assembly resolutions are only considered binding in relation to budgetary and internal procedural matters. The legality of Security Council resolutions is more ambiguous. It is not clear if all Security Council resolutions are binding or only those adopted under Chapter 7 of the Charter.[21] Under Article 25 of the Charter, UN member states are obligated to carry out "decisions of the Security Council in accordance with the present Charter," but it is unclear which kinds of resolutions are covered by the term "decisions." Regardless, it would be difficult to show that Israel has violated any Security Council resolutions on their wording and the Council has never sanctioned Israel for noncompliance.

MYTH

"The United Nations has demonstrated equal concern for the lives of Israelis and Palestinians."

FACT

While the UN routinely adopts resolutions critical of Israel's treatment of Palestinians, it has never adopted a resolution unequivocally condemning violence against Israeli citizens. One of the most dramatic examples of the institution's double-standard came in 2003 when Israel offered a draft resolution in the General Assembly for the first time in 27 years.

The resolution called for the protection of Israeli children from terrorism, but it did not receive enough support from the members of the General Assembly to even come to a vote. Israel had introduced the resolution in response to the murder of dozens of Israeli children in terrorist attacks, and after a similar resolution had been adopted by a UN committee (later adopted by the full Assembly) calling for the protection of Palestinian children from "Israeli aggression." Israel's ambassador withdrew the proposed draft after it became clear that members of the nonaligned movement were determined to revise it in such a way that it would have ultimately been critical of Israel.[22]

Notes

1. Chaim Herzog, *Who Stands Accused?*, (NY: Random House, 1978), pp. 4–5.
2. Israel's Mission to the UN.
3. *Jerusalem Post,* (September 4, 2003).
4. *Jerusalem Post,* (April 26, 2004).
5. Reuters, (March 1, 2005).
6. *Jerusalem Post,* (August 18, 2005).
7. *New York Times,* (March 31, 1983).
8. Anne Bayefsky, "Israel second-class status at the UN," *National Post,* (February 18, 2003).

9. "Israel and the UN—An Uneasy Relationship," Israel's Mission to the UN.

10. Speech before the UN, December 8, 1983, quoted in Harris Schoenberg, *Mandate For Terror: The United Nations and the PLO,* (NY: Shapolsky, 1989), p. 296.

11. Speech to UN seminar on religious tolerance and freedom, delivered December 5, 1984, quoted in Anti-Defamation League, *News,* (February 7, 1985).

12. Morris Abram, "Israel Under Attack: Anti-Semitism in the United Nations," *The Earth Times,* (December 16-31, 1997).

13. Ibid.

14. *Washington Times,* (July 11, 2005).

15. Morris B. Abram, "Anti-Semitism in the United Nations," UN Watch, (February 1998).

16. *New York Times,* (December 17, 1991).

17. U.S. State Department.

18. *Washington Post,* (July 26, 2002).

19. *"Voting Practices at the United Nations—2004,"* U.S. State Department.

20. *Jerusalem Post,* (September 5, 2001).

21. Bruno Simma, ed., *The Charter of the United Nations: A Commentary,* (NY: Oxford University Press, 1994), pp. 237-241; 407-418.

22. *Jerusalem Post,* (November 26, 2003).

13. Refugees

MYTH

"One million Palestinians were expelled by Israel from 1947–49."

FACT

The Palestinians left their homes in 1947–49 for a variety of reasons. Thousands of wealthy Arabs left in anticipation of a war, thousands more responded to Arab leaders' calls to get out of the way of the advancing armies, a handful were expelled, but most simply fled to avoid being caught in the cross fire of a battle.

Many Arabs claim that 800,000 to 1,000,000 Palestinians became refugees in 1947–49. The last census was taken by the British in 1945. It found approximately 1.2 million permanent Arab residents in *all* of Palestine. A 1949 Government of Israel census counted 160,000 Arabs living in the country after the war. In 1947, a total of 809,100 Arabs lived in the same area.[1] This meant no more than 650,000 Palestinian Arabs could have become refugees. A report by the UN Mediator on Palestine arrived at an even lower figure—472,000, and calculated that only about 360,000 Arab refugees required aid.[2]

MYTH

"Palestinians were the only people who became refugees as a result of the Arab-Israeli conflict."

FACT

Although much is heard about the plight of the Palestinian refugees, little is said about the Jews who fled from Arab states. Their situation had long been precarious. During the 1947 UN debates, Arab leaders threatened them. For example, Egypt's delegate told the General Assembly: "The lives of one million Jews in Muslim countries would be jeopardized by partition."[3]

The number of Jews fleeing Arab countries for Israel in the years following Israel's independence was nearly double the number of Arabs leaving Palestine. Many Jews were allowed to take little more than the shirts on their backs. These refugees had no desire to be repatriated. Little is heard about them because they did not remain refugees for long. Of the 820,000 Jewish refugees between 1948 and 1972, 586,000 were resettled in Israel at great expense, and without any offer of compensa-

Map 20 Jewish Refugees from Arab States 1948-1972

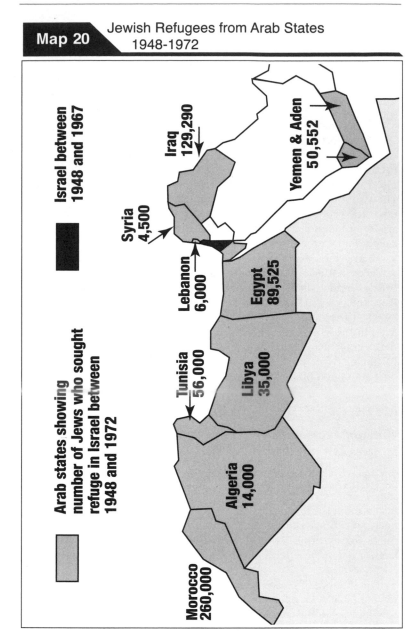

Israel between 1948 and 1967

Arab states showing number of Jews who sought refuge in Israel between 1948 and 1972

Iraq 129,290

Yemen & Aden 50,552

Syria 4,500

Lebanon 6,000

Egypt 89,525

Tunisia 56,000

Libya 35,000

Algeria 14,000

Morocco 260,000

tion from the Arab governments who confiscated their possessions.[4] Israel has consequently maintained that any agreement to compensate the Palestinian refugees must also include Arab reparations for Jewish refugees. To this day, the Arab states have refused to pay anything to the hundreds of thousands of Jews who were forced to abandon their property before fleeing those countries. Through November 2003, 101 of the 681 UN resolutions on the Middle East conflict referred directly to Palestinian refugees. Not one mentioned the Jewish refugees from Arab countries.[5]

The contrast between the reception of Jewish and Palestinian refugees is even starker when one considers the difference in cultural and geographic dislocation experienced by the two groups. Most Jewish refugees traveled hundreds—and some traveled thousands—of miles to a tiny country whose inhabitants spoke a different language. Most Arab refugees never left Palestine at all; they traveled a few miles to the other side of the truce line, remaining inside the vast Arab nation that they were part of linguistically, culturally and ethnically.

MYTH

"The Jews made clear from the outset they had no intention of living peacefully with their Arab neighbors."

FACT

In numerous instances, Jewish leaders urged the Arabs to remain in Palestine and become citizens of Israel. The Assembly of Palestine Jewry issued this appeal on October 2, 1947:

> We will do everything in our power to maintain peace, and establish a cooperation gainful to both [Jews and Arabs]. It is now, here and now, from Jerusalem itself, that a call must go out to the Arab nations to join forces with Jewry and the destined Jewish State and work shoulder to shoulder for our common good, for the peace and progress of sovereign equals.[6]

On November 30, the day after the UN partition vote, the Jewish Agency announced: "The main theme behind the spontaneous celebrations we are witnessing today is our community's desire to seek peace and its determination to achieve fruitful cooperation with the Arabs...."[7]

Israel's Proclamation of Independence, issued May 14, 1948, also invited the Palestinians to remain in their homes and become equal citizens in the new state:

> In the midst of wanton aggression, we yet call upon the Arab inhabitants of the State of Israel to preserve the ways of peace

and play their part in the development of the State, on the basis of full and equal citizenship and due representation in all its bodies and institutions.... We extend our hand in peace and neighborliness to all the neighboring states and their peoples, and invite them to cooperate with the independent Jewish nation for the common good of all.

MYTH

*"The Jews created the refugee problem
by expelling the Palestinians."*

FACT

Had the Arabs accepted the 1947 UN resolution, not a single Palestinian would have become a refugee. An independent Arab state would now exist beside Israel. The responsibility for the refugee problem rests with the Arabs.

The beginning of the Arab exodus can be traced to the weeks immediately following the announcement of the UN partition resolution. The first to leave were roughly 30,000 wealthy Arabs who anticipated the upcoming war and fled to neighboring Arab countries to await its end. Less affluent Arabs from the mixed cities of Palestine moved to all-Arab towns to stay with relatives or friends.[8] By the end of January 1948, the exodus was so alarming the Palestine Arab Higher Committee asked neighboring Arab countries to refuse visas to these refugees and to seal their borders against them.[9]

On January 30, 1948, the Jaffa newspaper, *Ash Sha'ab,* reported: "The first of our fifth-column consists of those who abandon their houses and businesses and go to live elsewhere.... At the first signs of trouble they take to their heels to escape sharing the burden of struggle."[10]

Another Jaffa paper, *As Sarih* (March 30, 1948) excoriated Arab villagers near Tel Aviv for "bringing down disgrace on us all by 'abandoning the villages.' "[11]

Meanwhile, a leader of the Arab National Committee in Haifa, Hajj Nimer el-Khatib, said Arab soldiers in Jaffa were mistreating the residents. "They robbed individuals and homes. Life was of little value, and the honor of women was defiled. This state of affairs led many [Arab] residents to leave the city under the protection of British tanks."[12]

John Bagot Glubb, the commander of Jordan's Arab Legion, said: "Villages were frequently abandoned even before they were threatened by the progress of war."[13]

Contemporary press reports of major battles in which large numbers of Arabs fled conspicuously fail to mention any forcible expulsion by the Jewish forces. The Arabs are usually described as "fleeing" or "evacuating" their homes. While Zionists are accused of "expelling and dispossessing" the Arab inhabitants of such towns as Tiberias and Haifa, the truth is much different. Both of those cities were within the boundaries of the Jewish State under the UN partition scheme and both were fought for by Jews and Arabs alike.

Jewish forces seized Tiberias on April 19, 1948, and the entire Arab population of 6,000 was evacuated under British military supervision. The Jewish Community Council issued a statement afterward: "We did not dispossess them; they themselves chose this course.... Let no citizen touch their property."[14]

In early April, an estimated 25,000 Arabs left the Haifa area following an offensive by the irregular forces led by Fawzi al-Qawukji, and rumors that Arab air forces would soon bomb the Jewish areas around Mt. Carmel.[15] On April 23, the Haganah captured Haifa. A British police report from Haifa, dated April 26, explained that "every effort is being made by the Jews to persuade the Arab populace to stay and carry on with their normal lives, to get their shops and businesses open and to be assured that their lives and interests will be safe."[16] In fact, David Ben-Gurion had sent Golda Meir to Haifa to try to persuade the Arabs to stay, but she was unable to convince them because of their fear of being judged traitors to the Arab cause.[17] By the end of the battle, more than 50,000 Palestinians had left.

"Tens of thousands of Arab men, women and children fled toward the eastern outskirts of the city in cars, trucks, carts, and afoot in a desperate attempt to reach Arab territory until the Jews captured Rushmiya Bridge toward Samaria and Northern Palestine and cut them off. Thousands rushed every available craft, even rowboats, along the waterfront, to escape by sea toward Acre."

—New York Times, (April 23, 1948)

In Tiberias and Haifa, the Haganah issued orders that none of the Arabs' possessions should be touched, and warned that anyone who violated the orders would be severely punished. Despite these efforts, all but about 5,000 or 6,000 Arabs evacuated Haifa, many leaving with the assistance of British military transports.

Syria's UN delegate, Faris el-Khouri, interrupted the UN debate on Palestine to describe the seizure of Haifa as a "massacre" and said this action was "further evidence that the 'Zionist program' is to annihilate Arabs within the Jewish state if partition is effected."[18]

The following day, however, the British representative at the UN, Sir Alexander Cadogan, told the delegates that the fighting in Haifa had been provoked by the continuous attacks by Arabs against Jews a few days before and that reports of massacres and deportations were erroneous.[19]

The same day (April 23, 1948), Jamal Husseini, the chairman of the Palestine Higher Committee, told the UN Security Council that instead of accepting the Haganah's truce offer, the Arabs "preferred to abandon their homes, their belongings, and everything they possessed in the world and leave the town."[20]

The U.S. Consul-General in Haifa, Aubrey Lippincott, wrote on April 22, 1948, for example, that "local mufti-dominated Arab leaders" were urging "all Arabs to leave the city, and large numbers did so."[21]

An army order issued July 6, 1948, made clear that Arab towns and villages were not to be demolished or burned, and that Arab inhabitants were not to be expelled from their homes.[22]

The Haganah did employ psychological warfare to encourage the Arabs to abandon a few villages. Yigal Allon, the commander of the *Palmach* (the "shock force of the Haganah"), said he had Jews talk to the Arabs in neighboring villages and tell them a large Jewish force was in Galilee with the intention of burning all the Arab villages in the Lake Hula region. The Arabs were told to leave while they still had time and, according to Allon, they did exactly that.[23]

In the most dramatic example, in the Ramle-Lod area, Israeli troops seeking to protect their flanks and relieve the pressure on besieged Jerusalem, forced a portion of the Arab population to go to an area a few miles away that was occupied by the Arab Legion. "The two towns had served as bases for Arab irregular units, which had frequently attacked Jewish convoys and nearby settlements, effectively barring the main road to Jerusalem to Jewish traffic."[24]

As was clear from the descriptions of what took place in the cities with the largest Arab populations, these cases were clearly the exceptions, accounting for only a small fraction of the Palestinian refugees.

MYTH

"The Arab invasion had little impact on the Palestinian Arabs."

FACT

Once the invasion began in May 1948, most Arabs remaining in Palestine left for neighboring countries. Surprisingly, rather than acting as a strategically valuable "fifth-column" that would fight the Jews from within the country, the Palestinians chose to flee to the safety of the other Arab states, still confident of being able to return. A leading Palestinian nationalist of the time, Musa Alami, revealed the attitude of the fleeing Arabs:

> The Arabs of Palestine left their homes, were scattered, and lost everything. But there remained one solid hope: The Arab armies

were on the eve of their entry into Palestine to save the country and return things to their normal course, punish the aggressor, and throw oppressive Zionism with its dreams and dangers into the sea. On May 14, 1948, crowds of Arabs stood by the roads leading to the frontiers of Palestine, enthusiastically welcoming the advancing armies. Days and weeks passed, sufficient to accomplish the sacred mission, but the Arab armies did not save the country. They did nothing but let slip from their hands Acre, Sarafand, Lydda, Ramleh, Nazareth, most of the south and the rest of the north. Then hope fled.[25]

As the fighting spread into areas that had previously remained quiet, the Arabs began to see the possibility of defeat. As the possibility turned into reality, the flight of the Arabs increased—more than 300,000 departed after May 15—leaving approximately 160,000 Arabs in the State of Israel.[26]

Although most of the Arabs had left by November 1948, there were still those who chose to leave even after hostilities ceased. An interesting case was the evacuation of 3,000 Arabs from Faluja, a village between Tel Aviv and Beersheba:

Observers feel that with proper counsel after the Israeli-Egyptian armistice, the Arab population might have advantageously remained. They state that the Israeli Government had given guarantees of security of person and property. However, no effort was made by Egypt, Transjordan or even the United Nations Palestine Conciliation Commission to advise the Faluja Arabs one way or the other.[27]

"The [refugee] problem was a direct consequence of the war that the Palestinians—and ... surrounding Arab states—had launched."

—Israeli historian Benny Morris[28]

MYTH

"Arab leaders never encouraged the Palestinians to flee."

FACT

A plethora of evidence exists demonstrating that Palestinians were encouraged to leave their homes to make way for the invading Arab armies.

The *Economist,* a frequent critic of the Zionists, reported on October 2, 1948: "Of the 62,000 Arabs who formerly lived in Haifa not more than 5,000 or 6,000 remained. Various factors influenced their decision to seek safety in flight. There is but little doubt that the most potent of the factors were the announcements made over the air by the Higher Arab Executive, urging the Arabs to quit. . . . It was clearly intimated that those Arabs who remained in Haifa and accepted Jewish protection would be regarded as renegades."

Time's report of the battle for Haifa (May 3, 1948) was similar: "The mass evacuation, prompted partly by fear, partly by orders of Arab leaders, left the Arab quarter of Haifa a ghost city. . . . By withdrawing Arab workers their leaders hoped to paralyze Haifa."

Benny Morris, the historian who documented instances where Palestinians were expelled, also found that Arab leaders encouraged their brethren to leave. The Arab National Committee in Jerusalem, following the March 8, 1948, instructions of the Arab Higher Committee, ordered women, children and the elderly in various parts of Jerusalem to leave their homes: "Any opposition to this order . . . is an obstacle to the holy war . . . and will hamper the operations of the fighters in these districts."[29]

Morris also said that in early May units of the Arab Legion ordered the evacuation of all women and children from the town of Beisan. The Arab Liberation Army was also reported to have ordered the evacuation of another village south of Haifa. The departure of the women and children, Morris says, "tended to sap the morale of the menfolk who were left behind to guard the homes and fields, contributing ultimately to the final evacuation of villages. Such two-tier evacuation—women and children first, the men following weeks later—occurred in Qumiya in the Jezreel Valley, among the Awarna bedouin in Haifa Bay and in various other places."

In his memoirs, Haled al Azm, the Syrian Prime Minister in 1948–49, also admitted the Arab role in persuading the refugees to leave:

"Since 1948 we have been demanding the return of the refugees to their homes. But we ourselves are the ones who encouraged them to leave. Only a few months separated our call to them to leave and our appeal to the United Nations to resolve on their return." [30]

Who gave such orders? Leaders such as Iraqi Prime Minister Nuri Said, who declared: "We will smash the country with our guns and obliterate every place the Jews seek shelter in. The Arabs should conduct their wives and children to safe areas until the fighting has died down."[31]

The Secretary of the Arab League Office in London, Edward Atiyah, wrote in his book, *The Arabs:* "This wholesale exodus was due partly to the belief of the Arabs, encouraged by the boastings of an unrealistic Arabic press and the irresponsible utterances of some of the Arab leaders that it could be only a matter of weeks before the Jews were defeated by the armies of the Arab States and the Palestinian Arabs enabled to reenter and retake possession of their country."[32]

"The refugees were confident their absence would not last long, and that they would return within a week or two," Monsignor George Hakim, a Greek Orthodox Catholic Bishop of Galilee told the Beirut newspaper, *Sada al-Janub* (August 16, 1948). "Their leaders had promised them that the Arab Armies would crush the 'Zionist gangs' very quickly and that there was no need for panic or fear of a long exile."

On April 3, 1949, the Near East Broadcasting Station (Cyprus) said: "It must not be forgotten that the Arab Higher Committee encouraged the refugees' flight from their homes in Jaffa, Haifa and Jerusalem."[33]

"The Arab States encouraged the Palestine Arabs to leave their homes temporarily in order to be out of the way of the Arab invasion armies," according to the Jordanian newspaper *Filastin*, (February 19, 1949).

One refugee quoted in the Jordan newspaper, *Ad Difaa* (September 6, 1954), said: "The Arab government told us: Get out so that we can get in. So we got out, but they did not get in."

"The Secretary-General of the Arab League, Azzam Pasha, assured the Arab peoples that the occupation of Palestine and Tel Aviv would be as simple as a military promenade," said Habib Issa in the New York Lebanese paper, *Al Hoda* (June 8, 1951). "He pointed out that they were already on the frontiers and that all the millions the Jews had spent on land and economic development would be easy booty, for it would be a simple matter to throw Jews into the Mediterranean. . . . Brotherly advice was given to the Arabs of Palestine to leave their land, homes and property and to stay temporarily in neighboring fraternal states, lest the guns of the invading Arab armies mow them down."

The Arabs' fear was naturally exacerbated by stories of real and imagined Jewish atrocities following the attack on Deir Yassin. The native population lacked leaders who could calm them; their spokesmen, such as the Arab Higher Committee, were operating from the safety of neighboring states and did more to arouse their fears than to pacify them. Local military leaders were of little or no comfort. In one instance the commander of Arab troops in Safed went to Damascus. The following day, his troops withdrew from the town. When the residents realized they were defenseless, they fled in panic.[34]

According to Dr. Walid al-Qamhawi, a former member of the Executive Committee of the PLO, "it was collective fear, moral disintegration and chaos in every field that exiled the Arabs of Tiberias, Haifa and dozens of towns and villages."[35]

As panic spread throughout Palestine, the early trickle of refugees became a flood, numbering more than 200,000 by the time the provisional government declared the independence of the State of Israel.

Even Jordan's King Abdullah, writing in his memoirs, blamed Palestinian leaders for the refugee problem:

The tragedy of the Palestinians was that most of their leaders had paralyzed them with false and unsubstantiated promises that they were not alone; that 80 million Arabs and 400 million Muslims would instantly and miraculously come to their rescue.[36]

"The Arab armies entered Palestine to protect the Palestinians from the Zionist tyranny but, instead, they abandoned them, forced them to emigrate and to leave their homeland, and threw them into prisons similar to the ghettos in which the Jews used to live."

—Palestinian Authority (then) Prime Minister Mahmoud Abbas (Abu Mazen)[37]

MYTH

"The Palestinian Arabs had to flee to avoid being massacred as were the peaceful villagers in Deir Yassin."

FACT

The United Nations resolved that Jerusalem would be an international city apart from the Arab and Jewish states demarcated in the partition resolution. The 150,000 Jewish inhabitants were under constant military pressure; the 2,500 Jews living in the Old City were victims of an Arab blockade that lasted five months before they were forced to surrender on May 29, 1948. Prior to the surrender, and throughout the siege on Jerusalem, Jewish convoys tried to reach the city to alleviate the food shortage, which, by April, had become critical.

Meanwhile, the Arab forces, which had engaged in sporadic and unorganized ambushes since December 1947, began to make an organized attempt to cut off the highway linking Tel Aviv with Jerusalem—the city's only supply route. The Arabs controlled several strategic vantage points, which overlooked the highway and enabled them to fire on the convoys trying to reach the beleaguered city with supplies. Deir Yassin was situated on a hill, about 2,600 feet high, which commanded a wide view of the vicinity and was located less than a mile from the suburbs of Jerusalem. The population was 750.[38]

On April 6, Operation Nachshon was launched to open the road to Jerusalem. The village of Deir Yassin was included on the list of Arab villages to be occupied as part of the operation. The following day Haganah commander David Shaltiel wrote to the leaders of the Lehi and Irgun:

I learn that you plan an attack on Deir Yassin. I wish to point out that the capture of Deir Yassin and its holding are one stage in our general plan. I have no objection to your carrying out the operation provided you are able to hold the village. If you are unable to do so I warn you against blowing up the village which will result in its inhabitants abandoning it and its ruins and deserted houses being occupied by foreign forces.... Furthermore, if foreign forces took over, this would upset our general plan for establishing an airfield.[39]

The Irgun decided to attack Deir Yassin on April 9, while the Haganah was still engaged in the battle for Kastel. This was the first major Irgun attack against the Arabs. Previously, the Irgun and Lehi had concentrated their attacks against the British.

According to Irgun leader Menachem Begin, the assault was carried out by 100 members of that organization; other authors say it was as many as 132 men from both groups. Begin stated that a small open truck fitted with a loudspeaker was driven to the entrance of the village before the attack and broadcast a warning to civilians to evacuate the area, which many did.[40] Most writers say the warning was never issued because the truck with the loudspeaker rolled into a ditch before it could broadcast the warning.[41] One of the fighters said, the ditch was filled in and the truck continued on to the village. "One of us called out on the loudspeaker in Arabic, telling the inhabitants to put down their weapons and flee. I don't know if they heard, and I know these appeals had no effect."[42]

Contrary to revisionist histories that the town was filled with peaceful innocents, residents and foreign troops opened fire on the attackers. One fighter described his experience:

> My unit stormed and passed the first row of houses. I was among the first to enter the village. There were a few other guys with me, each encouraging the other to advance. At the top of the street I saw a man in khaki clothing running ahead. I thought he was one of ours. I ran after him and told him, "advance to that house." Suddenly he turned around, aimed his rifle and shot. He was an Iraqi soldier. I was hit in the foot.[43]

The battle was ferocious and took several hours. The Irgun suffered 41 casualties, including four dead.

Surprisingly, after the "massacre," the Irgun escorted a representative of the Red Cross through the town and held a press conference. The *New York Times'* subsequent description of the battle was essentially the same as Begin's. The *Times* said more than 200 Arabs were killed, 40 captured and 70 women and children were released. No hint of a massacre appeared in the report.[44]

"Paradoxically, the Jews say about 250 out of 400 village inhabitants [were killed], while Arab survivors say only 110 of 1,000."[45] A study by

Bir Zeit University, based on discussions with each family from the village, arrived at a figure of 107 Arab civilians dead and 12 wounded, in addition to 13 "fighters," evidence that the number of dead was smaller than claimed and that the village did have troops based there.[46] Other Arab sources have subsequently suggested the number may have been even lower.[47]

In fact, the attackers left open an escape corridor from the village and more than 200 residents left unharmed. For example, at 9:30 A.M., about five hours after the fighting started, the Lehi evacuated 40 old men, women and children on trucks and took them to a base in Sheikh Bader. Later, the Arabs were taken to East Jerusalem. Seeing the Arabs in the hands of Jews also helped raise the morale of the people of Jerusalem who were despondent from the setbacks in the fighting to that point.[48] Another source says 70 women and children were taken away and turned over to the British.[49] If the intent was to massacre the inhabitants, no one would have been evacuated.

After the remaining Arabs feigned surrender and then fired on the Jewish troops, some Jews killed Arab soldiers and civilians indiscriminately. None of the sources specify how many women and children were killed (the *Times* report said it was about half the victims; their original casualty figure came from the Irgun source), but there were some among the casualties.

At least some of the women who were killed became targets because of men who tried to disguise themselves as women. The Irgun commander reported, for example, that the attackers "found men dressed as women and therefore they began to shoot at women who did not hasten to go down to the place designated for gathering the prisoners."[50] Another story was told by a member of the Haganah who overheard a group of Arabs from Deir Yassin who said "the Jews found out that Arab warriors had disguised themselves as women. The Jews searched the women too. One of the people being checked realized he had been caught, took out a pistol and shot the Jewish commander. His friends, crazed with anger, shot in all directions and killed the Arabs in the area."[51]

Contrary to claims from Arab propagandists at the time, and some since, no evidence has ever been produced that any women were raped. On the contrary, every villager has denied these allegations. Like many of the claims, this was a deliberate propaganda ploy, but one that backfired. Hazam Nusseibi, who worked for the Palestine Broadcasting Service in 1948, admitted being told by Hussein Khalidi, a Palestinian Arab leader, to fabricate the atrocity claims. Abu Mahmud, a Deir Yassin resident in 1948 told Khalidi "there was no rape," but Khalidi replied, "We have to say this, so the Arab armies will come to liberate Palestine from the Jews." Nusseibeh told the BBC 50 years later, "This was our biggest mistake. We did not realize how our people would react. As soon as they heard that women had been raped at Deir Yassin, Palestinians fled in terror."[52]

The Jewish Agency, upon learning of the attack, immediately expressed its "horror and disgust." It also sent a letter expressing the Agency's shock and disapproval to Transjordan's King Abdullah.

The Arab Higher Committee hoped exaggerated reports about a "massacre" at Deir Yassin would shock the population of the Arab countries into bringing pressure on their governments to intervene in Palestine. Instead, the immediate impact was to stimulate a new Palestinian exodus.

Just four days after the reports from Deir Yassin were published, an Arab force ambushed a Jewish convoy on the way to Hadassah Hospital, killing 77 Jews, including doctors, nurses, patients, and the director of the hospital. Another 23 people were injured. This *massacre* attracted little attention and is never mentioned by those who are quick to bring up Deir Yassin. Moreover, despite attacks such as this against the Jewish community in Palestine, in which more than 500 Jews were killed in the first four months after the partition decision alone, Jews did not flee.

The Palestinians knew, despite their rhetoric to the contrary, the Jews were not trying to annihilate them; otherwise, they would not have been allowed to evacuate Tiberias, Haifa or any of the other towns captured by the Jews. Moreover, the Palestinians could find sanctuary in nearby states. The Jews, however, had no place to run had they wanted to. They were willing to fight to the death for their country. It came to that for many, because the Arabs *were* interested in annihilating the Jews, as Secretary-General of the Arab League Azzam Pasha made clear in an interview with the BBC on the eve of the war (May 15, 1948): "The Arabs intend to conduct a war of extermination and momentous massacre which will be spoken of like the Mongolian massacres and the Crusades."

References to Deir Yassin have remained a staple of anti-Israel propaganda for decades because the incident was unique.

MYTH

"Israel refused to allow Palestinians to return to their homes so Jews could steal their property."

FACT

Israel could not simply agree to allow all Palestinians to return, but consistently sought a solution to the refugee problem. Israel's position was expressed by David Ben-Gurion (August 1, 1948):

When the Arab states are ready to conclude a peace treaty with Israel this question will come up for constructive solution as part of the general settlement, and with due regard to our counterclaims in respect of the destruction of Jewish life and property, the long-term interest of the Jewish and Arab populations, the stability of the State of Israel and the durability of the basis of peace between it and its neighbors, the actual position and fate of the Jewish communities in the Arab countries, the responsibilities of the Arab governments for their war of aggression and their liability for reparation, will all be relevant in the question whether, to what extent, and under what conditions, the former Arab residents of the territory of Israel should be allowed to return.[53]

The Israeli government was not indifferent to the plight of the refugees; an ordinance was passed creating a Custodian of Abandoned Property "to prevent unlawful occupation of empty houses and business premises, to administer ownerless property, and also to secure tilling of deserted fields, and save the crops...."[54]

The implied danger of repatriation did not prevent Israel from allowing some refugees to return and offering to take back a substantial number as a condition for signing a peace treaty. In 1949, Israel offered to allow families that had been separated during the war to return, to release refugee accounts frozen in Israeli banks (eventually released in 1953), to pay compensation for abandoned lands and to repatriate 100,000 refugees.[55]

The Arabs rejected all the Israeli compromises. They were unwilling to take any action that might be construed as recognition of Israel. They made repatriation a precondition for negotiations, something Israel rejected. The result was the confinement of the refugees in camps.

Despite the position taken by the Arab states, Israel did release the Arab refugees' blocked bank accounts, which totaled more than $10 million, paid thousands of claimants cash compensation and granted thousands of acres as alternative holdings.

MYTH

"UN resolutions call for Israel to repatriate all Palestinian refugees."

FACT

The United Nations took up the refugee issue and adopted Resolution 194 on December 11, 1948. This called upon the Arab states and Israel to resolve all outstanding issues through negotiations either directly, or with the help of the Palestine Conciliation Commission established by this resolution. Furthermore, Point 11 resolves:

> that refugees wishing to return to their homes *and live at peace* with their neighbors should be permitted to do so at the earliest practicable date, and that compensation should be paid for property of those choosing not to return and for loss of or damage to property which under principles of international law or in equity should be made good by Governments or authorities responsible. Instructs the Conciliation Commission to facilitate the repatriation, *resettlement* and economic and social rehabilitation of refugees and payment of compensation . . . (emphasis added).

The emphasized words demonstrate that the UN recognized that Israel could not be expected to repatriate a hostile population that might endanger its security. The solution to the problem, like all previous refugee problems, would require at least some Palestinians to be resettled in Arab lands. Furthermore, the resolution uses the word "should" instead of "shall," which, in legal terms, is not mandatory language.

The resolution met most of Israel's concerns regarding the refugees, whom they regarded as a potential fifth-column if allowed to return unconditionally. The Israelis considered the settlement of the refugee issue a negotiable part of an overall peace settlement. As President Chaim Weizmann explained: "We are anxious to help such resettlement provided that real peace is established and the Arab states do their part of the job. The solution of the Arab problem can be achieved only through an all-around Middle East development scheme, toward which the United Nations, the Arab states and Israel will make their respective contributions."[56]

At the time the Israelis did not expect the refugees to be a major issue; they thought the Arab states would resettle the majority and some compromise on the remainder could be worked out in the context of an overall settlement. The Arabs were no more willing to compromise in 1949, however, than they had been in 1947. In fact, they unanimously rejected the UN resolution.

The UN discussions on refugees had begun in the summer of 1948, before Israel had completed its military victory; consequently, the Arabs still believed they could win the war and allow the refugees to return triumphant. The Arab position was expressed by Emile Ghoury, the Secretary of the Arab Higher Committee:

> It is inconceivable that the refugees should be sent back to their homes while they are occupied by the Jews, as the latter would hold them as hostages and maltreat them. The very proposal is an evasion of responsibility by those responsible. It will serve

as a first step towards Arab recognition of the State of Israel and partition.[57]

The Arabs demanded that the United Nations assert the "right" of the Palestinians to return to their homes, and were unwilling to accept anything less until after their defeat had become obvious. The Arabs then reinterpreted Resolution 194 as granting the refugees the absolute right of repatriation and have demanded that Israel accept this interpretation ever since. Regardless of the interpretation, 194, like other General Assembly resolutions, is not legally binding.

"The Palestinian demand for the 'right of return' is totally unrealistic and would have to be solved by means of financial compensation and resettlement in Arab countries."

—Egyptian President Hosni Mubarak[58]

MYTH

"Palestinians who wanted to return to their homes posed no danger to Israeli security."

FACT

When plans for setting up a state were made in early 1948, Jewish leaders in Palestine expected the new nation to include a significant Arab population. From the Israeli perspective, the refugees had been given an opportunity to stay in their homes and be a part of the new state. Approximately 160,000 Arabs had chosen to do so. To repatriate those who had fled would be, in the words of Foreign Minister Moshe Sharett, "suicidal folly."[59]

In the Arab world, the refugees were viewed as a potential fifth-column within Israel. As one Lebanese paper wrote:

> The return of the refugees should create a large Arab majority that would serve as the most effective means of reviving the Arab character of Palestine, while forming a powerful fifth-column for the day of revenge and reckoning.[60]

The Arabs believed the return of the refugees would virtually guarantee the destruction of Israel, a sentiment expressed by Egyptian Foreign Minister Muhammad Salah al-Din:

> It is well-known and understood that the Arabs, in demanding the return of the refugees to Palestine, mean their return as masters of the Homeland and not as slaves. With a greater clarity, they mean the liquidation of the State of Israel.[61]

The plight of the refugees remained unchanged after the Suez War. In fact, even the rhetoric stayed the same. In 1957, the Refugee Conference at Homs, Syria, passed a resolution stating:

> Any discussion aimed at a solution of the Palestine problem which will not be based on ensuring the refugees' right to annihilate Israel will be regarded as a desecration of the Arab people and an act of treason.[62]

A parallel can be drawn to the time of the American Revolution, during which many colonists who were loyal to England fled to Canada. The British wanted the newly formed republic to allow the loyalists to return to claim their property. Benjamin Franklin rejected this suggestion in a letter to Richard Oswald, the British negotiator, dated November 26, 1782:

> Your ministers require that we should receive again into our bosom those who have been our bitterest enemies and restore their properties who have destroyed ours: and this while the wounds they have given us are still bleeding![63]

MYTH

"The Palestinian refugees were ignored by an uncaring world."

FACT

The General Assembly voted on November 19, 1948, to establish the United Nations Relief For Palestinian Refugees (UNRPR) to dispense aid to the refugees. Since then, more than 100 resolutions have been adopted that refer to Palestinian refugees, roughly 15 percent of all the resolutions on the conflict.[64]

The UNRPR was replaced by the United Nations Relief and Works Agency (UNWRA) on December 8, 1949, and given a budget of $50 million. UNWRA was designed to continue the relief program initiated by the UNRPR, substitute public works for direct relief and promote economic development. The proponents of the plan envisioned that direct relief would be almost completely replaced by public works, with the remaining assistance provided by the Arab governments.

UNRWA had little chance of success, however, because it sought to solve a political problem using an economic approach. By the mid-1950s, it was evident neither the refugees nor the Arab states were prepared to cooperate on the large-scale development projects originally foreseen by the Agency as a means of alleviating the Palestinians' situation. The Arab governments, and the refugees themselves, were unwilling to contribute to any plan that could be interpreted as fostering resettlement. They preferred to cling to their interpretation of Resolution 194, which they believed would eventually result in repatriation.

Palestinian Refugees Registered by UNRWA[65]

Field of Operations	Official Camps	Registered Refugees	Registered Refugees in Camps
Jordan	10	1,780,701	283,183
Lebanon	12	400,582	210,952
Syria	10	424,650	112,882
West Bank	19	687,542	181,241
Gaza Strip	8	961,645	471,555
Total	59	4,255,120	1,259,813

MYTH

"The Arab states have provided most of the funds for helping the Palestinian refugees."

FACT

While Jewish refugees from Arab countries received no international assistance, Palestinians received millions of dollars through UNRWA. Initially, the United States contributed $25 million and Israel nearly $3 million. The total Arab pledges amounted to approximately $600,000. For the first 20 years, the United States provided more than two-thirds of the funds, while the Arab states continued to contribute a tiny fraction.

Israel donated more funds to UNRWA than most Arab states. The Saudis did not match Israel's contribution until 1973; Kuwait and Libya, not until 1980. As recently as 1994, Israel gave more to UNRWA than all the Arab countries except Saudi Arabia, Kuwait and Morocco. After transferring responsibility for virtually the entire Palestinian population in the West Bank and Gaza Strip to the Palestinian Authority, Israel no longer controlled any refugee camps and ceased contributing to UNRWA.

In 2004, the United States contributed more than $127 million (36.5%) of UNRWA's nearly $350 million budget. Despite their rhetorical support for the Palestinians, all of the Arab countries *combined* pledged only about $8 million (2%). The largest donation from an Arab nation—$1.8 million—came from Saudi Arabia.[66]

Meanwhile, in addition to receiving annual funding from UNRWA for the refugees, the PA has received billions of dollars in international aid and yet has failed to build a single house to allow even one family to move out of a refugee camp into permanent housing. Given the amount of aid (approximately $6 billion since 1993) the PA has received, it is shocking and outrageous that more than 650,000 Palestinians under PA control are being forced by their own leaders to remain in squalid camps.

MYTH

"The Arab states have always welcomed the Palestinians."

FACT

Jordan was the only Arab country to welcome the Palestinians and grant them citizenship (to this day Jordan is the only Arab country where Palestinians *as a group* can become citizens). King Abdullah considered the Palestinian Arabs and Jordanians one people. By 1950, he annexed the West Bank and forbade the use of the term Palestine in official documents.[67]

Although ample room for settlement existed in Syria, Damascus refused to consider accepting any refugees, except those who might refuse repatriation. Syria also declined to resettle 85,000 refugees in 1952–54, though it had been offered international funds to pay for the project. Iraq was also expected to accept a large number of refugees, but proved unwilling. Lebanon insisted it had no room for the Palestinians. In 1950, the UN tried to resettle 150,000 refugees from Gaza in Libya, but was rebuffed by Egypt.

After the 1948 war, Egypt controlled the Gaza Strip and its more than 200,000 inhabitants, but refused to allow the Palestinians into Egypt or permit them to move elsewhere. Egypt's handling of Palestinians in Gaza was so bad Saudi Arabian radio compared Nasser's regime in Gaza to Hitler's rule in occupied Europe in World War II.[68]

In 1952, the UNWRA set up a fund of $200 million to provide homes and jobs for the refugees, but it went untouched.

"The Arab States do not want to solve the refugee problem. They want to keep it as an open sore, as an affront to the United Nations and as a weapon against Israel. Arab leaders don't give a damn whether the refugees live or die."

—former UNRWA official Ralph Galloway, in August 1958[69]

Little has changed in succeeding years. Arab governments have frequently offered jobs, housing, land and other benefits to Arabs and non-Arabs, *excluding* Palestinians. For example, Saudi Arabia chose not to use unemployed Palestinian refugees to alleviate its labor shortage in the late 1970's and early 1980's. Instead, thousands of South Koreans and other Asians were recruited to fill jobs.

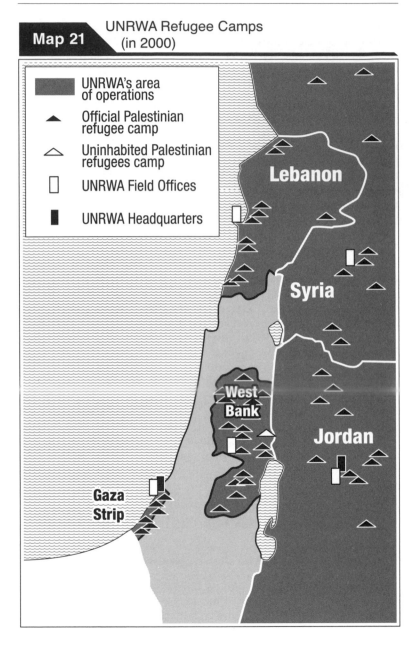

Map 21 — UNRWA Refugee Camps (in 2000)

UNRWA's area of operations

Official Palestinian refugee camp

Uninhabited Palestinian refugees camp

UNRWA Field Offices

UNRWA Headquarters

Lebanon

Syria

West Bank

Jordan

Gaza Strip

The situation grew even worse in the wake of the 1991 Gulf War. Kuwait, which employed large numbers of Palestinians but denied them citizenship, expelled more than 300,000 of them. "If people pose a security threat, as a sovereign country we have the right to exclude anyone we don't want," said Kuwaiti Ambassador to the United States, Saud Nasir Al-Sabah.[70]

Today, Palestine refugees in Lebanon do not have social and civil rights, and have very limited access to public health or educational facilities. The majority relies on UNRWA as the sole provider of education, health, relief and social services. Considered foreigners, Palestine refugees are prohibited by law from working in more than 70 trades and professions.[71]

The Palestinian refugees held the UN responsible for ameliorating their condition; nevertheless, many Palestinians were unhappy with the treatment they were receiving from their Arab brethren. Some, like Palestinian nationalist leader Musa Alami were incredulous: "It is shameful that the Arab governments should prevent the Arab refugees from working in their countries and shut the doors in their faces and imprison them in camps."[72] Most refugees, however, focused their discontentment on "the Zionists," whom they blamed for their predicament rather than the vanquished Arab armies.

MYTH

"Millions of Palestinians are confined to squalid refugee camps."

FACT

As of March 2005, the number of Palestinian refugees on UNRWA rolls had risen to nearly 4.3 million, several times the number that left Palestine in 1948. Fewer than one-third of the registered Palestine refugees, about 1.3 million, live in 59 recognized refugee camps in Jordan, Lebanon, Syria, the West Bank and Gaza Strip. The other two-thirds of the registered refugees live in and around the cities and towns of the host countries, and in the West Bank and the Gaza Strip, often in the environs of official camps.[73]

MYTH

"Israel forced the Palestinian refugees to stay in camps in the Gaza Strip."

FACT

During the years that Israel controlled the Gaza Strip, a consistent effort was made to get the Palestinians into permanent housing. The Palestinians opposed the idea because the frustrated and bitter inhabitants of the camps provided the various terrorist factions with their manpower. Moreover, the Arab states routinely pushed for the adoption of UN resolutions demanding that Israel desist from the removal of Palestinian refugees from camps in Gaza and the West Bank.[74] They preferred to keep the Palestinians as symbols of Israeli "oppression."

Now the camps are in the hands of the Palestinian Authority (PA), but little is being done to improve the lot of the Palestinians living in them. Journalist Netty Gross visited Gaza and asked an official why the camps there hadn't been dismantled. She was told the Palestinian Authority had made a "political decision" not to do anything for the more than 650,000 Palestinians living in the camps until the final-status talks with Israel took place.[75] Through 2005, the PA had still not spent one dime of the billions of dollars in foreign aid it had received to build permanent housing for the refugees.

MYTH

"Refugees have always been repatriated, only the Palestinians have been barred from returning to their homes."

FACT

Despite Arab intransigence, no one expected the refugee problem to persist. John Blandford Jr., the Director of UNRWA, wrote in his report on November 29, 1951, that he expected the Arab governments to assume responsibility for relief by July 1952. Moreover, Blandford stressed the need to end relief operations: "Sustained relief operations inevitably contain the germ of human deterioration."[76]

In fact, the Palestinians are the only displaced persons to have become wards of the international community.

Israel's agreement to pay compensation to the Palestinians who fled during 1948 can be contrasted with the treatment of the 12.5 million Germans in Poland and Czechoslovakia, who were expelled after World War II and allowed to take only those possessions they could carry. They received no compensation for confiscated property. World War II's effects on Poland's boundaries and population were considered "accomplished facts" that could not be reversed after the war. No one in Germany petitions today for the right of these millions of deportees and their children to return to the countries they were expelled from despite the fact that they and their ancestors had lived in those places for hundreds of years.

Another country seriously affected by the war was Finland, which was forced to give up almost one-eighth of its land and absorb more than 400,000 refugees (11 percent of the nation's population) from the Soviet Union. Unlike Israel, these were the *losers* of the war. There was no aid for their resettlement.

Perhaps an even better analogy can be seen in Turkey's integration of 150,000 Turkish refugees from Bulgaria in 1950. The difference between the Turks' handling of their refugees and the Arab states' treatment of the Palestinians was the attitude of the respective governments.

> Turkey has had a bigger refugee problem than either Syria or Lebanon and almost as big as Egypt has. . . . But you seldom hear about them because the Turks have done such a good job of resettling them. . . . The big difference is in spirit. The Turks, reluctant as they were to take on the burden, accepted it as a responsibility and set to work to clean it up as fast as possible.[77]

Had the Arab states wanted to alleviate the refugees' suffering, they could easily have adopted an attitude similar to Turkey's.

Another massive population transfer resulted from the partition of India and Pakistan in 1947. The eight *million* Hindus who fled Pakistan and the six *million* Muslims who left India were afraid of becoming a minority in their respective countries. Like the Palestinians, these people wanted to avoid being caught in the middle of the violence that engulfed their nations. In contrast to the Arab-Israeli conflict, however, the exchange of populations was considered the best solution to the problem of communal relations within the two states. Despite the enormous number of refugees and the relative poverty of the two nations involved, no special international relief organizations were established to aid them in resettlement.

> *". . . if there were a Palestinian state, why would its leaders want their potential citizens to be repatriated to another state? From a nation-building perspective it makes no sense. In fact, the original discussions about repatriation took place at a time that there was no hope of a Palestinian state. With the possibility of that state emerging, the Palestinians must decide if they want to view themselves as a legitimate state or if it is more important for them to keep their self-defined status as oppressed, stateless refugees. They really can't be both."*

> **—Fredelle Spiegel**[78]

MYTH

"Had the Palestinian refugees been repatriated, the Arab-Israeli conflict could have ended."

FACT

Israel consistently sought a solution to the refugee problem, but could not simply agree to allow all Palestinians to return.

No nation, regardless of past rights and wrongs, could contemplate taking in a fifth-column of such a size. And fifth-column it would be—people nurtured for 20 years [in 1967] in hatred of and totally dedicated to its destruction. The readmission of the refugees would be the equivalent to the admission to the U.S. of nearly 70,000,000 sworn enemies of the nation.[79]

The Arabs, meanwhile, adamantly refused to negotiate a separate agreement. The crux of the issue was the Arab states' unwillingness to accept Israel's existence. This was exemplified by Egyptian President Nasser's belligerent acts toward the Jewish State, which had nothing to do with the Palestinians. He was only interested in the refugees to the extent that they could contribute to his ultimate objective. As he told an interviewer on September 1, 1961: "If refugees return to Israel, Israel will cease to exist."[80]

MYTH

"Israel expelled more Palestinians in 1967."

FACT

After ignoring Israeli warnings to stay out of the war, King Hussein launched an attack on Jerusalem, Israel's capital. UNRWA estimated that during the fighting 175,000 of its registrants fled for a second time and approximately 350,000 fled for the first time. About 200,000 moved to Jordan, 115,000 to Syria and approximately 35,000 left Sinai for Egypt. Most of the Arabs who left came from the West Bank.

Israel allowed some West Bank Arabs to return. In 1967, more than 9,000 families were reunited and, by 1971, Israel had readmitted 40,000 refugees. By contrast, in July 1968, Jordan prohibited people intending to remain in the East Bank from emigrating from the West Bank and Gaza.[81]

When the Security Council empowered U Thant to send a representative to inquire into the welfare of civilians in the wake of the war, he instructed the mission to investigate the treatment of Jewish minorities in Arab countries, as well as Arabs in Israeli-occupied territory. Syria, Iraq and Egypt refused to permit the UN representative to carry out his investigation.[82]

MYTH

"UNRWA bears no responsibility for the terror and incitement that originates in the refugee camps."

FACT

Peter Hansen, commissioner-general of UNRWA admitted that the organization employed members of at least one Palestinian terrorist organization. "Oh I'm sure that there are Hamas members on the UNRWA payroll and I don't see that as a crime," he told the Canadian Broadcasting Corporation. "Hamas as a political organization does not mean that every member is a militant and we do not do political vetting and exclude people from one persuasion against another."[83] Although Hansen makes specious distinctions between members of Hamas, the United States and the European Union, the two largest contributors to UNRWA, have banned the military and civilian wings of the organization.

The fact is the refugee camps have long been nests of terrorism, but the evidence was not publicized until after Israel's Operation Defensive Shield in early 2002. The UNRWA-administered camps in the West Bank were found to have small-arms factories, explosives laboratories, arms caches and large numbers of suicide bombers and other terrorists using the refugees as shields.

Since 2001, 17 Palestinians employed by UNRWA have been arrested for alleged involvement in terrorist activities. Among them is the agency's director of food supplies for Gaza refugees, who admitted using his UN vehicle to transport arms, explosives, and people planning terrorist acts. A Hamas activist employed as an UNRWA ambulance driver admitted using his vehicle to forward weapons and messages to other members of Hamas.[84]

UNRWA's failure to report on these activities, or to prevent them, violate the UN's own conventions. Security Council resolutions oblige UNRWA representatives to take "appropriate steps to help create a secure environment" in all "situations where refugees [are] . . . vulnerable to infiltration by armed elements." With regard to Africa, UN Secretary-General Kofi Annan, said refugee camps should "be kept free of any military presence or equipment, including arms and ammunition.[85] The same rule applies to the disputed territories.

Schools under UNRWA's jurisdiction are also problematic. UNRWA takes credit for assisting in the development of the Palestinian curricula, which, among other things, does not show Israel on any maps. The schools are also filled with posters and shrines to suicide bombers. The State Department requested that UNRWA investigate allegations that Palestinian Authority curricular materials contained anti-Semitic references. One book taught that "Treachery and disloyalty are character traits of the Jews," but UNRWA said this was not offensive because it described actual "historical events." The State Department ultimately reported to Congress that the "UNRWA review did reveal instances of anti-Semitic characterizations and content" in the PA textbooks.[86]

Since the State Department's report, several studies have shown that while there has been marginal improvement in Palestinian texts, they still contain troubling content. For example, one report found that *Islamic Culture,* a book produced by the Palestinian Authority Ministry of Education, incites *jihad* and martyrdom, while another study of 35 books concluded that they lacked any commitment to peace and reconciliation with Israel.

MYTH

"All the Palestinian refugees have the right to return to their homes."

FACT

Does Israel have any obligation to take in the 4.3 million Palestinian refugees? Where would they live?

The current Israeli population is approximately 7 million, 5.3 million are Jews. If every Palestinian was allowed to move to Israel, the population would exceed 11 million and the Jewish proportion would shrink from 76% to 48%. The Jews would be a minority in their own country, the very situation they fought to avoid in 1948, and which the UN expressly ruled out in deciding on a partition of Palestine.

Current peace talks are based on UN Resolution 242. The Palestinians are not mentioned anywhere in Resolution 242. They are only alluded to in the second clause of the second article of 242, which calls for "a just settlement of the refugee problem." The generic term "refugee" may also be applied to the Jewish refugees from Arab lands.

Furthermore, most Palestinians now live in historic Palestine, which is an area including the Palestinian Authority and Jordan. When Palestinians speak of the right to return, however, they don't mean just to Palestine, but to the exact houses they lived in prior to 1948. These homes are either gone or inhabited now.

Even respected Palestinian leaders have begun to acknowledge that it is a mistake to insist that millions of refugees return to Israel. Palestinian intellectual Sari Nusseibeh, for example, said the refugees should be resettled in a future Palestinian state, "not in a way that would undermine the existence of the State of Israel as a predominantly Jewish state. Otherwise, what does a two-state solution mean?"[87]

In the context of a peace settlement, Israel could be expected to accept some refugees, as Ben-Gurion said he would do more than 50 years ago. If and when a Palestinian state is created, most, if not all, of the refugees should be allowed to move there, but the Palestinian leadership has expressed little interest in absorbing these people.

Notes

1. Arieh Avneri, *The Claim of Dispossession*, (NJ: Transaction Books, 1984), p. 272; Kedar, Benjamin, *The Changing Land Between the Jordan and the Sea*. (Israel: Yad Izhak Ben-Zvi Press, 1999), p. 206; Paul Johnson, *A History of the Jews*, (NY: Harper & Row, 1987), p. 529.

2. Progress Report of the United Nations Mediator on Palestine, Submitted to the Secretary-General for Transmission to the Members of the United Nations, General Assembly Official Records: Third Session, Supplement No. 11 (A\648), Paris, 1948, p. 47 and Supplement No. 11A (A\689, and A\689\Add. 1, p. 5; and "Conclusions From Progress Report of the United Nations Mediator on Palestine," (September 16, 1948), U.N. doc. A/648 (part one, p. 29; part two, p. 23 and part three, p. 11), (September 18, 1948).

3. *New York Times,* (November 25, 1947).

4. Avneri, p. 276.

5. *Jerusalem Post,* (December 4, 2003).

6. David Ben-Gurion, *Rebirth and Destiny of Israel,* (NY: Philosophical Library, 1954), p. 220.

7. Isi Liebler, *The Case For Israel,* (Australia: The Globe Press, 1972), p. 43.

8. Joseph Schechtman, *The Refugee in the World,* (NY: A.S. Barnes and Co., 1963), p. 184.

9. I.F. Stone, *This is Israel,* (NY: Boni and Gaer, 1948), p. 27.

10. *Ash Sha'ab,* (January 30, 1948).

11. *As Sarih,* (March 30, 1948).

12. Avneri, p. 270.

13. *London Daily Mail,* (August 12, 1948).

14. *New York Times,* (April 23, 1948).

15. Howard Sachar, *A History of Israel: From the Rise of Zionism to Our Time,* (NY: Alfred A. Knopf, 1979), p. 332; Avneri, p. 270.

16. Secret memo dated April 26, 1948, from the Superintendent of Police, regarding the general situation in Haifa. See also his April 29 memo.

17. Golda Meir, *My Life,* (NY: Dell, 1975), pp. 267-268.

18. *New York Times,* (April 23, 1948).

19. *London Times,* (April 24, 1948).

20. Schechtman, p. 190.

21. *Foreign Relations of the U.S. 1948,* Vol. V, (DC: GPO, 1976), p. 838.

22. Tom Segev, *1949: The First Israelis,* (NY: The Free Press, 1986), pp. 27-28.

23. Yigal Allon in *Sefer ha-Palmach,* quoted in Larry Collins and Dominique Lapierre, *O Jerusalem!,* (NY: Simon and Schuster, 1972), p. 337; Yigal Allon, *My Father's House,* (NY: W.W Norton and Company, Inc., 1976), p. 192.

24. Benny Morris, "Operation Dani and the Palestinian Exodus from Lydda and Ramle in 1948," *Middle East Journal,* (Winter 1986), pp. 82-83.

25. *Middle East Journal,* (October 1949).

26. Terence Prittie, "Middle East Refugees," in Michael Curtis, et al., *The Palestinians,* (NJ: Transaction Books, 1975), p. 52.

27. *New York Times,* (March 4, 1949).

28. *The Guardian* (February 21, 2002).

29. *Middle Eastern Studies,* (January 1986); See also Morris, *The Birth of the Palestinian Refugee Problem Revisited,* Cambridge: Cambridge University Press, 2004, pp. 263 & 590-591.

30. *The Memoirs of Haled al Azm,* (Beirut, 1973), Part 1, pp. 386-387.

31. Myron Kaufman, *The Coming Destruction of Israel,* (NY: The American Library Inc., 1970), pp. 26-27.

32. Edward Atiyah, *The Arabs,* (London: Penguin Books, 1955), p. 183.

33. Samuel Katz, *Battleground-Fact and Fantasy in Palestine,* (NY: Bantam Books, 1985), p. 15.

34. King Abdallah, *My Memoirs Completed,* (London: Longman Group, Ltd., 1978), p. xvi. [Abdullah generally, but spelled Abdallah in his memoir].

35. Schechtman, p. 186.
36. Yehoshofat Harkabi, *Arab Attitudes To Israel*, (Jerusalem: Israel Universities Press, 1972), p. 364.
37. *Falastin a-Thaura*, (March 1976).
38. "Dayr Yasin," Bir Zeit University.
39. Dan Kurzman, *Genesis 1948*, (OH: New American Library, Inc., 1970), p. 141.
40. Menachem Begin, *The Revolt*, (NY: Nash Publishing, 1977), pp. xx-xxi, 162-163.
41. See, for example, Amos Perlmutter, *The Life and Times of Menachem Begin*, (NY: Doubleday, 1987), p. 214; J. Bowyer Bell, *Terror Out Of Zion*, (NY: St. Martin's Press, 1977), p. 292-96; Kurzman, p. 142.
42. Uri Milstein, *History of Israel's War of Independence. Vol. IV*, (Lanham: University Press of America. 1999), p. 262.
43. Milstein, p. 262.
44. Dana Adams Schmidt, "200 Arabs Killed, Stronghold Taken," *New York Times*, (April 10, 1948).
45. Kurzman, p. 148.
46. Sharif Kanaana and Nihad Zitawi, "Deir Yassin," Monograph No. 4, Destroyed Palestinian Villages Documentation Project, (Bir Zeit: Documentation Center of Bir Zeit University, 1987), p. 55.
47. Sharif Kanaana, "Reinterpreting Deir Yassin," Bir Zeit University, (April 1998).
48. Milstein, p. 267
49. Rami Nashashibi, "Dayr Yasin," Bir Zeit University, (June 1996).
50. Yehoshua Gorodenchik testimony at Jabotinsky Archives.
51. Milstein, p. 276.
52. "Israel and the Arabs: The 50 Year Conflict," BBC.
53. Sachar, p. 335.
54. Schechtman, p. 268.
55. Prittie in Curtis, pp. 66-67.
56. *New York Times*, (July 17, 1949).
57. *Telegraph* (Beirut), (August 6, 1948), quoted in Schechtman, p. 210-211.
58. *Jerusalem Post*, (January 26, 1989).
59. Moshe Sharett, "Israel's Position and Problems," *Middle Eastern Affairs*, (May 1952), p. 136.
60. Lebanese newspaper, *Al Said*, (April 6, 1950), quoted in Prittie in Curtis, p. 69.
61. *Al-Misri*, (October 11, 1949).
62. *Beirut al Massa*, (July 15, 1957).
63. *The Writings of Benjamin Franklin*, (NY: The Macmillan Company, 1905), p. 626.
64. Melissa Radler, "UN marks partition plan anniversary with anti-Israel fest," *Jerusalem Post*, (December 4, 2003).
65. UNRWA, (as of March 31, 2005).
66. UNRWA Finances (as of March 31, 2005).
67. Speech to Parliament, April 24, 1950, Abdallah memoirs, p. 13; Aaron Miller, *The Arab States and the Palestine Question*, (DC: Center for Strategic and International Studies, 1986), p. 29.
68. Leibler, p. 48.
69. Prittie in Curtis, p. 71.
70. *Jerusalem Report*, (June 27, 1991).
71. UNRWA.
72. Musa Alami, "The Lesson of Palestine," *Middle East Journal*, (October 1949), p. 386.
73. UNRWA.
74. Arlene Kushner, "The UN's Palestinian Refugee Problem," *Azure*, (Autumn 2005).

75. *Jerusalem Report,* (July 6, 1998).
76. Schechtman, p. 220.
77. *Des Moines Register* editorial, (January 16, 1952).
78. *Jerusalem Report,* (March 26, 2001).
79. *New York Times* editorial, (May 14, 1967).
80. Leibler, p. 45.
81. UNRWA Annual Reports, (July 1, 1966-June 30, 1967), pp. 11-19; (July 1, 1967-June 30, 1968), pp. 4-10; (July 1, 1968-June 30, 1969), p. 6; (July 1, 1971-June 30, 1972), p. 3.
82. Maurice Roumani, *The Case of the Jews from Arab Countries: A Neglected Issue,* (Tel Aviv: World Organization of Jews from Arab Countries, 1977), p. 34.
83. Canadian Broadcasting Corporation, (October 4, 2004), quoted by Jewish Telegraphic Agency, (October 4, 2004).
84. Matthew Levitt, "Terror on the UN Payroll?," *Peace Watch,* DC: The Washington Institute for Near East Policy, (October 13, 2004); Greg Myre, "Israel Feuds With Agency Set Up to Aid Palestinians," *New York Times,* (October 18, 2004).
85. Isabel Kershner, "The Refugees' Choice?," *Jerusalem Report,* (August 12, 2002), p. 24.
86. David Tell, response to McCann, *The Weekly Standard,* (May 28, 2002).
87. Associated Press, (October 22, 2001).

14. The Treatment of Jews in Arab/Islamic Countries

MYTH

"Arabs cannot be anti-Semitic as they are themselves Semites."

FACT

The term "anti-Semite" was coined in Germany in 1879 by Wilhelm Marr to refer to the anti-Jewish manifestations of the period and to give Jew-hatred a more scientific sounding name.[1] "Anti-Semitism" has been accepted and understood to mean hatred of the Jewish people. Dictionaries define the term as: "Theory, action, or practice directed against the Jews" and "Hostility towards Jews as a religious or racial minority group, often accompanied by social, economic and political discrimination."[2]

The claim that Arabs as "Semites" cannot possibly be anti-Semitic is a semantic distortion that ignores the reality of Arab discrimination and hostility toward Jews. Arabs, like any other people, can indeed be anti-Semitic.

> *"The Arab world is the last bastion of unbridled, unashamed, unhidden and unbelievable anti-Semitism. Hitlerian myths get published in the popular press as incontrovertible truths. The Holocaust either gets minimized or denied. . . . How the Arab world will ever come to terms with Israel when Israelis are portrayed as the devil incarnate is hard to figure out."*
>
> **—Columnist Richard Cohen[3]**

MYTH

"Modern Arab nations are only anti-Israel and have never been anti-Jewish."

FACT

Arab leaders have repeatedly made clear their animosity toward Jews and Judaism. For example, on November 23, 1937, Saudi Arabia's King Ibn Saud told British Colonel H.R.P. Dickson: "Our hatred for the Jews dates from God's condemnation of them for their persecution and rejection of Isa (Jesus) and their subsequent rejection of His chosen Prophet."

He added "that for a Muslim to kill a Jew, or for him to be killed by a Jew ensures him an immediate entry into Heaven and into the august presence of God Almighty."[4]

When Hitler introduced the Nuremberg racial laws in 1935, he received telegrams of congratulation from all corners of the Arab world.[5] Later, during the war, one of his most ardent supporters was the Mufti of Jerusalem.

Jews were never permitted to live in Jordan. Civil Law No. 6, which governed the Jordanian-occupied West Bank, states explicitly: "Any man will be a Jordanian subject if he is not Jewish."[6]

After the Six-Day War in 1967, the Israelis found public school textbooks that had been used to educate Arab children in the West Bank. They were replete with racist and hateful portrayals of Jews.[7]

According to a study of Syrian textbooks, "the Syrian educational system expands hatred of Israel and Zionism to anti-Semitism directed at all Jews. That anti-Semitism evokes ancient Islamic motifs to describe the unchangeable and treacherous nature of the Jews. Its inevitable conclusion is that all Jews must be annihilated."[8]

An Arabic translation of Adolf Hitler's *Mein Kampf* was distributed in East Jerusalem and the territories controlled by the Palestinian Authority (PA) and became a bestseller. The official website of the Palestinian State Information Service also published an Arabic translation of the "Protocols of the Elders of Zion."[9]

Arab officials have also resorted to blood libels. King Faisal of Saudi Arabia, for example, said that Jews "have a certain day on which they mix the blood of non-Jews into their bread and eat it. It happened that two years ago, while I was in Paris on a visit, that the police discovered five murdered children. Their blood had been drained, and it turned out that some Jews had murdered them in order to take their blood and mix it with the bread that they eat on this day.".[10]

On November 11, 1999, during a Gaza appearance with First Lady Hillary Rodham Clinton, Suha Arafat, wife of Palestinian Authority Chairman Yasser Arafat stated: "Our people have been subjected to the daily and extensive use of poisonous gas by the Israeli forces, which has led to an increase in cancer cases among women and children." Other specious allegations have been made by other Palestinian officials, such as the claims that Israel dumped toxic waste in the West Bank, marketed carcinogenic juice to Palestinians, released wild pigs to destroy crops in the West Bank, infected Palestinians with the AIDS virus, dropped poison candy for children in Gaza from airplanes, and used a "radial spy machine" at checkpoints that killed a Palestinian woman.[11]

The Arab/Muslim press, which is almost exclusively controlled by the governments in each Middle Eastern nation, regularly publish anti-Semitic articles and cartoons. Today, it remains common to find anti-Semitic publications in Egypt. For example, the establishment *Al-Ahram* newspaper published an article giving the "historical" background of the blood libel tradition while accusing Israel of using the blood of Palestinian children to bake matzos up to the present time.[12]

Anti-Semitic articles also regularly appear in the press in Jordan and Syria. Many of the attacks deal with denial of the Holocaust, its "exploitation" by Zionism, and a comparison of Zionism and Israel to Nazism. To its credit, the Jordanian government canceled the 2005 broadcast of an anti-Semitic television series base on the "Protocols."[13]

In November 2001, a satirical skit aired on the second most popular television station in the Arab world, which depicted a character meant to be Ariel Sharon drinking the blood of Arab children as a grotesque-looking Orthodox Jew looked on. Abu Dhabi Television also aired a skit in which Dracula appears to take a bite out of Sharon, but dies because Sharon's blood is polluted. Protests that these shows were anti-Semitic were ignored by the network.[14]

"Syrian President Bashar Assad on Saturday [May 5] offered a vivid, if vile, demonstration of why he and his government are unworthy of respect or good relations with the United States or any other democratic country. Greeting Pope John Paul II in Damascus, Mr. Assad launched an attack on Jews that may rank as the most ignorant and crude speech delivered before the pope in his two decades of travel around the world. Comparing the suffering of the Palestinians to that of Jesus Christ, Mr. Assad said that the Jews 'tried to kill the principles of all religions with the same mentality in which they betrayed Jesus Christ and the same way they tried to betray and kill the Prophet Muhammad.' With that libel, the Syrian president stained both his country and the pope...."

—Washington Post editorial, (May 8, 2001)

The Palestinian Authority's media have also contained inflammatory and anti-Semitic material. A Friday sermon in the Zayed bin Sultan Aal Nahyan mosque in Gaza calling for the murder of Jews and Americans was broadcast live on the official Palestinian Authority television:

> Have no mercy on the Jews, no matter where they are, in any country. Fight them, wherever you are. Wherever you meet them, kill them. Wherever you are, kill those Jews and those Americans who are like them and those who stand by them they are all in one trench, against the Arabs and the Muslims because they established Israel here, in the beating heart of the Arab world, in Palestine....[15]

Even Palestinian crossword puzzles are used to delegitimize Israel and attack Jews, providing clues, for example, suggesting the Jewish trait is "treachery."[16]

MYTH

"Jews who lived in Islamic countries were well-treated by the Arabs."

FACT

While Jewish communities in Islamic countries fared better overall than those in Christian lands in Europe, Jews were no strangers to persecution and humiliation among the Arabs. As Princeton University historian Bernard Lewis has written: "The Golden Age of equal rights was a myth, and belief in it was a result, more than a cause, of Jewish sympathy for Islam."[17]

Muhammad, the founder of Islam, traveled to Medina in 622 A.D. to attract followers to his new faith. When the Jews of Medina refused to recognize Muhammad as their Prophet, two of the major Jewish tribes were expelled. In 627, Muhammad's followers killed between 600 and 900 of the men, and divided the surviving Jewish women and children amongst themselves.[18]

The Muslim attitude toward Jews is reflected in various verses throughout the Koran, the holy book of the Islamic faith. "They [the Children of Israel] were consigned to humiliation and wretchedness. They brought the wrath of God upon themselves, and this because they used to deny God's signs and kill His Prophets unjustly and because they disobeyed and were transgressors" (Sura 2:61). According to the Koran, the Jews try to introduce corruption (5:64), have always been disobedient (5:78), and are enemies of Allah, the Prophet and the angels (2:97–98).

Jews were generally viewed with contempt by their Muslim neighbors; peaceful coexistence between the two groups involved the subordination and degradation of the Jews. In the ninth century, Baghdad's Caliph al-Mutawakkil designated a yellow badge for Jews, setting a precedent that would be followed centuries later in Nazi Germany.[19]

At various times, Jews in Muslim lands lived in relative peace and thrived culturally and economically. The position of the Jews was never secure, however, and changes in the political or social climate would often lead to persecution, violence and death.

When Jews were perceived as having achieved too comfortable a position in Islamic society, anti-Semitism would surface, often with devastating results. On December 30, 1066, Joseph HaNagid, the Jewish vizier of Granada, Spain, was crucified by an Arab mob that proceeded to raze the Jewish quarter of the city and slaughter its 5,000 inhabitants. The riot was incited by Muslim preachers who had angrily objected to what they saw as inordinate Jewish political power.

Similarly, in 1465, Arab mobs in Fez slaughtered thousands of Jews, leaving only 11 alive, after a Jewish deputy vizier treated a Muslim woman in "an offensive manner." The killings touched off a wave of similar massacres throughout Morocco.[20] Other mass murders of Jews in Arab lands occurred in Morocco in the 8th century, where whole communities were wiped out by the Muslim ruler Idris I; North Africa in the 12th century, where the Almohads either forcibly converted or decimated several communities; Libya in 1785, where Ali Burzi Pasha murdered hundreds of Jews; Algiers, where Jews were massacred in 1805, 1815 and 1830; and Marrakesh, Morocco, where more than 300 Jews were murdered between 1864 and 1880.[21]

Decrees ordering the destruction of synagogues were enacted in Egypt and Syria (1014, 1293–4, 1301–2), Iraq (854–859, 1344) and Yemen (1676). Despite the Koran's prohibition, Jews were forced to convert to Islam or face death in Yemen (1165 and 1678), Morocco (1275, 1465 and 1790–92) and Baghdad (1333 and 1344).[22]

The situation of Jews in Arab lands reached a low point in the 19th century. Jews in most of North Africa (including Algeria, Tunisia, Egypt, Libya and Morocco) were forced to live in ghettos. In Morocco, which contained the largest Jewish community in the Islamic Diaspora, Jews were made to walk barefoot or wear shoes of straw when outside the ghetto. Even Muslim children participated in the degradation of Jews, by throwing stones at them or harassing them in other ways. The frequency of anti-Jewish violence increased, and many Jews were executed on charges of apostasy. Ritual murder accusations against the Jews became commonplace in the Ottoman Empire.[23]

As distinguished Orientalist G.E. von Grunebaum has written:

> It would not be difficult to put together the names of a very sizeable number Jewish subjects or citizens of the Islamic area who have attained to high rank, to power, to great financial influence, to significant and recognized intellectual attainment; and the same could be done for Christians. But it would again not be difficult to compile a lengthy list of persecutions, arbitrary confiscations, attempted forced conversions, or pogroms.[24]

The danger for Jews became even greater as a showdown approached in the UN. The Syrian delegate, Faris el-Khouri, warned: "Unless the Palestine problem is settled, we shall have difficulty in protecting and safeguarding the Jews in the Arab world."[25]

More than a thousand Jews were killed in anti-Jewish rioting during the 1940's in Iraq, Libya, Egypt, Syria and Yemen.[26] This helped trigger the mass exodus of Jews from Arab countries.

MYTH

"As 'People of the Book,' Jews and Christians are protected under Islamic law."

FACT

This argument is rooted in the traditional concept of the "dhimma" ("writ of protection"), which was extended by Muslim conquerors to Christians and Jews in exchange for their subordination to the Muslims. Yet, as French authority Jacques Ellul has observed: "One must ask: 'protected against whom?' When this 'stranger' lives in Islamic countries, the answer can only be: against the Muslims themselves." [27]

Peoples subjected to Muslim rule usually had a choice between death and conversion, but Jews and Christians, who adhered to the Scriptures, were usually allowed, as *dhimmis,* to practice their faith. This "protection" did little, however, to insure that Jews and Christians were treated well by the Muslims. On the contrary, an integral aspect of the *dhimma* was that, being an infidel, he had to acknowledge openly the superiority of the true believer—the Muslim.

In the early years of the Islamic conquest, the "tribute" (or *jizya*), paid as a yearly poll tax, symbolized the subordination of the *dhimmi.* [28] Later, the inferior status of Jews and Christians was reinforced through a series of regulations that governed the behavior of the *dhimmi.* *Dhimmis,* on pain of death, were forbidden to mock or criticize the Koran, Islam or Muhammad, to proselytize among Muslims, or to touch a Muslim woman (though a Muslim man could take a non-Muslim as a wife).

Dhimmis were excluded from public office and armed service, and were forbidden to bear arms. They were not allowed to ride horses or camels, to build synagogues or churches taller than mosques, to construct houses higher than those of Muslims or to drink wine in public. They were forced to wear distinctive clothing and were not allowed to pray or mourn in loud voices—as that might offend Muslims. The *dhimmi* also had to show public deference toward Muslims; for example, always yielding them the center of the road. The *dhimmi* was not allowed to give evidence in court against a Muslim, and his oath was unacceptable in an Islamic court. To defend himself, the *dhimmi* would have to purchase Muslim witnesses at great expense. This left the *dhimmi* with little legal recourse when harmed by a Muslim. [29]

By the twentieth century, the status of the *dhimmi* in Muslim lands had not significantly improved. H.E.W. Young, British Vice Consul in Mosul, wrote in 1909:

> The attitude of the Muslims toward the Christians and the Jews is that of a master towards slaves, whom he treats with a certain

lordly tolerance so long as they keep their place. Any sign of pretension to equality is promptly repressed.[30]

The Situation Today

The Jews of Algeria

1948 Jewish population: 140,000
2004: Less than 100[31]

Jewish settlement in present-day Algeria can be traced back to the first centuries of the Common Era. In the 14th century, with the deterioration of conditions in Spain, many Spanish Jews moved to Algeria. After the French occupation of the country in 1830, Jews gradually adopted French culture and were granted French citizenship.[32]

In 1934, Muslims, incited by events in Nazi Germany, rampaged in Constantine, killing 25 Jews and injuring many more. After being granted independence in 1962, the Algerian government harassed the Jewish community and deprived Jews of their economic rights. As a result, almost 130,000 Algerian Jews immigrated to France. Since 1948, 25,681 Algerian Jews have immigrated to Israel.

Most of the remaining Jews live in Algiers, but there are individual Jews in Oran and Blida. Jews practice their religion freely, and Jewish community leaders are included in ceremonial state functions. There is no resident rabbi.[33]

In 1994, the terrorist Armed Islamic Group—GIA declared its intention to eliminate Jews from Algeria.[34] Following the announcement, many Jews left Algeria and the single remaining synagogue was abandoned.[35] All other synagogues had previously been taken over for use as mosques.

The Jews of Egypt

1948 Jewish population: 75,000
2004: 100

Between June and November 1948, bombs set off in the Jewish Quarter of Cairo killed more than 70 Jews and wounded nearly 200.[36] In 1956, the Egyptian government used the Sinai Campaign as a pretext for expelling almost 25,000 Egyptian Jews and confiscating their property. Approximately 1,000 more Jews were sent to prisons and detention camps.

On November 23, 1956, a proclamation signed by the Minister of Religious Affairs, and read aloud in mosques throughout Egypt, declared that "all Jews are Zionists and enemies of the state," and promised that they would be soon expelled. Thousands of Jews were ordered to leave the country. They were allowed to take only one suitcase and a small sum of cash, and forced to sign declarations "donating" their property to the Egyptian government. Foreign observers reported that members of Jewish families were taken hostage, apparently to insure that those forced to leave did not speak out against the Egyptian government.[37]

When war broke out in 1967, Jewish homes and property were confiscated. Egypt's attitude toward Jews at that time was reflected in its treatment of former Nazis. Hundreds were allowed to take up residence in Egypt and given positions in the government. The head of the Polish Gestapo, Leopold Gleim (who had been sentenced to death in absentia), controlled the Egyptian secret police.

In 1979, following the signing of the Egypt-Israel peace treaty, the Egyptian Jewish community became the first in the Arab world to establish official contact with Israel. Israel now has an embassy in Cairo and a consulate general in Alexandria. At present, the few remaining Jews are free to practice Judaism without any restrictions or harassment. Shaar Hashamayim is the only functioning synagogue in Cairo. Of the many synagogues in Alexandria only the Eliahu Hanabi is open for worship.[38]

There have been no anti-Semitic incidents in recent years directed at the tiny Jewish community;[39] however, Anti-Semitism is rampant in the government-controlled press, and increased in late 2000 and 2001 following the outbreak of violence in Israel and the territories. In April 2001, columnist Ahmed Ragheb lamented Hitler's failure to finish the job of annihilating the Jews. In May 2001, an article in *Al-Akhbar* attacked Europeans and Americans for believing in the false Holocaust.[40] On March 18, 2004, 'Bad al-Ahab 'Adams, deputy editor of *Al Jumhuriya*, accused the Jews of the terrorist attack in Madrid on March 11 as well as of the September 11, 2001, attacks.[41]

A positive development was the announcement that a Cairo synagogue built in 1934, which had been closed because so few Jews remain in Egypt, would be reopened in July 2005. The head of Cairo's Jewish community, Carmen Weinstein, and Israel's ambassador to Egypt, Shalom Cohen, arranged to reopen the synagogue, which the Israeli Embassy will help to maintain.[42]

The Jews of Iran

1948 Jewish population, 100,000
2004: 10,900

The Jewish community of Persia, modern-day Iran, is one of the oldest in the Diaspora, and its historical roots reach back to the time of the First Temple. Under the Phalevi Dynasty, established in 1925, the country was secularized and oriented toward the West. This greatly benefited the Jews, who were emancipated and played an important role in the economy and cultural life.

On the eve of the Islamic Revolution in 1979, 80,000 Jews lived in Iran. In the wake of the upheaval, tens of thousands of Jews, especially the wealthy, left the country, leaving behind vast amounts of property. Iran's Jewish community, nevertheless, remains the largest in the Middle East outside Israel.

The Council of the Jewish Community, which was established after World War II, is the representative body of the community. The Jews also have a representative in parliament who is obligated by law to support Iranian foreign policy and its anti-Zionist position.

Despite the official distinction between "Jews," "Zionists," and "Israel," the most common accusation the Jews encounter is that of maintaining contacts with Zionists. The Jewish community does enjoy a measure of religious freedom, but is faced with constant suspicion of cooperating with the "Zionist state" and with "imperialistic America"—activities punishable by death. Jews who apply for a passport to travel abroad must do so in a special bureau and are immediately put under surveillance. The government does not generally allow all members of a family to travel abroad at the same time to prevent Jewish emigration. Jewish leaders fear government reprisals if they draw attention to official mistreatment of their community.

The Islamization of the country has brought about strict control over Jewish educational institutions. Before the revolution, there were some 20 Jewish schools functioning throughout the country. In recent years, most of these have been closed down. In the remaining schools, Jewish principals have been replaced by Muslims. In Teheran, Jewish pupils still constitute a majority in three schools. The curriculum is Islamic, and Persian is forbidden as the language of instruction for Jewish studies. Special Hebrew lessons are conducted on Fridays by the Orthodox Otzar ha-Torah organization, which is responsible for Jewish religious education. Saturday is no longer officially recognized as the Jewish sabbath, and Jewish pupils are compelled to attend school on that day. There are three synagogues in Teheran, but there has been no rabbi in Iran since 1994 and the bet din does not function.[43]

Following the overthrow of the shah and the declaration of an Islamic state in 1979, Iran severed relations with Israel. The country has subsequently supported many of the Islamic terrorist organizations that target Jews and Israelis, particularly the Lebanon-based Hizballah.

On the eve of Passover in 1999, 13 Jews from Shiran and Isfahan in southern Iran were arrested and accused of spying for Israel and the United States. Those arrested include a rabbi, a ritual slaughterer and teachers. In September 2000, an Iranian appeals court upheld a decision to imprison ten of the thirteen Jews accused of spying for Israel.

In the appeals court, ten of the accused were found guilty of cooperating with Israel and were given prison terms ranging from two to nine years. Three of the accused were found innocent in the first trial.[44] In March 2001, one of the imprisoned Jews was released, a second was freed in January 2002, the remaining eight were set free in late October 2002. The last five apparently were released on furlough for an indefinite period, leaving them vulnerable to future arrest. Three others were reportedly pardoned by Iran's Supreme Leader, Ayatollah Ali Khamenei.[45]

At least 17 Jews have been executed in Iran since the Islamic revolution 19 years ago, most of them for either religious reasons or their connection to Israel.

The Jews of Iraq

1948 Jewish population: 150,000
2004: Approximately 35

One of the longest surviving Jewish communities still lives in Iraq. In 722 B.C.E., the northern tribes of Israel were defeated by Assyria and some Jews were taken to what is now known as Iraq. A larger community was established in 586 B.C.E., when the Babylonians conquered the southern tribes of Israel and enslaved the Jews. In later centuries, the region became more hospitable to Jews and it became the home to some of the world's most prominent scholars who produced the Babylonian Talmud between 500 and 700 C.E.

By World War I, Jews accounted for one third of Baghdad's population. In 1922, the British received a mandate over Iraq and began transforming it into a modern nation-state. Iraq became an independent state in 1932.

Throughout this period, the authorities drew heavily on the talents of the well-educated Jews for their ties outside the country and proficiency in foreign languages. Iraq's first minister of finance, Yehezkel Sasson, was a Jew. Jews also played a vital role in the development of the judicial and postal systems.

Following the end of the British mandate, the 2,700-year-old Iraqi Jewish community suffered increasing persecution, particularly as the Zionist drive for a state intensified. In June 1941, Rashid Ali, inspired by the arrival of the exiled Mufti of Jerusalem, rebelled against British rule and took control of the Iraqi government. Ali sparked a pro-Nazi riot in Baghdad that left 180 Jews dead and 1,000 wounded. British forces struck back against Ali's army and crushed the rebellion.

Jews built a broad network of medical facilities, schools and cultural activity. Nearly all of the members of the Baghdad Symphony Orchestra were Jewish. Yet this flourishing environment abruptly ended in 1947, with the partition of Palestine and the fight for Israel's independence. Outbreaks of anti-Jewish rioting regularly occurred between 1947–49. After the establishment of Israel in 1948, Zionism became a capital crime. In 1950, Iraqi Jews were permitted to leave the country within a year provided they forfeited their citizenship. A year later, however, the property of Jews who emigrated was frozen and economic restrictions were placed on Jews who chose to remain in the country. From 1949 to 1951, 104,000 Jews were evacuated from Iraq in Operations Ezra and Nechemia; another 20,000 were smuggled out through Iran.[46]

In 1952, Iraq's government barred Jews from emigrating and publicly hanged two Jews after falsely charging them with hurling a bomb at the Baghdad office of the U.S. Information Agency.

With the rise of competing Ba'ath factions in 1963, additional restrictions were placed on the remaining Iraqi Jews. The sale of property was forbidden and all Jews were forced to carry yellow identity cards. After the Six-Day War, more repressive measures were imposed. Jewish property was expropriated; Jewish bank accounts were frozen; Jews were dismissed from public posts; businesses were shut; trading permits were cancelled and telephones were disconnected. Jews were placed under house arrest for long periods of time or restricted to the cities.

Persecution was at its worst at the end of 1968. Scores were jailed upon the discovery of a local "spy ring" composed of Jewish businessmen. Fourteen men—eleven of them Jews—were sentenced to death in staged trials and hanged in the public squares of Baghdad; others died of torture. On January 27, 1969, Baghdad Radio called upon Iraqis to "come and enjoy the feast." Some 500,000 men, women and children paraded and danced past the scaffolds where the bodies of the hanged Jews swung; the mob rhythmically chanted "Death to Israel" and "Death to all traitors." This display brought a worldwide public outcry that Radio Baghdad dismissed by declaring: "We hanged spies, but the Jews crucified Christ."[47] Jews remained under constant surveillance by the Iraqi government.

In response to international pressure, the Baghdad government quietly allowed most of the remaining Jews to emigrate in the early 1970's, even while leaving other restrictions in force.

In 1991, prior to the Gulf War, the State Department said "there is no recent evidence of overt persecution of Jews, but the regime restricts travel, (particularly to Israel) and contacts with Jewish groups abroad."

Only one synagogue continues to function in Iraq, "a crumbling buff-colored building tucked away in an alleyway" in Bataween, once Baghdad's main Jewish neighborhood. According to the synagogue's administrator, "there are few children to be bar-mitzvahed, or couples to be married. Jews can practice their religion but are not allowed to hold jobs in state enterprises or join the army."[48] The rabbi died in 1996 and only one of the remaining Jews can perform the liturgy; only a couple of people know Hebrew. The last wedding was held in 1980.[49]

Today, approximately 35 Jews live in Baghdad, and a handful more in the Kurdish-controlled northern parts of Iraq.[50] About half of those in Baghdad are elderly, poor and lacking basic needs such as clothing, medication and food. Jews face no direct threats. The one synagogue, the Meir Taweig Synagogue, remains to serve the needs of the small community. The youngest Jew living in Iraq is 38 years old, and acts as the volunteer lay rabbi and kosher slaughterer.[51]

The end of Saddam Hussein's regime created the possibility of an improvement in the living conditions of Jews and the return of some of the émigrés. Some hope also exists for rapprochement with Israel. Given the instability in Iraq since the fall of Saddam, it is unlikely any great changes will take place immediately. For now, at least, Iraq is no longer openly hostile toward Israel.

The Jews of Lebanon

1948 Jewish population: 20,000
2004: Fewer than 100

When Christian Arabs ruled Lebanon, Jews enjoyed relative toleration. In the mid-50's, approximately 7,000 Jews lived in Beirut. As Jews in an Arab country, however, their position was never secure, and the majority left in 1967.

Fighting in the 1975–76 Muslim-Christian civil war swirled around the Jewish Quarter in Beirut, damaging many Jewish homes, businesses and synagogues. Most of the remaining 1,800 Lebanese Jews emigrated in 1976, fearing the growing Syrian presence in Lebanon would curtail their freedom. Most Jews went to Europe (particularly France), the United States and Canada.

In the mid-1980's, Hizballah kidnapped several prominent Jews from Beirut—most were leaders of what remained of the country's tiny Jewish community. Four of the Jews were later found murdered.

Nearly all of the remaining Jews are in Beirut, where there is a committee that represents the community.[52] Because of the current political situation, Jews are unable to openly practice Judaism. In 2004, only 1 out of 5,000 Lebanese Jewish citizens registered to vote participated in the municipal elections. Virtually all of those registered have died or fled the country. The lone Jewish voter said that most of the community consists of old women.[53]

The Jewish cemetery in Beirut is decrepit and cared for by an elderly Shiite woman. The gravestones, written in Hebrew and French, are a testament to the Lebanese Jewish community that is now only a shadow of its former self.[54]

The Arab-Israeli conflict, and Israel's long military presence in Lebanon, provoked strong anti-Israel sentiment. All travel from Lebanon to Israel is strictly prohibited. Meanwhile, Hizballah uses southern Lebanon as a base for terrorist attacks against Israel.

The Jews of Libya

1948 Jewish population: 38,000
2004: 0

Jews had a presence in Libya at least since the time of Hellenistic rule under Ptolemy Lagos in 323 B.C.E. in Cyrene.[55] Once home to a very large and thriving Jewish community, Libya is now completely empty of Jews due to anti-Jewish pogroms and immigration to Israel.

A savage pogrom in Tripoli on November 5, 1945, killed more than 140 Jews and wounded hundreds more. Almost every synagogue was looted. In June 1948, rioters murdered another 12 Jews and destroyed 280 Jewish homes.[56]

Thousands of Jews fled the country after Libya was granted independence and membership in the Arab League in 1951. After the Six-Day War, the Jewish population of 7,000 was again subjected to pogroms in which 18 were killed, and many more injured, sparking a near-total exodus that left fewer than 100 Jews in Libya.

When Muammar Qaddafi came to power in 1969, all Jewish property was confiscated and all debts to Jews cancelled. In 1999, the synagogue in Tripoli was renovated, however, it was not reopened.[57]

The last Jew living in Libya, Esmeralda Meghnagi, died in February 2002. This marked the end of one of the world's oldest Jewish communities.[58]

The Jews of Morocco

1948 Jewish population: 265,000
2004: 4,000

Jews have been in Morocco since before the destruction of the Second Temple in 70 C.E., but the oldest archaeological evidence is from the 2nd century C.E. Thousands of Spanish Jews settled in Morocco and other locations throughout Africa due to increasing religious persecution in Spain. Throughout the Renaissance, Morocco was a haven for marranos, or "secret Jews" who had escaped the Inquisition.[59]

In June 1948, bloody riots in Oujda and Djerada killed 44 Jews and wounded scores more. That same year, an unofficial economic boycott was instigated against Moroccan Jews.

In 1956, Morocco declared its independence, and Jewish immigration to Israel was suspended. In 1963, emigration resumed, allowing more than 100,000 Moroccan Jews to reach Israel.[60]

In 1965, Moroccan writer Said Ghallab described the attitude of his fellow Muslims toward their Jewish neighbors:

> The worst insult that a Moroccan could possibly offer was to treat someone as a Jew.... My childhood friends have remained anti-Jewish. They hide their virulent anti-Semitism by contending that the State of Israel was the creature of Western imperialism.... A whole Hitlerite myth is being cultivated among the populace. The massacres of the Jews by Hitler are exalted ecstatically. It is even credited that Hitler is not dead, but alive and well, and his arrival is awaited to deliver the Arabs from Israel.[61]

Nonetheless, before his death in 1999, King Hassan tried to protect the Jewish population and, at present, Morocco has one of the most tolerant environments for Jews in the Arab world. Moroccan Jewish émigrés, even those with Israeli citizenship, freely visit friends and relatives in Morocco. Moroccan Jews have held leading positions in the business community and government.

The major Jewish organization representing the community is the Conseil des Communautes Israelites in Casablanca. Its functions include external relations, general communal affairs, communal heritage, finance, maintenance of holy places, youth activities, and cultural and religious life.[62]

In early 2004, Marrakesh had a small population of about 260 people, most over the age of 60. Casablanca has the largest community, about 3,000 people. There are synagogues, mikvaot, old-age homes, and kosher restaurants in Casablanca, Fez, Marrakesh, Mogador, Rabat, Tetuan and Tangier. In 1992, most Jewish schools were closed, but Casablanca has experienced a bit of a renewal and now 10 schools serve 800 students there.[63]

Morocco is perhaps Israel's closest friend in the Arab world. King Hassan often tried to be a behind-the-scenes catalyst in the Arab-Israeli peace process. In 1993, after signing the agreement with the PLO, Prime Minister Yitzhak Rabin paid a formal visit to Morocco.

In May 1999, King Hassan organized the first meeting of the World Union of Moroccan Jews, in Marrakech. In April and May 2000, the Moroccan government sponsored a series of events and lectures promoting respect among religions.[64] Andre Azoulay, royal counselor and a leading Jewish citizen, spoke about the need for interfaith respect and dialogue.

In October 2000, two Moroccan youths tried to vandalize a Tangiers synagogue. King Mohamed VI publicly declared in a televised speech on November 6, 2000, that the government would not tolerate mistreatment of Morocco's Jews. The youths were subsequently sentenced to one year in prison.[65]

On May 16, 2003, a series of suicide bombers attacked four Jewish targets in Casablanca, and a fifth attack was made against the Spanish consulate. No Jews were hurt in the attacks because it occurred on Shabbat when the buildings were empty of Jews. Twenty-nine Muslims were killed. Though the bombings affected the Jewish sense of security, they were viewed by most Moroccans as assaults on the country's social and political order, and a test of the young king's power, rather than an act of anti-Semitism. King Mohammed VI visited the site of one of the attacks the day it occurred and urged the Jewish community to rebuild. The government subsequently organized a large rally in the streets of Casablanca to demonstrate support for the Jewish community and the king reasserted his family's traditional protection for the country's Jews.[66]

The Jews of Syria

1948 Jewish population: 30,000
2004: Fewer than 100

Jewish history in Syria dates to biblical times. Due to the proximity of Syria with ancient Palestine, the Syrian Jewish community was once large and prosperous.

In 1944, after Syria gained independence from France, the new government prohibited Jewish immigration to Palestine, and severely restricted the teaching of Hebrew in Jewish schools. Attacks against Jews escalated, and boycotts were called against their businesses.

When partition was declared in 1947, Arab mobs in Aleppo devastated the 2,500-year-old Jewish community. Scores of Jews were killed and more than 200 homes, shops and synagogues were destroyed. Thousands of Jews illegally fled Syria for Israel.[67]

Shortly after, the Syrian government intensified its persecution of the Jewish population. Freedom of movement was severely restricted. Jews who attempted to flee faced either the death penalty or imprisonment at hard labor. Jews were not allowed to work for the government or banks, could not acquire telephones or driver's licenses, and were barred from buying property. Jewish bank accounts were frozen. An airport road was paved over the Jewish cemetery in Damascus; Jewish schools were closed and handed over to Muslims.

Syria's attitude toward Jews was reflected in its sheltering of Alois Brunner, one of the most notorious Nazi war criminals. Brunner, a chief aide to Adolf Eichmann, served as an adviser to the Assad regime.[68]

In 1987–88, the Syrian secret police seized 10 Jews on suspicion of violating travel and emigration laws, planning to escape and having taken unauthorized trips abroad. Several who were released reported being tortured while in custody.[69]

For years, the Jews in Syria lived in extreme fear. The Jewish Quarter in Damascus was under the constant surveillance of the secret police, who were present at synagogue services, weddings, bar-mitzvahs and other Jewish gatherings. Contact with foreigners was closely monitored. Travel abroad was permitted in exceptional cases, but only if a bond of $300–$1,000 was left behind, along with family members who served as hostages. U.S. pressure applied during peace negotiations helped convince President Hafez Assad to lift these restrictions, and those prohibiting Jews from buying and selling property, in the early 1990's.

In an undercover operation in late 1994, 1,262 Syrian Jews were brought to Israel. The spiritual leader of the Syrian Jewish community for 25 years, Rabbi Avraham Hamra, was among those who left Syria and went to New York (he now lives in Israel). Syria had granted exit visas on condition that the Jews not go to Israel.[70] The decision to finally free the Jews came about largely as a result of pressure from the United States following the 1991 Madrid peace conference. The remaining Syrian Jews were forbidden from seeking government employment, and they were the only citizens whose passports were required to state their religion.

By the end of 1994, the Joab Ben Zeruiah Synagogue in Aleppo, in continuous use for more than 1,600 years, was deserted. A year later, approximately 250 Jews remained in Damascus, all apparently staying by choice.[71] By the middle of 2001, Rabbi Huder Shahada Kabariti estimated that 150 Jews were living in Damascus, 30 in Haleb and 20 in Kamashili. Every two or three months, a rabbi visits from Istanbul, Turkey, to oversee preparation of kosher meat, which residents freeze and use until his next visit. Two synagogues remain open in Damascus.[72]

Although Jews were in the past subjected to violence by Palestinian protesters, the government has taken strict protective measures, including arresting assailants and guarding the remaining synagogues.[73]

Jews still have a separate primary school for religious instruction on Judaism and are allowed to teach Hebrew in some schools. About a dozen students still attend the Jewish school, which had 500 students as recently as 1992. Jews and Kurds are the only minorities not allowed to participate in the political system. In addition, "the few remaining Jews are generally barred from government employment and do not have military service obligations. They are the only minority whose passports and identity cards note their religion."

The government used mass media outlets to disseminate anti-Semitic materials throughout the country. In 2003, a private film company produced an anti-Semitic television series, "Ash-Shata" ("The Diaspora"), based on the infamous "Protocols of the Elders of Zion." The series claimed that Jews orchestrated both World Wars and manipulated world opinion to create Israel.

The Jews of Tunisia

1948 Jewish population: 105,000
2004: 1,200

Tunisia was the only Arab country to come under direct German occupation during World War II. According to Robert Satloff, "From November 1942 to May 1943, the Germans and their local collaborators implemented a forced-labor regime, confiscations of property, hostage-taking, mass extortion, deportations, and executions. They required thousands of Jews in the countryside to wear the Star of David, and they created special Judenrat-like committees of Jewish leaders to implement Nazi policies under threat of imprisonment or death."[74]

After Tunisia gained independence in 1956, a series of anti-Jewish government decrees were promulgated. In 1958, Tunisia's Jewish Community Council was abolished by the government and ancient synagogues, cemeteries and Jewish quarters were destroyed for "urban renewal."[75]

The increasingly unstable situation caused more than 40,000 Tunisian Jews to immigrate to Israel. By 1967, the country's Jewish population had shrunk to 20,000.

During the Six-Day War, Jews were attacked by rioting Arab mobs, and synagogues and shops were burned. The government denounced the violence, and President Habib Bourguiba apologized to the Chief Rabbi. The government appealed to the Jewish population to stay, but did not bar them from leaving. Subsequently, 7,000 Jews immigrated to France.

In 1982, attacks on Jews were reported in the towns of Zarzis and Ben Guardane. According to the State Department, the Tunisian government "acted decisively to provide protection to the Jewish community."[76]

In 1985, a Tunisian guard opened fire on worshipers in a synagogue in Djerba, killing five people, four of them Jewish. Since then, the government has sought to prevent further tragedy by giving Tunisian Jews heavy protection when necessary. Following Israel's October 1, 1985, bombing of the PLO headquarters near Tunis, "the government took extraordinary measures to protect the Jewish community."[77]

Djerba has one Jewish kindergarten. There are also six Jewish primary schools (three located in Tunis, two in Djerba and one in the coastal city of Zarzis) and four secondary schools (two in Tunis and two in Djerba). There are also yeshivas in Tunis and Djerba. The community has two homes for the aged. The country has several kosher restaurants and five officiating rabbis: the chief rabbi in Tunis, a rabbi in Djerba, and four others in Tunis. The majority of the Jewish community observes the laws of *kashrut*.

Today, the 1,300 Jews comprise the country's largest indigenous religious minority. "The Government assures freedom of worship for the Jewish community and pays the salary of the Grand Rabbi" of the community.[78]

In October 1999, the Jewish community elected a new Board of Directors for the first time since Tunisia's independence in 1956. They also gave the Board a new name: "The Jewish Committee of Tunisia."[79]

On April 11, 2002, a natural gas truck exploded at the outer wall of the Ghriba synagogue in Djerba. Tunisian officials at first said the truck accidentally struck the wall of the synagogue, but a group linked to Osama bin Laden's al-Qaeda network claimed responsibility for carrying out what was actually a terrorist attack on the oldest synagogue in Africa. The explosion killed 17 people, including 11 German tourists. In 2003, French authorities arrested German citizen Christian Ganczarski at Charles de Gaulle Airport for his alleged role in the Djerba attack.[80]

The Tunisian government increased its measures to protect synagogues during Jewish holidays, and actually encouraged Jewish expatriates to return to Djerba for an annual religious pilgrimage.

The Jews of Yemen

1948 Jewish population: 55,000 (in Aden: another 8,000)
2004: 200

In 1922, the government of Yemen reintroduced an ancient Islamic law requiring that Jewish orphans under age 12 be forcibly converted to Islam.

In 1947, after the partition vote, Muslim rioters, joined by the local police force, engaged in a bloody pogrom in Aden that killed 82 Jews and destroyed hundreds of Jewish homes. Aden's Jewish community was economically paralyzed, as most of the Jewish stores and businesses were destroyed. Early in 1948, the false accusation of the ritual murder of two girls led to looting.[81]

This increasingly perilous situation led to the emigration of virtually the entire Yemenite Jewish community—almost 50,000—between June 1949 and September 1950 in Operation "Magic Carpet." A smaller, continuous migration was allowed to continue into 1962, when a civil war put an abrupt halt to any further Jewish exodus.

Until 1976, when an American diplomat came across a small Jewish community in a remote region of northern Yemen, it was believed the Yemenite Jewish community was extinct. As a result, the plight of Yemenite Jews went unrecognized by the outside world.

It turned out some people stayed behind during Operation "Magic Carpet" because family members did not want to leave sick or elderly relatives behind. These Jews were forbidden from emigrating and not allowed to contact relatives abroad. They were isolated and trapped, scattered throughout the mountainous regions in northern Yemen and lacked food, clothing, medical care and religious articles. As a result, some Yemenite Jews abandoned their faith and converted to Islam. Today, Jews are the only indigenous religious minority besides a small number of Christians, Hindus and Baha'is. The small community that remains in the northern area of Yemen is tolerated and allowed to practice Judaism. It is believed that two synagogues are still functioning in Saiqaya and in Amlah. Jews are still treated as second-class citizens and cannot serve in the army or be elected to political positions. Jews are traditionally restricted to living in one section of a city or village and are often confined to a limited choice of employment, usually farming or handicrafts. Jews may, and do, own property.[82]

During the past few years, about 400 Jews have immigrated to Israel, despite the official ban on emigration.[83]

The State Department reported that in mid-2000 "the Government suspended its policy of allowing Yemeni-origin Israeli passport holders to travel to Yemen on laissez-passer documents. However, Yemeni, Israeli, and other Jews may travel freely to and within Yemen on non-Israeli passports."[84]

In January 2001, the ruling "General People's Party" placed a Yemeni Jewish citizen on the slate for parliamentary elections for the first time. The candidate, Ibrahim Ezer, was reportedly recommended by President Ali Abdallah Salah as a gesture to the incoming Bush administration in a bid to receive economic aid for Yemen. The General Election Committee, subsequently rejected Ezer's application on grounds that a candidate must be the child of two Muslim parents. Political analysts speculated that the true reason was a desire not to establish a precedent of allowing a Jew to run for office.[85]

Notes

1. Vamberto Morais, *A Short History of Anti-Semitism,* (NY: W.W Norton and Co., 1976), p. 11; Bernard Lewis, *Semites & Anti-Semites,* (NY: WW Norton & Co., 1986), p. 81.
2. *Oxford English Dictionary; Webster's Third International Dictionary.*
3. *Washington Post,* (October 30, 2001).
4. Official British document, Foreign Office File No. 371/20822 E 7201/22/31; Elie Kedourie, *Islam in the Modern World,* (London: Mansell, 1980), pp. 69–72.
5. Howard Sachar, *A History of Israel: From the Rise of Zionism to Our Time,* (NY: Alfred A. Knopf, 1979), p. 196.
6. Jordanian Nationality Law, Official Gazette, No. 1171, Article 3(3) of Law No. 6, 1954, (February 16, 1954), p. 105.
7. Modern World History, Jordanian Ministry of Education, 1966, p. 150.
8. Meyrav Wurmser, *The Schools of Ba'athism: A Study of Syrian Schoolbooks,* (Washington, D.C.: Middle East Media and Research Institute (MEMRI), 2000), p. xiii.
9. Aaron Klein, "Official PA site publishes 'Protocols' in Arabic," *WorldNetDaily,* (May 21, 2005).
10. *Al-Mussawar,* (August 4, 1972).

11. Middle East Media and Research Institute (MEMRI); *Al-Hayat Al-Jadeeda,* (May 15, 1997); *Jerusalem Post,* (May 23, 2001); Palestine News Agency WAFA, (April 28, 2005).
12. *Al-Ahram,* (October 28, 2000).
13. "Anti-Semitic TV Series Cancelled by Jordan," History News Network, (October 27, 2005).
14. *Jerusalem Post,* (November 19, 2001).
15. Palestinian Authority television, (October 14, 2000).
16. Palestinian Media Watch, (March 15, 2000).
17. Bernard Lewis, "The Pro-Islamic Jews," *Judaism,* (Fall 1968), p. 401.
18. Bat Ye'or, *The Dhimmi,* (NJ: Fairleigh Dickinson University Press, 1985), pp. 43-44.
19. Bat Ye'or, pp. 185-86, 191, 194.
20. Norman Stillman, *The Jews of Arab Lands,* (PA: The Jewish Publication Society of America, 1979), p. 84; Maurice Roumani, *The Case of the Jews from Arab Countries: A Neglected Issue,* (Tel Aviv: World Organization of Jews from Arab Countries, 1977), pp. 26-27; Bat Ye'or, p. 72; Bernard Lewis, *The Jews of Islam,* (NJ: Princeton University Press, 1984) p. 158.
21. Stillman, pp. 59, 284.
22. Roumani, pp. 26-27.
23. G.E. Von Grunebaum, "Eastern Jewry Under Islam," *Viator,* (1971), p. 369.
24. *New York Times,* February 19, 1947).
25. Roumani, pp. 30-31; Norman Stillman, *The Jews of Arab Lands in Modern Times,* (NY: Jewish Publication Society, 1991), pp. 119-122.
26. Bat Ye'or, p. 61.
27. Bat Ye'or, p. 30.
28. Louis Gardet, *La Cite Musulmane: Vie sociale et politique,* (Paris: Etudes musulmanes, 1954), p. 348.
29. Bat Ye'or, pp. 56-57.
30. *Middle Eastern Studies,* (1971), p. 232.
31. David Singer, ed., *American Jewish Year Book 2004.* NY: American Jewish Committee, 2004. The American Jewish Committee Yearbook is the source for all Jewish population figures in this chapter.
32. Jewish Communities of the World, World Jewish Congress (WJC), Copyright 1997; Institute of the World Jewish Congress. *Country Reports on Human Rights Practices for 1997.*
33. *Country Reports on Human Rights Practices for 1991,* (DC: Department of State, 1992), p. 1339.
34. *Country Reports on Human Rights Practices for 1997,* (DC: Department of State, 1998).
35. U.S. Department of State, *2000 Annual Report on International Religious Freedom,* Released by the Bureau for Democracy, Human Rights, and Labor Washington, DC, September 5, 2000.
36. Sachar, p. 401.
37. Associated Press, (November 26, 1956); *New York World Telegram,* (November 29, 1956).
38. Jewish Communities of the World.
39. U.S. Department of State, *2000 Annual Report on International Religious Freedom,* Released by the Bureau for Democracy, Human Rights, and Labor Washington, DC, (September 5, 2000).
40. U.S. Department of State, *2001 Annual Report on International Religious Freedom,* Released by the Bureau for Democracy, Human Rights, and Labor Washington, DC, (October 26, 2001).

41. U.S. Department of State, *2004 Report on Global Anti-Semitism,* Released by the Bureau for Democracy, Human Rights, and Labor Washington, DC, (January 5, 2005).
42. Jewish Telegraphic Agency, (July 13, 2005).
43. World Jewish Congress, Jewish Communities of the World.
44. Schneider, Howard. "Iran Court Reduces Penalties for Jews." *Washington Post,* (September 22, 2000).
45. *Jerusalem Post,* (January 16, 2002); *Washington Jewish Week,* (October 31, 2002).
46. *Jerusalem Post,* (Dec. 13, 1997); Arieh Avneri, *The Claim of Dispossession,* (Tel Aviv: Hidekel Press, 1984), p. 274; Roumani, pp. 29–30; Stillman (1991), pp. 117–119; Sachar, p. 399.
47. Judith Miller and Laurie Mylroie, *Saddam Hussein and the Crisis in the Gulf,* (NY: Random House, 1990), p. 34.
48. *New York Times Magazine,* (February 3, 1985).
49. Associated Press, (March 28, 1998).
50. *Jerusalem Post,* (September 28, 2002).
51. "The Last Jews of Baghdad," National Public Radio, (May 22, 2003).
52. *Maariv,* (June 21, 1991); Jewish Telegraphic Agency, (July 22, 1993); Jewish Communities of the World.
53. Majdoline Hatoum, "Of 5,000 Jewish Lebanese, only 1 voted," *The Daily Star,* (May 10, 2004).
54. Stephen Talbot, "Syria/Lebanon: The Occupier and the Occupied," PBS Frontline, (2004).
55. *Encyclopedia Judaica,* CD-Rom edition, 1997.
56. Sachar, p. 400; Stillman (1991), p. 145.
57. U.S. Department of State, *2000 Annual Report on International Religious Freedom,* Released by the Bureau for Democracy, Human Rights, and Labor Washington, DC, September 5, 2000.
58. *Jerusalem Report,* (March 11, 2002).
59. *Encyclopedia Judaica,* CD-Rom edition, 1997.
60. Roumani, pp. 32–33.
61. Said Ghallab, "Les Juifs sont en enfer," in *Les Temps Modernes,* (April 1965), pp. 2247–2251.
62. *Country Reports on Human Rights Practices for 1996,* (DC: Department of State, 1997); Jewish Communities of the World; *Country Reports on Human Rights Practices for 1997.*
63. Jewish Telegraphic Agency, (March 17, 2004).
64. U.S. Department of State, *2000 Annual Report on International Religious Freedom,* Released by the Bureau for Democracy, Human Rights, and Labor Washington, DC, (September 5, 2000).
65. U.S. Department of State, *2001 Annual Report on International Religious Freedom,* Released by the Bureau for Democracy, Human Rights, and Labor Washington, DC, (October 26, 2001).
66. Jewish Telegraphic Agency, (March 17, 2004).
67. Sachar, p. 400; Roumani, p. 31; Stillman (1991), p. 146.
68. *Newsday,* (November 1, 1987); information provided by Rep. Michael McNulty.
69. Middle East Watch, *Human Rights in Syria,* (NY: Middle East Watch, 1990), p. 94.
70. *Jerusalem Post,* (October 18, 1994).
71. *Jerusalem Post,* (May 27, 1995).
72. Associated Press, (January 27, 2000).
73. U.S. Department of State, *2000 Annual Report on International Religious Freedom,* Released by the Bureau for Democracy, Human Rights, and Labor Washington, DC, (September 5, 2000).

74. Robert Satloff, "In Search of "Righteous Arabs," Commentary, (July 04, 2004).
75. Roumani, pp. 33; Stillman (1991), p. 127.
76. *Country Reports on Human Rights Practices for 1982,* (DC: Department of State, 1983), pp. 1290-91.
77. *Country Reports on Human Rights Practices for 1985,* (DC: Department of State, 1986), p. 1321.
78. *Country Reports on Human Rights Practices for 1997.*
79. *Washington Post,* (April 17 & 23, 2002).
80. "French Say Suspect is Qaeda Big," CBS News, (June 12, 2003).
81. Sachar, pp. 397-98; Roumani, pp. 32-33; Stillman (1991), p. 498.
82. Jewish Communities of the World; *Country Reports on Human Rights Practices for 1997.*
83. Jewish Communities of the World.
84. U.S. Department of State, *2001 Annual Report on International Religious Freedom,* Released by the Bureau for Democracy, Human Rights, and Labor Washington, DC, (October 26, 2001).
85. *Jerusalem Post,* (January 30, 2001).

15. Human Rights in Israel and the Territories

MYTH

"Israel discriminates against its Arab citizens."

FACT

Israel is one of the most open societies in the world. Out of a population of nearly 7 million, about 1.4 million—20 percent of the population—are non-Jews (approximately 1.2 million Muslims, 130,000 Christians and 100,000 Druze).[1]

Arabs in Israel have equal voting rights; in fact, it is one of the few places in the Middle East where Arab women may vote. Arabs currently hold 9 seats in the 120-seat Knesset. Israeli Arabs have also held various government posts, including one who served as Israel's ambassador to Finland and the current deputy mayor of Tel Aviv. Oscar Abu Razaq was appointed Director General of the Ministry of Interior, the first Arab citizen to become chief executive of a key government ministry. Ariel Sharon's original cabinet included the first Arab minister, Salah Tarif, a Druze who served as a minister without portfolio. An Arab is also a Supreme Court justice. In October 2005, an Arab professor was named Vice President of Haifa University.

Arabic, like Hebrew, is an official language in Israel. More than 300,000 Arab children attend Israeli schools. At the time of Israel's founding, there was one Arab high school in the country. Today, there are hundreds of Arab schools.[2]

In 2002, the Israeli Supreme Court ruled that the government cannot allocate land based on religion or ethnicity, and may not prevent Arab citizens from living wherever they choose.[3]

The sole legal distinction between Jewish and Arab citizens of Israel is that the latter are not required to serve in the Israeli army. This is to spare Arab citizens the need to take up arms against their brethren. Nevertheless, Bedouins have served in paratroop units and other Arabs have volunteered for military duty. Compulsory military service is applied to the Druze and Circassian communities at their own request.

Some economic and social gaps between Israeli Jews and Arabs result from the latter not serving in the military. Veterans qualify for many benefits not available to non-veterans. Moreover, the army aids in the socialization process.

On the other hand, Arabs do have an advantage in obtaining some jobs during the years Israelis are in the military. In addition, industries like construction and trucking have come to be dominated by Israeli Arabs.

Although Israeli Arabs have occasionally been involved in terrorist activities, they have generally behaved as loyal citizens. During the 1967, 1973 and 1982 wars, none engaged in any acts of sabotage or disloyalty. Sometimes, in fact, Arabs volunteered to take over civilian functions for reservists. During the Palestinian War that began in September 2000, Israeli Arabs for the first time engaged in widespread protests with some violence.

The United States has been independent for almost 230 years and still has not integrated all of its diverse communities. Even today, 60 years after civil rights legislation was adopted, discrimination has not been eradicated. It should not be surprising that Israel has not solved all of its social problems in only 57 years.

MYTH

"Israeli Arabs are barred from buying land."

FACT

In the early part of the century, the Jewish National Fund was established by the World Zionist Congress to purchase land in Palestine for Jewish settlement. This land, and that acquired after Israel's War of Independence, was taken over by the government. Of the total area of Israel, 92 percent belongs to the State and is managed by the Land Management Authority. It is not for sale to anyone, Jew or Arab. The remaining 8 percent of the territory is privately owned. The Arab Waqf (the Muslim charitable endowment), for example, owns land that is for the express use and benefit of Muslim Arabs. Government land can be leased by anyone, regardless of race, religion or sex. All Arab citizens of Israel are eligible to lease government land.

MYTH

"Israeli Arabs are discriminated against in employment."

FACT

Israeli law prohibits discrimination in employment. According to the State Department, all Israeli workers "may join and establish labor organizations freely."[4] Most unions are part of the Histadrut or the smaller Histadrut Haovdim Haleumit (National Federation of Labor), both of which are independent of the Government.

MYTH

"Israel uses administrative detention to imprison peaceful Arabs without trial."

FACT

Israel inherited and continued certain laws adopted by the British. One is the use of administrative detention, which is permitted under certain circumstances in security cases. The detainee is entitled to be represented by counsel, and may appeal to the Israeli Supreme Court. The burden is on the prosecution to justify holding closed proceedings. Often, officials believe presenting evidence in open court would compromise its methods of gathering intelligence and endanger the lives of individuals who have provided information about planned terrorist activities.

Administrative detention is not necessary in much of the Arab world because the authorities frequently arrest people and throw them in jail without due process. No lawyers, human rights organizations or independent media can protest. Even in the United States, with its exceptionally liberal bail policy, people may be held for extended periods awaiting trial, and special legal standards have been applied to allow the prolonged incarceration of Taliban and al-Qaida members captured in Afghanistan.

"One does not judge a democracy by the way its soldiers immediately react, young men and women under tremendous provocation. One judges a democracy by the way its courts react, in the dispassionate cool of judicial chambers. And the Israeli Supreme Court and other courts have reacted magnificently. For the first time in Mideast history, there is an independent judiciary willing to listen to grievances of Arabs—that judiciary is called the Israeli Supreme Court."

—Alan Dershowitz[5]

MYTH

"Arabs held in Israeli jails are tortured, beaten and killed."

FACT

Prison is not a pleasant place for anyone and complaints about the treatment of prisoners in American institutions abound. Israel's prisons are probably among the most closely scrutinized in the world. One reason is the government has allowed representatives of the Red Cross and other groups to inspect them regularly.

Israeli law prohibits the arbitrary arrest of citizens. In addition, defendants are considered innocent until proven guilty and have the right to writs of *habeas corpus* and other procedural safeguards. Israel holds no political prisoners and maintains an independent judiciary.

Some prisoners, particularly Arabs suspected of involvement in terrorism, were interrogated using severe methods that have been criticized as excessive. Israel's Supreme Court issued a landmark ruling in 1999 prohibiting the use of a variety of practices that were considered abusive.

The death penalty has been applied just once, in the case of Adolf Eichmann, the man largely responsible for the "Final Solution." No Arab has ever been given the death penalty, even after the most heinous acts of terrorism.

"The Israeli regime is not apartheid. It is a unique case of democracy."

—South African Interior Minister Chief Mangosuthu Buthelezi[6]

MYTH

"Israel's treatment of Palestinians is similar to the treatment of blacks in apartheid South Africa."

FACT

Even before the State of Israel was established, Jewish leaders consciously sought to avoid the situation that prevailed in South Africa. As David Ben-Gurion told Palestinian nationalist Musa Alami in 1934:

> We do not want to create a situation like that which exists in South Africa, where the whites are the owners and rulers, and the blacks are the workers. If we do not do all kinds of work, easy and hard, skilled and unskilled, if we become merely landlords, then this will not be our homeland.[7]

Today, within Israel, Jews are a majority, but the Arab minority are full citizens who enjoy equal rights and are represented in all the branches of government. Under apartheid, black South Africans could not vote and were not citizens of the country in which they formed the overwhelming majority of the population. Laws dictated where they could live, work and travel. And, in South Africa, the government killed blacks who protested against its policies. By contrast, Israel allows freedom of movement, assembly and speech. Some of the government's harshest critics are Israeli Arabs who are members of the Knesset.

The situation of Palestinians in the territories is different. The security requirements of the nation, and a violent insurrection in the territories, forced Israel to impose restrictions on Arab residents of the West Bank and Gaza Strip that are not necessary inside Israel's pre-1967 borders. The Palestinians in the territories, typically, dispute Israel's right to exist whereas blacks did not seek the destruction of South Africa, only the apartheid regime.

If Israel were to give Palestinians full citizenship, it would mean the territories had been annexed. No Israeli government has been prepared to take that step. Instead, through negotiations, Israel agreed to give the Palestinians increasing authority over their own affairs. It is likely that a final settlement will allow most Palestinians to become citizens of their own state. The principal impediment to Palestinian independence is not Israeli policy, it is the unwillingness of the Palestinian leadership to give up terrorism and agree to live in peace beside Israel.

Despite all their criticism, when asked what governments they admire most, more than 80 percent of Palestinians consistently choose Israel because they can see up close the thriving democracy in Israel, and the rights the Arab citizens enjoy there. By contrast, Palestinians place Arab regimes far down the list, and their own Palestinian Authority at the bottom, with only 20 percent saying they admired the corrupt Arafat regime in 2003.[8]

"There is still one other question arising out of the disaster of nations which remains unsolved to this day, and whose profound tragedy, only a Jew can comprehend. This is the African question. Just call to mind all those terrible episodes of the slave trade, of human beings who, merely because they were black, were stolen like cattle, taken prisoner, captured and sold. Their children grew up in strange lands, the objects of contempt and hostility because their complexions were different. I am not ashamed to say, though I may expose myself to ridicule for saying so, that once I have witnessed the redemption of the Jews, my people, I wish also to assist in the redemption of the Africans."

—Theodor Herzl[9]

MYTH

"Israel is pursuing a policy of genocide toward the Palestinians comparable to the Nazis' treatment of the Jews."

FACT

This is perhaps the most odious claim made by Israel's detractors. The Nazis' objective was the systematic extermination of every Jew in Europe. Israel is seeking peace with its Palestinian neighbors. More than one million Arabs live as free and equal citizens in Israel. Of the Palestinians in the territories, 98 percent live under the civil administration of the Palestinian Authority. While Israel sometimes employs harsh measures against Palestinians in the territories to protect Israeli citizens—Jews and non-Jews—from the incessant campaign of terror waged by the PA and Islamic radicals, there is no plan to persecute, exterminate, or expel the Palestinian people.

In response to one such comparison, by a poet who referred to the "Zionist SS," *The New Republic*'s literary editor Leon Wieseltier observed:

> The view that Zionism is Nazism—there is no other way to understand the phrase "Zionist SS"—is not different in kind from the view that the moon is cheese. It is not only spectacularly wrong, it is also spectacularly unintelligent. I will not offend myself (that would be self-hate speech!) by patiently explaining why the State of Israel is unlike the Third Reich, except to say that nothing that has befallen the Palestinians under Israel's control may responsibly be compared to what befell the Jews under Germany's control, and that a considerable number of the people who have toiled diligently to find peace and justice for the Palestinians, and a solution to this savage conflict, have been Israeli, some of them even Israeli prime ministers. There is no support for the Palestinian cause this side of decency that can justify the locution "Zionist SS."[10]

The absurdity of the charge is also clear from the demography of the disputed territories. While detractors make outrageous claims about Israel committing genocide or ethnic cleansing, the Palestinian population has continued to explode. In Gaza, for example, the population increased from 731,000 in July 1994 to 1,324,991 in 2004, an increase of 81 percent. The growth rate was 3.8 percent, one of the highest in the world. According to the UN, the total Palestinian population in all the disputed territories (they include Gaza, the West Bank, and East Jerusalem) was 1,006,000 in 1950, 1,094,000 in 1970, and grew to 2,152,000 in 1990. Anthony Cordesman notes the increase "was the result of improvements in income and health services" made by Israel. The Palestinian population has continued to grow exponentially and was estimated in 2004 at more than 3.6 million.[11]

MYTH

"Palestinians have the lowest standard of living in the Middle East."

FACT

When Israel captured the West Bank and Gaza Strip in 1967, officials took measures to improve the conditions that Palestinians had lived under during Jordan's 19-year occupation of the West Bank, and Egypt's occupation of Gaza. Universities were opened, Israeli agricultural innovations were shared, modern conveniences were introduced, and health care was significantly upgraded. More than 100,000 Palestinians were employed in Israel, and were paid the same wages as Israeli workers, which stimulated economic growth.

The rise in violence during the 1990s, and then the war instigated by Palestinian terrorists beginning in 2000, has taken a heavy toll on the Palestinian economy. To protect its citizens from suicide bombers and other terrorists, Israel was forced to take measures that had a deleterious impact on the economy in the Palestinian Authority. The most serious step was to limit the number of Palestinian laborers entering Israel to reduce the risk of terrorists pretending to be workers slipping into the country. This raised the level of unemployment, which, in turn, had a negative spillover effect on the rest of the Palestinian economy.

Despite the collapse of the PA economy from five years of war, Palestinian Arabs are still better off than many of their neighbors. The most recent Human Development Report from the United Nations ranks the PA 102nd in terms of life expectancy, educational attainment and adjusted real income out of the 177 countries and territories in the world, placing it in the "medium human development" category along with most of the other Middle Eastern states (only the Gulf sheikdoms are ranked "high"). The PA is ranked just 12 places below Jordan and one behind Iran; it is rated ahead of Syria (#105), Algeria (#108), Egypt (#120) and Morocco (#125).[12]

Few Palestinians would trade places with Arabs in neighboring countries. Well, perhaps, with one exception. They might aspire to the standard of living in the country ranked 22nd by the UN—Israel.

MYTH

"Israeli checkpoints unnecessarily prevent Palestinians from receiving medical attention."

FACT

Israel has instituted checkpoints for one reason—to prevent Palestinian terrorists from infiltrating Israel. If the Palestinian Authority was fulfilling its road map obligations to dismantle the terrorist networks and disarm the terrorists, and its security forces were taking adequate measures to prevent Palestinians from planning and launching attacks, the checkpoints would be unnecessary.

Israel tries to balance its security concerns with the welfare of the Palestinians, and is especially sensitive to the medical needs of Palestinians. Thus, many Palestinians are allowed to enter Israel to receive treatment from some of the finest medical facilities in the world.

Unfortunately, Palestinian terrorists have tried to take advantage of Israel's goodwill. In December 2004, for example, a Hamas agent with forged documents claiming that he was a cancer patient in need of medical treatment from an Israeli hospital was arrested by security forces. Hamed A-Karim Hamed Abu Lihiya was to meet up with another terrorist, obtain weapons from allies inside Israel, and carry out an attack. That same month, a man recruited by the al-Aqsa Martyrs Brigade to plant a bomb on the railway tracks near Netanya tried to use false papers indicating he needed hospital treatment to enter Israel. Another Hamas terrorist planning a suicide bombing was arrested in March 2005 after pretending to be a kidney donor.[13]

"Israeli hospitals extend humanitarian treatment to Palestinians from the Gaza Strip and West Bank. These efforts continued when all other cooperation between Palestinians and Israelis came to a halt during the most recent intifada."

—Palestinian obstetrician and gynecologist Dr. Izzeldin Abuelaish[14]

On June 20, 2005, Wafa Samir Ibrahim Bas was arrested attempting to smuggle an explosives belt through the Erez crossing. Bas aroused the suspicion of soldiers at the checkpoint when a biometric scanner revealed she was hiding explosives. When she realized they had discovered the explosive belt, she attempted unsuccessfully to detonate it.[15]

Bas had been admitted on humanitarian grounds to Soroka Medical Center in Beersheba several months earlier for treatment of massive burns she received as a result of a cooking accident. After her arrest, she admitted that the Fatah al-Aqsa Martyrs Brigade had instructed her to use her personal medical authorization documents to enter into Israel to carry out a suicide attack. In an interview shown on Israeli television, Bas said her "dream was to be a martyr" and that her intent was to kill 40 or 50 people—as many young people as possible.

Dr. Izzeldin Abuelaish, a Palestinian obstetrician and gynecologist from the Jabalya refugee camp in the Gaza Strip, who has worked at the Soroka Hospital, wrote that he was "outraged at the cynical and potentially deadly suicide bombing attempt." Dr. Abuelaish said he does research at the hospital's Genetic Institute and has warm relations with his colleagues. "I make a point, whenever I'm at the hospital, of visiting Palestinian patients," he said. "I also schedule appointments for other Gaza residents, and even bring medication from Soroka to needy patients in the Strip.... On the very day that she planned to detonate her bomb, two Palestinians in critical condition were waiting in Gaza to be taken for urgent treatment at Soroka."

Dr. Abuelaish added, "Wafa was sent to kill the very people in Israel who are healing Palestinians from the Gaza Strip and West Bank. What if

Israeli hospitals now decide to bar Palestinians seeking treatment? How would those who sent Bas feel if their own relatives, in need of medical care in Israel, are refused treatment?"[16]

The Israeli checkpoint saved the lives not only of countless Israelis, but of the Palestinian would-be suicide bomber. By using this tactic, the Palestinians have reinforced the necessity of retaining the checkpoints and forced Israel to carry out more stringent inspections, yet another example of how terrorists are making life unnecessarily difficult for innocent Palestinians.

MYTH

"Israel prevents Palestinian ambulances from taking sick and injured Palestinians to hospitals."

FACT

One of the unfortunate results of the violence during the Palestinian War has been the allegations of Israeli abuse against Palestinian Red Crescent ambulances, which it is alleged, has resulted in inconveniences, medical complications and even death to the sick passengers on board. These accounts tend to portray the delays as wanton acts of cruelty on the part of Israeli soldiers against Palestinians in need of medical attention.

According to IDF guidelines, any Palestinian in need of urgent medical care is allowed passage through checkpoints. The severity of the medical condition is determined by the checkpoint commander, who is to make decisions in favor of the Palestinian if there is any doubt. Palestinians are also allowed to enter Israel for routine medical care unless there is a security problem. Even then, Palestinians can appeal decisions and are also offered other options, such as transfer to neighboring states.

Ambulances are still stopped and searched at Israeli checkpoints because they have frequently been used as a means to transport terrorist bombs, and many of the murderers who have triggered suicide bombings in Israel gained access by driving or riding in Red Crescent ambulances. For example:

- In October 2001, Nidal Nazal, a Hamas operative in Kalkilya, was arrested by the IDF. He was an ambulance driver for the Palestinian Red Crescent who served as a messenger between the Hamas headquarters in several West Bank towns.[17]

- In January 2002, Wafa Idris blew herself up on the crowded Jaffa Street in Jerusalem, becoming one of the first female suicide bombers. She was an ambulance driver for the Palestinian Red Crescent, as was Mohammed Hababa, the Tanzim operative who sent her on her mission. She left the West Bank by way of an ambulance.[18]

- On March 27, 2002, a Tanzim member who worked as a Red Crescent ambulance driver was captured with explosives in his ambulance. A child disguised as a patient was riding in the ambulance along with the child's family. The explosives were found under the stretcher the "sick" child was laying on.[19]

- On May 17, 2002, an explosive belt was found in a Red Crescent ambulance at a checkpoint near Ramallah. The bomb, the same type generally used in suicide bombings, was hidden under a gurney on which a sick child was lying. The driver, Islam Jibril, was already wanted by the IDF, and admitted that this was not the first time that an ambulance had been used to transport explosives or terrorists. In a statement issued the same day, the International Committee of the Red Cross said that it "understands the security concerns of the Israeli authorities, and has always acknowledged their right to check ambulances, provided it does not unduly delay medical evacuations." The sick passengers in the ambulance were escorted by soldiers to a nearby hospital.[20]

- On June 30, 2002, Israeli troops found 10 suspected Palestinian terrorists hiding in two ambulances in Ramallah. They were caught when soldiers stopped the vehicles for routine checks.[21]

- In December 2003, Rashed Tarek al-Nimr, who worked as a chemist in hospitals in Nablus and Bethlehem, supplied chemicals from the hospitals to Hamas for use in making bombs and admitted he used ambulances to transport the chemicals. He also said the Hamas commanders would hide in hospitals to avoid arrest.[22]

The accusations leveled against Israel by its critics have frequently been based on statements of international law, such as the Fourth Geneva Convention. It is true that the Geneva Convention does place particular emphasis on the immunity and neutrality of ambulances and emergency medical personnel. But the conclusion that Israel must ignore a clear and present danger to its citizens, or else violate international law, is a distortion. By using ambulances to smuggle explosives into Israel, it is the Palestinian terrorists who are compromising the Red Crescent's immunity and neutrality.

MYTH

"Israel uses checkpoints to deny Palestinians their rights and humiliate them."

FACT

It is not unusual for nations to guard their borders and to establish checkpoints to prevent people from illegally entering their countries. The United States has checkpoints at its borders and airports and, as

Americans saw on September 11, these are necessary but not foolproof security precautions.

In the case of Israel, the necessity for checkpoints has been created by the Palestinians. By pursuing a violent campaign of terror against Israel's citizens, they have forced Israel to set up barriers to make it as difficult as possible for terrorists to enter Israel or travel through the territories to carry out acts of violence. The checkpoints are an inconvenience to innocent Palestinians, but they do in fact prevent terror and save lives.

For example, on November 2, 2002, a van carrying boxes of jeans pulled up at a checkpoint. Soldiers checked the IDs of the men in the van and discovered one of the passengers was a wanted man. The van was unloaded and it was not until the soldiers opened the last box that they discovered an explosive belt that was being delivered to a suicide bomber. Two weeks later, a taxi pulled up to the same checkpoint. Soldiers found two computers in the trunk that seemed unusually heavy. They opened the boxes and found two explosive belts. They also found a bag with a gun.[23]

Hyperbolic media reports and anti-Israel propaganda have suggested Israel is harassing Palestinian women at checkpoints. It is unfortunate that women cannot be ignored as potential security threats. Border policemen at a checkpoint north of Jerusalem, for example, arrested a

Case Study

Picture a 19-year-old soldier commanding a checkpoint. An ambulance arrives, and inside is a woman who is seemingly pregnant. The woman appears to be in pain and her husband is also highly anxious. But the soldier has been warned about an ambulance bearing a pregnant woman who is not really pregnant. The intelligence said that underneath the stretcher in the ambulance a wanted terrorist is hiding with an explosive belt for a suicide attack. It is a hot day and there is a long line of cars. His commanders are yelling at him on the two-way radio, "Do not let ambulances go through because there is a terrorist in an ambulance!" To complicate the picture, a news video crew is present.

The soldier has to make an incredible number of decisions in a very short time. He is only 19 and has no medical training. He knows that if he lets the ambulance go through and it contains a terrorist, then innocent people will die and he will have failed in his mission. On the other hand, if there is not a terrorist in this particular ambulance, and he delays a truly pregnant woman from reaching a hospital, the lives of the mother and baby could be endangered.

What would you do?

Palestinian woman pushing a baby stroller that concealed a pistol, two ammunition clips and a knife. On another occasion, troops searching a West Bank house for a wanted Hamas activist found his sister hiding his gun in her underpants. A woman hid a hand grenade under her baby during another raid.[24]

Commercial goods, food, medicine, ambulances, and medical crews continue to circulate freely, hampered only by continuing attacks. Palestinian workers going to jobs in Israel also may pass through the checkpoints with the proper identification; restrictions are only imposed when necessitated by the security situation.

Barriers are not set up to humiliate Palestinians, but to ensure the safety of Israeli citizens. Unfortunately, every time Israel has relaxed its policy and withdrawn checkpoints, Palestinian terrorists have taken advantage of the opportunity to launch new attacks on innocent Israelis.

MYTH

"Israeli textbooks are just as bad as those in the Palestinian Authority."

FACT

The best hope for the future is that Israeli and Arab children will grow up with a greater understanding and tolerance of one another. Unfortunately, the textbooks in Arab countries, and the Palestinian Authority, in particular, do not promote coexistence. By contrast, Israeli textbooks are oriented toward peace and tolerance. The Palestinians are accepted as Palestinians. Islam and Arab culture are referred to with respect. Islamic holy places are discussed along with Jewish ones. Stereotypes are avoided to educate against prejudice.

More than 20 years ago, it was true that some Israeli textbooks used stereotyped images of Arabs; however, the books in use in public schools today are very different. Israeli texts go out of their way to avoid prejudices and to guard against generalizations. In one seventh grade lesson, students are given the following problem:

Many people think: The dove is a bird that pursues peace. This belief is incorrect; it is a prejudice: people believe it without checking it. There are a lot of prejudices. For example:

1. The Jews control the world and exploit all those who live in it.

2. The blacks are inferior; they are incapable of being scientists.

3. The Arabs only understand the language of force ...

Be ready to explain orally why these are prejudices. (*I Understand*, 1993, p. 259)

In an elementary textbook on reading comprehension, students read how a Jewish girl was saved by an Arab woman. The book notes, "The Arabs are like the Jews.... There are nasty people among them and there are decent people and ... they should not be labeled" (What is the Interpretation? Comprehension B, pp. 184-188).

Contrary to suggestions that Israelis do not accept the idea that Palestinians are a people, Israeli textbooks explain the origins of Palestinian nationalism. For example, a 9th grade text observes that "during the 1930's, Arab nationalist movements evolved all over the Middle East. Many of the Arabs of Eretz Yisrael also began formulating a national consciousness—in other words, the perception that they are not just part of the larger Arab nation, but are also Palestinians" (*The Twentieth Century—On the Threshold of Tomorrow,* Grade 9, 1999, p. 44).

While Palestinian texts omit references to Jewish contributions to the world, the Israeli books recognize the achievements of Arabs and Muslims. One text highlights the Arab role as creators of culture: "... they were the first to discover the existence of infectious diseases. They were also the first to build public hospitals. Because of their considerable contribution to various scientific fields, there are disciplines that to this day are called by their Arabic names, such as algebra." Islam's contributions are also acknowledged in the same passage: "The Islamic religion also influenced the development of culture. The obligation to pray in the direction of Mecca led to the development of astronomy, which helped identify the direction according to the heavenly bodies. The duty to make a pilgrimage developed geography and gave a push to the writing of travel books. These books, and the Arabs' high capability in map drawing, helped develop trade. To this day, merchants use Arabic words, such as bazaar, check and tariff" (*From Generation to Generation,* Vol. b, 1994, p. 220).

Palestinian textbooks also negate the Jewish connection to the Holy Land while Israeli texts show respect for the Arab/Muslim attachment to the land. "The Land of Israel in general, and Jerusalem in particular, have been sanctified more and more in Islamic thought—as Islam has developed and spread, both religiously and geographically. As Islam absorbed more and more of the world conquered by it, so it adapted and Islamized the values that it absorbed, including the holiness of the Land of Israel, its flora and its water, living in it, the sanctity of being buried in it and the like. All these became from that time onwards part of orthodox Islam" (H. Peleg, G. Zohar, *This is the Land—Introduction to Land of Israel Studies for the Upper Grades,* 2000, pp. 161-162).

Israeli textbooks contain a plurality of views, including those that conflict with conventional research and are critical of Israeli policies. Controversial topics, such as the disputed territories, the refugee issue, and the status of Israeli Arabs are covered from multiple viewpoints. For example, one book quotes historian Benny Morris's unconventional position attributing the flight of Palestinians in 1947–1948 more to the actions of Jewish forces than the instructions of the leaders of Arab countries (*From Exile to Independence—The History of the Jewish People in Recent Generations,* vol. 2, 1990, p. 312).

The Arab-Israeli conflict is factually described as an ongoing conflict between two national entities over the same territory. The Arab point of view is also represented. For example, a history text notes how Israel's government treated Anwar Sadat's 1971 peace proposal "with scorn out of the feeling of power and superiority that had taken hold of Israeli society following the Six-Day War. After his proposal had been rejected and the political stalemate continued, Sadat decided to go to war" (K. Tabibian, *Journey to the Past—The Twentieth Century, By Dint of Freedom,* 1999, p. 313).

The content of the peace treaties between Israel and Egypt and Jordan is detailed, along with the implications of those agreements. Agreements with the Palestinians are discussed as well, and the atlas used in Israeli schools shows the Palestinian Authority.[21a]

Israeli texts also use simulation games to help students understand different perspectives on an issue. In one, students are told to divide into groups representing Jewish and Palestinian journalists and prepare a report on the discussion in the United Nations leading to the partition resolution. Students are then asked to discuss the differences between the reports of the Jewish and Palestinian journalists (K. Tabibian, *Journey To The Past—The Twentieth Century, By Dint of Freedom,* 1999, p. 294).

Israel is not perfect and exceptions do exist. Some generalizations and patronizing terminology are found in textbooks used in the ultra-Orthodox schools. These schools comprise less than 10 percent of the Israeli educational system, and the same Israeli watchdog organizations that have pointed out problems in Palestinian textbooks have also publicized the need to remove the handful of inappropriate references from school books in this system.[25]

MYTH

"Israel is a theocracy and should not be a Jewish State."

FACT

It often makes people uncomfortable to refer to Israel as "the Jewish State" because it suggests a theocracy and, therefore, the demise of Israel as a Jewish state is viewed by some people as a positive development. Israel is not a theocracy; however, it is governed by the rule of law as drafted by a democratically elected parliament. It is informed by Jewish values and adheres to many Jewish religious customs (such as holidays), but this is similar to the United States and other nations that are shaped by the Judeo-Christian heritage and also have expressly religious elements (e.g., church-state separation in the U.S. does not preclude the recognition of Christmas as a holiday). Israel has no state religion, and all faiths enjoy freedom of worship; yet, it is attacked for its Jewish character, whereas the Arab states that all have Islam as their official religion are regarded as legitimate.

Why shouldn't the Jews have a state? The Jewish people are a nation with a shared origin, religion, culture, language, and history. No one suggests that Arabs are not entitled to a nation of their own (and they have not one, but twenty-one) or Swedes or Germans, or that Catholics are not entitled to a state (Vatican City) headed by a theocrat (the Pope). To suggest that Zionism, the nationalist movement of the Jewish people, is the only form of nationalism that is illegitimate is pure bigotry. It is especially ironic that the Jewish nation should be challenged given that Jewish statehood preceded the emergence of most modern nation-states by thousands of years.

It is also not unusual that one community should be the majority within a nation and seek to maintain that status. In fact, this is true in nearly every country in the world. Moreover, societies usually reflect the cultural identity of the majority. India and Pakistan were established at the same time as Israel through a violent partition, but no one believes these nations are illegitimate because one is predominantly Hindu and the other has a Muslim majority, or that these nations shouldn't be influenced by those communities (e.g., that cows in India should not be treated as sacred).

In the United States, a vigorous debate persists over the boundaries between church and state. Similar discussions regarding "synagogue and state" are ongoing in Israel, with philosophical disagreements over whether Israel can be a Jewish and a democratic state, and practical arguments over Sabbath observance, marriage and divorce laws, and budgets for religious institutions. Nevertheless, most Jews take for granted that Israel is, and must remain, a Jewish state. Arab citizens also understand that Israel is a Jewish state and, while they might prefer that it was not, they have still chosen to live there (nothing prevents Arabs from moving to any of the 180-odd non-Jewish states in the world). Both Jews and Arabs realize that if Jews cease to be a majority in Israel, Israel will no longer have a Jewish character or serve as a haven for persecuted Jews, and that is one of the elements underlying peace negotiations between Israel and the Palestinians.

MYTH

"Israel is persecuting Christians."

FACT

While Christians are unwelcome in Islamic states such as Saudi Arabia, and most have been driven out of their longtime homes in Lebanon,

Christians continue to be welcome in Israel. Christians have always been a minority in Israel, but it is the only Middle East nation where the Christian population has grown in the last half century (from 34,000 in 1948 to 145,000 today), in large measure because of the freedom to practice their religion.

By their own volition, the Christian communities have remained the most autonomous of the various religious communities in Israel, though they have increasingly chosen to integrate their social welfare, medical and educational institutions into state structures. The ecclesiastical courts of the Christian communities maintain jurisdiction in matters of personal status, such as marriage and divorce. The Ministry of Religious Affairs deliberately refrains from interfering in their religious life, but maintains a Department for Christian Communities to address problems and requests that may arise.

In Jerusalem, the rights of the various Christian churches to custody of the Christian holy places were established during the Ottoman Empire. Known as the "status quo arrangement for the Christian holy places in Jerusalem," these rights remain in force today in Israel.

It was during Jordan's control of the Old City from 1948 until 1967 that Christian rights were infringed and Israeli Christians were barred from their holy places. The Christian population declined by nearly half, from 25,000 to 12,646. Since then, the population has slowly been growing.

Some Christians have been among those inconvenienced by Israel's construction of the security fence, but they have not been harmed because of their religious beliefs. They simply live in areas where the fence is being built. Like others who can show they have suffered some injury, Christians are entitled to compensation. Suggestions that Israel is persecuting Christians were publicized by columnist Bob Novak, who has a long history of vitriolic attacks on Israel. Novak actually presented no specific evidence that any Christians have been harmed or their religious freedom infringed.[26] He cited a single source, whose bias was obvious, to support the charge that the fence is hurting Christians in East Jerusalem, but failed to mention that the fence is helping to save Christian lives that might otherwise be lost in the indiscriminate attacks of Palestinian terrorists.

The hypocrisy of Novak's critique is clear from his failure to raise the very real concerns about the fate of Christians under Arab rule, especially under the Palestinian Authority, where a rapidly declining population of 27,000 Christians live among 3 million Muslims. The proportion of Christians in the Palestinian territories has dropped from 15 percent of the Arab population in 1950 to less than 1 percent today. Three-fourths of all Bethlehem Christians now live abroad, and the majority of the city's population is Muslim. The Christian population declined 29 percent in the West Bank and 20 percent in the Gaza Strip from 1997 to 2002. By contrast, in the period 1995–2003, Israel's Arab Christian population *grew* 14.1 percent.[27]

Jonathan Adelman and Agota Kuperman noted that Yasser Arafat "tried to erase the historic Jesus by depicting him as the first radical Palestinian armed *fedayeen* (guerrilla). Meanwhile, the Palestinian Authority has adopted Islam as its official religion, used *shari'a* Islamic codes, and allowed even officially appointed clerics to brand Christians (and Jews) as infidels in their mosques." The authors add that the "militantly Islamic rhetoric and terrorist acts of Hamas, Islamic Jihad, and Hizballah . . . offer little comfort to Christians."

David Raab observed that "Palestinian Christians are perceived by many Muslims—as were Lebanon's Christians—as a potential fifth column for Israel. In fact, at the start of the Palestinian War in 2000, Muslim Palestinians attacked Christians in Gaza." Raab also wrote that "anti-Christian graffiti is not uncommon in Bethlehem and neighboring Beit Sahur, proclaiming: 'First the Saturday people (the Jews), then the Sunday people (the Christians),' " and that "Christian cemeteries have been defaced, monasteries have had their telephone lines cut, and there have been break-ins at convents." In 2002, Palestinian terrorists holed up in the Church of the Nativity in Bethlehem, endangering the shrine and provoking a tense standoff with Israeli troops.

When Arafat died, Vatican Radio correspondent Graziano Motta said, "The death of the president of the Palestinian National Authority has come at a time when the political, administrative and police structures often discriminate against [Christians]." Motta added that Christians "have been continually exposed to pressures by Muslim activists, and have been forced to profess fidelity to the intifada."

While Novak charged Israel with bulldozing Christian houses, without any evidence, he ignored reports by journalists such as Motta who reported, "Frequently, there are cases in which the Muslims expropriate houses and lands belonging to Catholics, and often the intervention of the authorities has been lacking in addressing acts of violence against young women, or offenses against the Christian faith."[28]

In September 2005, Muslims attacked the Christian town of Taibe a few days after a Muslim woman was allegedly killed by her family for having become involved in a relationship with a Christian from Taibe. It took hours before any police responded. "It was like a war," said one Taibe resident. Hours passed before the Palestinian Authority security and fire services arrived.[29]

It certainly wouldn't be difficult for Novak to find evidence of mistreatment of Christians in the PA if he were interested, but unlike Christians who enjoy freedom of speech as well as religion in Israel, beleaguered Palestinian Christians are afraid to speak out. "Out of fear for their safety, Christian spokesmen aren't happy to be identified by name when they complain about the Muslims' treatment of them . . . off the record they talk of harassment and terror tactics, mainly from the gangs of thugs who looted and plundered Christians and their property, under the protection of Palestinian security personnel."[30]

Notes

1. Israeli Central Bureau of Statistics.
2. Israeli Central Bureau of Statistics.
3. Alan Dershowitz, *The Case for Israel.* (NY: John Wiley & Sons, 2003), p. 157.
4. U.S. Department of State, 2001 Annual Report on International Religious Freedom, Released by the Bureau for Democracy, Human Rights, and Labor Washington, DC, (October 26, 2001).
5. Speech to AIPAC Policy Conference, (May 23, 1989).
6. *Haaretz,* (September 23, 2003).
7. Shabtai Teveth, *Ben-Gurion and the Palestinian Arabs: From Peace to War,* (London: Oxford University Press, 1985), p. 140.
8. James Bennet, "Letter from the Middle East; Arab Showplace? Could It Be the West Bank?" *New York Times,* (April 2, 2003).
9. Golda Meir, *My Life,* (NY: Dell Publishing Co., 1975), pp. 308–309.
10. *The New Republic,* (December 30, 2002).
11. Anthony Cordesman, "From Peace to War: Land for Peace or Settlements for War," (DC: Center for Strategic and International Studies, August 15, 2003), pp. 12–13; CIA World Factbook, 2004.
12. "Human Development Report 2004," United Nations Development Programme, 2005.
13. *Jerusalem Post,* (June 20, 2005).
14. *Jerusalem Post,* (June 24, 2005).
15. *Jerusalem Post,* (June 20, 2005); BBC, (June 21, 2005).
16. *Jerusalem Post,* (June 24, 2005).
17. Israeli Foreign Ministry.
18. *Washington Post,* (January 31, 2002).
19. Israeli Foreign Ministry.
20. "Bomb found in Red Crescent Ambulance," *Haaretz,* (June 12, 2002).
21. Jewish Telegraphic Agency, (June 30, 2002).
22. Margot Dudkevitch, "Palestinian Transported Bomb Materials in Ambulances," *Jerusalem Post,* (December 11, 2003).
23. *Haaretz,* (November 28, 2002).
24. *Maariv,* (October 14, 2003); Efrat Weiss, "Palestinian girl hides gun in undies," Ynetnews.com, (April 15, 2005); Ali Daraghmeh, "Woman Found Hiding Grenade Under Baby," Associated Press, (October 22, 2005).
25. Center for Monitoring the Impact on Peace, Newsletter, (February 2004).
26. Bob Novak, "Hyde fights for overlooked Christians," *Chicago Sun-Times,* (April 18, 2005).
27. Alex Safian, "New York Times Omits Major Reason Christians are Leaving Bethlehem," (December 24, 2004), CAMERA.
28. "Christians in Palestine Concerned About their future Zenit," Zenit News Agency, (November 14, 2004).
29. *Jerusalem Post,* (September 4, 2005).
30. *Maariv,* (December 24, 2001).

16. The Palestinian War, 2000–2005*

MYTH

"The Palestinian War, dubbed by Arabs the 'al-Aksa intifada,' was provoked by Ariel Sharon's September 2000 visit to the Temple Mount."

FACT

To believe Palestinian spokesmen, the five-year war was caused by the desecration of a Muslim holy place—*Haram al-Sharif* (the Temple Mount)—by Likud leader Ariel Sharon and the "thousands of Israeli soldiers" who accompanied him. The violence was carried out through unprovoked attacks by Israeli forces, which invaded Palestinian-controlled territories and "massacred" defenseless Palestinian civilians, who merely threw stones in self-defense. The only way to stop the violence, then, was for Israel to cease-fire and remove its troops from the Palestinian areas.

The truth is dramatically different.

Imad Faluji, the Palestinian Authority Communications Minister, admitted months after Sharon's visit that the violence had been planned in July, far in advance of Sharon's "provocation." "It [the violence] had been planned since Chairman Arafat's return from Camp David, when he turned the tables on the former U.S. president and rejected the American conditions."[1]

"The Sharon visit did not cause the 'Al-Aksa Intifada.'"

—Conclusion of the Mitchell Report, (May 4, 2001)[2]

The violence started before Sharon's September 28, 2000, visit to the Temple Mount. The day before, for example, an Israeli soldier was killed at the Netzarim Junction. The next day, in the West Bank city of Kalkilya, a Palestinian police officer working with Israeli police on a joint patrol opened fire and killed his Israeli counterpart.

On September 29, the Voice of Palestine, the PA's official radio station sent out calls "to all Palestinians to come and defend the al-Aksa mosque." The PA closed its schools and bused Palestinian students to the Temple Mount to participate in the organized riots.

Just prior to Rosh Hashanah (September 30), the Jewish New Year, when hundreds of Israelis were worshipping at the Western Wall, thousands of Arabs began throwing bricks and rocks at Israeli police and Jewish worshippers. Rioting then spread to towns and villages throughout Israel, the West Bank and Gaza Strip.

Internal Security Minister Shlomo Ben-Ami permitted Sharon to go to the Temple Mount—Judaism's holiest place—only after calling Palestinian security chief Jabril Rajoub and receiving his assurance that if Sharon did not enter the mosques, no problems would arise. The need to protect Sharon arose when Rajoub later said that the Palestinian police would do nothing to prevent violence during the visit.

Sharon did not attempt to enter any mosques and his 34 minute visit to the Temple Mount was conducted during normal hours when the area is open to tourists. Palestinian youths—eventually numbering around 1,500—shouted slogans in an attempt to inflame the situation. Some 1,500 Israeli police were present at the scene to forestall violence.

There were limited disturbances during Sharon's visit, mostly involving stone throwing. During the remainder of the day, outbreaks of stone throwing continued on the Temple Mount and in the vicinity, leaving 28 Israeli policemen injured. There are no accounts of Palestinian injuries on that day. Significant and orchestrated violence was initiated by Palestinians the next day following Friday prayers.

The real desecration of holy places was perpetrated by Palestinians, not Israelis. In October 2000, Palestinian mobs destroyed a Jewish shrine in Nablus—Joseph's Tomb—tearing up and burning Jewish prayer books. They stoned worshipers at the Western Wall, attacked Rachel's Tomb in Bethlehem with firebombs and automatic weapons, and destroyed synagogues left in the Gaza Strip after Israel evacuated the area in August 2005.

None of the violent attacks following Sharon's visit were initiated by Israeli security forces, which in all cases responded to Palestinian violence that went well beyond stone throwing. It included massive attacks with automatic weapons and the lynching of Israeli soldiers. Most armed attackers were members of the Tanzim—Arafat's own militia.

MYTH

"A handful of Israelis have been murdered in the war while thousands of innocent Palestinians have been killed by Israeli troops."

FACT

During the Palestinian War, the number of Palestinian casualties has been higher than the figure for Israelis; however, the gap narrowed as Palestinian suicide bombers used increasingly powerful bombs to kill larger numbers of Israelis in their terror attacks. When the war unofficially concluded at the end of September 2005, more than 2,100 Palestinians and 1,061 Israelis had been killed. The disproportionate number of Palestinian casualties was primarily a result of the number of Palestinians involved in violence and was the inevitable result of an irregular, ill-trained group of terrorists attacking a well-trained regular army. The unfortunate death of noncombatants was largely due to the habit of Palestinian terrorists using civilians as shields.

What is more revealing than the tragic totals, however, is the specific breakdown of the casualties. According to one study, Palestinian noncombatants were mostly teenage boys and young men. "This completely contradicts accusations that Israel has 'indiscriminately targeted women and children,' " according to the study. "There appears to be only one reasonable explanation for this pattern: that Palestinian men and boys engaged in behavior that brought them into conflict with Israeli armed forces."

By contrast, the number of women and older people among the noncombatant Israeli casualties illustrates the randomness of Palestinian attacks, and the degree to which terrorists have killed Israelis for the "crime" of being Israeli.[3] Israeli troops do not target innocent Palestinians, but Palestinian terrorists do target Israeli civilians.

> *"It is not a mistake that the Koran warns us of the hatred of the Jews and put them at the top of the list of the enemies of Islam.... The Muslims are ready to sacrifice their lives and blood to protect the Islamic nature of Jerusalem and al-Aksa!"*
>
> **—Sheikh Hian Al-Adrisi[4]**

MYTH

"Violence is an understandable and legitimate reaction to Israel's policies."

FACT

The basis of the peace process is that disputes should be resolved through negotiations. One of the conditions Israel set before agreeing to negotiate with the PLO was that the organization renounce terrorism. It formally did so in 1993; however, the PLO and other Palestinian groups and individuals have consistently resorted to violence since the agreements. Whether or not Israel made concessions, Palestinians have still committed heinous attacks. In some instances atrocities are perpetrated because of alleged mistreatment; in other cases, they are deliberate efforts to sabotage negotiations. Even after Israel completely withdrew from the Gaza Strip, attacks continued. The Palestinian Authority, which has a nearly 40,000-person police force (larger than allowed under the peace agreements), and multiple intelligence agencies, must be held responsible for keeping the peace.

> *"Deliberately and systematically killing civilians violates the most fundamental principles of humanity. Political parties, community leaders and government officials should speak out unequivocally against these atrocities and support every effort to bring the perpetrators to justice."*
>
> **—Sarah Leah Whitson, Human Rights Watch.**[5]

MYTH

"Israel created Hamas."

FACT

Israel had nothing to do with the creation of Hamas. The organization grew out of the ideology and practice of the Islamic fundamentalist Muslim Brotherhood movement that arose in Egypt in the 1920s.

Hamas was legally registered in Israel in 1978 as an Islamic Association by Sheikh Ahmad Yassin. Initially, the organization engaged primarily in social welfare activities and soon developed a reputation for improving the lives of Palestinians, particularly the refugees in the Gaza Strip.

Though Hamas was committed from the outset to destroying Israel, it took the position that this was a goal for the future, and that the more immediate focus should be on winning the hearts and minds of the people through its charitable and educational activities. Its funding came primarily from Jordan and Saudi Arabia.

The PLO was convinced that Israel was helping Hamas in the hope of triggering a civil war. Since Hamas did not engage in terror at first, Israel did not see it as a serious short-term threat, and some Israelis believed the rise of fundamentalism in Gaza would have the beneficial impact of weakening the PLO, and this is what ultimately happened.

Hamas certainly didn't believe it was being supported by Israel. As early as February 1988, the group put out a primer on how its members should behave if confronted by the Shin Bet. Several more instructional documents were distributed by Hamas to teach followers how to confront the Israelis and maintain secrecy.

Israel's assistance was more passive than active, that is, it did not interfere with Hamas activities or prevent funds from flowing into the organization from abroad. Israel also may have provided some funding to allow its security forces to infiltrate the organization.[6] Meanwhile, Jordan was actively helping Hamas, with the aim of undermining the PLO and strengthening Jordanian influence in the territories.

Though some Israelis were very concerned about Hamas before rioting began in December 1987, Israel was reluctant to interfere with an Islamic organization, fearing that it might trigger charges of violating the Palestinians' freedom of religion. It was not until early in the intifada, when Hamas became actively involved in the violence, that the group began to be viewed as a potentially greater threat than the PLO. The turning point occurred in the summer of 1988 when Israel learned that Hamas was stockpiling arms to build an underground force and Hamas issued its covenant calling for the destruction of Israel. At this point it became clear that Hamas was not going to put off its *jihad* to liberate Palestine and was shifting its emphasis from charitable and educational activity to terrorism. Israel then began to crack down on Hamas and wiped out its entire command structure. Hamas has been waging a terror war against Israel ever since.[7]

MYTH

"The Palestinian Authority arrests terrorists and confiscates illegal weapons."

FACT

At times cooperation between Israeli and Palestinian security forces has been good, and Israel has publicly commended the Palestinian Authority. More often, however, the PA has failed to take adequate measures to prevent attacks against Israelis. While some terrorists have been apprehended, they are usually released shortly afterward and many have subsequently been involved in assaults against Jews.[8]

The PA is also filled with illegal weapons, including machine guns, hand grenades, rockets, explosives and mortars. Despite repeated promises, no effort has been made to collect the weapons. On the contrary, the PA has been actively stockpiling them and President Abbas has explicitly said he has no intention of disarming the terrorists.[9] This is a serious violation of the agreements signed with Israel, one that provokes mistrust and threatens Israeli security.

MYTH

"Palestinians do not encourage children to engage in terror."

FACT

Most Palestinians who adopt terror in the hope of either "ending the occupation" or destroying Israel do so because they freely choose murder over any other option. Palestinian terrorists also use children, however, to do their dirty work.

On March 15, 2004, Israeli security forces caught an 11-year-old boy attempting to smuggle a bomb through a roadblock. The boy was promised a large sum of money by Tanzim activists in Nablus if he delivered a bag containing a bomb stuffed with bolts to a woman on the other side of the checkpoint. If the boy was stopped and searched, the terrorists who sent him planned to use a cell phone to immediately detonate the 15 to 22 pounds of explosives he was carrying, murdering nearby soldiers as well as the boy. The plan was foiled by an alert Israeli soldier, and the bomb apparently malfunctioned when the terrorists tried to remotely detonate it. A week later, on March 24, 2004, a 14-year-old Palestinian child was found to be carrying explosives when attempting to pass through the Israeli army checkpoint at Hawara, at the entrance of the town of Nablus.[10]

Just over a year later, on May 22, 2005, a 14-year-old boy was again arrested at the Hawara checkpoint with two pipe bombs strapped to a belt he was wearing. A few days later, a 15-year-old tried to get through the checkpoint with two more pipe bombs. Yet another teen, a 16-year-old, was caught on July 4, 2005, attempting to smuggle a bomb and homemade handgun. In August, another 14-year-old boy was caught carrying three pipe bombs packed with explosives, shrapnel and glass balls.[11]

These were just the latest examples of the cynical use of children by Palestinians waging war on Israel. Young Palestinians are routinely indoctrinated and coerced into the cult of martyrdom.

"Using children to carry out or assist in armed attacks of any kind is an abomination. We call on the Palestinian leadership to publicly denounce these practices."

—Amnesty International[12]

Despite occasional claims that terror is only promoted by "extremists," the truth is the Palestinian Authority has consistently incited its youth to violence. Children are taught that the greatest glory is to die for Allah in battle as a *Shahada*. The PA regularly broadcast television shows that encouraged children to embrace this concept. One film used the death of Muhammad Al-Dura, the child killed in the crossfire of a shootout between Palestinian gunmen and Israeli forces, to show that life after death is paradise. An actor playing Al-Dura is shown in an amusement park, playing on the beach, and flying a kite. The Al-Dura in the film invited viewers to follow him. Similar messages extolling the virtue of the *Shahid* can be found in school textbooks and sermons by Muslim clergy.[13]

The indoctrination is having an impact. According to one Palestinian newspaper, 79–80% of children told pollsters they were willing to be *Shahids*.[14]

Palestinian children now play death games, competing to see who will be the *Shahid*. They also collect "terrorist cards" the way American kids collect baseball cards. The maker of the Palestinian cards sold 6 million in just over two years. "I take hundreds of these pictures from children every day and burn them," said Saher Hindi, a teacher at a Nablus elementary school. "They turn children into extremists."[15]

Many Palestinian youngsters have gone from pretending to carrying out actual terrorist attacks. More than two dozen suicide bombers have been under the age of 18. Between 2001 and March 2004, more than 40 minors involved in planning suicide bombings were arrested. In those years, 22 shootings and bombings were carried out by minors. For example, teens ages 11–14 attempted to smuggle munitions from Egypt into the Gaza Strip; three teenagers, ages 13–15, were arrested on their way to carry out a shooting attack in Afula; and a 17-year-old blew himself up in an attempted suicide attack. In just the first five months of 2005, 52 more Palestinian minors were caught wearing explosive belts or attempting to smuggle weapons through checkpoints in the West Bank.[16]

The situation has finally gotten so out of hand that Palestinian families are starting to protest. The mother of one of the three teenagers sent to carry out the Afula attack said of the letter he had left behind, "My son doesn't know how to write a letter like that and has never belonged to one of the organizations. Some grownup wrote the letter for him." The boy's father added, "Nobody can accept to send his children to be slaughtered. I am sure that whoever recruits children in this kind of unlawful activity will not recruit his own children."[17]

Martin Fletcher interviewed the parents of the 15-year-old stopped at the Hawara checkpoint. His parents expressed their anger at the Al-Aqsa Martyrs' Brigades, calling its operatives criminals and saying that Allah would punish them. The correspondent spoke with the boy and read him a letter from his mother asking him to confess and to give Israel all the information in his possession about the men who had sent him.[18]

Whenever the use of children in terror operations provokes an outcry, the terrorist groups either claim ignorance or promise never to do it again. Meanwhile, the Palestinian Authority does nothing to stop the recruitment of children or to dismantle the organizations responsible for drafting them in their terror war.

"As one of the Islamic fanatics who inspired al-Qaida said: 'We are not trying to negotiate with you. We are trying to destroy you.'... They wish to destroy the whole basis of Western society—secular democracy, individual liberty, equality before the law, toleration and pluralism—and replace it with a theocracy based on a perverted and dogmatic interpretation of the Koran.... The idea that we should try to appease the terrorists is wrong in every respect. It would not protect us, for nothing acts as a greater incentive to terrorists than the realization that their target is weak and frightened. And it would only weaken the institutions we are trying to protect, and demonstrate to the terrorists that we are—as they frequently allege—too decadent and craven to defend the way of life to which we claim to be attached."

—**London** *Daily Telegraph*[19]

MYTH

"Palestinian women are becoming suicide bombers because of their commitment to 'liberate' Palestine."

FACT

It may be that some Palestinian women share the ideology of the terrorists who believe that blowing up innocent men, women, and children will achieve their political objective, but many others are being blackmailed into carrying out suicide attacks by sadistic and manipulative Palestinian men.

More than 20 Palestinian women have engaged in suicide attacks and the terrorist organizations that recruit them do so in part because they believe women will generate less suspicion, and that Israeli soldiers will be more reticent to search them.

Some of the women have been convinced to engage in terrorist attacks to rehabilitate their reputations in their community if they have acquired a bad name or done something to bring shame upon their family. Shame is a powerful force in Arab society, and women who are promiscuous, engage in adultery, become pregnant out of wedlock, or behave in other ways deemed improper may be ostracized or severely punished (e.g., husbands may kill wives who shamed them in so-called "honor crimes").

Terrorist organizations have used emotional blackmail against these often vulnerable women to convince them that by carrying out a suicide attack against Jews, they may restore their honor or that of their family. Israeli intelligence declassified a report that said Fatah operatives went so far as to seduce women and then, after they became pregnant, used their condition to blackmail them into committing heinous crimes. The report cited two specific cases, one involved a 21-year-old from Bethlehem who blew herself up in the Mahane Yehuda market in Jerusalem, killing six and wounding more than 60, and the other was an 18-year-old from the Dehaishe refugee camp who blew up a Jerusalem supermarket and killed two people and wounded 22 others.[20]

These examples show the merciless way Palestinian terrorists treat not only their victims, but their own people.

MYTH

"Palestinians interested in peace and preventing terror are respected and allowed freedom of speech by the Palestinian Authority."

FACT

One of the principal deterrents to speaking out against Palestinian irredentism and terror in the Palestinian Authority is the threat of being murdered. By the end of the first intifada in the early 1990s, more Palestinians were killed by their fellow Palestinians than died in clashes with Israeli security forces. During the Palestinian War, intimidation and murder have again been used to muzzle dissent. Usually those seeking peace or an end to terror are labeled "collaborators" and, if they are lucky, arrested by the Palestinian Authority. The unlucky ones are murdered, often in grisly and public ways, such as stringing them up from lamp posts in public squares to send the message that a similar fate awaits anyone who dares cross those seeking Israel's destruction.

A Palestinian need not be interested in peace to become a target of violence; one need only express opposition or offer a challenge to the ruling Fatah party. For example, after student elections at Bir Zeit University in Ramallah resulted in the Islamic Bloc of Hamas and Islamic Jihad receiving more votes than Fatah, Palestinian security forces and members of Fatah attacked members of the Islamic groups and their supporters. Security forces opened fire on the crowd and wounded more than 100 students.[21] When the president of the Gaza-based National Institute of Strategic Studies, Riad al-Agha, criticized the Palestinian security forces on Palestine TV for failing to impose law and order after Israel's disengagement, he was arrested.[22]

There are no exact figures for the number of Palestinians killed in the internecine war; however, Amnesty International reported that "scores of Palestinians" had been unlawfully killed and that the PA "consistently failed to investigate these killings and none of the perpetrators was brought to justice."[23] The Independent Commission for Human Rights, a Palestinian organization that monitors slayings of Palestinians by Palestinians, recorded 43 such murders in 2002; 56 in 2003, and 93 in 2004.

By October, 151 Palestinians had already been killed in 2005, more than had died in clashes with Israeli troops.[24]

MYTH

"Israel uses excessive force to respond to children who are just throwing stones."

FACT

Palestinians, young and old, attack Israeli civilians and soldiers with a variety of weapons. When they throw stones, they are not pebbles, but large rocks that can and do cause serious injuries.

Typically, Israeli troops under attack have numbered fewer than 20, while their assailants, armed with Molotov cocktails, pistols, assault rifles, machine guns, hand grenades and explosives, have numbered in the hundreds. Moreover, mixed among rock throwers have been Palestinians, often policemen, armed with guns. Faced with an angry, violent mob, Israeli police and soldiers often have no choice but to defend themselves by firing rubber bullets and, in life-threatening situations, live ammunition.

The use of live-fire by the Palestinians has effectively meant that Israeli forces have had to remain at some distance from those initiating the violence. In addition, the threat of force against Israelis has been a threat of lethal force. Both factors have inhibited the use of traditional methods of riot control.

According to the rules of engagement for Israeli troops in the territories, the use of weapons is authorized solely in life-threatening situations or, subject to significant limitations, in the exercise of the arrest of an individual suspected of having committed a grave security offense. In all cases, IDF activities have been governed by an overriding policy of restraint, the requirement of proportionality and the necessity to take all possible measures to prevent harm to innocent civilians.

Meanwhile, the Palestinians escalated their violent attacks against Israelis by using mortars and anti-tank missiles illegally smuggled into the Gaza Strip. The Palestinian Authority has also been stockpiling weapons smuggled into Gaza by sea and underground tunnels linked to Egypt.

The possession and use of these weapons and other arms by the Palestinians violates commitments they made in various agreements with Israel. Under the Oslo accords, the only weapons allowed in the Palestinian-controlled areas are handguns, rifles and machine guns, and these are to be held only by PA security officers.[25]

The number of Palestinian casualties in clashes is regrettable, but it is important to remember that no Palestinian would be in any danger or risk injury if they were not waging a terror campaign. If children were in school or at home with their families, rather than throwing rocks in the streets, they too would have little to fear. And children throw more than rocks. Abu Mazen, revealed that children are paid to carry out terrorist attacks against Israel. He told a Jordanian newspaper that "at least 40 children in Rafah lost arms from the throwing of Bangalore torpedoes [explosive charges]. They received five shekels [approximately $1.00] in order to throw them."[26]

Also, while the number of Palestinians who have died is greater than the number of Israelis, that should not minimize the traumatic loss of life on the Israeli side. Contrary to Palestinian assertions that they are fighting a war against armed forces, fewer than one-third of the Israelis that have been killed were soldiers. In 2004, Palestinians successfully carried out 15 suicide attacks and Israeli security forces thwarted 367 others.[27]

Consider how police in the United States and other nations react to mob violence. Abuses do sometimes occur when police are under attack, but no one expects them to stand by and allow their lives to be put in danger to assuage international opinion. In fact, the PA itself does not hesitate to use lethal force against protestors. For example, after the U.S. coalition attacked Afghanistan, Hamas organized a rally in the Gaza Strip in which thousands of Palestinians marched in support of Osama bin Laden. Palestinian police killed two protestors when they tried to break it up.[28]

It is only Israelis who are denied their right to self-defense or see it used as a propaganda weapon against them.

"If Muslims claim that we are against violence, why aren't we demonstrating in the streets against suicide bombings? Why is it so much easier to draw us into protest against a French ban on the hijab, but next to impossible to exorcise ourselves about slavery, stonings and suicide killings? Where's our collective conscience?"

—Muslim author Irshad Manji[29]

MYTH

"The shooting of a child being protected by his father shown on TV proves Israel does not hesitate to kill innocent Palestinian children."

FACT

Perhaps the most vivid image of the Palestinian War was the film of a Palestinian father trying unsuccessfully to shield his son from gunfire. Israel was universally blamed for the death of 12-year-old Mohammed Aldura, but subsequent investigations found that the boy was most likely killed by Palestinian bullets.

The father and son took cover adjacent to a Palestinian shooting position at the Netzarim junction in the Gaza Strip. After Palestinian policemen fired from this location and around it toward an IDF position opposite, IDF soldiers returned fire toward the sources of the shooting. During the exchange of fire, the Palestinian child was hit and killed.

Contrary to the conventional belief that the footage of the incident was live, it was actually edited before it was broadcast around the world. Though a number of cameramen were in the area, only one, a Palestinian working for France 2, recorded the shooting. Raw footage of the day shows a far more complex picture of what was taking place and raised questions about the universal assumption that Israel had killed the boy.

An IDF investigation of the incident released November 27, 2000, found that Aldura was most likely killed by a Palestinian policeman and not by IDF fire. This report was confirmed by an independent investigation by German ARD Television, which said the footage of Aldura's death was censored by the Palestinians to look as if he had been killed by the Israelis when, in fact, his death was caused by Palestinian gunfire.[30]

James Fallows revisited the story and found that "the physical evidence of the shooting was in all ways inconsistent with shots coming from the IDF outpost." In addition, he cites a number of unanswered questions, which have led some to conclude the whole incident was staged. For example, Fallows asks, "Why is there no footage of the boy after he was shot? Why does he appear to move in his father's lap, and to clasp a hand over his eyes after he is supposedly dead? Why is one Palestinian policeman wearing a Secret Service-style earpiece in one ear? Why is another Palestinian man shown waving his arms and yelling at others, as if 'directing' a dramatic scene? Why does the funeral appear—based on the length of shadows—to have occurred before the apparent time of the shooting? Why is there no blood on the father's shirt just after they are shot? Why did a voice that seems to be that of the France 2 cameraman yell, in Arabic, 'The boy is dead' before he had been hit? Why do ambulances appear instantly for seemingly everyone else and not for al-Dura?"[31]

More recently, Denis Jeambar, editor-in-chief of the French news weekly *l'Express,* and filmmaker Daniel Leconte, a producer and owner of the film company Doc en Stock, saw raw, unedited video of the shooting and said the boy could not have been shot by Israeli soldiers. "The only ones who could hit the child were the Palestinians from their position. If they had been Israeli bullets, they would be very strange bullets because they would have needed to go around the corner." France 2 claimed that the gunshots that struck al-Durra were bullets that ricocheted off the ground, but Leconte dismissed the argument. "It could happen once, but that there should be eight or nine of them, which go around a corner?"[32]

Despite the growing body of evidence that the report was inaccurate, France 2 refuses to retract the story.

"I think when you are attacked by a terrorist and you know who the terrorist is and you can fingerprint back to the cause of the terror, you should respond."

—U.S. Secretary of State Colin Powell[33]

MYTH

"Israel's use of F-16 fighter jets typifies the disproportionate use of force applied by Israel against innocent Palestinian civilians."

FACT

How do you determine the proportionate use of military force? When Palestinian terrorists plant bombs at Israeli shopping malls and kill and maim dozens of civilians, would the proportionate response be for Israelis to plant bombs in Palestinian malls? No one in Israel believes this would be a legitimate use of force. Thus, Israel is left with the need to take measured action against specific targets in an effort to either deter Palestinian violence or stop it.

In the specific case of Israel's use of F-16s, Major General Giora Eiland, Head of the IDF Operation Branch, explained Israel's reasoning:

> I know that the F-16 was not designed to attack targets in Palestinian cities. But we have to remember that although we use this kind of aircraft, it is still very accurate. All the targets were military targets.... it was rather a tactical decision, simply because the targets were big enough, were strong enough or solid enough that attack helicopters were considered not effective enough to penetrate or to hit these specific targets. So when we decided or we chose these targets then we were looking for the best ammunition for them and in this specific case it was F-16.[34]

Israel's deployment of the fighters came after 88 Israelis had already lost their lives, including 55 civilians. The civilians were not killed accidentally, they were deliberately targeted. In the previous two-and-a-half months, Palestinians had attempted to place 28 bombs inside Israel. The F-16 attack came in direct response to one that exploded at a Netanya shopping mall May 18, 2001, killing five Israelis.

A month before deploying the F-16s, the U.S. State Department accused Israel of an "excessive and disproportionate" response to Palestinian violence when it launched air strikes against targets in Gaza, even though the spokesman admitted the retaliation was "precipitated by the provocative Palestinian mortar attacks on Israel."[35] The U.S. position is ironic given the so-called Powell Doctrine enunciated by Secretary of State Colin Powell, which holds that "America should enter fights with every bit of force available or not at all."[36] Consider a few examples of the application of this doctrine:

- General Powell insisted on deploying overwhelming force before going to war against Iraq in the Gulf War. The Allied force of more than half a million troops demolished Saddam Hussein's army at a cost of fewer than 200 American lives while approximately 35,000 Iraqis were killed, including many civilians.

- Powell also oversaw the invasion of Panama, which required the deployment of 25,000 troops and the use of F-117 Stealth bombers for the first time. Thousands of Panamanian civilians were injured and displaced and at least 100 killed. He said later, "Use all the force necessary, and do not apologize for going in big if that is what it takes. Decisive force ends wars quickly and in the long run saves lives."[37]

- In reaction to an attempt to assassinate President Bush in 1993, the U.S. launched 23 cruise missiles at Iraq's intelligence headquarters and hit a civilian neighborhood in the process. Powell later said this was an "appropriate, proportional" response.[38]

- The U.S. also deployed massive force in the Balkans and, in 1999, accidentally bombed the Chinese embassy in Belgrade killing three and injuring 20.

- The U.S. has relied heavily on fighter planes and bombers to conduct its post-September 11 war in Afghanistan. A number of incidents have subsequently been reported in which civilians have been killed, including the bombing of a wedding party that killed 48.[39]

The United States has not hesitated to use overwhelming force against its adversaries, even though the threats have been distant and in no way posed a danger to the existence of the nation or the immediate security of its citizens. While U.S. military objectives were accomplished, they also were routinely accompanied by errors and collateral damage that resulted in the loss of civilian lives.

Israel is in a different position. The threat it faces is immediate in time and physical proximity, and poses a direct danger to Israeli citizens. Still, Israel has not used its full might as the Powell Doctrine dictates. The use of force has been judicious and precise. In those instances where mistakes occur—as inevitably happens in war—the incidents are investigated.

The bottom line is that Israel would have no need to respond with military force if the Palestinians were not attacking its citizens and soldiers.

MYTH

"Israel's policy of assassinating Palestinian terrorists is immoral and counterproductive."

FACT

Israel is faced with a nearly impossible situation in attempting to protect its civilian population from Palestinians who are prepared to blow themselves up to murder innocent Jews. One strategy for dealing with the problem has been to pursue negotiations to resolve all of the conflicts with the Palestinians and offer to trade land for peace. After Israel gave back much of the West Bank and Gaza Strip, and offered virtually all of the remainder, however, the Palestinians chose to use violence to try to force Israel to capitulate to all their demands.

> *"The assassination of Hamas head Sheikh Ahmed Yassin in 2004 played in the world as the killing of a crippled holy man by Israeli rockets as he was leaving the mosque in a wheelchair after morning prayers. Because of secrecy surrounding the operation, no file was prepared to explain why he was being killed, that he was an arch-terrorist who had, two days previously, sent two Gaza suicide bombers into Ashdod Port in an attempt to cause a mega-blast of the fuel and nitrates stored there. Or that he had been directly responsible for the deaths of scores, if not hundreds, of Israelis."*
>
> **—Columnist Hirsh Goodman[40]**

A second strategy is for Israel to "exercise restraint," that is, not respond to Palestinian terror. The international community lauds Israel when it turns the other cheek after heinous attacks. While this restraint might win praise from world leaders, it does nothing to assuage the pain of the victims or to prevent further attacks. Moreover, the same nations that urge Israel to exercise control have often reacted forcefully when put in similar situations. For example, the British assassinated Nazis after World War II and targeted IRA terrorists in Northern Ireland. The Clinton Administration attempted to assassinate Osama bin Laden in 1998 in retaliation for his role in the bombings of the United States embassies in Tanzania and Kenya. The Administration of George W. Bush has said it also would not hesitate to kill bin Laden and has targeted a number of other al-Qaeda operatives.[41] On November 4, 2002, for example, the United States killed six suspected al-Qaeda members in Yemen with a Hellfire missile fired from an unmanned CIA drone at the car in which they were traveling.[42]

In April 1986, after the U.S. determined that Libya had directed the terrorist bombing of a West Berlin discotheque that killed one American and injured 200 others, it launched a raid on a series of Libyan targets, including President Muammar Qaddafi's home. Qaddafi escaped, but his infant daughter was killed and two of his other children were wounded. In addition, a missile went off track and caused fatalities in a civilian neighborhood. President Reagan justified the action as self-defense against Libya's state-sponsored terrorism. "As a matter of self-defense, any nation victimized by terrorism has an inherent right to respond with force to deter new acts of terror. I felt we must show Qaddafi that there was a price he would have to pay for that kind of behavior and that we wouldn't let him get away with it."[43] More recently, George W. Bush ordered "hits" on the Iraqi political leadership during the 2003 war in Iraq.

Israel has chosen a third option—eliminating the masterminds of terror attacks. It is a policy that is supported by a vast majority of the public (70 percent in an August 2001 *Haaretz* poll supported the general policy and a similar percentage in 2003 specifically backed the attempt to kill the leader of Hamas). The policy is also supported by the American public according to an August 2001 poll by the America Middle East Information Network. The survey found that 73 percent of respondents felt Israel was justified in killing terrorists if it had proof they were planning bombings or other attacks that could kill Israelis.[44]

Then Deputy Chief of Staff Major-General Moshe Ya'alon explained the policy this way:

> There are no executions without a trial. There is no avenging someone who had carried out an attack a month ago. We are acting against those who are waging terror against us. We prefer to arrest them and have detained over 1,000. But if we can't, and the Palestinians won't, then we have no other choice but to defend ourselves.[45]

The Israeli government also went through a legal process before adopting the policy of targeted killings. Israel's attorney general reviewed the policy and determined that it is legal under Israeli and international law.[46]

Targeting the terrorists has a number of benefits. First, it places a price on terror: Israelis can't be attacked with impunity anymore, for terrorists know that if they target others, they will become targets themselves. Second, it is a method of self-defense: pre-emptive strikes eliminate the people who would otherwise murder Israelis. While it is true that there are others to take their place, they can do so only with the knowledge they too will become targets, and leaders are not easily replaceable. Third, it throws the terrorists off balance. Extremists can no longer nonchalantly plan an operation; rather, they must stay on the move, look over their shoulders at all times, and work much harder to carry out their goals.

Of course, the policy also has costs. Besides international condemnation, Israel risks revealing informers who often provide the information needed to find the terrorists. Soldiers also must engage in sometimes high-risk operations that occasionally cause tragic collateral damage to property and persons.

The most common criticism of "targeted killings" is that they do no good because they perpetuate a cycle of violence whereby the terrorists seek revenge. This is probably the least compelling argument against the policy, because the people who blow themselves up to become martyrs could always find a justification for their actions. They are determined to bomb the Jews out of the Middle East and will not stop until their goal is achieved.

Case Study

In August 2002, we had all the leadership of Hamas—Sheikh Yassin and all his military commanders . . . in one room in a three-story house and we knew we needed a 2,000-pound bomb to eliminate all of them—the whole leadership, 16 people, all the worst terrorists. Think about having Osama bin Laden and all the top leadership of al-Qaeda in one house. However, due to the criticism in Israeli society and in the media, and due to the consequences of innocent Palestinians being killed, a 2,000-pound bomb was not approved and we hit the building with a much smaller bomb. There was a lot of dust, a lot of noise, but they all got up and ran away and we missed the opportunity. So the ethical dilemmas are always there.[47]

MYTH

"Israel indiscriminately murders terrorists and Palestinian civilians."

FACT

It is always a tragedy when innocent civilians are killed in a counterterrorism operation. Civilians would not be at risk, however, if the Palestinian Authority arrested the terrorists, the murderers did not choose to hide among noncombatants and the civilians refused to protect the killers.

Israel does not attack Palestinian areas indiscriminately. On the contrary, the IDF takes great care to target people who are planning terrorist attacks against Israeli civilians. Israeli forces have a history of accuracy in such assaults, nevertheless, mistakes are sometimes made. Whereas the terrorists make no apology for their attacks on civilians, and purposely target them, Israel always investigates the reasons for any errors and takes steps to prevent them from reoccurring.

Israel is not alone in using military force against terrorists or in sometimes inadvertently harming people who are not targets. For example, on the same day that American officials were condemning Israel because a number of civilians died when Israel assassinated a leader of Hamas, news reports disclosed that the United States bombed a village in Afghanistan in an operation directed at a Taliban leader that instead killed 48 Afghan civilians at a wedding party. In both cases, flawed intelligence played a role in the tragic mistakes.

The terrorists themselves do not care about the lives of innocent Palestinians and are ultimately responsible for any harm that comes to them. The terrorists' behavior is a violation of international law, specifically Article 51 of the 1977 amendment to the 1949 Geneva Conventions, which prohibits the use of civilians to "shield, favor or impede military operations."[48]

"In Gaza last week, crowds of children reveled and sang while adults showered them with candies. The cause for celebration: the cold-blooded murder of at least seven people—five of them Americans—and the maiming of 80 more by a terrorist bomb on the campus of Jersualem's Hebrew University."

—Historian Michael Oren[49]

MYTH

"Israel perpetrated a massacre in the Jenin refugee camp in April 2002."

FACT

Secretary of State Colin Powell concisely refuted Palestinian claims that Israel was guilty of atrocities in Jenin. "I see no evidence that would support a massacre took place."[50] Powell's view was subsequently confirmed by the United Nations, Human Rights Watch and an investigation by the European Union.[51]

The Palestinians repeatedly claimed that a massacre had been committed in the days immediately following the battle. Spokesman Saeb Erekat, for example, told CNN on April 17 that at least 500 people were massacred and 1,600 people, including women and children, were missing. The Palestinians quickly backpedaled when it became clear they could not produce any evidence to support the scurrilous charge, and their own review committee reported a death toll of 56, of whom 34 were combatants. No women or children were reported missing.[52]

Israel did not arbitrarily choose to raid the refugee camp in Jenin. It had little choice after a series of suicide bombings had terrorized Israeli civilians for the preceding 18 months. To defend itself and bring about hope for peace, Israeli forces went into Jenin to root out one of the principal terrorist bases.

The Palestinian Authority's own documents call Jenin the "suiciders capital." The camp has a long history as a base for extremists, and no less than 28 suicide attacks were launched from this terror nest during the wave of violence that preceded Israel's action. These terrorists violated the cease-fire agreed to by Israel and undermined Israeli efforts to resume political negotiations toward a peace agreement.

Palestinian snipers targeted soldiers from a girls' school, a mosque, and a UNRWA building and, in returning fire and pursuing terrorists, some noncombatants were hit. Any civilian casualty is a tragedy, but some were unavoidable because Palestinian terrorists used civilians as shields. The majority of casualties were gunmen.

"Philosophically, the difference between me and the terrorist is that he wants to hurt me and my children and my wife, while I want to hit him and spare his children and his wife ... because even the killing of one innocent person is unfortunate and should be avoided."

—Senior Israeli Air Force pilot[53]

While Israel could have chosen to bomb the entire camp, the strategy employed by the U.S. in Afghanistan, the IDF deliberately chose a riskier path to reduce the likelihood of endangering civilians. Soldiers went house to house and 23 were killed in bitter combat with Palestinian terrorists using bombs, grenades, booby-traps and machine guns to turn the camp into a war zone.

Also, contrary to media reports, Israel had "carefully worked out ambulance evacuation routes with local Jenin medical officials and the International Red Cross."[54] Israel also kept the hospital running in Jenin. Lt. Col. Fuad Halhal, the Druze commander of the district coordinating body for the IDF, personally delivered a generator to the hospital under fire during the military operation.[55]

Television pictures gave a distorted perspective of the damage in the camp as well. Jenin was not destroyed. The Israeli operation was conducted in a limited area of the refugee camp, which itself comprises a small fraction of the city. The destruction that did occur in the camp was largely caused by Palestinian bombs.

Palestinians have learned from fabricating atrocity stories in the past that a false claim against Israel will get immediate media attention and attract sympathy for their cause. The corrections that inevitably follow these specious charges are rarely seen, read, or noticed.

MYTH

"Rachel Corrie was murdered by Israel while she was peacefully protesting against the illegal demolition of a Palestinian home."

FACT

American Rachel Corrie was killed in the Gaza Strip on March 16, 2003, when she entered an area where Israeli forces were carrying out a military operation. The incident occurred while IDF forces were removing shrubbery along the security road near the border between Israel and Egypt at Rafah to uncover explosive devices, and destroying tunnels used by Palestinian terrorists to illegally smuggle weapons from Egypt to Gaza. Corrie was not demonstrating for peace or trying to shield innocent civilians, she was interfering with a military operation to legally demolish an empty house used to conceal one of these tunnels.

A misleading photo published by the Associated Press gave the impression that Corrie was standing in front of the bulldozer and shouting at the driver with a megaphone, trying to prevent the driver from tearing down a building in the refugee camp. This photo, which was taken by a member of Corrie's organization, was not shot at the time of her death, however, but hours earlier. The photographer said that Corrie was actually sitting and waving her arms when she was struck.[56]

"No matter how you turn the question, Rachel Corrie's death Sunday is a tragedy.... But Corrie's death is no more tragic than the deaths of other young people—some of them young Americans who had traveled to Israel—who died in bombings committed by Palestinian terrorists. They're also worth remembering this day. However you feel about Corrie's actions, whether she was a martyr or misguided, she at least made her choice. Palestinian terrorists didn't give the young people killed in their bombings any choice in their deaths. That, it seems to us, is another kind of tragedy for these young Americans and their families."

—OregonLive.com[57]

Israel's Judge Advocate's Office investigated the incident and concluded that the driver of the bulldozer never saw or heard Corrie because she was standing behind debris that obstructed the view of the driver whose field of view was limited by the small armored windows of his cab. An autopsy found that the cause of Corrie's death was falling debris.[58]

The State Department warned Americans not to travel to Gaza, and Israel made clear that civilians who enter areas where troops are engaged in counter-terror operations put themselves unnecessarily at risk.

This was not the first time protestors tried to obstruct Israeli operations, but the case received worldwide publicity because it was the first such incident where a protestor was killed. In fact, the army had told Corrie and other demonstrators from the anti-Israel International Solidarity Movement (ISM) to move out of the way. "It's possible they [the protesters] were not as disciplined as we would have liked," admitted Thom Saffold, a founder and organizer of ISM.[59]

The death of an innocent civilian is always tragic, and the best way to avoid such tragedies in the future is, first and foremost, by the Palestinian Authority putting an end to violence, and stopping the smuggling operations that have brought huge quantities of illegal weapons into the Gaza Strip. Activists interested in peace should be protesting the Palestinian actions. Demonstrators have every right to express their views about Israel's policies, but they should take care to avoid the appearance of siding with the terrorists or placing themselves in positions where they could be inadvertently caught in the crossfire of a counter-terror operation or otherwise endangered by entering an area where military operations are being conducted.

> *"The intifada is in its death throes. These are the final stages. . . . Not only was the intifada a failure, but we are a total failure. We achieved nothing in 50 years of struggle; we've achieved only our survival."*
>
> **—Zakariya Zubeidi, leader of the al-Aqsa Martyrs Brigades in the West Bank**[60]

MYTH
"Israel poisoned Yasser Arafat."

FACT
Farouk Kaddoumi claimed that Israel poisoned Yasser Arafat because it wants Palestinian leaders who obey it and agree with its policies.[61] This was just the most recent of a number of such allegations that have persisted since Arafat's death.

We don't know for sure what killed Arafat, but even then Foreign Minister Nabil Shaath ruled out poisoning.[62] At the time of his death, the French government, constrained by privacy laws, discounted the possibility of foul play when it announced, "If the doctors had had the slightest doubt, they would have referred it to the police."[63] Moreover, members of Arafat's family, including ones who have made the poisoning charge, have had access to the records and produced nothing to substantiate the rumors. Arafat's wife, Suha, could have released the findings of French physicians, and you can be sure she would have done so if they would have implicated Israel in her husband's death.

Notes

*The war was never formally declared, but began in September 2000 with a surge of Palestinian terrorist attacks in Israel. The war also had no formal ending resulting in a cease-fire or peace agreement. The Israeli Defense Forces succeeded in suppressing the violence to the point where the war had petered out by the end of September 2005.

1. *Jerusalem Post,* (March 4, 2001).
2. Conclusion of the Mitchell Report, (May 4, 2001).
3. "An Engineered Tragedy: Statistical Analysis of Casualties in the Palestinian-Israeli Conflict, September 2000-June 2002," International Policy Institute for Counter-Terrorism, (June 2002).
4. Quoted in Sharm El-Sheikh Fact-Finding Committee First Statement of the Government of Israel, Israeli Foreign Ministry, (December 28, 2000).
5. "Egypt/Israel: Attacks on Civilians Are Unjustifiable Crimes," Human Rights Watch
6. Richard Sale, "Hamas history tied to Israel," UPI, (June 18, 2002).
7. Ze'ev Schiff and Ehud Ya'ari, *Intifada: The Palestinian Uprising—Israel's Third Front.* (NY: Simon and Schuster, 1990), pp. 227-239.
8. *Jerusalem Report,* (May 21, 2001).
9. *Jerusalem Post,* (September 22, 2005).
10. Associated Press; *Jerusalem Post; New York Post,* (March 16, 2004); CNN.com (March 25, 2004).
11. *Jerusalem Post,* (May 25, July 5, August, 29, 2005).
12. Amnesty International, Press Release, (March 24, 2004).
13. Itamar Marcus, "Ask for Death," *The Review,* (March 2003).
14. *Al-Hayat Al-Jadida,* (June 18, 2002).
15. *Jerusalem Post,* (December 25, 2003).
16. *Jerusalem Post,* (March 15, 2004, May 25, 2005).
17. Associated Press, (March 1, 2004).
18. MSNBC, (May 27, 2005).
19. London *Daily Telegraph,* (March 15, 2004).
20. "Blackmailing Young Women into Suicide Terrorism," Israeli Foreign Ministry, (February 12, 2003).
21. NewsFirstClass, (December 12, 2003).
22. Khaled Abu Toameh, "PA arrests academic voicing criticism," *Jerusalem Post,* (July 4, 2005).
23. *Country Reports on Human Rights Practices—2002,* The State Department, March 31, 2003; B'tselem, Amnesty International, January–December 2002; *Jerusalem Post,* (August 25, 2002).
24. Mohammed Daraghmeh, "Palestinian Vigilante Killings on the Rise," Associated Press, (October 6, 2005).
25. *Near East Report,* (March 5, 2001).
26. *Almazen* [Kuwait], (June 20, 2002).
27. *Jerusalem Report,* (February 25, 2002); *Maariv,* (July 31, 2002); Israeli Foreign Ministry, *Washington Post,* (April 2, 2004).
28. Jewish Telegraphic Agency, (October 8, 2001).
29. Pearl Sheffy Gefen, "Irshad Manji, Muslim Refusenik," *Lifestyles Magazine,* (Summer 2004), p. 29.

30. CNN, Israel Defense Forces, *Jerusalem Post,* (November 28, 2000); Jewish Telegraphic Agency, (March 21, 2002).
31. James Fallows, "Who Shot Mohammed al-Dura?" *The Atlantic Monthly,* (June 2003).
32. Eva Cahen, "French TV Sticks by Story That Fueled Palestinian Intifada," CNSNews. com, (February 15, 2005).
33. News Conference, (September 12, 2001).
34. Briefing by Major General Giora Eiland, Head of the IDF Operation Branch, to the Foreign Press Association, Jerusalem, (May 20, 2001).
35. State Department Briefing, (April 17, 2001).
36. *Time,* (April 19, 2001).
37. Collin Powell, *My American Journey,* (NY: Random House, 1995), p. 434.
38. *Washington Post,* (June 28, 1993).
39. CNN, (July 16, 2002).
40. Hirsh Goodman, "A Lesson Learned," *Jerusalem Report,* (September 19, 2005).
41. *Washington Post,* (September 14 and 18, 2001).
42. CNN, (November 4, 2002).
43. RonaldReagan.com, *Washington Post* and other news sources.
44. Jewish Telegraphic Agency, (August 30, 2001).
45. *Jerusalem Post,* (August 10, 2001).
46. Jewish Telegraphic Agency, (November 30, 2001).
47. Amos Yadlin, "Updating the Concept of War: The Ethics of Fighting Terrorism," *The Review,* (January 2005), p. 27.
48. *Near East Report,* Year End Reports, (1991–1993).
49. Michael Oren, "Palestinians Cheer Carnage," *Wall Street Journal,* (August 7, 2002).
50. *Jerusalem Post,* (April 25, 2002).
51. *Jerusalem Post,* (April 28, 2002); *Forward,* (June 28, 2002); MSNBC, (July 31, 2002).
52. *New York Post,* (May 3, 2002).
53. Christian Lowe and Barbara Opall-Rome, "Israel Air Force Seeks Expanded Anti-Terror Role," *Defense News,* (March 28, 2005).
54. "Anatomy of Anti-Israel Incitement: Jenin, World Opinion and the Massacre That Wasn't," Anti-Defamation League, 2002 [http://www.adl.org/Israel/jenin/default.asp].
55. *Jerusalem Report,* (December 30, 2002).
56. *Christian Science Monitor,* (April 2, 2003).
57. *OregonLive.com,* (March 18, 2003).
58. *Jerusalem Post,* (June 26, 2003).
59. *Washington Post,* (March 17, 2003).
60. *Jerusalem Post,* (August 4, 2004).
61. Khaled Abu Toameh, "Kaddoumi claims Israel poisoned Arafat," *Jerusalem Post,* (March 30, 2005).
62. Associated Press, (November 17, 2004).
63. John Ward Anderson, "Conspiracy Theories Persist on Arafat's Death," *Washington Post,* (November 18, 2004), p. A36.

17. Jerusalem

MYTH

"Jerusalem is an Arab City."

FACT

Jews have been living in Jerusalem continuously for nearly two millennia. They have constituted the largest single group of inhabitants there since the 1840's. Jerusalem contains the Western Wall of the Temple Mount, the holiest site in Judaism.

Jerusalem was never the capital of any Arab entity. In fact, it was a backwater for most of Arab history. Jerusalem never served as a provincial capital under Muslim rule nor was it ever a Muslim cultural center. For Jews, the entire city is sacred, but Muslims revere a site—the Dome of the Rock—not the city. "To a Muslim," observed British writer Christopher Sykes, "there is a profound difference between Jerusalem and Mecca or Medina. The latter are holy places containing holy sites." Besides the Dome of the Rock, he noted, Jerusalem has no major Islamic significance.[1]

Jerusalem's Population[2]

Year	Jews	Muslims	Christians	Total
1844	7,120	5,000	3,390	15,510
1876	12,000	7,560	5,470	25,030
1896	28,112	8,560	8,748	45,420
1922	33,971	13,411	4,699	52,081
1931	51,222	19,894	19,335	90,451
1948	100,000	40,000	25,000	165,000
1967	195,700	54,963	12,646	263,309
1987	340,000	121,000	14,000	475,000
1990	378,200	131,800	14,400	524,400
2000	530,400	204,100	14,700	758,300

MYTH

"The Temple Mount has always been a Muslim holy place and Judaism has no connection to the site."

FACT

During the 2000 Camp David Summit, Yasser Arafat said that no Jewish Temple ever existed on the Temple Mount.[3] A year later, the Palestinian Authority-appointed Mufti of Jerusalem, Ikrima Sabri, told the German publication *Die Welt*, "There is not [even] the smallest indication of the existence of a Jewish temple on this place in the past. In the whole city, there is not even a single stone indicating Jewish history."

These views are contradicted by a book entitled *A Brief Guide to al-Haram al-Sharif*, published by the Supreme Moslem Council in 1930. The Council, the principal Muslim authority in Jerusalem during the British Mandate, said in the guide that the Temple Mount site "is one of the oldest in the world. Its sanctity dates from the earliest times. Its identity with the site of Solomon's Temple is beyond dispute. This, too, is the spot, according to universal belief, on which David built there an altar unto the Lord, and offered burnt offerings and peace offerings."

In a description of the area of Solomon's Stables, which Islamic Waqf officials converted into a new mosque in 1996, the guide states: "...little is known for certain about the early history of the chamber itself. It dates probably as far back as the construction of Solomon's Temple ...According to Josephus, it was in existence and was used as a place of refuge by the Jews at the time of the conquest of Jerusalem by Titus in the year 70 A.D."[4]

More authoritatively, the Koran—the holy book of Islam—describes Solomon's construction of the First Temple (34:13) and recounts the destruction of the First and Second Temples (17:7).

The Jewish connection to the Temple Mount dates back more than 3,000 years and is rooted in tradition and history. When Abraham bound his son Isaac upon an altar as a sacrifice to God, he is believed to have done so atop Mount Moriah, today's Temple Mount. The First Temple's Holy of Holies contained the original Ark of the Covenant, and both the First and Second Temples were the centers of Jewish religious and social life until the Second Temple's destruction by the Romans. After the destruction of the Second Temple, control of the Temple Mount passed through several conquering powers. It was during the early period of Muslim control that the Dome of the Rock was built on the site of the ancient temples.

Strictly observant Jews do not visit the Temple Mount for fear of accidentally treading upon the Holy of Holies, since its exact location on the Mount is unknown. Other Jews and non-Muslims are permitted to visit.

"The Zionist movement has invented that this was the site of Solomon's Temple. But this is all a lie."

—Sheik Raed Salah, a leader of the Islamic Movement in Israel[5]

MYTH

"Jerusalem need not be the capital of Israel."

FACT

Ever since King David made Jerusalem the capital of Israel more than 3,000 years ago, the city has played a central role in Jewish existence. The Western Wall in the Old City is the object of Jewish veneration and the focus of Jewish prayer. Three times a day, for thousands of years, Jews have prayed "To Jerusalem, thy city, shall we return with joy," and have repeated the Psalmist's oath: "If I forget thee, O Jerusalem, let my right hand forget her cunning."

Jerusalem "has known only two periods of true greatness, and these have been separated by 2,000 years. Greatness has only happened under Jewish rule," Leon and Jill Uris wrote in *Jerusalem*. "This is so because the Jews have loved her the most, and have remained constant in that love throughout the centuries of their dispersion.... It is the longest, deepest love affair in history."[6]

"For three thousand years, Jerusalem has been the center of Jewish hope and longing. No other city has played such a dominant role in the history, culture, religion and consciousness of a people as has Jerusalem in the life of Jewry and Judaism. Throughout centuries of exile, Jerusalem remained alive in the hearts of Jews everywhere as the focal point of Jewish history, the symbol of ancient glory, spiritual fulfillment and modern renewal. This heart and soul of the Jewish people engenders the thought that if you want one simple word to symbolize all of Jewish history, that word would be 'Jerusalem.'"

—Teddy Kollek[7]

MYTH

"Unlike the Jews, the Arabs were willing to accept the internationalization of Jerusalem."

FACT

When the United Nations took up the Palestine question in 1947, it recommended that all of Jerusalem be internationalized. The Vatican and many predominantly Catholic delegations pushed for this status, but a key reason for the UN decision was the Soviet Bloc's desire to embarrass Transjordan's King Abdullah and his British patrons by denying Abdullah control of the city.

The Jewish Agency, after much soul-searching, agreed to accept internationalization in the hope that in the short-run it would protect the city from bloodshed and the new state from conflict. Since the partition resolution called for a referendum on the city's status after 10 years, and Jews comprised a substantial majority, the expectation was that the city would later be incorporated into Israel. The Arab states were as bitterly opposed to the internationalization of Jerusalem as they were to the rest of the partition plan.

In May 1948, Jordan invaded and occupied East Jerusalem, dividing the city for the first time in its history, and driving thousands of Jews—whose families had lived in the city for centuries—into exile. The UN partition plan, including its proposal that Jerusalem be internationalized, was overtaken by events. Prime Minister David Ben-Gurion subsequently declared that Israel would no longer accept the internationalization of Jerusalem.

"You ought to let the Jews have Jerusalem; it was they who made it famous."

—Winston Churchill[8]

MYTH

"Internationalization is the best solution to resolve the conflicting claims over Jerusalem."

FACT

The seeming intractability of resolving the conflicting claims to Jerusalem has led some people to resurrect the idea of internationalizing the city. Curiously, the idea had little support during the 19 years Jordan controlled the Old City and barred Jews and Israeli Muslims from their holy sites.

The fact that Jerusalem is disputed, or that it is of importance to people other than Israeli Jews, does not mean the city belongs to others or should be ruled by some international regime. There is no precedent for such a setup. The closest thing to an international city was post-war Berlin when the four powers shared control of the city and that experiment proved to be a disaster.

Even if Israel were amenable to such an idea, what conceivable international group could be entrusted to protect the freedoms Israel already guarantees? Surely not the United Nations, which has shown no understanding of Israeli concerns since partition. Israel can count only on the support of the United States, and it is only in the UN Security Council that an American veto can protect Israel from political mischief by other nations.

MYTH

"From 1948 through 1967, Jordan ensured freedom of worship for all religions in Jerusalem."

FACT

From 1948–67, Jerusalem was divided between Israel and Jordan. Israel made western Jerusalem its capital; Jordan occupied the eastern section. Because Jordan maintained a state of war with Israel, the city became, in essence, two armed camps, replete with concrete walls and bunkers, barbed-wire fences, minefields and other military fortifications.

Under paragraph eight of the 1949 Armistice Agreement, Jordan and Israel had were to establish committees to arrange the resumption of the normal functioning of cultural and humanitarian institutions on Mt. Scopus, use of the cemetery on the Mount of Olives, and free access to holy places and cultural institutions. Jordan violated the agreement, however, and denied Israelis access to the Western Wall and to the cemetery on the Mount of Olives, where Jews have buried their dead for more than 2,500 years.

Under Jordanian rule, "Israeli Christians were subjected to various restrictions during their seasonal pilgrimages to their holy places" in Jerusalem, noted Teddy Kollek. "Only limited numbers were grudgingly permitted to briefly visit the Old City and Bethlehem at Christmas and Easter."[9]

In 1955 and 1964, Jordan passed laws imposing strict government control on Christian schools, including restrictions on the opening of new schools, state control over school finances and appointment of teachers and the requirements that the Koran be taught. In 1953 and 1965, Jordan adopted laws abrogating the right of Christian religious and charitable institutions to acquire real estate in Jerusalem.

In 1958, police seized the Armenian Patriarch-elect and deported him from Jordan, paving the way for the election of a patriarch supported by King Hussein's government. Because of these repressive policies, many Christians emigrated from Jerusalem. Their numbers declined from 25,000 in 1949 to fewer than 13,000 in June 1967.[10]

These discriminatory laws were abolished by Israel after the city was reunited in 1967.

MYTH

"Jordan safeguarded Jewish holy places."

FACT

Jordan desecrated Jewish holy places. King Hussein permitted the construction of a road to the Intercontinental Hotel across the Mount of Olives cemetery. Hundreds of Jewish graves were destroyed by a highway that could have easily been built elsewhere. The gravestones, honoring the memory of rabbis and sages, were used by the engineer corps of the Jordanian Arab Legion as pavement and latrines in army camps (inscriptions on the stones were still visible when Israel liberated the city).

The ancient Jewish Quarter of the Old City was ravaged, 58 Jerusalem synagogues—some centuries old—were destroyed or ruined, others were turned into stables and chicken coops. Slum dwellings were built abutting the Western Wall.[11]

MYTH

"Under Israeli rule, religious freedom has been curbed in Jerusalem."

FACT

After the 1967 war, Israel abolished all the discriminatory laws promulgated by Jordan and adopted its own tough standard for safeguarding access to religious shrines. "Whoever does anything that is likely to violate the freedom of access of the members of the various religions to the places sacred to them," Israeli law stipulates, is "liable to imprisonment for a term of five years." Israel also entrusted administration of the holy places to their respective religious authorities. Thus, for example, the Muslim Waqf has responsibility for the mosques on the Temple Mount.

Les Filles de la Charite de l'Hospice Saint Vincent de Paul of Jerusalem repudiated attacks on Israel's conduct in Jerusalem a few months after Israel took control of the city:

> Our work here has been made especially happy and its path smoother by the goodwill of Israeli authorities ... smoother not only for ourselves, but (more importantly) for the Arabs in our care.[12]

Former President Jimmy Carter acknowledged that religious freedom has been enhanced under Israeli rule. There is "no doubt" that Israel did a better job safeguarding access to the city's holy places than did Jordan. "There is unimpeded access today," Carter noted. "There wasn't from 1948-67."[13]

The State Department notes that Israeli law provides for freedom of worship, and the Government respects this right.[14]

"I also respect the fact that Israel allows for a multifaith climate in which every Friday a thousand Muslims pray openly on the Temple Mount in Jerusalem. When I saw that, I had to ask myself, where in the Islamic world can 1,000 Jews get together and pray in full public view?"

—Muslim author Irshad Manji[15]

MYTH

"Israel denies Muslims and Christians free access to their holy sites."

FACT

Since 1967, hundreds of thousands of Muslims and Christians—many from Arab countries that remain in a state of war with Israel—have come to Jerusalem to see their holy places.

According to Islam, the prophet Muhammad was miraculously transported from Mecca to Jerusalem, and it was from there that he made his ascent to heaven. The Dome of the Rock and the al-Aksa Mosque, both built in the seventh century, made definitive the identification of Jerusalem as the "Remote Place" that is mentioned in the Koran, and thus a holy place after Mecca and Medina.

After reuniting Jerusalem during the Six-Day War, Defense Minister Moshe Dayan permitted the Islamic authority, the Waqf, to continue its civil authority on the Temple Mount even though it part of the holiest site in Judaism. The Waqf oversees all day-to-day activity there. An Israeli presence is in place at the entrance to the Temple Mount to ensure access for people of all religions.

Arab leaders are free to visit Jerusalem to pray if they wish to, just as Egyptian President Anwar Sadat did at the al-Aksa mosque. For security reasons, restrictions are sometimes imposed on the Temple Mount temporarily, but the right to worship is not abridged and other mosques remain accessible even in times of high tension. In October 2004, for example, despite high alerts for terrorism and the ongoing Palestinian war, an estimated 140,000 Muslim worshipers attended Ramadan prayers on the Temple Mount.[16]

For Christians, Jerusalem is the place where Jesus lived, preached, died and was resurrected. While it is the heavenly rather than the earthly Jerusalem that is emphasized by the Church, places mentioned in the New Testament as the sites of Jesus' ministry have drawn pilgrims and devoted worshipers for centuries. Among these sites are the Church of the Holy Sepulcher, the Garden of Gethsemane, the site of the Last Supper, and the Via Dolorosa with the fourteen Stations of the Cross.

The rights of the various Christian churches to custody of the Christian holy places in Jerusalem were defined in the course of the nineteenth century, when Jerusalem was part of the Ottoman Empire. Known as the "status quo arrangement for the Christian holy places in Jerusalem," these rights remained in force during the period of the British Mandate and are still upheld today in Israel.

> *"There is only one Jerusalem. From our perspective, Jerusalem is not a subject for compromise. Jerusalem was ours, will be ours, is ours and will remain as such forever."*
>
> **—Prime Minister Yitzhak Rabin**[17]

MYTH

"Israeli policy encourages attacks by Jewish fanatics against Muslim and Christian residents and their holy sites."

FACT

Israeli authorities have consistently attempted to stop fanatics—of all faiths—from desecrating religious sites or committing acts of violence near them. When it has been unable to stop such acts from occurring, Israel has severely punished the perpetrators. Allen Goodman, a deranged Israeli who in 1982 went on a shooting rampage on the Temple Mount, for example, was sentenced to life imprisonment.

In 1984, Israeli authorities infiltrated a Jewish group that planned acts of violence against non-Jewish sites and civilians. The terrorists were tried and imprisoned.

In 1990, the Temple Mount Faithful, a Jewish extremist group, sought to march to the Temple Mount on Sukkot to lay the cornerstone for the Third Temple. The police, worried that such a march would anger Muslims and exacerbate an already tense situation created by the intifada and events in the Persian Gulf, denied them the right to march. That decision was upheld by the Israeli Supreme Court, a fact communicated immediately to Muslim religious leaders and the Arab press. Despite Israel's preemptive action, "Muslim leaders and intifada activists persisted in inciting their faithful to confrontation."[18] As a result, a tragic riot ensued in which 17 Arabs were killed.

Since that time, Israel has been especially vigilant, and done everything possible to prevent any provocation by groups or individuals that might threaten the sanctity of the holy places of any faith. In 2005, for example, Israel banned non-Muslims from the Temple Mount to forestall a planned rally by Jewish ultra-nationalists.

MYTH

"Israel has not acknowledged Palestinian claims to Jerusalem."

FACT

Jerusalem was never the capital of any Arab entity. Palestinians have no special claim to the city; they simply demand it as their capital.

Israel has recognized that the city has a large Palestinian population, that the city is important to Muslims, and that making concessions on the sovereignty of the city might help minimize the conflict with the Palestinians. The problem has been that Palestinians have shown no reciprocal appreciation for the Jewish majority in the city, the significance of Jerusalem to the Jewish people or the fact that it is already the nation's capital.

The Israeli-Palestinian Declaration of Principles (DoP) signed in 1993 left open the status of Jerusalem. Article V said only that Jerusalem is one of the issues to be discussed in the permanent status negotiations. The agreed minutes also mention Jerusalem, stipulating that the Palestinian Council's jurisdiction does not extend to the city. Prime Minister Yitzhak Rabin said that Jerusalem will "not be included in any sphere of the prerogatives of whatever body will conduct Palestinian affairs in the territories. Jerusalem will remain under Israeli sovereignty."

> *"Anyone who relinquishes a single inch of Jerusalem is neither an Arab nor a Muslim."*
>
> **—Yasser Arafat**[19]

The overwhelming majority of Israelis oppose any division of Jerusalem. Still, efforts have been made to find some compromise that could satisfy Palestinian interests. For example, while the Labor Party was in power under Yitzhak Rabin and Shimon Peres, Knesset Member Yossi Beilin reportedly reached a tentative agreement that would allow the Palestinians to claim the city as their capital without Israel sacrificing sovereignty over its capital. Beilin's idea was to allow the Palestinians to set up their capital in a West Bank suburb of Jerusalem—Abu Dis. The PA subsequently constructed a building for its parliament in the city.

Prime Minister Ehud Barak offered dramatic concessions that would have allowed the Arab neighborhoods of East Jerusalem to become the capital of a Palestinian state, and given the Palestinians control over the Muslim holy places on the Temple Mount. These ideas were discussed at the White House Summit in December 2000, but rejected by Yasser Arafat.

Barak's proposals were controversial. Giving up sovereignty over the Temple Mount would place potentially hostile Arabs literally over the heads of Jews praying at their holiest site. Other suggested compromises involving a division of sovereignty over the Old City run into practical complications created by the labyrinthine nature of the city, and the intertwining of the Muslim, Christian, Jewish and Armenian quarters.

In February 2001, Ariel Sharon ran for Prime Minister against Barak—and was overwhelmingly elected—on a platform specifically repudiating the concessions Barak offered on Jerusalem. The prospect for a compromise now depends in large measure on whether the Palestinians will recognize Jewish claims to Jerusalem and offer their own concessions.

"I'll urge the Muslims to launch jihad and to use all their capabilities to restore Muslim Palestine and the holy al-Aksa mosque from the Zionist usurpers and aggressors. The Muslims must be united in the confrontation of the Jews and those who support them."

—Saudi King Fahd[20]

MYTH

"Israel has restricted the political rights of Palestinian Arabs in Jerusalem."

FACT

Along with religious freedom, Palestinian Arabs in Jerusalem have unprecedented political rights. Arab residents were given the choice of whether to become Israeli citizens. Most chose to retain their Jordanian citizenship. Moreover, regardless of whether they are citizens, Jerusalem Arabs are permitted to vote in municipal elections and play a role in the administration of the city.

MYTH

"Under UN Resolution 242, East Jerusalem is considered 'occupied territory.' Israel's annexation of Jerusalem therefore violates the UN resolution."

FACT

One drafter of the UN Resolution was then-U.S. Ambassador to the UN Arthur Goldberg. According to Goldberg, "Resolution 242 in no way refers to Jerusalem, and this omission was deliberate.... Jerusalem was a discrete matter, not linked to the West Bank." In several speeches at the UN in 1967, Goldberg said: "I repeatedly stated that the armistice lines of 1948 were intended to be temporary. This, of course, was particularly true of Jerusalem. At no time in these many speeches did I refer to East Jerusalem as occupied territory."[21]

Because Israel was defending itself from aggression in the 1948 and 1967 wars, former President of the International Court of Justice Steven Schwebel wrote, it has a better claim to sovereignty over Jerusalem than its Arab neighbors.[22]

> *"The basis of our position remains that Jerusalem must never again be a divided city. We did not approve of the status quo before 1967; in no way do we advocate a return to it now."*
>
> **—President George Bush**[23]

MYTH

"East Jerusalem should be part of a Palestinian state because all its residents are Palestinian Arabs and no Jews have ever lived there."

FACT

Before 1865, the entire population of Jerusalem lived behind the Old City walls (what today would be considered part of the eastern part of the city). Later, the city began to expand beyond the walls because of population growth, and both Jews and Arabs began to build in new areas of the city.

By the time of partition, a thriving Jewish community was living in the eastern part of Jerusalem, an area that included the Jewish Quarter of the Old City. This area of the city also contains many sites of importance to the Jewish religion, including the City of David, the Temple Mount and the Western Wall. In addition, major institutions such as Hebrew University and the original Hadassah Hospital are on Mount Scopus—in eastern Jerusalem.

The only time that the eastern part of Jerusalem was exclusively Arab was between 1949 and 1967, and that was because Jordan occupied the area and forcibly expelled all the Jews.

MYTH

"The United States does not recognize Jerusalem as Israel's capital."

FACT

Only two countries have embassies in Jerusalem—Costa Rica and El Salvador. Of the 180 nations with which America has diplomatic relations,

Israel is the only one whose capital is not recognized by the U.S. government. The U.S. embassy, like most others, is in Tel Aviv, 40 miles from Jerusalem. The United States does maintain a consulate in East Jerusalem, however, that deals with Palestinians in the territories and works independently of the embassy, reporting directly to Washington. Today, then, we have the anomaly that American diplomats refuse to meet with Israelis in their capital because Jerusalem's status is negotiable, but make their contacts with Palestinians in the city.

In 1990, Congress passed a resolution declaring that "Jerusalem is and should remain the capital of the State of Israel" and "must remain an undivided city in which the rights of every ethnic and religious group are protected." During the 1992 Presidential campaign, Bill Clinton said: "I recognize Jerusalem as an undivided city, the eternal capital of Israel, and I believe in the principle of moving our embassy to Jerusalem." He never reiterated this view as President; consequently, official U.S. policy remained that the status of Jerusalem is a matter for negotiations.

"I would be blind to disclaim the Jewish connection to Jerusalem."

—Sari Nusseibeh, President of Al Quds University[24]

In an effort to change this policy, Congress overwhelmingly passed The Jerusalem Embassy Act of 1995. This landmark bill declared that, as a statement of official U.S. policy, Jerusalem should be recognized as the undivided, eternal capital of Israel and required that the U.S. embassy in Israel be established in Jerusalem no later than May 1999. The law also included a waiver that allowed the President to essentially ignore the legislation if he deemed doing so to be in the best interest of the United States. President Clinton exercised that option.

During the 2000 presidential campaign George W. Bush promised that as President he would immediately "begin the process of moving the United States ambassador to the city Israel has chosen as its capital."[25] As President, however, Bush has followed Clinton's precedent and repeatedly used the presidential waiver to prevent the embassy from being moved.

While critics of Congressional efforts to force the administration to recognize Jerusalem as Israel's capital insist that such a move would harm the peace process, supporters of the legislation argue the opposite is true. By making clear the United States position that Jerusalem should remain unified under Israeli sovereignty, they say, unrealistic Palestinian expectations regarding the city can be moderated and thereby enhance the prospects for a final agreement.

MYTH

"The Palestinians have been careful to preserve the archaeological relics of the Temple Mount."

FACT

Though it has refused to recognize Israeli sovereignty over the Temple Mount, the Waqf cooperated with Israeli inspectors when conducting work on the holy site. After the 1993 Oslo accords, however, the Jordanian-controlled Waqf was replaced with representatives beholden to the Palestinian Authority. Following the riots that accompanied Israel's decision to open an exit from the Western Wall tunnel, the Waqf ceased cooperating with Israel.

The Waqf has subsequently prevented Israeli inspectors from overseeing work done on the Mount that has caused irreparable damage to archaeological remains from the First and Second Temple periods. Israeli archaeologists found that during extensive construction work, thousands of tons of gravel—which contained important relics—was removed from the Mount and discarded in the trash. Experts say that even the artifacts that were not destroyed were rendered archaeologically useless because the Palestinian construction workers mixed finds from diverse periods when they scooped up earth with bulldozers.[26]

Given the sensitivity of the Temple Mount, and the tensions already existing between Israelis and Palestinians over Jerusalem, the Israeli government has not interfered in the Waqf's activities. Meanwhile, the destruction of the past continues.

"For us, there is only one Jerusalem, and no other. It will be ours forever, and will never again be in the hands of foreigners. We will honor and cherish all lovers of Jerusalem, of all faiths and religions. We will carefully guard all its sites of prayer, churches and mosques, and freedom of worship will be ensured, which was not the case when others ruled it. We will fearlessly face the entire world and will ensure the future of united Jerusalem. For Jerusalem is the anchor, root of life, and faith of the Jewish people and we will never again part with it."

—Ariel Sharon[27]

Notes

1. *Encounter*, (February 1968).
2. John Oesterreicher and Anne Sinai, eds., *Jerusalem*, (NY: John Day, 1974), p. 1; Israel Central Bureau of Statistics; Jerusalem Foundation; Municipality of Jerusalem. The figures for 2000 include 9,000 with no religion classified.
3. Interview with Dennis Ross, Fox News Sunday, (April 21, 2002).

4. *Jerusalem Post,* (January 26, 2001).
5. Jewish Telegraphic Agency, (February 12, 2001).
6. Leon and Jill Uris, *Jerusalem,* (New York: Doubleday and Company, 1981), p. 13.
7. Teddy Kollek, *Jerusalem,* (DC: Washington Institute For Near East Policy, 1990), pp. 19-20.
8. Sir Eveyln Shuckburgh, *Descent to Suez; Diaries 1951-56,* (London, 1986).
9. Kollek, p. 15.
10. Kollek, p. 16.
11. Kollek, p. 15.
12. *Catholic Herald of London,* (October 6, 1967).
13. *Near East Report,* (April 2, 1990).
14. U.S. Department of State, "2001 Annual Report on International Religious Freedom," Released by the Bureau for Democracy, Human Rights, and Labor, (Washington, D.C., December 2001).
15. Pearl Sheffy Gefen, "Irshad Manji, Muslim Refusenik," *Lifestyles Magazine,* (Summer 2004), p. 29.
16. *Jerusalem Post,* (October 22, 2004).
17. Jerusalem Day Address to Knesset, (May 29, 1995).
18. Kollek, p. 62.
19. Voice of Palestine, Algiers, (September 2, 1993).
20. Saudi Press Agency, (July 15, 1986).
21. *New York Times,* (March 12, 1980).
22. *American Journal of International Law,* (April 1970), pp. 346-47.
23. Letter from President George Bush to Jerusalem Mayor Teddy Kollek, (March 20, 1990).
24. *Jerusalem Post,* (November 12, 2001).
25. Speech to AIPAC Policy Conference, (May 22, 2000).
26. Jewish Telegraphic Agency, (February 12, 2001).
27. Address by Prime Minister Sharon at the Jerusalem Day Ceremony Ammunition Hill, (June 6, 2005).

18. U.S. Middle East Policy

MYTH

"The creation of Israel resulted solely from U.S. pressure."

FACT

When the UN took up the question of Palestine, President Harry Truman explicitly said the United States should not "use threats or improper pressure of any kind on other delegations."[1] Some pressure was nevertheless exerted and the U.S. played a key role in securing support for the partition resolution. U.S. influence was limited, however, as became clear when American dependents such as Cuba and Greece voted against partition, and El Salvador and Honduras abstained.

Many members of the Truman Administration opposed partition, including Defense Secretary James Forrestal, who believed Zionist aims posed a threat to American oil supplies and its strategic position in the region. The Joint Chiefs of Staff worried that the Arabs might align themselves with the Soviets if they were alienated by the West. These internal opponents undermined U.S. support for the establishment of a Jewish state.[2]

Although much has been written about the tactics of the supporters of partition, the behavior of the Arab states has been largely ignored. They were, in fact, actively engaged in arm-twisting of their own at the UN trying to scuttle partition.[3]

MYTH

"The United States favored Israel over the Arabs in 1948 because of the pressures of the Jewish lobby."

FACT

Truman supported the Zionist movement because he believed the international community was obligated to fulfill the promise of the Balfour Declaration and because he believed it was the humanitarian thing to do to ameliorate the plight of the Jewish survivors of the Holocaust. He did not believe the rights of the Arabs should or would be compromised. A sense of his attitude can be gleaned from a remark he made with regard to negotiations as to the boundaries of a Jewish state:

> The whole region waits to be developed, and if it were handled
> the way we developed the Tennessee River basin, it could sup-

port from 20 to 30 million people more. To open the door to this kind of future would indeed be the constructive and humanitarian thing to do, and it would also redeem the pledges that were given at the time of World War I.[4]

The American public supported the President's policy. According to public opinion polls, 65 percent of Americans supported the creation of a Jewish state. During the third quarter of 1947 alone, 62,850 postcards, 1,100 letters and 1,400 telegrams flooded the White House, most urging the President to use American influence at the UN.[5]

This public support was reflected in Congress where a resolution approving the Balfour Declaration was adopted in 1922. In 1944, both national parties called for the restoration of the Jewish Commonwealth and, in 1945, a similar resolution was adopted by Congress.

Rather than giving in to pressure, Truman tended to react negatively to the "Jewish lobby." He complained repeatedly about being pressured and talked about putting propaganda from the Jews in a pile and striking a match to it. In a letter to Rep. Claude Pepper, Truman wrote: "Had it not been for the unwarranted interference of the Zionists, we would have had the matter settled a year and a half ago."[6] This was hardly the attitude of a politician overly concerned with Jewish votes.

MYTH

"The United States and Israel have nothing in common."

FACT

The U.S.-Israel relationship is based on the twin pillars of shared values and mutual interests. Given this commonality of interests and beliefs, it should not be surprising that support for Israel is one of the most pronounced and consistent foreign policy values of the American people.

Although Israel is geographically located in a region that is relatively undeveloped and closer to the Third World than the West, Israel has emerged in less than 60 years as an advanced nation with the characteristics of Western society. This is partially attributable to the fact that a high percentage of the population came from Europe or North America and brought with them Western political and cultural norms. It is also a function of the common Judeo-Christian heritage.

Simultaneously, Israel is a multicultural society with people from more than 100 nations. Today, nearly half of all Israelis are Eastern or Oriental Jews who trace their origins to the ancient Jewish communities of the Islamic countries of North Africa and the Middle East.

While they live in a region characterized by autocracies, Israelis have a commitment to democracy no less passionate than that of Americans. All citizens of Israel, regardless of race, religion or sex, are guaranteed equality before the law and full democratic rights. Freedom of speech, assembly and press is embodied in the country's laws and traditions. Israel's independent judiciary vigorously upholds these rights.

The political system does differ from America's—Israel's is a parliamentary democracy—but it is still based on free elections with divergent parties. And though Israel does not have a formal constitution, it has adopted "Basic Laws" that establish similar legal guarantees.

Americans have long viewed Israelis with admiration, at least partly because they see much of themselves in their pioneering spirit and struggle for independence. Like the United States, Israel is also a nation of immigrants. Despite the burden of spending nearly one-fifth of its budget on defense, it has had an extraordinary rate of economic growth for most of its history. It has also succeeded in putting most of the newcomers to work. As in America, immigrants to Israel have tried to make better lives for themselves and their children. Some have come from relatively undeveloped societies like Ethiopia or Yemen and arrived with virtually no possessions, education or training and become productive contributors to Israeli society.

Israelis also share Americans' passion for education. Israelis are among the most highly educated people in the world.

From the beginning, Israel had a mixed economy, combining capitalism with socialism along the British model. The economic difficulties Israel has experienced—created largely in the aftermath of the 1973 Yom Kippur War by increased oil prices and the need to spend a disproportionate share of its Gross National Product on defense—have led to a gradual movement toward a free market system analogous to that of the United States. America has been a partner in this evolution.

In the 1980's, attention increasingly focused on one pillar of the relationship—shared interests. This was done because of the threats to the region and because the means for strategic cooperation are more easily addressed with legislative initiatives. Despite the end of the Cold War, Israel continues to have a role to play in joint efforts to protect American interests, including close cooperation in the war on terror. Strategic cooperation has progressed to the point where a de facto alliance now exists. The hallmark of the relationship is consistency and trust: The United States knows it can count on Israel.

It is more difficult to devise programs that capitalize on the two nations' shared values than their security interests; nevertheless, such programs do exist. In fact, these *Shared Value Initiatives* cover a broad range of areas such as the environment, energy, space, education, occupational safety and health. More than 400 American institutions in 47 states, the District of Columbia and Puerto Rico have received funds from binational programs with Israel. Little-known relationships like the Free Trade Agreement, the Cooperative Development Research Program, the Middle East Regional Cooperation Program and various memoranda of understanding with virtually every U.S. governmental agency demonstrate the depth of the special relationship. Even more important may be the broad ties between Israel and each of the individual 50 states and the District of Columbia.

MYTH

"Most Americans oppose a close U.S. relationship with Israel."

FACT

Support for Israel is not restricted to the Jewish community. Americans of all ages, races and religions sympathize with Israel. This support is also nonpartisan, with a majority of Democrats and Republicans consistently favoring Israel by large margins over the Arabs.

The best indication of Americans' attitude toward Israel is found in the response to the most consistently asked question about the Middle East: "In the Middle East situation, are your sympathies more with Israel or with the Arab nations?" The organization that has conducted the most surveys is Gallup. Support for Israel in Gallup Polls has remained consistently around the 50 percent mark since 1967.

In 76 Gallup polls, going back to 1967, Israel has had the support of an average of 46 percent of the American people compared to just under 12 percent for the Arab states/Palestinians. Americans have slightly more sympathy for the Palestinians than for the Arab states, but the results of polls asking respondents to choose between Israel and the Palestinians have not differed significantly from the other surveys.

Some people have the misperception that sympathy for Israel was once much higher, but the truth is that before the Gulf War the peak had been 56 percent, reached just after the Six-Day War. In January 1991, sympathy for Israel reached a record high of 64 percent, according to Gallup. Meanwhile, support for the Arabs dropped to 8 percent and the margin was a record 56 points.

The most recent poll, reported by Gallup in February 2005, found that sympathy for Israel was 52 percent compared to only 18 percent for the Palestinians. Despite the violence of the preceding three years, and a steady stream of negative media coverage, this is nearly the same level of support Israel enjoyed after the 1967 war, when many people mistakenly believe that Israel was overwhelmingly popular. The figure for the Palestinians is the highest ever (on a few occasions questions asking about the "Arabs" received higher levels of support).

Polls also indicate the public views Israel as a reliable U.S. ally, a feeling that grew stronger during the Gulf crisis. A January 1991 Harris Poll, for example, found that 86 percent of Americans consider Israel a "close ally" or "friendly." This was the highest level ever recorded in a Harris Poll. The figure in 2005 was 72 percent, ranking

Israel fourth after Great Britain, Canada, and Australia. In a 2005 ADL poll, the figure was 71 percent, and a May 2003 survey sponsored by ARNSI, the Alliance for Research on National Security Issues, reported that 63 percent of Americans believe Israel is "a reliable ally of the U.S. in the fight against terrorism."

> *"The allied nations with the fullest concurrence of our government and people are agreed that in Palestine shall be laid the foundations of a Jewish Commonwealth."*
>
> **—President Woodrow Wilson, March 3, 1919**[7]

MYTH

"U.S. policy has always been hostile toward the Arabs."

FACT

Arabs rarely acknowledge the American role in helping the Arab states achieve independence. President Wilson's stand for self-determination for all nations, and the U.S. entry into World War I, helped cause the dissolution of the Ottoman Empire and stimulate the move toward independence in the Arab world.

The Arabs have always asserted that Middle East policy must be a zero-sum game whereby support for their enemy, Israel, necessarily puts them at a disadvantage. Thus, Arab states have tried to force the United States to choose between support for them or Israel. The U.S. has usually refused to fall into this trap. The fact that the U.S. has a close alliance with Israel while maintaining good relations with several Arab states is proof the two are not incompatible.

The U.S. has long sought friendly relations with Arab leaders and has, at one time or another, been on good terms with most Arab states. In the 1930s, the discovery of oil led U.S. companies to become closely involved with the Gulf Arabs. In the 1950s, U.S. strategic objectives stimulated an effort to form an alliance with pro-Western Arab states. Countries such as Iraq and Libya were friends of the U.S. before radical leaders took over those governments. Egypt, which was hostile toward the U.S. under Nasser, shifted to the pro-Western camp under Sadat.

Since World War II, the U.S. has poured economic and military assistance into the region and today is the principal backer of nations such as Jordan, Saudi Arabia, Morocco, Egypt and the Gulf sheikdoms. Although the Arab states blamed the U.S. for their defeats in wars they initiated with Israel, the truth is most of the belligerents had either been given or offered American assistance at some time.

MYTH

*"The United States has supported Israel
automatically ever since 1948."*

FACT

The United States has been Israel's closest ally throughout its history; nevertheless, the U.S. has acted against the Jewish State's wishes many times.

The U.S. effort to balance support for Israel with placating the Arabs began in 1948 when President Truman showed signs of wavering on partition and advocating trusteeship. After the surrounding Arab states invaded Israel, the U.S. maintained an arms embargo that severely restricted the Jews' ability to defend themselves.

Ever since the 1948 war, the U.S. has been unwilling to insist on projects to resettle Arab refugees. The U.S. has also been reluctant to challenge Arab violations of the UN Charter and resolutions. Thus, for example, the Arabs were permitted to get away with blockading the Suez Canal, imposing a boycott on Israel and committing acts of terrorism. In fact, the U.S. has taken positions against Israel at the UN more often than not, and did not use its Security Council veto to block an anti-Israel resolution until 1972.

Perhaps the most dramatic example of American policy diverging from that of Israel came during the Suez War when President Eisenhower took a strong stand against Britain, France and Israel. After the war, U.S. pressure forced Israel to withdraw from the territory it conquered. David Ben-Gurion relied on dubious American guarantees that sowed the seeds of the 1967 conflict.

At various other times, American Presidents have taken action against Israel. In 1981, for example, Ronald Reagan suspended a strategic cooperation agreement after Israel annexed the Golan Heights. On another occasion, he held up delivery of fighter planes because of unhappiness over an Israeli raid in Lebanon.

In 1991, President Bush held a press conference to ask for a delay in considering Israel's request for loan guarantees to help absorb Soviet and Ethiopian Jews because of his disagreement with Israel's settlement policy. In staking his prestige on the delay, Bush used intemperate language that inflamed passions and provoked concern in the Jewish community that anti-Semitism would be aroused.

Though often described as the most pro-Israel President in history, Bill Clinton also was critical of Israel on numerous occasions. George W. Bush's administration has also shown no reluctance to criticize Israel for actions it deems contrary to U.S. interests, but has generally been more reserved in its public statements. During the first year of the Palestinian War, the U.S. imposed an arms embargo on spare parts for helicopters because of anger over the use of U.S.-made helicopters in targeted killings. The Bush Administration also punished Israel for agreeing to sell military equipment to China in 2005.[8]

MYTH

"The U.S. has always given Israel arms to insure it would have a qualitative edge over the Arabs."

FACT

The United States provided only a limited amount of arms to Israel, including ammunition and recoilless rifles, prior to 1962. In that year, President Kennedy sold Israel HAWK anti-aircraft missiles, but only after the Soviet Union provided Egypt with long-range bombers.

By 1965, the U.S. had become Israel's main arms supplier. This was partially necessitated by West Germany's acquiescence to Arab pressure, which led it to stop selling tanks to Israel. Throughout most of the Johnson Administration, however, the sale of arms to Israel was balanced by corresponding transfers to the Arabs. Thus, the first U.S. tank sale to Israel, in 1965, was offset by a similar sale to Jordan.[9]

The U.S. did not provide Israel with aircraft until 1966. Even then, secret agreements were made to provide the same planes to Morocco and Libya, and additional military equipment was sent to Lebanon, Saudi Arabia and Tunisia.[10]

As in 1948, the U.S. imposed an arms embargo on Israel during the Six-Day War, while the Arabs continued to receive Soviet arms. Israel's position was further undermined by the French decision to embargo arms transfers to the Jewish State, effectively ending their role as Israel's only other major supplier.

It was only after it became clear that Israel had no other sources of arms, and that the Soviet Union had no interest in limiting its sales to the region, that President Johnson agreed to sell Israel Phantom jets that gave the Jewish State its first qualitative advantage. "We will henceforth become the principal arms supplier to Israel," Assistant Secretary of Defense Paul Warnke told Israeli Ambassador Yitzhak Rabin, "involving us even more intimately with Israel's security situation and involving more directly the security of the United States."[11]

From that point on, the U.S. began to pursue a policy whereby Israel's qualitative edge was maintained. The U.S. has also remained committed, however, to arming Arab nations, providing sophisticated missiles, tanks and aircraft to Jordan, Morocco, Egypt, Saudi Arabia and the Gulf states. Thus, when Israel received F-15s in 1978, so did Saudi Arabia (and Egypt received F-5Es). In 1981, Saudi Arabia, for the first time, received a weapons system that gave it a qualitative advantage over Israel—AWACS radar planes.

Today, Israel buys near top-of-the-line U.S. equipment, but many Arab states also receive some of America's best tanks, planes and missiles. The qualitative edge may be intact, but it is undoubtedly narrow.

"Our society is illuminated by the spiritual insights of the Hebrew prophets. America and Israel have a common love of human freedom, and they have a common faith in a democratic way of life."

—President Lyndon Johnson[12]

MYTH

"U.S. aid in the Middle East has always been one-sided, with the Arabs getting practically nothing."

FACT

After Israel's victory in its War of Independence, the U.S. responded to an appeal for economic aid to help absorb immigrants by approving a $135 million Export-Import Bank loan and the sale of surplus commodities. In those early years of Israel's statehood (also today), U.S. aid was seen as a means of promoting peace.

In 1951, Congress voted to help Israel cope with the economic burdens imposed by the influx of Jewish refugees from the displaced persons camps in Europe and from the ghettos of the Arab countries. Arabs then complained the U.S. was neglecting them, though they had no interest in or use for American aid then. In 1951, Syria rejected offers of U.S. aid. Oil-rich Iraq and Saudi Arabia did not need U.S. economic assistance, and Jordan was, until the late 1950s, the ward of Great Britain. After 1957, when the United States assumed responsibility for supporting Jordan and resumed economic aid to Egypt, assistance to the Arab states soared. Also, the United States was by far the biggest contributor of aid to the Palestinians through UNRWA, a status that continues to the present.

Israel has received more direct aid from the United States since World War II than any other country, but the amounts for the first half of this period were relatively small. Between 1949 and 1973, the U.S. provided Israel with an average of about $122 million a year, a total of $3.1 billion (and actually more than $1 billion of that was loans for military equipment in 1971–73). Prior to 1971, Israel received a total of only $277 million in military aid, all in the form of loans as credit sales. The bulk of the economic aid was also lent to Israel. By comparison, the Arab states received nearly three times as much aid before 1971, $4.4 billion, or $170 million per year. Moreover, unlike Israel, which receives nearly all its aid from the United States, Arab nations have gotten assistance from Asia, Eastern Europe, the Soviet Union and the European Community.

"It is my responsibility to see that our policy in Israel fits in with our policy throughout the world; second, it is my desire to help build in Palestine a strong, prosperous, free and independent democratic state. It must be large enough, free enough, and strong enough to make its people self-supporting and secure."

—President Harry Truman[13]

Israel did not begin to receive large amounts of assistance until 1974, following the 1973 war, and the sums increased dramatically after the Camp David agreements. Altogether, since 1949, Israel has received more than $90 billion in assistance. Though the totals are impressive, the value of assistance to Israel has been eroded by inflation.

Arab states that have signed agreements with Israel have also been rewarded. Since signing the peace treaty with Israel, Egypt has been the second largest recipient of U.S. foreign aid ($1.8 billion in 2005, Israel received $2.6 billion). Jordan has also been the beneficiary of higher levels of aid since it signed a treaty with Israel (increasing from less than $40 million to approximately $250 million). The multibillion dollar debts to the U.S. of both Arab nations were also forgiven.

After the Oslo agreements, the United States also began providing aid to the Palestinians. Funding for the West Bank and Gaza between 1993 and 2004 totaled approximately $1.3 billion. In May 2005, Congress passed a $200 million emergency aid package for the Palestinians aimed at promoting development projects in the West Bank and Gaza Strip. In an effort to strengthen Palestinian President Mahmoud Abbas, President Bush agreed to provide the Palestinian Authority with $50 million in direct aid. Past assistance had been indirect, paid through nongovernmental organizations, but these funds were deposited in a special account managed by Palestinian Finance Minister Salam Fayyad, who is widely credited with making the PA's finances more transparent. The money "is to be used to build housing, schools, roads, water facilities and health clinics in Gaza to help ease the transition as Israelis withdraw."[14]

MYTH

"Israel continues to demand large amounts of economic aid even though it is now a rich country that no longer needs help."

FACT

Starting with fiscal year 1987, Israel annually received $1.2 billion in all grant economic aid and $1.8 billion in all grant military assistance. In

1998, Israel offered to voluntarily reduce its dependence on U.S. economic aid. According to an agreement reached with the Clinton Administration and Congress, the economic aid package will be reduced by $120 million each year so that it will be phased out over 10 years. Half of the annual savings in economic assistance each year ($60 million) will be added to Israel's military aid package in recognition of its increased security needs.

Israel made the offer because it does not have the same need for assistance it once did. The foundation of Israel's economy today is strong; still, Israel remains saddled with past debts to the U.S., which, unlike those of Jordan and Egypt, were not forgiven. In addition, Israel still can use American help. The country has the tremendous financial burden of absorbing thousands of immigrants, a very high rate of unemployment and an alarmingly high number of people who fall below the poverty line. The situation was further exacerbated by the Palestinian War, which devastated the tourist industry and all related service sectors of the economy. Furthermore, concessions made in peace negotiations have required the dismantling of military bases and the loss of valuable resources that must be replaced. The cost of disengaging from Gaza alone is estimated at more than $2 billion.

In 2005, economic aid to Israel was expected to be reduced to $360 million while military aid was to be increased to $2.2 billion.

MYTH

"Israel boasts that it is the fourth strongest nation in the world, so it certainly doesn't need U.S. military assistance."

FACT

Israel has peace treaties with only two of its neighbors. It remains technically at war with the rest of the Arab/Islamic world, and several countries, notably Iran, are openly hostile. Given the potential threats, it is a necessity that Israel continue to maintain a strong defense.

As the arms balance chart in the Appendix indicates, Israel faces formidable enemies that could band together, as they have in the past, to threaten its security. It must, therefore, rely on its qualitative advantage to insure it can defeat its enemies, and that can only be guaranteed by the continued purchase of the latest weapons. New tanks, missiles and planes carry high price tags, however, and Israel cannot afford what it needs on its own, so continued aid from the United States is vital to its security. Furthermore, Israel's enemies have numerous suppliers, but Israel must rely almost entirely on the United States for its hardware.

MYTH

*"U.S. military aid subsidizes Israeli defense contractors
at the expense of American industry."*

FACT

Contrary to popular wisdom, the United States does not simply write
billion dollar checks and hand them over to Israel to spend as they like.
Only about 25 percent ($555 million of $2.2 billion in 2004) of what
Israel receives in Foreign Military Financing (FMF) can be spent in Is-

The Value of Foreign Military Financing (FMF) Orders by State[15]

Alabama	$78,276,940	Montana	$64,553
Arkansas	$81,801	North Carolina	$8,411,180
Arizona	$22,691,178	Nebraska	$240,000
California	$140,040,580	New Hampshire	$10,538,391
Colorado	$13,929,613	New Jersey	$40,998,939
Connecticut	$29,994,359	New Mexico	$118,093
D.C.	$44,555	Nevada	$518,921
Delaware	$225,251	New York	$114,131,158
Florida	$58,534,433	Ohio	$55,781,273
Georgia	$4,043,891	Oklahoma	$3,089,217
Hawaii	$65,000	Oregon	$3,458,387
Iowa	$2,745,748	Pennsylvania	$12,377,050
Illinois	$22,372,828	Rhode Island	$63,750
Indiana	$2,218,757	South Carolina	$1,215,324
Kansas	$19,194,285	South Dakota	$90,000
Kentucky	$33,275,716	Tennessee	$16,465,058
Louisiana	$36,900,038	Texas	$65,216,418
Massachusetts	$20,555,992	Utah	$347,871
Maryland	$41,821,169	Virginia	$10,094,379
Michigan	$30,304,390	Vermont	$180,929
Minnesota	$5,701,158	Washington	$3,630,537
Missouri	$2,563,271	Wisconsin	$6,523,873
Mississippi	$6,152,867	West Virginia	$35,910

rael for military procurement. The remaining 74 percent is spent in the United States to generate profits and jobs. More than 1,000 companies in 47 states, the District of Columbia and Puerto Rico have signed contracts worth billions of dollars through this program over the last several years. The figures for 2004 are on page 225.

MYTH

"Israel was never believed to have any strategic value to the United States."

FACT

In 1952, Gen. Omar Bradley, head of the Joint Chiefs of Staff, believed the West required 19 divisions to defend the Middle East and that Israel could supply two. He also expected only three states to provide the West air power in Middle Eastern defense by 1955: Great Britain, Turkey and Israel. Bradley's analysis was rejected because the political echelon decided it was more important for the United States to work with Egypt, and later Iraq. It was feared that integration of Israeli forces in Western strategy would alienate the Arabs.[16]

Israel's crushing victory over the combined Arab forces in 1967 caused this view to be revised. The following year, the United States sold Israel sophisticated planes (Phantom jets) for the first time. Washington shifted its Middle East policy from seeking a balance of forces to ensuring that Israel enjoyed a qualitative edge over its enemies.

Israel proved its value in 1970 when the United States asked for help in bolstering King Hussein's regime. Israel's willingness to aid Amman, and movement of troops to the Jordanian border, persuaded Syria to withdraw the tanks it had sent into Jordan to support PLO forces challenging the King during "Black September."[17]

By the early 1970s it was clear that no Arab state could or would contribute to Western defense in the Middle East. The Baghdad Pact had long ago expired, and the regimes friendly to the United States were weak compared to the anti-Western forces in Egypt, Syria and Iraq. Even after Egypt's reorientation following the signing of its peace treaty with Israel, the United States did not count on any Arab government for military assistance.

The Carter Administration began to implement a form of strategic cooperation (it was not referred to as such) by making Israel eligible to sell military equipment to the United States. The willingness to engage in limited, joint military endeavors was viewed by President Carter as a means of rewarding Israel for "good behavior" in peace talks with Egypt.

Though still reluctant to formalize the relationship, strategic cooperation became a major focus of the U.S.-Israel relationship when Ronald Reagan entered office. Before his election, Reagan had written: "Only by full appreciation of the critical role the State of Israel plays in our strategic calculus can we build the foundation for thwarting Moscow's designs on territories and resources vital to our security and our national well-being."[18]

Reagan's view culminated in the November 30, 1981, signing of a Memorandum of Understanding on "strategic cooperation." On November 29, 1983, a new agreement was signed creating the Joint Political-Military Group (JPMG) and a group to oversee security assistance, the Joint Security Assistance Planning Group (JSAP).

In 1987, Congress designated Israel as a major non-NATO ally. This law formally established Israel as an ally, and allowed its industries to compete equally with NATO countries and other close U.S. allies for contracts to produce a significant number of defense items.

"Since the rebirth of the State of Israel, there has been an ironclad bond between that democracy and this one."

—President Ronald Reagan[19]

In April 1988, President Reagan signed another MOU encompassing all prior agreements. This agreement institutionalized the strategic relationship.

By the end of Reagan's term, the U.S. had prepositioned equipment in Israel, regularly held joint training exercises, began co-development of the Arrow Anti-Tactical Ballistic Missile and was engaged in a host of other cooperative military endeavors. Since then, U.S.-Israel strategic cooperation has continued to evolve. Israel now regularly engages in joint training exercises with U.S. forces and, in 2005, for the first time, also trained and exercised with NATO forces.

Today, strategic ties are stronger than ever and Israel has become a de facto ally of the United States.

MYTH

"The employment of Jonathan Pollard to spy on the United States is proof that Israel works against American interests."

FACT

In November 1985, the FBI arrested Jonathan Pollard, a U.S. Navy intelligence analyst, on charges of selling classified material to Israel. Pollard was subsequently sentenced to life imprisonment. His wife, Anne, was sentenced to five years in jail for assisting her husband.

Immediately upon Pollard's arrest, Israel apologized and explained that the operation was unauthorized. "It is Israel's policy to refrain from any intelligence activity related to the United States," an official government statement declared, "in view of the close and special relationship of friendship" between the two countries. Prime Minister Shimon Peres stated: "Spying on the United States stands in total contradiction to our policy."[20] The United States and Israel worked together to investigate the Pollard affair. The Israeli inquiry revealed that Pollard was not working for Israeli military intelligence or the Mossad. He was directed by a small, independent scientific intelligence unit. Pollard initiated the contact with the Israelis.

A subcommittee of the Knesset's Defense and Foreign Affairs Committee on Intelligence and Security Services concluded: "Beyond all doubt . . . the operational echelons (namely: the Scientific Liaison Unit headed by Rafael Eitan) decided to recruit and handle Pollard without any check or consultation with the political echelon or receiving its direct or indirect approval." The Knesset committee took the government to task for not properly supervising the scientific unit.

As promised to the U.S. government, the spy unit that directed Pollard was disbanded, his handlers punished and the stolen documents returned.[21] The last point was crucial to the U.S. Department of Justice's case against Pollard.

Pollard denied spying "against" the United States. He said he provided only information he believed was vital to Israeli security and was being withheld by the Pentagon. This included data on Soviet arms shipments to Syria, Iraqi and Syrian chemical weapons, the Pakistani atomic bomb project and Libyan air defense systems.[22]

Pollard was convicted of espionage. His life sentence was the most severe prison term ever given for spying for an ally. It also was far greater than the average term imposed for spying for the Soviet Union and other enemies of the United States.[23]

Though initially shunned by Israel, the government of Benjamin Netanyahu admitted that Pollard had worked for Israeli intelligence and granted him citizenship. Netanyahu requested clemency for Pollard during Middle East peace talks at the Wye Plantation in Maryland in 1998. Since then, Israeli officials have made additional entreaties on Pollard's behalf.

Pollard's supporters in the United States also routinely request that he be pardoned. President Clinton reportedly considered a pardon, but defense and intelligence agency officials vigorously opposed the idea. At the end of Clinton's term, the issue was again raised and Sen. Richard Shelby (R-AL), chairman of the Senate's Select Committee on Intelligence, along with a majority of senators argued against a pardon. "Mr. Pollard is a convicted spy who put our national security at risk and endangered the lives of our intelligence officers," Shelby said. "There not terms strong enough to express my belief that Mr. Pollard should serve every minute of his sentence. . . ."[24]

In November 2003, a federal judge rejected requests by Pollard to appeal his life sentence and review classified government documents that Pollard said would prove his spying was not as damaging or as extensive as prosecutors had charged. The judge said that Pollard had waited too long—more than a decade after it was imposed—to object to his sentence and ruled that Pollard's attorneys offered no compelling justification for seeing the sealed intelligence documents.[25]

A U.S. federal appeals court in July 2005 rejected Pollard's claim that he had inadequate counsel in his original trial and denied his request to downgrade his life sentence. The court also denied Pollard's attorneys access to classified information they hoped would help in their attempt to win presidential clemency for their client. The rulings leave Pollard with little recourse but the Supreme Court to change his fate.[26]

MYTH

"U.S. dependence on Arab oil has decreased over the years."

FACT

In 1973, the Arab oil embargo dealt the U.S. economy a major blow. This, combined with OPEC's subsequent price hikes and a growing American dependence on foreign oil, triggered the recession in the early seventies.

In 1973, foreign oil accounted for 35 percent of total U.S. oil demand. By 2005, the figure had risen to 57 percent, and Arab OPEC countries accounted for 26 percent of 2004 U.S. imports (with non-Arab countries Indonesia, Venezuela, and Nigeria, the figure is 50 percent). Saudi Arabia ranked number three and Iraq (#6), Algeria (#7) and Kuwait (#12) were among the top 20 suppliers of petroleum products to the United States in 2004. The Persian Gulf states alone supply 24 percent of U.S. petroleum imports.[27]

The growing reliance on imported oil has also made the U.S. economy even more vulnerable to price jumps, as occurred in 1979, 1981, 1982, 1990, 2000 and 2005. Oil price increases have also allowed Arab oil-producers to generate tremendous revenues at the expense of American consumers. These profits have subsidized large weapons purchases and nonconventional weapons programs such as Iran's.

America's dependence on Arab oil has occasionally raised the specter of a renewed attempt to blackmail the United States to abandon its support for Israel. In April 2002, for example, Iraq suspended oil shipments for a month to protest Israel's operation to root out terrorists in the West Bank. No other Arab oil producers followed suit and the Iraqi action had little impact on oil markets and no effect on policy.

The good news for Americans is that the top two suppliers of U.S. oil today—Canada and Mexico—are more reliable and better allies than the Persian Gulf nations.

MYTH

"America's support of Israel is the reason that terrorists attacked the World Trade Center and Pentagon on September 11."

FACT

The heinous attacks against the United States were committed by Muslim fanatics who had a variety of motivations for these and other terrorist attacks. These Muslims have a perverted interpretation of Islam and believe they must attack infidels, particularly Americans and Jews, who do not share their beliefs. They oppose Western culture and democracy and object to any U.S. presence in Muslim nations. They are particularly angered by the existence of American military bases in Saudi Arabia and other areas of the Persian Gulf. This would be true regardless of U.S. policy toward the Israeli-Palestinian conflict. Nevertheless, an added excuse for their fanaticism is the fact that the United States is allied with Israel. Previous attacks on American targets, such as the *USS Cole* and U.S. embassies in Kenya and Tanzania, were perpetrated by suicide bombers whose anger at the United States had little or nothing to do with Israel.

> *"Osama bin Laden made his explosions and then started talking about the Palestinians. He never talked about them before."*
>
> **—Egyptian President Hosni Mubarak**[28]

Osama bin Laden claimed he was acting on behalf of the Palestinians, and that his anger toward the United States was shaped by American support for Israel. This was a new invention by bin Laden clearly intended to attract support from the Arab public and justify his terrorist acts. Bin Laden's antipathy toward the United States has never been related to the Arab-Israeli conflict. Though many Arabs were taken in by bin Laden's transparent effort to drag Israel into his war, Dr. Abd Al-Hamid Al-Ansari, dean of Shar'ia and Law at Qatar University was critical, "In their hypocrisy, many of the [Arab] intellectuals linked September 11 with the Palestinian problem—something that completely contradicts seven years of Al-Qaida literature. Al-Qaida never linked anything to Palestine."[29]

Even Yasser Arafat told the *Sunday Times* of London that bin Laden should stop hiding behind the Palestinian cause. Bin Laden "never helped us, he was working in another completely different area and against our interests," Arafat said.[30]

Though Al-Qaida's agenda did not include the Palestinian cause, the organization has begun to take a more active role in terror against Israeli targets, starting with the November 28, 2002, suicide bombing at an Israeli-owned hotel in Kenya that killed three Israelis and 11 Kenyans, and the attempt to shoot down an Israeli airliner with a missile as it was taking off from Kenya that same day.[31] Al-Qaida operatives have also now has begun to infiltrate the Palestinian Authority.[32]

MYTH

"The hijacking of four airliners in one day, on September 11, was an unprecedented act of terror."

FACT

The scale of the massacre and destruction on September 11 was indeed unprecedented, as was the use of civilian aircraft as bombs. The coordinated hijackings, however, were not new.

On September 6, 1970, members of the Popular Front for the Liberation of Palestine (PFLP) hijacked three jets (Swissair, TWA and Pan Am) with more than 400 passengers on flights to New York. A fourth plane, an El Al flight, was also targeted, but Israeli security agents foiled the hijacking in mid-air and killed one of the two terrorists when they tried to storm the cockpit. On the 9th, a British BOAC jet was also hijacked by the PFLP.[33]

The UN could not muster a condemnation of the hijackings. A Security Council Resolution only went so far as to express grave concern, and did not even bring the issue to a vote.

Instead of flying their planes into buildings, they landed them on airfields (three in Jordan, one in Egypt). All four hijacked planes were blown up on the ground—after the passengers were taken off the planes—on September 12.

More than three dozen Americans were among the passengers who were then held hostage in Jordan as the terrorists attempted to blackmail the Western governments and Israel to swap the hostages for Palestinian terrorists held in their jails. On September 14, after releasing all but 55 hostages, the terrorists said all American hostages would be treated as Israelis. A tense standoff ensued. Seven terrorists were ultimately set free by Britain, Germany and Switzerland in exchange for the hostages.[34]

After the hijackings, shocked members of Congress called for immediate and forceful action by the United States and international community. They insisted on quick adoption of measures aimed at preventing air piracy, punishing the perpetrators and recognizing the responsibility of nations that harbor them.[35] Virtually nothing was done until 31 years later.

The PFLP as an organization, and some of the individual participants responsible for those hijackings still are alive and well, supported by Syria, the Palestinian Authority and others. In fact, Leila Khaled, the person who tried to hijack the El Al jet, was going to be admitted into the territories to attend the Palestine National Council meetings in 1996, but she still refused to disavow terrorism. Today, she is said to live in Amman.

MYTH

"Israel's Mossad carried out the bombing of the World Trade Center to provoke American hatred of Arabs."

FACT

Syrian Defense Minister Mustafa Tlass told a delegation from Great Britain that Israel was responsible for the September 11, 2001, attacks on the United States. He claimed the Mossad had warned thousands of Jewish employees not to go to work that day at the World Trade Center. He was the highest-ranking Arab public official to publicly voice a view that is widespread in the Arab world that the attacks were part of a Jewish conspiracy to provoke U.S. retaliation against the Arab world and to turn American public opinion against Muslims. One poll published in the Lebanese newspaper *An Nahar,* for example, found that 31 percent of the respondents believed Israel was responsible for the hijackings while only 27 percent blamed Osama bin Laden. A *Newsweek* poll found that a plurality of Egyptians believed the Jews were responsible for the Trade Center bombings.[36]

The conspiracy theory is also being circulated by American Muslim leaders. Imam Mohammed Asi of the Islamic Center of Washington said Israeli officials decided to launch the attack after the United States refused their request to put down the Palestinian intifada. "If we're not going to be secure, neither are you," was the Israelis' thinking following the U.S. response, according to Asi.[37]

No U.S. authority has suggested, nor has any evidence been produced, to suggest any Israeli or Jew had any role in the terrorist attacks. These conspiracy theories are complete nonsense and reflect the degree to which many people in the Arab world are prepared to accept anti-Semitic fabrications and the mythology of Jewish power. They may also reflect a refusal to believe that Muslims could be responsible for the atrocities and the hope that they could be blamed on the Jews.

MYTH

"Groups like Hizballah, Islamic Jihad, Hamas and the PFLP are freedom fighters and not terrorists."

FACT

When the United States declared a war on terrorists and the nations that harbor them after September 11, Arab states and their sympathizers argued that many of the organizations that engage in violent actions against

Americans and Israelis should not be targets of the new American war because they are "freedom fighters" rather than terrorists. This has been the mantra of the terrorists themselves, who claim that their actions are legitimate forms of resistance against the "Israeli occupation."

This argument is deeply flawed. First, the enemies of Israel rationalize any attacks as legitimate because of real and imagined sins committed by Jews since the beginning of the 20th century. Consequently, the Arab bloc and its supporters at the United Nations have succeeded in blocking the condemnation of any terrorist attacks against Israel. Instead, they routinely sponsor resolutions criticizing Israel when it retaliates.

Second, nowhere else in the world is the murder of innocent men, women and children considered a "legitimate form of resistance." The long list of heinous crimes includes snipers shooting infants, suicide bombers blowing up pizzerias and discos, hijackers taking and killing hostages, and infiltrators murdering Olympic athletes. Hizballah, Islamic Jihad, Hamas, the PFLP, and a number of other groups, mostly Palestinian, have engaged in these activities for decades and rarely been condemned or brought to justice. All of them qualify as terrorist groups according to the U.S. government's own definition—"Terrorism is the unlawful use of force or violence against persons or property to intimidate or coerce a government, the civilian population, or any segment thereof, in furtherance of political or social objectives"[38]—and therefore should be targets of U.S. efforts to cut off their funding, to root out their leaders and to bring them to justice.

In the case of the Palestinian groups, there is no mystery as to who the leaders are, where their funding comes from and which nations harbor them. American charitable organizations have been linked to funding some of these groups and Saudi Arabia, Syria, Lebanon, Iraq, Iran and the Palestinian Authority all shelter and/or financially and logistically support them.

"You can't say there are good terrorists and there are bad terrorists."

—U.S. National Security Adviser Condoleezza Rice[39]

MYTH

"American universities should divest from companies that do business in Israel to force an end to Israeli 'occupation' and human rights abuses."

FACT

The word "peace" does not appear in divestment petitions, which makes clear the intent is not to resolve the conflict but to delegitimize Israel. Petitioners blame Israel for the lack of peace and demand that it make unilateral concessions without requiring anything of the Palestinians, not even the cessation of terrorism. Divestment advocates also ignore Israel's efforts during the Oslo peace process, and at the summit meetings with President Clinton, to reach historic compromises with the Palestinians that would have created a Palestinian state. Even after Israel completely withdrew from the Gaza Strip, certain individuals and groups persisted in their campaign to undermine Israel and further demonstrated that they are interested in Israel's destruction rather than any territorial compromise.

The divestment campaign against South Africa was specifically directed at companies that were using that country's racist laws to their advantage. In Israel no such racist laws exist; moreover, companies doing business there adhere to the same standards of equal working rights that are applied in the United States.

Harvard University President Lawrence Summers observed that the divestment efforts are anti-Semitic. "Profoundly anti-Israel views are increasingly finding support in progressive intellectual communities," said Summers. "Serious and thoughtful people are advocating and taking actions that are anti-Semitic in their effect, if not their intent."[40]

Peace in the Middle East will come only from direct negotiations between the parties, and only after the Arab states recognize Israel's right to exist, and the Palestinians and other Arabs cease their support of terror. American universities cannot help through misguided divestment campaigns that unfairly single out Israel as the source of conflict in the region. Divestment proponents hope to tar Israel with an association with apartheid South Africa, an offensive comparison that ignores the fact that all Israeli citizens are equal under the law.

MYTH

"Advocates for Israel try to silence critics by labeling them anti-Semitic."

FACT

Criticizing Israel does not necessarily make someone anti-Semitic. The determining factor is the intent of the commentator. Legitimate critics accept Israel's right to exist, whereas anti-Semites do not. Anti-Semites use double standards when they criticize Israel, for example, denying Israelis the right to pursue their legitimate claims while encouraging the Palestinians to do so. Anti-Semites deny Israel the right to defend itself, and ignore Jewish victims, while blaming Israel for pursuing their murderers. Anti-Semites rarely, if ever, make positive statements about Israel. Anti-Semites describe Israelis using pejorative terms and hate-speech, suggesting, for example, that they are "racists" or "Nazis."

Natan Sharansky has suggested a "3-D" test for differentiating legitimate criticism of Israel from anti-Semitism. The first "D" is the test of whether Israel or its leaders are being demonized or their actions blown out of proportion. Equating Israel with Nazi Germany is one example of demonization. The second "D" is the test of double standards. An example is when Israel is singled out for condemnation at the United Nations for perceived human rights abuses while nations that violate human rights on a massive scale, such as Iran, Syria, and Saudi Arabia, are not even mentioned. The third "D" is the test of delegitimization. Questioning Israel's legitimacy, that is, its right to exist is always anti-Semitic.[41]

No campaign exists to prevent people from expressing negative opinions about Israeli policy. In fact, the most vociferous critics of Israel are Israelis themselves who use their freedom of speech to express their concerns every day. A glance at any Israeli newspaper will reveal a surfeit of articles questioning particular government policies. Anti-Semites, however, do not share Israelis' interest in improving the society; their goal is to delegitimize the state in the short-run, and destroy it in the long-run. There is nothing Israel could do to satisfy these critics.

MYTH

"Arab-Americans are a powerful voting bloc that U.S. presidential candidates must pander to for votes."

FACT

Arab-Americans represent a tiny fraction (less than one-half of one percent) of the U.S. population. Unlike American Jews, who are overwhelmingly supportive of Israel, Arab-Americans are not a monolithic group. There are approximately 1.2 million Arabs in the United States, and they tend to reflect the general discord of the Arab world, which has twenty-one states with competing interests.

While the Palestinian cause receives most of the media's attention, because of the salience of the Arab-Israeli conflict and the omnipresence of a handful of activists and vocal Palestinian spokespersons, the reality is that only about 70,000 Palestinians (6 percent of all Arab-Americans) live in the United States. Roughly 38 percent of Arab-Americans are Lebanese, primarily Christians.

In addition, while attention has focused on the allegedly growing political strength of Muslims in the United States, fewer than one-fourth of all Arab-Americans are Muslims.[42] Christian Arabs, especially those from Lebanon, do not typically support the Palestinians' anti-Israel agenda, largely because of their history of mistreatment by Palestinians and Muslims.

Consequently, Arab-American voters do not pursue a positive agenda of strengthening U.S.-Arab ties; instead, they focus on weakening U.S.-Israel relations. Presidential candidates, however, and most Americans, historically view Israel as an ally that supports American interests, and are unwilling to support a reversal of this longstanding policy. The divisions were apparent in 2000 when George W. Bush was viewed with suspicion by most Jewish voters and considered likely to be more sympathetic to the Arab cause by Arab-Americans. In that election, 45 percent of Arab-Americans nationwide voted for George Bush, 38 percent for Al Gore, and 13 percent for Ralph Nader (who, incidentally, is of Lebanese descent).[43] The situation changed dramatically in 2004 when Arab-Americans perceived Bush as pro-Israel, and were disturbed by his support for security measures that they viewed as threats to their civil liberties. Consequently, John Kerry received 63 percent of the Arab-American vote, while President Bush won 28 percent.[44] Once again, this constituency did not change the outcome.

Even if Arab-Americans vote as a bloc, their influence is marginal, and restricted to a handful of states. About half of the Arab population is concentrated in five states—California, Florida, Michigan, New Jersey, and New York—that are all key to the electoral college. Still, the Arab population is dwarfed by that of the Jews in every one of these states except Michigan.

Jewish and Arab Populations in Key States[45]

State	Arab Population	Arabs as % of Total State Population	Jewish Population	Jews as % of Total State Population
CA	142,805	.48	999,000	2.9
FL	49,206	.38	628,000	3.9
MI	76,504	.82	110,000	1.1
NJ	46,381	.60	485,000	5.7
NY	94,319	.52	1,657,000	8.7

MYTH

"The United States must be 'engaged' to advance the peace process."

FACT

The European Union, Russia, and the UN all have pursued largely one-sided policies in the Middle East detrimental to Israel, which has disqualified them as honest brokers. The United States is the only country that has the trust of both the Israelis and the Arabs and is therefore the only third party that can play a constructive role in the peace process. This has led many people to call for greater involvement by the Bush Administration in negotiations. While the United States can play a valuable role as a mediator, history shows that American peace initiatives have never succeeded, and that it is the parties themselves who must resolve their differences.

The Eisenhower Administration tried to ease tensions by proposing the joint Arab-Israeli use of the Jordan River. The plan would have helped the Arab refugees by producing more irrigated land and would have reduced Israel's need for more water resources. Israel cautiously accepted the plan, the Arab League rejected it.

President Johnson outlined five principles for peace. "The first and greatest principle," Johnson said, "is that every nation in the area has a fundamental right to live and to have this right respected by its neighbors." The Arab response came a few weeks later: "no peace with Israel, no recognition of Israel, no negotiations with it...."

President Nixon's Secretary of State, William Rogers, offered a plan that sought to "balance" U.S. policy, but leaned on the Israelis to withdraw to the pre-1967 borders, to accept many Palestinian refugees, and to allow Jordan a role in Jerusalem. The plan was totally unacceptable to Israel and, even though it tilted toward the Arab position, was rejected by the Arabs as well.

President Ford's Secretary of State, Henry Kissinger, had a little more success in his shuttle diplomacy, arranging the disengagement of forces after the 1973 war, but he never put forward a peace plan, and failed to move the parties beyond the cessation of hostilities to the formalization of peace.

Jimmy Carter was the model for presidential engagement in the conflict. He wanted an international conference at Geneva to produce a comprehensive peace. While Carter spun his wheels trying to organize a conference, Egyptian President Anwar Sadat decided to bypass the Americans and go directly to the Israeli people and address the Knesset.

Despite revisionist history by Carter's former advisers, the Israeli-Egyptian peace agreement was negotiated largely *despite* Carter. Menachem Begin and Sadat had carried on secret contacts long before Camp David and had reached the basis for an agreement before Carter's intervention. Carter's mediation helped seal the treaty, but Sadat's decision to go to Jerusalem was stimulated largely by his conviction that Carter's policies were misguided.

In 1982, President Reagan announced a surprise peace initiative that called for allowing the Palestinians self-rule in the territories in association with Jordan. The plan rejected both Israeli annexation and the creation of a Palestinian state. Israel denounced the plan as endangering Israeli security. The plan had been formulated largely to pacify the Arab states, which had been angered by the expulsion of the PLO from Beirut, but they also rejected the Reagan Plan.

George Bush's Administration succeeded in convening a historic regional conference in Madrid in 1991, but it ended without any agreements and the multilateral tracks that were supposed to resolve some of the more contentious issues rarely met and failed to resolve anything. Moreover, Bush's perceived hostility toward Israel eroded trust and made it difficult to convince Israelis to take risks for peace.

President Clinton barely had time to get his vision of peace together when he discovered the Israelis had secretly negotiated an agreement with the Palestinians in Oslo. The United States had nothing to do with the breakthrough at Oslo and very little influence on the immediate aftermath. In fact, the peace process became increasingly muddled as the United States got more involved.

Peace with Jordan also required no real American involvement. The Israelis and Jordanians already were agreed on the main terms of peace, and the main obstacle had been King Hussein's unwillingness to sign a treaty before Israel had reached an agreement with the Palestinians. After Oslo, he felt safe to move forward and no American plan was needed.

In a last ditch effort to save his presidential legacy, Clinton put forward a peace plan to establish a Palestinian state. Again, it was Prime Minister Ehud Barak's willingness to offer dramatic concessions that raised the prospects for an agreement rather than the President's initiative. Even after Clinton was prepared to give the Palestinians a state in virtually all the West Bank and Gaza, and to make east Jerusalem their capital, the Palestinians rejected the deal.

President George W. Bush also offered a plan, but it was undercut by Yasser Arafat, who obstructed the required reforms of the Palestinian Authority, and refused to dismantle the terrorist infrastructure and stop the violence. Bush's plan morphed into the road map, which drew the support of Great Britain, France, Russia, and the United Nations, but has not been implemented because of the continuing Palestinian violence. The peace process only began to move again when Prime Minister Ariel Sharon made his disengagement proposal, a unilateral approach the State Department had long opposed. Rather than try to capitalize on the momentum created by Israel's evacuation of the Gaza Strip, however, the Bush Administration remains wedded to its plan, which stalled because Mahmoud Abbas has been unable and/or unwilling to fulfill his commitments.

History has shown that Middle East peace is not made in America. Only the parties can decide to end the conflict, and the terms that will be acceptable. No American plan has ever succeeded, and it is unlikely one will bring peace. The end to the Arab-Israeli conflict will not be achieved through American initiatives or intense involvement; it will be possible only when Arab leaders have the courage to follow the examples of Sadat and Hussein and resolve to live in peace with Israel.

Notes

1. *Foreign Relations of the United States 1947,* (DC: GPO, 1948), pp. 1173-4, 1198-9, 1248, 1284. [Henceforth FRUS 1947.]
2. Mitchell Bard, *The Water's Edge And Beyond,* (NJ: Transaction Publishers, 1991), p. 132.
3. FRUS 1947, p. 1313.
4. Harry Truman, *Years of Trial and Hope,* Vol. 2, (NY: Doubleday, 1956), p. 156.
5. John Snetsinger, *Truman, The Jewish Vote and the Creation of Israel,* (CA: Hoover Institution Press, 1974), pp. 9-10; David Schoenbaum, "The United States and the Birth of Israel," *Wiener Library Bulletin,* (1978), p. 144n.
6. Peter Grose, *Israel in the Mind of America,* (NY: Alfred A. Knopf, 1983), p. 217; Michael Cohen, "Truman, The Holocaust and the Establishment of the State of Israel," *Jerusalem Quarterly,* (Spring 1982), p. 85.
7. Mitchell Bard, *U.S.-Israel Relations: Looking to the Year 2000,* AIPAC Papers on U.S.-Israel Relations, (1991), p. 3.
8. Nathan Guttman, "US Stopped parts sales during intifada," *Jerusalem Post,* (September 22, 2005); Ze'ev Schiff, "U.S. Sanctions still in place, despite deal over security exports," *Haaretz,* (August 28, 2005).
9. Memorandum of conversation regarding Harriman-Eshkol talks, (February 25, 1965); Memorandum of conversation between Ambassador Avraham Harman and W. Averill Harriman, Ambassador-at-Large, (March 15, 1965), LBJ Library; Yitzhak Rabin, *The Rabin Memoirs,* (MA: Little Brown and Company, 1979), pp. 65-66.
10. Robert Trice, "Domestic Political Interests and American Policy in the Middle East: Pro-Israel, Pro-Arab and Corporate Non-Governmental Actors and the Making of American Foreign Policy, 1966-1971," (Unpublished Ph.D. Dissertation, University of Wisconsin-Madison, 1974), pp. 226-230.
11. Memorandum of conversation between Yitzhak Rabin et al., and Paul Warnke et al., (November 4, 1968), LBJ Library.
12. Speech to B'nai B'rith on September 10, 1968, cited in Bernard Reich, *Quest for Peace,* (NJ: Transaction Books, 1977), p. 423n.
13. Truman campaign speech, Madison Square Garden, (October 28, 1948).
14. USAID; *Washington Post,* (May 27, 2005).
15. Israeli Ministry of Defense.
16. Dore Gold, *America, the Gulf, and Israel,* (CO: Westview Press, 1988), p. 84.
17. Yitzhak Rabin, address to conference on "Strategy and Defense in the Eastern Mediterranean," sponsored by the Washington Institute for Near East Policy and Israel Military Correspondents Association, Jerusalem, (July 9-11, 1986).
18. Ronald Reagan, "Recognizing the Israeli Asset," *Washington Post,* (August 15, 1979).
19. Reagan Address to B'nai B'rith, September 3, 1980, cited in Mitchell Bard, *U.S.-Israel Relations: Looking to the Year 2000,* AIPAC Papers on U.S.-Israel Relations, p. 6.
20. Wolf Blitzer, *Territory of Lies,* (NY: Harper & Row, 1989), p. 201.
21. *New York Times,* (December 2 and 21, 1985).
22. Blitzer, pp. 166-171.
23. Alan Dershowitz, *Chutzpah,* (MA: Little Brown, & Co., 1991), pp. 289-312.
24. *Washington Post,* (December 23, 2000).
25. *Washington Post,* (November 14, 2003).

26. Matthew E. Berger, "After court denies his appeal, Pollard left with few legal options," Jewish Telegraphic Agency, (July 24, 2005).
27. Energy Information Administration; Oak Ridge National Laboratory.
28. *Newsweek,* (October 29, 2001).
29. *Al-Raya* (Qatar), (January 6, 2002).
30. *Washington Post,* (December 16, 2002).
31. CNN, (December 3, 2002).
32. *Maariv,* (October 17, 2005).
33. Henry Kissinger, *The White House Years.* (MA: Little Brown & Co., 1979), pp. 600-617.
34. *Guardian Unlimited,* (January 1, 2001).
35. *Near East Report,* (September 16, 1970).
36. *Jerusalem Post,* (October 19, 2001); *Newsweek* poll quoted in "Protocols," *The New Republic Online,* (October 30, 2001).
37. Jewish Telegraphic Agency, (November 2, 2001).
38. *Washington Post,* (September 13, 2001).
39. *Jerusalem Post,* (October 17, 2001).
40. Address at morning prayers, Memorial Church, Cambridge, Massachusetts, (September 17, 2002), Office of the President, Harvard University.
41. Natan Sharansky, "Antisemitism in 3-D," *Forward,* (January 21, 2005), p. 9.
42. Alex Ionides, "Getting Their House Together," *Egypt Today,* (November 2003).
43. "Poll: Bush losing Arab-American support," Zogby International, (March 13, 2004).
44. James Zogby, "Arab Americans in election 2004," Arab American Institute—November 15, 2004, in American Muslim Perspective, [http://www.ampolitics.ghazali.net/html/arab_americans2.html].
45. U.S. Census Bureau (2000).

19. The Peace Process

MYTH

"Anwar Sadat deserves all of the credit for the Egyptian-Israeli peace treaty."

FACT

The peace drive did not begin with President Anwar Sadat's November 1977 visit to Jerusalem. Sadat's visit was unquestionably a courageous act of statesmanship. But it came only after more than a half-century of efforts by early Zionist and Israeli leaders to negotiate peace with the Arabs.

"For Israel to equal the drama," said Simcha Dinitz, former Israeli Ambassador to the U.S., "we would have had to declare war on Egypt, maintain belligerent relations for years, refuse to talk to them, call for their annihilation, suggest throwing them into the sea, conduct military operations and terrorism against them, declare economic boycotts, close the Strait of Tiran to their ships, close the Suez Canal to their traffic, and say they are outcasts of humanity. Then Mr. Begin would go to Cairo, and his trip would be equally dramatic. Obviously, we could not do this, because it has been our policy to negotiate all along."[1]

Nonetheless, Israeli Prime Minister Menachem Begin proved that, like Sadat, he was willing to go the extra mile to achieve peace. Although he faced intense opposition from within his Likud Party, Begin froze Israeli settlements in the West Bank to facilitate the progress of negotiations. Despite the Carter Administration's tilt toward Egypt during the talks, Begin remained determined to continue the peace process. In the end, he agreed to give the strategically critical Sinai—91 percent of the territory won by Israel during the Six-Day War—back to Egypt in exchange for Sadat's promise to make peace.

In recognition of his willingness to join Sadat in making compromises for peace, Begin shared the 1978 Nobel Peace Prize with the Egyptian leader.

MYTH

"Egypt made all the concessions for peace."

FACT

Israel made tangible concessions to Egypt in exchange only for promises.

Israel—which had repeatedly been the target of shipping blockades, military assaults and terrorist attacks staged from the area—made far greater economic and strategic sacrifices in giving up the Sinai than Egypt did in normalizing relations with Israel. While it received additional U.S. aid for withdrawing, Israel gave up much of its strategic depth in the Sinai, returning the area to a neighbor that had repeatedly used it as a launching point for attacks. Israel also relinquished direct control of its shipping lanes to and from Eilat, 1,000 miles of roadways, homes, factories, hotels, health facilities and agricultural villages.

Because Egypt insisted that Jewish civilians leave the Sinai, 7,000 Israelis were uprooted from their homes and businesses, which they had spent years building in the desert. This was a physically and emotionally wrenching experience, particularly for the residents of Yamit, who had to be forcibly removed from their homes by soldiers.

Israel also lost electronic early-warning stations situated on Sinai mountaintops that provided data on military movement on the western side of the Suez Canal, as well as the areas near the Gulf of Suez and the Gulf of Eilat, which were vital to defending against an attack from the east. Israel was forced to relocate more than 170 military installations, airfields and army bases after it withdrew.

By turning over the Sinai to Egypt, Israel may have given up its only chance to become energy-independent. The Alma oil field in the southern Sinai, discovered and developed by Israel, was transferred to Egypt in November 1979. When Israel gave up this field, it had become the country's largest single source of energy, supplying half the country's energy needs. Israel, which estimated the value of untapped reserves in the Alma field at $100 billion, had projected that continued development there would make the country self-sufficient in energy by 1990.

Israel also agreed to end military rule in the West Bank and Gaza, withdraw its troops from certain parts of the territories and work toward Palestinian autonomy. The Begin government did this though no Palestinian Arab willing to recognize Israel came forward to speak on behalf of residents of the territories.

In 1988, Israel relinquished Taba—a resort built by Israel in what had been a barren desert area near Eilat—to Egypt. Taba's status had not been resolved by the Camp David Accords. When an international arbitration panel ruled in Cairo's favor on September 29, 1988, Israel turned the town over to Egypt.

MYTH

"The Palestinian question is the core of the Arab-Israeli conflict."

FACT

In reality, the Palestinian Arab question is the result of the conflict, which stems from Arab unwillingness to accept a Jewish State in the Middle East.

Had Arab governments not gone to war in 1948 to block the UN partition plan, a Palestinian state would be celebrating more than half a century of independence. Had the Arab states not supported terrorism directed at Israeli civilians and provoked seven subsequent Arab-Israeli wars, the conflict could have been settled long ago, and the Palestinian problem resolved.

From 1948–67, the West Bank and Gaza were under Arab rule, and no Jewish settlements existed there, but the Arabs never set up a Palestinian state. Instead, Gaza was occupied by Egypt, and the West Bank by Jordan. No demands for a West Bank/Gaza independent state were heard until Israel took control of these areas in the Six-Day War.

> *"Israel wants to give the Palestinians what no one else gave them—a state. Not the Turks, the British, the Egyptians, or the Jordanians gave them this possibility."*
>
> **—Prime Minister Ariel Sharon²**

MYTH

"If the Palestinian problem was solved, the Middle East would be at peace."

FACT

The Palestinian problem is but one of many simmering ethnic, religious and nationalistic feuds plaguing the region. Here is but a partial list of other conflicts from the end of the 20th century: the 1991 Gulf War; the Iran-Iraq War; the Lebanese Civil War; Libya's interference in Chad; the Sudanese Civil War; the Syria-Iraq conflict and the war between the Polisario Front and Morocco.

"Almost every border in that part of the world, from Libya to Pakistan, from Turkey to Yemen, is either ill-defined or in dispute," scholar Daniel Pipes noted. "But Americans tend to know only about Israel's border problems, and do not realize that these fit into a pattern that recurs across the Middle East."[3]

If the Palestinian problem was solved, it would have negligible impact on the many inter-Arab rivalries that have spawned numerous wars in the region. Nor would it eliminate Arab opposition to Israel. Syria, for example, has a territorial dispute with Israel unrelated to the Palestinians. Other countries, such as Iran, whose president threatened to wipe Israel off the map, maintain a state of war with Israel despite having no territorial disputes.

MYTH

*"Israel's opposition to the creation of a Palestinian
state is the cause of the present conflict."*

FACT

For many years, the consensus in Israel was that the creation of a Palestinian state would present a grave risk to Israeli security. These fears were well founded given the longstanding Palestinian commitment to the destruction of Israel, and the later adoption of the phased plan whereby the Palestinians expressed a reluctant willingness to start with a small state in the short-term and use it as a base from which to pursue the longer-term goal of replacing Israel.

Israelis still believe a Palestinian state will present a threat, especially given the Palestinians' illegal smuggling of weapons into the Palestinian Authority, and continuing support for terrorism; nevertheless, a radical shift in opinion has occurred and even most "right-wing" Israelis are now reconciled to the establishment of a Palestinian state, and are prepared to accept the risks involved in exchange for peace.

> *"In the end we [Israel and the Palestinians] will reach a solution in which there will be a Palestinian state, but it has to be a Palestinian state by agreement and it has to be a demilitarized Palestinian state."*
>
> **—Ariel Sharon[4]**

MYTH

"A Palestinian state will pose no danger to Israel."

FACT

Though reconciled to the creation of a Palestinian state, and hopeful that it will coexist peacefully, Israelis still see such an entity as a threat to their security. Even after returning much of the West Bank and all of Gaza, and allowing the Palestinians to govern themselves, terrorism against Israelis has continued. So far, no concessions by Israel have been sufficient to prompt the Palestinian Authority to end the violence. This has not reassured Israelis; on the contrary, it has made them more reluctant to give up additional territory for a Palestinian state.

Israelis also fear that a Palestinian state will become dominated by Islamic extremists and serve as a staging area for terrorists. The greatest danger, however, would be that a Palestinian state could serve as a forward base in a future war for Arab nations that have refused to make peace with Israel.

"In Israeli hands, the West Bank represents a tremendous defensive asset whose possession by Israel deters Arab foes from even considering attack along an 'eastern front,'" a report by the Institute for Advanced Strategic and Political Studies notes. Today, an Arab coalition attacking from east of the Jordan "would face very difficult fighting conditions" because "it would be fighting uphill from the lowest point on the face of the earth: the Dead Sea and the Rift Valley that runs below it." The mountain ranges in the West Bank constitute "Israel's main line of defense against Arab armies from the east."[5]

MYTH

"The Palestinians have never been offered a state of their own."

FACT

The Palestinians have actually had numerous opportunities to create an independent state, but have repeatedly rejected the offers:

- In 1937, the Peel Commission proposed the partition of Palestine and the creation of an Arab state.

- In 1939, the British White Paper proposed the creation of an Arab state alone, but the Arabs rejected the plan.

- In 1947, the UN would have created an even larger Arab state as part of its partition plan.

- The 1979 Egypt-Israel peace negotiations offered the Palestinians autonomy, which would almost certainly have led to full independence.

- The Oslo process that began in 1993 was leading toward the creation of a Palestinian state before the Palestinians violated their commitments and scuttled the agreements.

- In 2000, Prime Minister Ehud Barak offered to create a Palestinian state, but Yasser Arafat rejected the deal.

In addition, from 1948 to 1967, Israel did not control the West Bank. The Palestinians could have demanded an independent state from the Jordanians.

A variety of reasons have been given for why the Palestinians have in Abba Eban's words, "never missed an opportunity to miss an opportunity." Historian Benny Morris has suggested that the Palestinians have religious, historical, and practical reasons for opposing an agreement with Israel. He says that "Arafat and his generation cannot give up the vision of the greater land of Israel for the Arabs. [This is true because] this is a holy land, *Dar al-Islam* [the world of Islam]. It was once in the hands of the Muslims, and it is inconceivable [to them] that infidels like us [the Israelis] would receive it." The Palestinians also believe that time is on their side. "They feel that demographics will defeat the Jews in one hundred or two hundred years, just like the Crusaders." The Palestinians also hope the Arabs will acquire nuclear weapons in the future that will allow them to defeat Israel. "Why should they accept a compromise that is perceived by them as unjust today?"[6]

"Barak made a proposal that was as forthcoming as anyone in the world could imagine, and Arafat turned it down. If you have a country that's a sliver and you can see three sides of it from a high hotel building, you've got to be careful what you give away and to whom you give it."

—U.S. Defense Secretary Donald Rumsfeld[7]

MYTH

"Yasser Arafat rejected Barak's proposals in 2000 because they did not offer the Palestinians a viable state."

FACT

Israeli Prime Minister Ehud Barak offered to withdraw from 97 percent of the West Bank and 100 percent of the Gaza Strip. In addition, he agreed to dismantle 63 isolated settlements. In exchange for the 3 percent annexation of the West Bank, Israel would increase the size of the Gaza territory by roughly a third.

Barak also made previously unthinkable concessions on Jerusalem, agreeing that Arab neighborhoods of East Jerusalem would become the capital of the new state. The Palestinians would maintain control over their holy places and have "religious sovereignty" over the Temple Mount.

According to U.S. peace negotiator Dennis Ross, Israel offered to create a Palestinian state that was contiguous, and not a series of cantons. Even in the case of the Gaza Strip, which must be physically separate from the West Bank unless Israel were to be cut into non-contiguous pieces, a solution was devised whereby an overland highway would connect the two parts of the Palestinian state without any Israeli checkpoints or interference. The proposal also addressed the refugee issue, guaranteeing them the right of return to the Palestinian state and reparations from a $30 billion international fund that would be collected to compensate them.

Israel also agreed to give the Palestinians access to water desalinated in its territory.

Arafat was asked to agree to Israeli sovereignty over the parts of the Western Wall religiously significant to Jews (i.e., not the entire Temple Mount), and three early warning stations in the Jordan valley, which Israel would withdraw from after six years. Most important, however,

Arafat was expected to agree that the conflict was over at the end of the negotiations. This was the true deal breaker. Arafat was not willing to end the conflict. "For him to end the conflict is to end himself," said Ross.[8]

The prevailing view of the Camp David/White House negotiations— that Israel offered generous concessions, and that Yasser Arafat rejected them to pursue the war that began in September 2000—was acknowledged for more than a year. To counter the perception that Arafat was the obstacle to peace, the Palestinians and their supporters then began to suggest a variety of excuses for why Arafat failed to say "yes" to a proposal that would have established a Palestinian state. The truth is that if the Palestinians were dissatisfied with any part of the Israeli proposal, all they had to do was offer a counterproposal. They never did.

"In his last conversation with President Clinton, Arafat told the President that he was "a great man." Clinton responded, "The hell I am. I'm a colossal failure, and you made me one." [9]

MYTH

"Israel and the Palestinians were on the verge of reaching a peace deal during negotiations at Taba in 2001, but Ariel Sharon's election torpedoed the agreement."

FACT

Even after Yasser Arafat rejected Ehud Barak's unprecedented offer to create a Palestinian state in 97 percent of the West Bank, members of the Israeli government still hoped a peace agreement was possible with the Palestinians. In hopes of a breakthrough before the scheduled Israeli election, and the end of President Clinton's term, Israel sent a delegation of some of its most dovish officials, all of whom favored a two-state solution, to the Egyptian port city of Taba in January 2001. The Israelis believed that even though Arafat would not even offer a counterproposal to Barak, they might induce a Palestinian delegation without the PLO chairman to make sufficient compromises to at least narrow the gap between the Barak proposal and Arafat's maximalist demands.

The Israelis discovered, however, that the Palestinians were not willing to negotiate on the basis of what Barak had proposed. Instead, they withdrew many of the concessions they had offered. For example, at Camp David, the Palestinians agreed that Israel could retain two settlement blocs that would incorporate most of the Jews into Israel. At Taba, the Palestinians called for the evacuation of 130 out of 146 settlements and refused to accept the creation of settlement blocs. In fact, while the

Palestinians now falsely claim that Barak offered them only cantons at Camp David, instead of a contiguous state, it is actually the Palestinians at Taba who sought to create isolated Jewish Bantustans that would be dependent on strings of access roads.

Besides other disagreements over settlements, many of which represented backsliding from earlier Palestinian positions, the parties remained deeply divided over the status of Jerusalem. Barak had offered to allow the Palestinians to make their capital in the predominantly Arab parts of East Jerusalem, and to share sovereignty over the Temple Mount. Arafat had insisted on complete Palestinian control over the holy site, and denied Jews had any connection to it. At Taba, the Palestinians also refused to recognize the area was holy to the Jews and insisted on controlling most, if not all, of the Western Wall.

On the third key final status issue, refugees, no agreement was reached. The Palestinians did not accept Israeli proposals on the number of refugees that would be allowed into Israel or the amount of compensation that should be paid to the rest. Beilin said the Palestinians should tell the refugees that once peace is achieved, and their state is established, "they will be allowed to immigrate to [the Palestinians state] and live in it in dignity. Not in Haifa."[10]

Despite a positive joint statement issued at the end of the negotiations, the truth is that no agreement was reached at Taba and, according to the Palestinians themselves, the parties left the talks farther apart on the issues than they had been at Camp David. Abu Alaa, one of the lead Palestinian negotiators told *Al-Ayyam* after the talks that "there has never before been a clearer gap in the positions of the two sides."[11]

MYTH

"The Palestinians are being asked to accept only 22 percent of Palestine for their state while Israel keeps 78 percent."

FACT

The government of Israel has agreed to a two-state solution to the conflict with the Palestinians. Once Israel agreed to give the Palestinians the independence they say they want, they shifted their complaint to the size of the state they were being offered. Many "moderates," such as Hanan Ashrawi, who say they can coexist with Israel, have adopted the refrain that Israel is doing the Palestinians no favors by offering them a state in the disputed territories because it is asking them to accept a state in only 22 percent of Palestine while Israel keeps 78 percent. This is a very convincing point to show the unfairness of the Palestinians' plight and to suggest Israel's peace overtures are niggardly; that is, unless you know the history of Palestine and recognize that the truth is exactly the reverse.

Historic Palestine included not only Israel and the West Bank, but also all of modern Jordan. It is *Israel,* including the disputed territories, that is only 22 percent of Palestine. If Israel were to withdraw completely from the West Bank and Gaza Strip, it would possess only about 18 percent. And from Israel's perspective, it is the Zionists who have made the real sacrifice by giving up 82 percent of the Land of Israel. In fact, by accepting the UN's partition resolution, they were prepared to accept only about 12 percent of historic Israel before the Arab states attacked and tried to destroy the nascent state of Israel.

Meanwhile, of the approximately 9 million Palestinians worldwide, three-fourths live in historic Palestine.

MYTH

"Ariel Sharon has made clear that he does not want peace and no deal is possible as long as he is Prime Minister."

FACT

Ariel Sharon has been demonized by the Arabs and caricatured by the media, which often insists on referring to him as the "right-wing" or "hard-line" Prime Minister, appellations rarely affixed to any other foreign leaders. Sharon has spent most of his life as a soldier and public servant trying to bring peace to his nation.

It was Ariel Sharon who gave then Prime Minister Menachem Begin the critical backing that made the Israel-Egypt Peace Treaty possible. At a crucial moment at Camp David, the negotiations were on the verge of collapse over Egyptian President Anwar Sadat's insistence that all Israeli settlements in the Sinai be dismantled. Begin called Sharon and asked if he should give up the settlements; Sharon not only advised him to do so, but ultimately was the one who implemented the decision to remove the settlers, some by force.[12]

Sharon's views have also evolved over time. While he was once fiercely opposed to the creation of a Palestinian state, as Prime Minister he has endorsed the idea. Since taking office, Sharon has repeatedly offered to negotiate with the Palestinians on condition only that they end the violence. He asked for only seven days of peace—a demand some found onerous despite the fact that the Palestinians had promised at Oslo eight years of peace—and later even dropped that demand. When he did, the Palestinians answered his gesture with the Passover massacre, the suicide bombing of a religious observance in a Netanya hotel in which 29 people were killed.

Even when Saudi Crown Prince Abdullah proposed a peace initiative that was filled with provisions the Saudi knew Israel could never accept, Sharon did not reject the plan, and called for direct negotiations to discuss it. Sharon also agreed to negotiate with the Palestinians according to the road map formula devised by the United States, Russia, the European Union, and the United Nations, despite serious reservations about many elements of the plan.

Although Sharon is one of the fathers of the settlement movement, he has said "not all the settlements in Judea and Samaria today will remain."[13] He also ordered the evacuation of four settlements in Samaria and all of those in Gaza despite virulent opposition from his own party.

If the Arabs doubt Sharon's commitment to peace, all they need do is put him to the test—end the violence and begin negotiations. So long as the Palestinians keep up their terrorist attacks, no Israeli Prime Minister can offer them concessions.

"To keep 3.5 million people under occupation is bad for us and them. . . . I want to say clearly that I have come to the conclusion that we have to reach a [peace] agreement."

—Prime Minister Ariel Sharon[14]

MYTH

"Israel must help Mahmoud Abbas improve his standing among Palestinians to facilitate the peace process."

FACT

The death of Yasser Arafat, stimulated hope that a new Palestinian leader would emerge with the courage and vision of Anwar Sadat and King Hussein, and agree to the establishment of a Palestinian state that will live in peace beside Israel. The Palestinians chose Mahmoud Abbas to lead them. Abbas was involved in past peace negotiations and his election was welcomed by Israel. Still, Israelis had no illusions about Abbas. He was the number two person in the PLO and a founder of the Fatah terrorist organization. He had made numerous irredentist statements in the past and during his campaign. His uncompromising position on the "right of return" of Palestinian refugees, for example, bodes ill for negotiations. On the other hand, he also demonstrated the courage to publicly criticize the Palestinian War, and said that violence has not helped the Palestinian cause. He declared a readiness to make peace with Israel.

Israel has been repeatedly called on to make gestures to Abbas to help him consolidate his power; however, Israel owes him nothing. It is Abbas who must show that he has both the will and ability to reform the Palestinian Authority, to dismantle the terrorist networks, and to end the violence. Words are insufficient; he must take action. The agreements signed by the Palestinians are unequivocal about what is required of them; they cannot evade their responsibilities with conciliatory statements to the press in English or cease-fires with groups such as Hamas that remain committed to Israel's destruction.

Though it has no obligation to do so, Israel has taken steps to show its goodwill, including facilitating the Palestinian elections (which international observers reported were unfettered by Israel[15]), releasing prisoners, and withdrawing troops from parts of the West Bank. More important, Israel evacuated all of its civilians and soldiers from the Gaza Strip.

The hope for a negotiated settlement of the conflict between Israelis and Palestinians now rests on the shoulders of Abbas. He has taken steps to consolidate his power. He has persuaded Hamas at different times to accept a cease-fire. He ordered Palestinian security forces to stop attacks by terrorists on Israelis and he sent a police contingent to the Gaza Strip to impose order. He also declared that only policemen and security personnel will be allowed to carry weapons. To date, however, he has had limited success in implementing these decisions and many Israelis question whether he is politically strong enough to impose order.

Coexistence is impossible unless Palestinian violence stops. There can be no attacks on Jews anywhere, no mortars or rockets fired into Israel, and no incitement to violence. This is not a case of giving extremists a veto over negotiations; Israel has not said that Abbas must stop 100 percent of the incidents before it will talk, but Israel does insist that he demonstrate a 100 percent effort to stop them. To date, he has not done so.

> *"I confirm that the resistance will continue after the withdrawal from Gaza, and the resistance's weapons will remain to protect this achievement."*
>
> **—Hamas representative Osama Hamdan[16]**

MYTH

"The disengagement plan was a trick to allow Israel to hold onto the West Bank."

FACT

Prime Minister Sharon, as well as President Bush, have made it clear that the disengagement plan is consistent with the road map. Sharon has also repeatedly stated his acceptance of the establishment of a contiguous Palestinian state in the West Bank and Gaza Strip, which would require the evacuation of additional communities in the West Bank.

Sharon's motives were questioned despite the political risks he took in pursuing his plan. After all, few people inside or outside of Israel would have predicted as recently as the year 2000 that the man considered the father of the settlement movement would defy much of his own party and evacuate Jews from their homes in the territories.

Moreover, the disengagement plan was not restricted to Gaza; it also involved the dismantling of four Jewish communities in Samaria. While the number of Jews evacuated was small (approximately 550), the area that Israel evacuated was actually larger than the entire Gaza Strip.[17]

The Jews who live in the West Bank did not believe the evacuation of Gaza was meant to solidify their position. On the contrary, the reason so many Jews in Judea and Samaria defended the rights of the Jews in Gaza was because they saw their removal as a precedent that will eventually be followed in the West Bank. Sharon has only expressed commitments to retain the large settlement blocs that the overwhelming majority of Israelis agree should be incorporated into Israel, and many of the Jews living in smaller, isolated communities saw the disengagement as the first step toward their eventual evacuation.

"I think if they (Palestinians) can't achieve progress in the time of the current (Israeli) prime minister, it will be very difficult to make any progress in peace. He (Sharon) is capable of pursuing peace, and he is capable of reaching solutions, if he wants to."

—Egyptian President Hosni Mubarak[18]

MYTH

"Israel evacuated Gaza, but turned it into a prison by preventing the movement of people or goods."

FACT

Israel decided to completely evacuate its soldiers and civilians from Gaza to improve the lives of Palestinians and Israelis. The Palestinian Authority now has full control over the population in Gaza. No one there is "under occupation." Gaza Palestinians can now move freely within Gaza, live and work where they choose, and pursue normal lives, subject only to the restrictions imposed by their leaders.

Prior to disengagement, Israel established a development team to improve the economic circumstances in Gaza. Israel offered to provide assistance in building desalination facilities, sewage systems, hospitals, and a power station. Another team was created to facilitate trade with the Palestinians.[19] In addition, Israel has agreed to allow guarded convoys to travel between the Gaza Strip and the West Bank, and proposed building a railway linking the two, demonstrating that Israel has no intention of isolating the two territories.[20]

Still, Israel is accused of imprisoning Gazans by refusing to allow the Palestinians use of a seaport or airport. Israel is prepared to allow the use of these facilities, but neither is ready for use now. Moreover, Palestinian businessmen and economists have said the construction of a seaport, which will take many months, is not a priority. If relations with Israel are good, Palestinians can use the Israeli port of Ashdod or Port Said in Egypt.[21]

Israel and the PA reached an agreement in November 2005 to allow greater freedom of movement in and out of Gaza, and to permit the Palestinians to begin building a seaport and airport. The deal stipulated that the Rafah crossing would be monitored by Palestinian and Egyptian officials, with outside observers from the European Union on site. Israel will have access to closed-circuit cameras to watch traffic going through the crossing, and will be able to voice objections over any person that they regard as suspicious, but will not have the power to veto an individual's access to the other side of the border.[22]

> *"I thank Allah the exalted for His support in the Jihad of our people and for the liberation of the beloved Gaza Strip, and I ask him to help us to liberate Jerusalem and the West Bank, Acre, Haifa, Jaffa, Safed, Nazareth, Ashkelon, and all of Palestine."*
>
> **—Muhammad Deif, Commander of the ʿIzz Al-Din Al-Qassam Brigades[23]**

The Palestinians were unwilling to negotiate a peace agreement in conjunction with Israel's disengagement from Gaza; therefore, Israel has no assurance the area will not be used as a terrorist base. Hamas and other terrorist groups explicitly say they plan to continue their war to destroy Israel. The PA, meanwhile, refuses to honor its road map obligations to disarm the terrorists and dismantle the infrastructure. Given these conditions, and memories of the *Karine-A*—the ship laden with Iranian weapons meant for the PA that Israel seized in 2002—Israel cannot put its population at risk by allowing Palestinians to bring material in by air and sea without any inspection, or to go to and from the West Bank without scrutiny. Israelis and Palestinians have been discussing how to provide Israel with the necessary security safeguards to allow for the quicker movement of goods and people over the border.[24]

MYTH

"Israel should be replaced by a binational state where Jews and Palestinians live together."

FACT

The idea of a binational state is not new; it was first proposed by prominent Jews such as Judah Magnes in the 1920s. As is the case today, however, the suggestion enjoyed no popular support.

The utopian view of the advocates of binationalism was that the Jews and Arabs both had legitimate claims to the land and should live in peace together in one state. This idea negated the Jewish right to its historic homeland and also assumed the Arabs were prepared to coexist peacefully with the Jews within the same state. This was proven wrong through two decades of violence by Arabs against Jews in Palestine, and by the Arab rejection of the British White Paper of 1939, which offered them just such an arrangement.

> *"A Palestinian state will never be built on a foundation of violence. Now is the time for every true friend of the Palestinian people, every leader in the Middle East, and the Palestinian people themselves, to cut off all money and support for terrorists and actively fight terror on all fronts. Only then can Israel be secure and the flag rise over an independent Palestine."*
>
> **—President George W. Bush**[25]

As early as 1937, it had become clear that the two peoples could not live together and needed to have states of their own. As a result, the Peel Commission proposed a partition in that year and the UN approved the same approach a decade later. Nothing has changed since that time to suggest any other solution can end the conflict.

Since Palestinian Arabs already constitute approximately 46 percent of the population living between the Mediterranean Sea and the Jordan River, and their birth rate is double that of Israeli Jews, they would soon become the majority of the population in a binational state. The Jewish character of the nation would then erode and disappear, and Israeli Jews would lose political control over the one safe haven for Jews.

Given the historical mistreatment of minorities, especially Jews, in Arab lands, this idea would be a recipe for the persecution of Jews (and Christians). One proponent of the idea of a binational state suggested that an international force would protect the Jews, but no leader would entrust the fate of the Jewish people to such an unreliable guarantor. More important, if advocates of binationalism acknowledge that Jews would need protection in such a state, what is the basis for believing this is a solution to the conflict?

MYTH

"The Palestinians have been educating their children about Israel and a future of coexistence with Israeli Jews."

FACT

Rather than use education to promote peace with their Jewish neighbors, the Palestinians have persistently indoctrinated their children with anti-Semitic stereotypes, anti-Israel propaganda and other materials designed more to promote hostility and intolerance than coexistence.

For example, a Palestinian children's television show called the "Children's Club" uses a "Sesame Street" formula involving interaction between children, puppets and fictional characters to encourage a hatred for Jews and the perpetration of violence against them in a *jihad* (holy war). In one song, young children are shown singing about wanting to become "suicide warriors" and taking up machine guns against Israelis. Another song features young children singing a refrain, "When I wander into Jerusalem, I will become a suicide bomber." Children on the show also say, "We will settle our claims with stones and bullets," and call for a "jihad against Israel."

Palestinians also called on their youth to join the battle against Israel in commercials on Palestinian TV that tell children to drop their toys, pick up rocks, and do battle with Israel. In one commercial, actors recreate the incident where a child was killed in the crossfire of a confrontation between Israelis and Palestinians. The commercial shows the child in paradise urging other children to "follow him."[26]

> *"We have found books with passages that are so anti-Semitic, that if they were published in Europe, their publishers would be brought up on anti-racism charges."*
>
> **—French lawyer and European Parliament member Francois Zimeray**[27]

Similar messages are conveyed in Palestinian textbooks, many of which were prepared by the Palestinian Ministry of Education. The 5th grade textbook *Muqarar al-Tilawa Wa'ahkam Al-Tajwid* describes Jews as cowards for whom Allah has prepared fires of hell. In a text for 8th graders, *Al-Mutala'ah Wa'alnussus al-Adabia,* Israelis are referred to as the butchers in Jerusalem. Stories glorifying those who throw stones at soldiers are found in various texts. A 9th grade text, *Al-Mutala'ah Wa'alnussus al-Adabia,* refers to the bacteria of Zionism that has to be uprooted out of the Arab nation.

Newer textbooks are less strident, but still problematic. For example, they describe the Palestinian nation as one comprised of Muslims and Christians. No mention is made of Jews or the centuries-old Jewish communities of Palestine that predated Zionism. The State of Israel also is not mentioned, though many problems of Palestinian society are attributed to the Arab-Israeli conflict. References to Jews are usually stereotypical and are often related in a negative way to their opposition to Muhammad and refusal to convert to Islam. A lesson on architecture describes prominent mosques and churches, but makes no mention of Jewish holy places.[28] A recent study concludes:

> Despite the evident reduction in anti-Semitic references, compared to the old textbooks, the history of the relationship between Muslims, Christians and Jews in the new textbooks strengthen classical stereotypes of Jews in both Islamic and Christian cultures. The linkage of present conflicts with ancient disputes of the time of Jesus or Muhammad implies that nothing has really changed.

The lessons don't end in school. Summer camp teaches Palestinian children how to resist the Israelis and that the greatest glory is to be a martyr. Campers stage mock kidnappings and learn how to slit the throats of Israelis. Four "Paradise Camps" run by Islamic Jihad in the Gaza Strip offer 8–12 year-olds military training and encourage them to become suicide bombers. The BBC filmed children marching in formation and practicing martial arts.[29]

The Palestinian authorities also try to convince children that Israel is out to kill them by all sorts of devious methods. For example, the Palestinian daily newspaper, *Al Hayat Jadida,* reported that Israeli aircraft were dropping poisonous candy over elementary and junior high schools in the Gaza Strip.[30]

These teachings violate the letter and spirit of the peace agreements.

"We are teaching the children that suicide bombs make Israeli people frightened. . . . We teach them that after a person becomes a suicide bomber he reaches the highest level of paradise."

—Palestinian "Paradise Camp" counselor speaking to BBC interviewer[31]

MYTH

"Palestinians no longer object to the creation of Israel."

FACT

One of the primary Palestinian obligations under the road map for peace is to affirm Israel's right to exist in peace and security. How then does one interpret Palestinian Authority Chairman Mahmoud Abbas's description of the decision to create a Jewish state in 1948 as a crime?[32]

While Israelis were still celebrating the 57th anniversary of their independence, Abbas and other Palestinians were mourning the establishment of Israel on what they call Nakba Day. Had the Palestinians and the Arab states accepted the partition resolution in 1947, the State of Palestine would have also been celebrating its birthday, and Palestinians would not be lamenting *Al Nakba* ("The Catastrophe").

Palestinians are understandably bitter about their history over these last six decades, but we are often told that what they object to today is the "occupation" of the territories Israel captured in 1967. If that is true, then why isn't their Nakba Day celebrated each June on the anniversary of the Arab defeat in the Six-Day War?

The reason is that the Palestinians consider the creation of Israel the original sin, and their focus on that event is indicative of a refusal, even today, to reconcile themselves with the Jewish State. Abbas's comments on the occasion, along with those by PA Prime Minister Ahmed Korei, who said "our wound is still bleeding 57 years later," hardly inspires confidence in their willingness to end the conflict with Israel.[33]

> *"Terrorism will have no positive results, and there will be no chance to establish an independent Palestinian state as long as violence and terrorism continue."*
>
> **—German Foreign Minister Joschka Fischer[34]**

And Hamas, which has never left any doubt about its refusal to accept Israel's existence, said that Israel is a "cancer" and promised to continue fighting "until the liberation of the last inch of our land and the last refugee heads back to his home."[35] This is the organization that could win upcoming elections in the PA and would then presumably have a greater say in policy toward Israel.

Another disturbing aspect of Nakba Day was that traffic stopped and people stood straight and silent as sirens of mourning sounded, intentionally mimicking the Israeli practice on Holocaust Remembrance Day. This was an insidious way to make the odious comparison between the Holocaust and the creation of Israel.

It may be that the current leadership does not truly represent the feelings of the Palestinian people. A May 2005 poll, for example, found that 54 percent of Palestinians are prepared to accept a two-state solution.[36] This is a hopeful sign, however, as long as the Palestinian Authority treats Israel's creation as a catastrophe on a par with the Holocaust, the prospects for coexistence will remain bleak.

Map 22 The Palestinian Authority's Map of Palestine

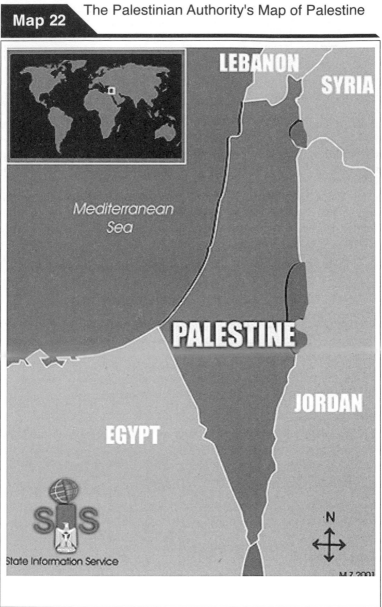

MYTH

*"The Palestinians have given up their
maximalist dream of destroying Israel."*

FACT

The Palestinian Authority continues to promote the maximalist vision
in its school textbooks and, especially, by its maps. The most dramatic
expression of the goal is in Map 22, a map of Palestine published on its
official web site, which shows Palestine as encompassing not only the
West Bank and Gaza Strip, but all of Israel as well. Similar maps appear in
textbooks, which never show Israel.[37]

Israelis have expressed a willingness to live in peace with a Palestinian state beside Israel. As Map 22 vividly indicates, however, the Palestinians continue to dream of a Palestinian state that replaces Israel.

MYTH

"Palestinians are driven to terror by desperation."

FACT

The situation many Palestinians find themselves in is unfortunate and
often quite severe. Many live in poverty, see the future as hopeless, and
are unhappy with the way they are treated by Israelis. None of these are
excuses for engaging in terrorism. In fact, many of the terrorists are not
poor, desperate people at all. The world's most wanted terrorist, Osama
bin Laden, for example, is a Saudi millionaire.

When asked about two Palestinian suicide bombers who blew themselves up on a pedestrian mall in Jerusalem, killing 10 people between
the ages of 14 and 21, the cousin of one of the men said "these two
were not deprived of anything."[38]

A report by the National Bureau of Economic Research concluded
that "economic conditions and education are largely unrelated to
participation in, and support for, terrorism." The researchers said the
violence in the region cannot be blamed on deteriorating economic
conditions because there is no connection between terrorism and
economic depression. Furthermore, the authors found that support for
violent action against Israel, including suicide bombing, does not vary
much according to social background.[39]

Amnesty International published a study that condemned all attacks
by Palestinians against Israeli civilians and said that no Israeli action
justified them. According to the report, "The attacks against civilians by
Palestinian armed groups are widespread, systematic and in pursuit of
an explicit policy to attack civilians. They therefore constitute crimes
against humanity under international law."[40]

Terrorism is not Israel's fault. It is not the result of "occupation." And it certainly is not the only response available to the Palestinians' discontentment. Palestinians have an option for improving their situation, it is called negotiations. And that is not the only option. The Palestinians could also choose the nonviolent path taken by Martin Luther King or Gandhi. Unfortunately, they have chosen to pursue a war of terror instead of a process for peace. Israel has proven time and again a willingness to trade land for peace, but it can never concede land for terror.

"The use of suicide bombing is entirely unacceptable. Nothing can justify this."

—UN Special Representative for the protection of children in armed conflict, Under Secretary-General Olara Otunnu[41]

MYTH

"Palestinians are helpless to stop the terrorists."

FACT

The media has helped create the misperception that the Palestinian Authority cannot dismantle the terrorist network in its midst because of the strength and popularity of the radical Islamic Palestinian terrorist groups.

Hamas and Islamic Jihad are not huge armed forces. Together, the armed wings of both organizations total fewer than 1,500 men. By contrast, the PA has 35,000 people in a variety of police, intelligence, and security forces.[42] Not only does the PA have overwhelming superiority of manpower and firepower, it also has the intelligence assets to find most, if not all, of the terrorists.

It is true these Islamic groups have achieved some popularity, but polls show that together they still are only supported by about one-fourth of the Palestinian population. The PA is not a democracy, so its leaders do not base their decisions on public opinion, but the data shows that it is not hindered from acting by any overwhelming sympathy for the radical factions.

The PA could follow the example of the Jordanian government, which has not allowed Hamas to establish a foothold in the kingdom. King Abdullah closed their offices in Amman, as well as their newspaper, and has arrested and deported numerous members of the organization.[43]

Despite the suffering the terrorists have brought them, the Palestinian public has not called for an end to the violence. No equivalent to Israel's Peace Now movement has emerged.

Still, on an individual basis, it is possible for Palestinians to say no to terror. When the suicide bombing recruiter phoned the wife of former Hamas leader Abdel Aziz al-Rantisi to ask if her son was available for an operation, she turned him down.[44] In other countries, including Israel (where they helped prompt a withdrawal from Lebanon), mothers have often helped stimulate positive change. When enough Palestinian mothers stand up to the terror recruiters, and to their political leaders, and say that they will no longer allow their children to be used as bombs, the prospects for peace will improve. So long as they prefer their children to be martyrs rather than doctors, bombers rather than scholars, and murderers rather than lawyers, the violence will continue, and young Palestinians will continue to die needlessly.

> *"The Palestinian Authority, despite consistent promises by its leadership, has made no progress on its core obligation to take immediate action on the ground to end violence and combat terror, and to reform and reorganize the Palestinian Authority."*
>
> **—UN Mideast envoy Terje Roed-Larsen[45]**

MYTH

"Palestinians are justified in using violence because the peace process has not allowed them to achieve their national aspirations."

FACT

The premise from the beginning of the Oslo peace process was that disputes would be resolved by talking, not shooting. The Palestinians have never accepted this most basic of principles for coexistence. The answer to complaints that Israel is not withdrawing far enough or fast enough should be more negotiations, more confidence-building measures and more demonstrations of a desire to live together without using violence.

To understand why the Oslo process failed, and why Palestinians and Israelis are not living peacefully beside each other, it is useful to look at the first Arab-Israeli peace process that did work, the Egyptian-Israeli negotiations. Though the peace agreement was hammered out in intensive negotiations at Camp David, the route to peace was a long, tortuous one that took years to navigate. What made it possible, however, was the commitment both nations made to peace and the actions they took to insure it.

Egypt maintained a state of war with Israel for more than 25 years before Anwar Sadat seriously talked about peace. Bloody conflicts were fought in 1948, 1956, 1967, 1968–70 and 1973. The anger, heartache and distrust of a quarter century did not dissipate overnight. The process began after the 1973 war when Henry Kissinger facilitated the negotiation of a disengagement agreement in which both sides made significant concessions.

Egypt had demanded that Israel make a substantial withdrawal from Sinai and commit to abandon all its territorial gains from 1967, but Israel gave up only a tiny area of the Sinai. Rather than resort to violence, the Egyptians engaged in more negotiations.

The first agreement was signed in January 1974. It took about a year and a half before a second agreement was reached. It wasn't easy. Israel was criticized for "inflexibility," and the Egyptians were no less difficult. Anwar Sadat agreed to limit anti-Israel propaganda in the Egyptian press and to end his country's participation in the Arab boycott. Yitzhak Rabin also made difficult territorial concessions, giving up oil fields and two critical Sinai passes.

"If the Israelis can make compromises and you can't, I should go home. You have been here 14 days and said no to everything. These things will have consequences. Failure will end the peace process...."

—President Clinton to Yasser Arafat[46]

After "Sinai II," Egypt still had not recovered all of its territory. Sadat was dissatisfied and was pilloried by the other Arabs for going as far as he did toward peace with Israel. Nevertheless, he did not resort to violence. There was no unleashing of *fedayeen,* as Nasser had done in the 1950s. Instead, he continued talking.

It took three more years before the Camp David Accords were signed and another six months after that before the final peace treaty was negotiated. It took five years to work out issues that were as complex as those in the current impasse.

In return for its tangible concessions, Israel received a promise of a new future of peaceful relations. Israel could take this risk because Egypt had demonstrated over the previous five years that it would resolve disputes with Israel peacefully, and that it no longer wished to destroy its neighbor.

Egypt still wasn't completely satisfied. Sadat demanded a small sliver of land that Israel retained in the Sinai. It took another nine years before international arbitration led Israel to give up Taba. Rather than using this dispute as a pretext for violating the peace treaty, Egypt negotiated.

MYTH

"The Palestinian Authority has seized illegal weapons and fulfilled its obligation to restrict the possession of arms to the authorized police force."

FACT

According to the Interim Agreement signed by Israel and the Palestinians, "no organization, group or individual in the West Bank and the Gaza Strip shall manufacture, sell, acquire, possess, import or otherwise introduce into the West Bank or the Gaza Strip any firearms, ammunition, weapons, explosives, gunpowder or any related equipment" except the Palestinian police. The agreement's annex further specifies that the police are only permitted a limited number of pistols, rifles and machine guns and that all weapons must be registered. By accepting the road map, the Palestinian Authority agreed also to confiscate all illegal weapons.

During the Palestinian War, the Palestinians abandoned all pretense of fulfilling what Israel viewed as a crucial security requirement in the Oslo accords. The most dramatic example was the PA's attempt in January 2002 to smuggle in 50 tons of Iranian and Russian-made weapons, including long-range Katyusha rockets, LAW anti-tank missiles, Sagger anti-tank missiles, long-range mortar bombs, mines, sniper rifles, ammunition and more than two tons of high explosives. After the IDF captured the *Karine-A* with its illicit cargo, Yasser Arafat denied having anything to do with the ship; however, Omar Akawi, a PA naval officer who captained the Palestinian-owned and operated vessel, admitted the smuggling operation was ordered by the PA.[47]

Between the time of the capture of the arms ship and the evacuation from Gaza, Israeli forces fought a constant battle to prevent Palestinians from smuggling weapons through tunnels in the Gaza Strip. After the disengagement from Gaza, Israel and Egypt signed an agreement stating that Egypt was now in charge of patrolling the "Philadelphi Route" along the Egyptian-Gaza border. Egypt opened the border with Gaza for a short time after the Israelis evacuated in August 2005, and this allowed Palestinians to bring weapons and ammunition into Gaza to attack Israelis.

According to Major Gen. Doron Almog, "The term 'smuggling' does not do justice to the problem of the Philadelphi corridor...It involves the illegal importation into Gaza of significant quantities of arms and materiel, on a scale sufficient to turn Gaza into launching pad for ever-deeper attacks against Israel proper."[48]

In addition to its unwillingness to stem the flow of illegal weapons, the PA has also flouted its road map commitment by repeatedly saying that terrorist groups will not be disarmed.[49] Now dozens of armed militias have formed that are prohibited by the peace agreements. They have used rifles, machine guns, mortars, grenades and other explosives to carry out terrorist attacks against Israel. Every time a photo is shown of a Palestinian holding a weapon—and they appear in the press all the time—it is evidence the Palestinians are breaking their promises and reinforces Israeli concerns about Palestinian intentions and the threat that a future Palestinian state might pose to Israel's security.

MYTH

"The Palestinians have fulfilled their commitment to arrest and prosecute terrorists."

FACT

The Palestinians have arrested suspected terrorists from time to time; however, they have had a revolving door whereby most of them are subsequently released.[50] To give one example of the failure to act against the terrorists, the head of Hamas, Sheikh Ahmed Yassin, was not arrested until the end of June 2002, and then he was only placed under house arrest. Shortly thereafter, he attended a rally in the Gaza Strip. Despite leading the organization most responsible for the suicide bombing campaign against Israeli civilians, Yassin was never jailed.

The Palestinian Authority's treatment of Palestinians suspected of terrorism against Israel is in stark contrast to how it handles Palestinians accused of collaborating with Israel or opposing the policies of the leadership. Palestinians who commit "crimes" against the Palestinian people are usually arrested and, in several instances, quickly executed.[51]

The unwarranted release of those accused of violence against Israel sends the message to the Palestinian public that terrorism is acceptable. It also allows the terrorists themselves to continue their campaign of violence against Israel.

> *"We will not arrest the sons of our people in order to appease Israel. Let our people rest assured that this won't happen."*
>
> **—Chief of the PA Preventive Security in the West Bank, Jabril Rajoub[52]**

MYTH

"Palestinian terrorists only attack Israelis; they never assault Americans."

FACT

The PLO has a long history of brutal violence against innocent civilians of many nations, including the United States. Palestinian Muslim terrorist groups are a more recent phenomenon, but they have not spared Americans either. Here are a few examples of Palestinian terrorist incidents involving American citizens:

■ More than three dozen Americans were among the passengers who were held hostage when the Popular Front for the Liberation of Palestine (PFLP) hijacked four jets in September 1970.

■ In 1972, the PLO attempted to mail letter bombs to President Nixon, former Secretary of State William Rogers and Secretary of Defense Melvin Laird.

■ On March 2, 1973, members of the PLO murdered U.S. Ambassador to the Sudan Cleo Noel and chargé d'affaires George Moore. The killers were captured by Sudan and admitted they had gotten orders directly from the PLO. U.S. intelligence officials were believed to also have evidence directly tying Yasser Arafat to the killings, but for unknown reasons suppressed it. All the terrorists were released.[53]

■ On March 11, 1978, PLO terrorists landed on Israel's coast and murdered an American photographer walking along the beach. The terrorists then commandeered a bus along the coastal road, shooting and lobbing grenades from the bus window at passersby. When Israeli troops stopped their deadly ride, 34 civilians were dead and another 82 wounded.

■ In October 1985, a PLF terror squad commanded by Abul Abbas hijacked the ocean liner Achille Lauro. Leon Klinghoffer, a wheelchair-bound American passenger was murdered.

■ In March 1988, Arafat's Fatah declared it had attempted to murder Secretary of State George Shultz by planting a car bomb near his Jerusalem hotel.[54]

■ On April 9, 1995, an Islamic Jihad suicide bomber blew up an Israeli bus killing eight people, including 20-year-old Brandeis University student Alisa Flatow.

■ August 9, 2001, Shoshana Yehudit Greenbaum, was among 15 people killed in a suicide bombing at the Sbarro pizzeria in downtown Jerusalem. Hamas and the Islamic Jihad claimed responsibility for the attack.

■ July 31, 2002, a bomb exploded at the Hebrew University cafeteria killing seven and wounding 80. Five Americans were among the dead.

■ June 11, 2003, a bus bombing in Jerusalem killed one American and injured the daughter of New Jersey State Senator Robert Singer.

■ June 20, 2003, a shooting attack on a car driving through the West Bank killed Tzvi Goldstein, and injured his father, mother, and wife.

- August 19, 2003, a suicide bombing on a bus in Jerusalem killed five Americans, including children aged 9, 3, and 3 months; an 11-year-old American was injured.

- October 15, 2003, Palestinian terrorists ambushed an American convoy in the Gaza Strip killing three U.S. citizens on contract to the U.S. embassy in Tel Aviv.

- September 24, 2004, A mortar strike on a housing community killed dual citizen Tiferet Tratner.

"The bombing yesterday [August 9, 2001] of a crowded pizza restaurant in downtown Jerusalem, which killed at least 14 people and injured around 100, was an atrocity of the sort that must be distinguished from everything else that goes on in the Palestinian-Israeli conflict. . . . the deliberate targeting of civilians, including children . . . is a simple savagery that no country can reasonably be expected to tolerate. Israel's determination last night to respond was entirely legitimate. . . .

It was Mr. Arafat who released dozens of Islamic militants from custody and has refused to rearrest them since. Terrorist attack was the altogether predictable consequence. It was Mr. Arafat as well who has consistently failed to bring violence to heel and stop official incitement against Israel. The Palestinian Authority, having stoked Palestinian anger and jettisoned a viable political process, cannot now shift the blame for deadly attacks by groups it is knowingly protecting."

—*Washington Post* Editorial[55]

MYTH

"Hamas is a force for moderation in the territories. It advocates Muslim-Jewish harmony and reconciliation."

FACT

Hamas, the Islamic Resistance Movement, is opposed to Israel's existence in any form. Its platform states that "there is no solution for the Palestinian question except through *jihad* (holy war)." The group warns that any Muslim who leaves "the circle of struggle with Zionism" is guilty of "high treason." Hamas's platform calls for the creation of an Islamic republic in Palestine that would replace Israel.[56]

MYTH

*"There is a distinction between the political
and terror wings of Hamas."*

FACT

Apologists for Palestinian terror, especially in the media, sometimes argue that Hamas shouldn't be labeled a terrorist organization because only some members engage in murder while others perform charitable activity. The ombudsman for the *Washington Post,* for example, argued that, since Hamas is a "nationalist movement" engaged in "some social work," the perpetrators of Palestinian suicide and other attacks should be described in the press as "militants" or "gunmen."[57] A false distinction is made between the "political" and "military" wings of Hamas. All of the activities of Hamas are intertwined, and serve the organization's primary objective laid out in its covenant, namely, to "raise the banner of Allah over every inch of Palestine."

Hamas's leader, Sheikh Ahmed Yassin, denied that Hamas has un-coordinated wings: "We cannot separate the wing from the body. If we do so, the body will not be able to fly. Hamas is one body."[58] And the "political" leaders of Hamas freely admit their relationship to the murderers. "The political leadership," Hamas spokesman, 'Abd al-'Aziz ar-Rantisi said, "has freed the hand of the ['Izz ad-Din al-Qassam] brigades to do whatever they want against the brothers of monkeys and pigs [i.e., Jews]."[59]

While Hamas does engage in social work, this is closely connected to the "armed struggle." Various charitable activities are used to recruit young Palestinians for terrorist operations. Hospitals, mosques, sport clubs, libraries, and schools serve not only their expected roles but also act as covers for hiding weapons, obtaining supplies, and indoctrinating future suicide bombers.

The education system is used to incite young Palestinians to become martyrs. "The children of the kindergarten are the *shahids* [martyrs] of tomorrow," read signs in a Hamas-run school, while placards in classrooms at al-Najah University in the West Bank and at Gaza's Islamic University declare that "Israel has nuclear bombs; we have human bombs."[60]

Hamas operatives use Islamic charities and social welfare programs to skim and launder funds, and to earn money to live on while they engage in terrorism. Recipients of Hamas charity also understand there is a quid pro quo. If they are asked to provide assistance, whether it be to hide weapons, provide a safe house for a fugitive, or act as a courier, few are likely to refuse.[61]

The United States government recognizes the connection between the charitable activities of Hamas and its terrorist campaign, which is why the Treasury Department designated six senior Hamas political leaders and five charities as terrorist entities. According to the Treasury Department, "the political leadership of Hamas directs its terrorist networks just as they oversee their other activities."

> "... any culture that takes pride in having the next generation as a ready supply of cheap weapons has already lost its future. Any leader who cultivates or condones suicide as its war plan has lost all moral standing. What do we say about societies that practice human sacrifice?"
>
> **—Columnist Ellen Goodman**[62]

MYTH

"Palestinians have no need for propaganda because the truth about Israeli behavior makes clear their barbarity."

FACT

Palestinian and other Arab leaders routinely use their media outlets to spread outrageous libels against Israel and the Jews to inflame their populations. Palestinians have become masters of the technique perfected by Adolf Hitler known as the "big lie." As Hitler explained in *Mein Kampf:*

> The size of a lie is a definite factor in causing it to be believed, for the vast masses of a nation are in the depths of their hearts more easily deceived than consciously and intentionally bad. The primitive simplicity of their minds renders them a more easy prey to a big lie than a small one, for they themselves often tell little lies but would be ashamed to tell big ones.

One example of the Palestinian big lie came on March 11, 1997, when the Palestinian representative to the UN Human Rights Commission claimed the Israeli government had injected 300 Palestinian children with the HIV virus.[63]

Palestinians claimed in 2002 that Israel was dropping poisoned candies from helicopters in front of schools to poison children. That lie was updated in 2003 with the fabrication that Israel is making "bombs and mines designed as toys" and dropping them into the Palestinian territories from airplanes so children will play with them and be blown up.[64] In 2005, the Palestinians announced that Israel was using a "radial spy machine" at checkpoints, and that the device killed a 55-year-old Palestinian woman.[65]

The Palestinians also regularly try to inflame the Muslim world by falsely claiming the Jews are going to blow up the Temple Mount or the al-Aksa Mosque. For example, on September 29, 2000, the Voice of

Palestine, the PA's official radio station, sent out calls "to all Palestinians to come and defend the al-Aksa mosque." This was the day *after* Ariel Sharon's visit to the Temple Mount, and the subsequent riots marked the unofficial beginning of the Palestinian War.

In the midst of that war, the Palestinian Authority TV "Message to the World" broadcast announced: "The Zionist criminals are planning to destroy the al-Aksa mosque on the ground that they are searching for the Holy Temple, which they falsely claim is under the mosque."[66]

One of the most outrageous lies circulated throughout the Middle East was that 4,000 Israelis did not report to work on September 11, or "called in sick" that morning because they knew an attack was coming. Israel and the Mossad are also said to be responsible for the atrocities. Of course, this was also a lie, but it is the type of conspiracy theory that is widely believed by Arabs who maintain the forgery, the *Protocols of the Elders of Zion*, is factual.

> *"I'll remind those who focus on the road map that the first thing the road map said was that there must be security in order for peace to advance, that there must be a collective effort to fight terror."*
>
> **—President George W. Bush**[67]

MYTH

"Releasing Palestinian prisoners would build confidence for the peace process without endangering Israeli security."

FACT

Israel has released Palestinian prisoners from its jails on a number of occasions because the Palestinians have made this a major issue and said that it would build confidence in the peace process. To date, however, it is difficult to find evidence that these prisoner releases have done anything to improve the prospects for peace. The Israeli concession has not moderated Palestinian behavior or prompted the PA to fulfill its road map obligations to dismantle terrorist networks and confiscate illegal weapons.

Israel has naturally been reluctant to release prisoners because these individuals are in jail for a good reason, they committed crimes, often violent ones. Moreover, when Israel has made these political and humanitarian gestures, the criminals have often resumed their terrorist activities. In the summer of 2003, for example, Ariel Sharon responded to the entreaties of the Palestinians, and the international community, to release prisoners as a way to help bolster the stature of then Prime Minister Mahmoud Abbas. Even though the road map says nothing about the subject, Sharon released 350 Palestinians. Not long after, two of the former prisoners, under the command of a third, carried out suicide bombings at Café Hillel in Jerusalem and the Tzrifin army base, killing 15 civilians and soldiers, and wounding more than 80.[68]

After Mahmoud Abbas was elected president of the Palestinian Authority, and prior to Israel's disengagement from Gaza, nearly 1,000 Palestinians were released. The terror continued.

Releasing prisoners is another example of one of the great risks that Israel has often taken for peace without any reciprocal gesture from the Palestinians.

"The problem is the same problem that has been there for the three years that I have been working in this account. And that is terrorism, terrorism that still emanates from Hamas, Palestinian Islamic Jihad, and other organizations that are not interested in peace, not interested in a state for the Palestinian people. They're interested in the destruction of Israel."

—Secretary of State Colin Powell[69]

MYTH

"Israel's security fence won't stop terrorism."

FACT

Along much of the frontier separating Israel from the West Bank, there are either no barriers of any kind, or easily avoidable ones. In response to dozens of suicide bombings, and daily terrorist attacks against its civilians, Israel decided to construct a security fence near the Green Line (the 1949 armistice line) to prevent Palestinian terrorists from infiltrating into Israel.

A large majority of Israelis support the construction of the security fence. Israelis living along the Green Line, both Jews and Arabs, favor the fence to prevent penetration by thieves and vandals as well as terrorists. In fact, the fence has caused a revolution in the daily life of some Israeli Arab towns because it has brought quiet, which has allowed a significant upsurge in economic activity.[70]

Even Israelis who are not enthusiastic about the establishment of a Palestinian state argue the fence is needed to reduce the number of terror attacks. The head of the Shin Bet, Avi Dichter, for example, has said that a physical barrier can be a deterrent and cites the example of the fence that was built to separate Israel from the Gaza Strip.[71] Since its construction no suicide bombers have penetrated the barrier, while approximately 250 came from the West Bank during the Palestinian War.

The fence is not impregnable. It is possible that some terrorists will manage to get past the barrier; nevertheless, the obstacle makes it far more difficult for incursions and thereby minimizes the number of attacks. During the 34 months from the beginning of the violence in September 2000 until the construction of the first continuous segment of the security fence at the end of July 2003, Samaria-based terrorists carried out 73 attacks in which 293 Israelis were killed and 1,950 wounded. In the 11 months between the erection of the first segment at the beginning of August 2003 and the end of June 2004, only three attacks were successful, and all three occurred in the first half of 2003. Since construction of the fence began, the number of attacks has declined by more than 90 percent.

The number of Israelis murdered and wounded has decreased by more than 70 percent and 85 percent, respectively, after erection of the fence. The success of the anti-terrorist fence in Samaria means that the launching point for terrorists has been moved to Judea, where there is not yet a continuous fence.[72]

MYTH

"Israel is the only country that believes a fence can secure its borders."

FACT

It is not unreasonable or unusual to build a fence for security purposes. Israel already has fences along the frontiers with Lebanon, Syria, and Jordan, so building a barrier to separate Israel from the Palestinian Authority is not revolutionary. Most nations have fences to protect their borders and several use barriers in political disputes:

- The United States is building a fence to keep out illegal Mexican immigrants.

- Spain built a fence, with European Union funding, to separate its enclaves of Ceuta and Melilla from Morocco to prevent poor people from sub-Saharan Africa from entering Europe.

- India constructed a 460-mile barrier in Kashmir to halt infiltrations supported by Pakistan.

- Saudi Arabia built a 60-mile barrier along an undefined border zone with Yemen to halt arms smuggling.

- Turkey built a barrier in the southern province of Alexandretta, which was formerly in Syria and is an area that Syria claims as its own.

- In Cyprus, the UN sponsored a security fence reinforcing the island's de facto partition.

■ British-built barriers separate Catholic and Protestant neighborhoods in Belfast.[73]

Ironically, after condemning Israel's barrier, the UN announced plans to build its own fence to improve security around its New York headquarters.[74]

MYTH

"The security fence should be built along the pre-1967 border."

FACT

Critics have complained that the fence is being built beyond Israel's pre-1967 border, but the so-called Green Line was not an internationally recognized border, it was an armistice line between Israel and Jordan pending the negotiation of a final border. As Israel's Supreme Court noted in its ruling on the route of the barrier, building the fence along that line would have been a political statement and would not accomplish the principal goal of the barrier, namely, the prevention of terror.

The route of the fence must take into account topography, population density, and threat assessment of each area. To be effective in protecting the maximum number of Israelis, it also must incorporate some of the settlements in the West Bank.

Most of the fence runs roughly along the Green Line. In some places, the fence is actually *inside* this line. The fence is about a mile to the east in three places that allows the incorporation of the settlements of Henanit, Shaked, Rehan, Salit, and Zofim. One of the most controversial questions has been whether to build the fence around Ariel, a town of approximately 20,000 people, the second largest Jewish settlement in the territories. To incorporate Ariel, the fence would have to extend approximately 12 miles into the West Bank. In the short-run, Israel decided to build a separate fence around Ariel, but said in February 2005 it would be incorporated within the main fence at a later stage.

Palestinians complain that the fence creates "facts on the ground," but most of the area incorporated within the fence is expected to be part of Israel in any peace agreement with the Palestinians. Israeli negotiators have always envisioned the future border to be the 1967 frontier with modifications to minimize the security risk to Israel and maximize the number of Jews living within the State, and a growing number of Israelis have come to the conclusion that the best solution to the conflict with the Palestinians is separation.

The original route was 458 miles; however, the plan has been repeatedly modified. As a result of the June 2004 Supreme Court decision, the route is being altered further to move the barrier closer to the 1967 cease-fire line and to make it less burdensome to the Palestinians. The fence is now expected to cover approximately 385 miles and incorporate just 7 percent of the West Bank—less than 160 square miles—on its "Israeli side," while 2,100 square miles will be on the "Palestinian side."

To date, more than 140 miles of the fence has been completed. After the fence is finished, Israel will have to decide whether to allow Jews to remain in communities on the "wrong" side of the fence (where they would not benefit from the security the fence provides), offer them compensation to move, or forcibly evacuate them to the Israeli side.

If and when the Palestinians decide to negotiate an end to the conflict, the fence may be torn down or moved. Even without any change, a Palestinian state could now theoretically be created in 93 percent of the West Bank (the PA now controls 100 percent of the Gaza Strip). This is very close to the 97 percent Israel offered to the Palestinians at Camp David in 2000, which means that while other difficult issues remain to be resolved, the territorial aspect of the dispute will be reduced to a negotiation over roughly 90 square miles.

MYTH

"Israel is creating a Palestinian ghetto."

FACT

Palestinian charges that a fence would have the effect of creating a ghetto are nonsense. Prime Minister Sharon has accepted the establishment of a contiguous Palestinian state on their side of the barrier.

When the Palestinians stop the violence, as required by the road map for peace, and negotiate in good faith, it may be possible to remove the fence, move it, or open it in a way that offers freedom of movement. Israel moved a similar fence when it withdrew from southern Lebanon. Until the terror stops, however, Israel must take precautions to protect its citizens, and finishing the fence is one of the most vital safeguards. The fence may help stimulate the Palestinians to take positive steps because it has shown them there is a price to pay for sponsoring terrorism.

In the short-run, Palestinians benefit from the fence because it reduces the need for Israeli military operations in the territories, and the deployment of troops in Palestinian towns. Onerous security measures, such as curfews and checkpoints, have in many areas become unnecessary or dramatically scaled back.

Every effort is being made to exclude Palestinian villages from the area within the fence and no territories are being annexed. The land used in building the security fence is seized for military purposes, not confiscated, and it remains the property of the owner. Legal procedures are already in place to allow every owner to file an objection to the seizure of their land. In addition, Israel has budgeted $22 million to compensate Palestinians for the use of their land.

Israel is doing its best to minimize the negative impact on Palestinians in the area of construction and is providing agricultural passageways to allow farmers to continue to cultivate their lands, and crossing points to allow the movement of people and the transfer of goods. Moreover, property owners are offered compensation for the use of their land and for any damage to their trees. Contractors are responsible for carefully uprooting and replanting the trees. So far, more than 60,000 olive trees have been relocated in accordance with this procedure.

Despite Israel's best efforts, the fence has caused some injury to residents near the fence. Israel's Supreme Court took up the grievances of Palestinians and ruled the government had to reduce the infringement upon local inhabitants by altering the path of the fence in an area near Jerusalem. Though the Court's decision made the government's job of securing the population from terrorist threats more difficult, costly, and time-consuming, the Prime Minister immediately accepted the ruling.

MYTH

"Israel's security fence is just like the Berlin Wall."

FACT

Although critics have sought to portray the security fence as a kind of "Berlin Wall," it is nothing of the sort. First, unlike the Berlin Wall, the fence does not separate one people, Germans from Germans, and deny freedom to those on one side. Israel's security fence separates two peoples, Israelis and Palestinians, and offers freedom and security for both. Second, while Israelis are fully prepared to live with Palestinians, and 20 percent of the Israeli population is already Arab, it is the Palestinians who say they do not want to live with any Jews and call for the West Bank to be *judenrein*. Third, the fence is not being constructed to prevent the citizens of one state from escaping; it is designed solely to keep terrorists out of Israel.

Finally, of the 385 miles scheduled to be constructed, only a tiny fraction of that (less than 3 percent or about 15 miles) is actually a 30-foot-high concrete wall, and that is being built in areas where it will prevent Palestinian snipers in the terrorist hotbeds of Kalkilya and Tulkarm from shooting at cars along the Trans-Israel Highway, one of the country's main roads. The wall also takes up less space than the other barriers, only about seven feet, so it did not have a great impact on the area where it was built.

Most of the barrier will be a chain-link type fence, similar to those used all over the United States, combined with underground and long-range sensors, unmanned aerial vehicles, trenches, landmines and guard paths. Manned checkpoints will constitute the only way to travel back and forth through the fence. The barrier is altogether about 160 feet wide in most places.

Israel did not want to build a fence, and resisted doing so for more than 35 years. If anyone is to blame for the construction, it is Hamas, Islamic Jihad and the other Palestinian terrorists. Perhaps the construction of the security fence may help stimulate the Palestinians to take action against the terrorists because the barrier has shown them there is a price to pay for sponsoring terrorism.

MYTH

"Israel's Supreme Court ruled that the security fence is illegal."

FACT

In 1989, Alan Dershowitz observed, "For the first time in Mideast history, there is an independent judiciary willing to listen to grievances of Arabs—that judiciary is called the Israeli Supreme Court.[75] That court took up the grievances of Palestinians who claimed the Israeli security fence causes hardships for them, is illegal according to Israeli and international law, and is meant to disguise the Israeli objective of annexing additional territory to Israel.

The Court ruled that a small segment of the fence—an 18-mile stretch near Jerusalem (out of the 125 miles built at that time)—needed to be rerouted because of the hardships caused to the Palestinians in the area who were cut off from their farms, schools and villages.

The Court also said, however, that it could not accept the argument that the fence's route was determined by politics rather than security. The Justices specifically rejected the idea that the fence should be constructed on the Green Line, noting that "it is the security perspective—and not the political one—which must examine a route based on its security merits alone, without regard for the location of the 'Green Line.' "

The Justices also concluded "it is permitted, by the international law applicable to an area under belligerent occupation to take possession of an individual's land in order to erect a separation fence upon it, on the condition that this is necessitated by military needs. To the extent that construction of the Fence is a military necessity, it is permitted, therefore, by international law. Indeed, the obstacle is intended to take the place of combat military operations, by physically blocking terrorist infiltration into Israeli population centers."

The fundamental question for the Court was how to satisfy Israel's security concerns without causing disproportionate injury to the residents affected by the fence. The Justices ruled that international humanitarian law and Israeli administrative law "require making every possible effort to ensure that injury will be proportionate. Where con-

struction of the Separation Fence demands that inhabitants be separated from their lands, access to these lands must be ensured, in order
to minimize the damage to the extent possible."
The Justices acknowledged that the ruling would have an impact on
the fight against terrorism. "We are aware this decision does not make
it easier to deal with that reality. This is the destiny of a democracy: She
does not see all means as acceptable, and the ways of her enemies are
not always open before her. A democracy must sometimes fight with
one arm tied behind her back. Even so, a democracy has the upper
hand. The rule of law and individual liberties constitute an important
aspect of her security stance. At the end of the day, they strengthen her
spirit and this strength allows her to overcome her difficulties."

*"In the length of the fence involved, in the number of villages and people
affected, the [Israeli Supreme Court] decision is hardly momentous. But
as a statement of principle, it is head and shoulders above anything any
other Middle East government would permit—never mind implement."*

—Richard Cohen[76]

The Supreme Court once again demonstrated that in Israel the rule
of law and judicial review is applied even to matters of national security and that it can balance the State's need to protect its citizens with
humanitarian matters.
Though the Court's decision made the government's job of protecting its citizens from terrorist threats more difficult, costly, and time-
consuming, the government accepted the ruling and began to reroute
the section of the fence near Jerusalem. In addition, the Court's ruling is
also being factored into the planning of the rest of the barrier.

MYTH

*"Hundreds of Israeli soldiers are refusing to serve in the
territories. This proves that Israel's policies are unjust."*

FACT

About 400 Israelis serving in the reserves (out of 445,000—0.08 percent) signed a petition in 2002 saying they would no longer serve in
the territories. They received a lot of publicity because it is so unusual
for Israeli soldiers to refuse to serve their country. What attracted no
media attention was the reaction of most Israelis to the call to serve in
Operation Defensive Shield. The response was more than 100 percent.

Israelis who were not obligated to report because they were too old, had disabilities, or were otherwise excused from service volunteered to go to the territories.

In a democracy, such as Israel, people may protest their government's policies, but the voices of a minority do not carry more weight than the majority. In fact, a poll from Tel Aviv University showed that nearly 80 percent of the public rejected the refuseniks' argument. Total support for their point of view was 15 percent. In addition, a counterpetition was published in Israeli newspapers in February signed by more than 1,000 other reservists who said they were "amazed and ashamed" by the original letter written by a group of what they called "draft dodgers." Also, more than 4,500 reservists volunteered for additional duty.[77]

The soldiers raised important issues about the treatment of Palestinians by the military that were taken seriously by the Israeli public and government, but their actions were also politically motivated and not mere acts of conscience. Shlomo Gazit, a former head of Israeli military intelligence, and someone who sympathized with the political goals of the refusenik soldiers, wrote an impassioned plea for them to give up their protest. He pointed out that Israeli security depends on soldiers' absolute loyalty to the elected officials of the nation and the apolitical nature of the security system. Gazit noted that soldiers can't decide which orders they wish to carry out and said that if the refuseniks' principles were adopted they could find that many other soldiers would take the exact opposite views and, say, refuse to carry out orders to evacuate settlements or withdraw from the territories, which is precisely what happened three years later when another handful of soldiers objected to the disengagement from Gaza. As Gazit also observed, soldiers can carry out their missions without losing their humanity and can refuse *illegal* orders.[78]

In addition, Israel's democratic society gives the soldiers other outlets to pursue their political agenda, such as creating a new political movement or using an existing one to change Israeli policy. Another option is to take their grievances before the judiciary. Eight of the Israeli reservists did just that, and their case was heard by Israel's Supreme Court. In December 2002, the court ruled that reservists cannot choose their assignments. The court said allowing them to do so could lead to a situation in which each army unit operates according to its own moral code.[79]

While the small minority of "refuseniks" created a sensation in 2002, the number of Israelis who have resisted service in the territories has declined ever since. In 2002, 129 reservists were jailed; in 2003, the figure fell to 26.[80] In November 2004, an all-time high of motivation to serve in IDF combat units was recorded when 92 percent of fresh conscripts asked to be deployed in these units.[81]

MYTH

"The Palestinian Authority protects Jewish holy sites."

FACT

Less than 24 hours after the last IDF soldier withdrew from the Gaza Strip, Palestinian Authority bulldozers began to raze synagogues that were left behind by Jewish residents. Thousands of Palestinians also stormed the former Gaza settlements and set fire to several synagogues and yeshivas while PA security forces stood and watched. Several Palestinians belonging to terrorist groups climbed the roofs of synagogues and placed green flags on top while other members inside set fire to the buildings and looted items that the Jews left behind.[82]

Israel decided not to dismantle the 19 synagogues and yeshivas in Gaza and the evacuated northern Samaria settlements. "It would be a historic Jewish mistake to destroy the synagogues," said Defense Minister Shaul Mofaz.[83]

United Nations Secretary-General Kofi Annan was told by Israel that since the disengagement plan was implemented, the "PA now had the moral responsibility to protect the synagogues as places with religious significance."[84] Earlier in the week, Ministry of Defense workers placed signs that read "Holy Place" in Arabic and English on synagogue walls throughout Gaza so the Palestinians would know not to destroy them.[85]

Palestinian Authority President Mahmoud Abbas defended the razing of Gaza synagogues by claiming, "There are no synagogues here." Abbas said the buildings that were formally synagogues were now emptied and in danger of collapsing, and must be demolished to build homes for thousands of Palestinians.[86] The PA maintained that the synagogues were symbols of Israeli occupation, and boycotted the ceremony marking the handover of Gaza to the Palestinians in protest of Israel's decision to leave the synagogues intact.[87]

This was not the first instance when the PA has failed to protect Jewish holy places:

- In September 1996, Palestinian rioters destroyed a synagogue at Joseph's Tomb in Nablus.

- Rachel's Tomb near Bethlehem has been repeatedly attacked since 1996.

- In October 2000, Joseph's Tomb was torched after the Israeli garrison guarding it was temporarily withdrawn. It was subsequently rebuilt as a mosque.

- Also in October 2000, the ancient synagogue in Jericho was destroyed by arson and a second historic synagogue was damaged.

PA textbooks continue to teach young Palestinians that Jews have no connection to the Land of Israel and to disparage Judaism, so it should not be surprising that Jewish institutions are not shown respect. This is one reason why Israel is reluctant to make any compromises regarding Jerusalem that might allow Palestinians to threaten the sanctity of the shrines of any religion.

MYTH

"Peace with Syria has been prevented only by Israel's obstinate refusal to withdraw from the Golan Heights."

FACT

Given past history, Israel is understandably reluctant to give away the strategic high ground and its early-warning system. Nevertheless, Israel had repeatedly expressed a willingness to negotiate the future of the Golan Heights. One possible compromise might be a partial Israeli withdrawal, along the lines of its 1974 disengagement agreement with Syria. Another would be a complete withdrawal, with the Golan becoming a demilitarized zone.

After losing the 1999 election, Benjamin Netanyahu confirmed reports that he had engaged in secret talks with Syrian President Hafez Assad to withdraw from the Golan and maintain a strategic early-warning station on Mount Hermon. Publicly, Assad continued to insist on a total withdrawal with no compromises and indicated no willingness to go beyond agreeing to a far more limited "non-belligerency" deal with Israel than the full peace treaty Israel has demanded.

The election of Ehud Barak stimulated new movement in the peace process, with intensive negotiations held in the United States in January 2000 between Barak and Syrian Foreign Minister Farouk al-Sharaa. These talks raised new hope for the conclusion of a peace treaty, but the discussions did not bear fruit. Hafez Assad died in June 2000 and no further talks have been held as Assad's son and successor, Bashar, has not indicated any shift in Syria's position on the Golan.

Israel has made clear it is prepared to compromise on the Golan and make significant territorial concessions. The only obstacle is Assad's unwillingness to say yes to peace with Israel.

MYTH

"Israel's continued occupation of Lebanese territory is the only impediment to the conclusion of a peace treaty."

FACT

Israel has never had any hostile intentions toward Lebanon, but has been forced to fight as a result of the chaotic conditions in southern Lebanon that have allowed terrorists, first the PLO, and now Hizballah, to menace citizens living in northern Israel. In 1983, Israel did sign a peace treaty with Lebanon, but Syria forced President Amin Gemayel to renege on the agreement.

Israel pulled all its troops out of southern Lebanon on May 24, 2000. The Israeli withdrawal was conducted in coordination with the UN, and, according to the UN, constituted an Israeli fulfillment of its obligations under Security Council Resolution 425. Still, Hizballah and the Lebanese government insist that Israel holds Lebanese territory in a largely uninhabited patch called Shebaa Farms. This claim provides Hizballah with a pretext to continue its attacks against Israel. The Israelis maintain, however, that the land was captured from Syria.

Syria, meanwhile, has used its influence over Lebanon to discourage any peace negotiations until its claims on the Golan Heights are resolved. Once Israel and Syria reach an agreement, the expectation is that Lebanon would quickly do so afterward.

"Palestine is not only a part of our Arab homeland, but a basic part of southern Syria."

—Syrian President Hafez Assad[88]

MYTH

"Israel has a surplus of water and its refusal to share with its neighbors could provoke the next war."

FACT

The supply of water is a matter of life and death, war and peace for the peoples of the Middle East. A *Jerusalem Post* headline concisely stated the security threat for Israel, "The hand that controls the faucet rules the country."[89]

King Hussein said in 1990 the one issue that could bring Jordan to war again is water, so it is not surprising that an agreement on water supplies was critical to the negotiation of the peace treaty with Israel. Jordan now receives an annual allotment of water from Israel.[90]

Israel has had an ongoing water deficit for a number of years. Simply put, the amount of water consumed is greater than the amount of water collected from rainfall. In a drought year, the situation worsens, because the amount of water in reservoirs and the amount of water flowing in rivers and streams is significantly decreased.

The situation is growing more dangerous each year as the population of the region continues to grow exponentially, political disputes over existing water supplies become more pronounced, and Israel and the Palestinians negotiate rights to the water in the West Bank and Gaza Strip.

Israel has three main water sources: the coastal and mountain aquifers and Lake Kinneret (Sea of Galilee). Each supply approximately 25 percent of the total consumed. Roughly 20 percent is derived from smaller aquifers. The remaining 5 percent comes from the Shafdan project that recycles sewage in metropolitan Tel Aviv.

"In Old Testament times, there were two ways of solving disputes over water, which has always been scarce in our region. One was to fight over it. The other was to jointly place over the mouth of the well, a stone so large that five shepherds were needed to lift it, creating the need for cooperation."

—Former Israeli Agriculture Minister Yaacov Tzur

The coastal aquifer's water quality is deteriorating because of overpumping and contamination from sewage. Lake Kinneret requires a delicate water level balance. If the level is too low, salty water from neighboring springs seeps in. If the level rises too high, it can flood. The mountain aquifer is in the best condition.

The mountain aquifer is also the most politically contentious. Prior to 1967, Israel used 95 percent of this water, the Arabs only 5 percent. Since then, the Arab share has more than tripled, but the Palestinians are still demanding that these proportions be reversed. They argue that since the aquifer lies under the West Bank, it should come under the control of the Palestinian Authority. The Palestinians maintain that Israel is "stealing" their water, but Israel wants to retain control over the lion's share of the water.

The water issue clearly affects Israel's economy and security. One danger, for example, is that pumping of water in Judea and Samaria by Palestinians could increase to a degree that would completely eliminate pumping in Israel. The Palestinians have also demanded the right to expand their agricultural sector, using the same limited water resources that Israel's State Comptroller said were inadequate to expand Israel's agricultural production. Meanwhile, Palestinian water authorities have said as much as 50 percent of domestic water is lost because of old, inefficient supply systems. The PA's dilemma is even worse in Gaza, where the sole aquifer is already virtually unusable because of contamination and salinity.

The amount of water to be supplied to the territories by Israel was determined in negotiations between the two sides, and Israel has ful-

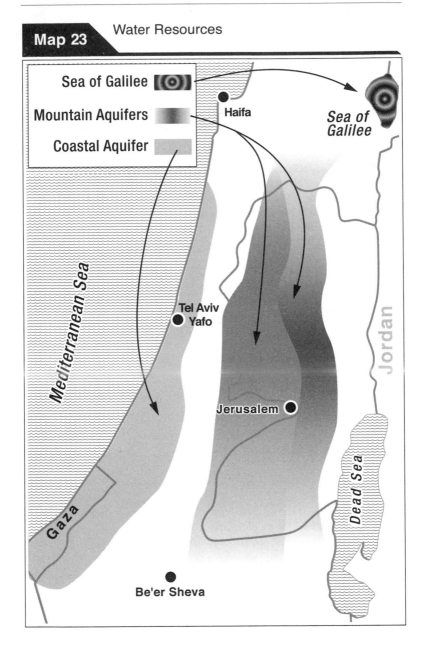

Map 23   Water Resources

filled all of its obligations under the Interim Agreement. In addition, the United States agreed to fund a pipeline to bring water to Gaza from Israel's desalinization plant in Ashkelon.[91]

In response to the threat to water supplies posed by the Palestinian War, Palestinian and Israeli water officials issued a joint statement in January 2001 opposing any damage to water and wastewater infrastructure, and expressing the intent to ensure the water supply to the Palestinian and Israeli cities, towns and villages in the West Bank and Gaza Strip.[92]

Israel could secure its water future by maintaining control over three West Bank regions comprising 20 percent of the land; however, pressure from the international community and the momentum of the peace process may force Israel to give up some or all of these territories.

"Israel has no right even to a single drop of water in this region."

—Syrian Foreign Minister Farouk al-Sharaa[93]

Water is also an issue in negotiations with the Syrians. Syria demands the full return of the Golan Heights in return for peace with Israel. According to water expert Joyce Starr, an Israeli government that concedes territory on the Golan without a guaranteed supply of Yarmuk waters, or some alternative source of water, would be putting the nation in "grave jeopardy."[94]

Israel is taking steps to ameliorate the water issue by beginning construction of major desalination plants that are scheduled to provide, by 2006, nearly one-fourth of Israel's needs. An agreement has also been reached that will allow Israel to import water from Turkey. Israel has offered to build a desalination plant in Hadera for the Palestinians in the West Bank, but they have rejected the idea.

MYTH

"Saudi Arabia is a force for peace and moderation that does not sponsor terror."

FACT

"The Saudis are active at every level of the terror chain, from planners to financiers, from cadre to foot-soldier, from ideologist to cheerleader," said Laurent Murawiec, a Rand Corporation analyst in a secret briefing to a top Pentagon advisory board. "Saudi Arabia," he added, "supports our enemies and attacks our allies."[95]

The most dramatic evidence of Saudi involvement in terror is the fact that 15 of the 19 September 11 terrorists were from Saudi Arabia. Despite this, the Saudi government refused to cooperate with the U.S. investigation of the attacks and rejected American requests to stop the flow of money through charitable organizations to terrorist groups. Many such charities are based in the United States and are being investigated by the Treasury Department.

Saudi support for terrorism and al-Qaida, in particular, is not restricted to extremists in the kingdom. A classified American intelligence report revealed that an October 2001 survey of educated Saudis between the ages of 25 and 41 found that 95 percent of the respondents supported Osama bin Laden's cause.[96] According to a UN report, "al-Qaida was able to receive between $300 and $500 million over the last 10 years from wealthy businessmen and bankers whose fortunes represent about 20 percent of the Saudi GNP, through a web of charities and companies acting as fronts."[97]

The Saudis have been heavily involved in supporting Palestinian terror. They were the largest financial backer of Hamas during the 1990s, providing perhaps as much as $10 million annually. At one point, Abu Mazen even complained to the governor of Riyadh that Saudi money wasn't reaching the "martyrs," but was going directly to Hamas.[98]

The Saudis held a terror telethon on April 11, 2002, which raised more than $100 million for families of Palestinian "martyrs," including the families of suicide bombers[99] and, during Operation Defensive Shield, the Israelis found numerous documents linking the Saudis to terror. One, for example, itemized their allocations line by line, detailing the circumstances of the death of Palestinians whose families received assistance, and making clear the allocation was for suicide attacks. The information came from the Saudi Committee for Aid to the Al-Quds Intifada, which is headed by Saudi Minister of the Interior, Prince Nayef bin 'Abd al-Aziz.

Israeli authorities arrested an Israeli-Arab Hamas activist in September 2005 who confessed to receiving instructions for Hamas field operatives and hundreds of thousands of dollars from the Hamas headquarters in Saudi Arabia. Hamas leaders in Saudi Arabia provided funding to establish a "communications office" to report developments on the ground to Hamas operatives abroad. Money was also transferred, often under the cover of charity work, to the families of suicide bombers, imprisoned terrorists and Hamas institutions.[100]

MYTH

"The Arab world's commitment to peace is reflected by its abandonment of the boycott against Israel."

FACT

The Arab League declared a boycott against the Jews before Israel was established, and most of its members have pursued a diplomatic and economic embargo against the Jewish State since its establishment. The boycott's influence waned after Egypt and Jordan made peace with Israel, the Palestinians became engaged in peace negotiations, and several Gulf states started ignoring the blacklist, but it was never abandoned, and several nations, most notably Saudi Arabia, have energetically enforced it for decades.

To give an indication of how entrenched the boycott is within the Arab world, the Bureau for Boycotting Israel held its *72nd* conference in April 2004. Representatives from 19 Arab countries met in Syria to discuss tightening the boycott, and blacklisting new companies that do business with the Jewish state.[101]

To their credit, Mauritania, Egypt and Jordan, which have diplomatic ties with Israel, stayed away from the meeting. The Palestinians, however, did participate, and the head of their delegation, Ali Abo al-Hawa, asked the conference to respond to the Arab public's call for boycotting Israel, particularly in commercial relations. This was a violation of the PLO promise to oppose the boycott made in the September 28, 1995, Joint Declaration of the Washington Summit. Delegates to the 2004 conference also wanted to take measures to prevent Israeli companies from trying to penetrate the Iraqi market, but removed the issue from the agenda after the Iraqi delegate, Sabah al-Imam, assured the group, "there is no Israeli activity in Iraq "approved by Iraqi authorities.

Syria subsequently banned a Greek, a Danish and two Maltese ships from its ports because they'd made stops in Israeli ports, and has placed nine Israeli companies on a black list. And Libya, which had pledged to provide entry visas to all qualified participants, announced that it would not allow any Israelis to participate in the World Chess Championships in Tripoli in June 2004.[102]

In 2005, Saudi Arabia announced it would end its economic embargo of Israeli goods to win acceptance to the World Trade Organization.[103] Nevertheless, the continued effort to isolate Israel economically and diplomatically demonstrates that many Arab states are still unwilling to recognize Israel. Until the boycott is terminated, and the Arab League members accept the existence of Israel, the prospects for regional peace will remain dim.

Notes

1. Speech to AIPAC Policy Conference, (May 8, 1978).
2. Reuters, (September 24, 2001).
3. Daniel Pipes, *The Long Shadow: Culture and Politics in the Middle East*, (NJ: Transaction Publishers, 1989), pp. 273-74.
4. Reuters, (November 11, 2001).
5. Michael Widlanski, *Can Israel Survive A Palestinian State?*, (Jerusalem: Institute for Advanced Strategic and Political Studies, 1990), pp. 10, 35.
6. *Yediot Aharonot*, (November 23, 2001).
7. *Yediot Aharonot*, (August 7, 2002).

8. *Maariv,* (April 6, 2001); Interview with Dennis Ross, Fox News Sunday, (April 21, 2002); President Clinton, Press Conference, (July 25, 2000); "Camp David: An Exchange." *The New York Review of Books,* (September 20, 2001); Fred Barnes, "Myths of the Intifada," *The Daily Standard,* (April 25, 2002).

9. MSNBC, (March 26, 2002).

10. *Yediot Aharonot,* (August 18, 2003).

11. David Makovsky, "Taba Mythchief," *The National Interest,* (February 26, 2003).

12. Steven Spiegel, *The Other Arab-Israeli Conflict: Making America's Middle East Policy from Truman to Reagan,* (IL: University of Chicago Press, 1986), p. 358; Ariel Sharon, *Warrior,* (NY: Touchstone Books, 2001), pp. 400–401.

13. CBC News, (August 29, 2005).

14. Associated Press, (May 26, 2003).

15. Herb Keinon, "Observer teams validate PA elections," *Jerusalem Post,* (January 11, 2005).

16. *Jerusalem Post,* (November 4, 2004).

17. Speech by Ambassador Dennis Ross, University of Michigan, (March 13, 2005).

18. *Jerusalem Post,* (December 2, 2004).

19. *Globes,* (April 26, 2005).

20. *Haaretz,* (June 7, 2005); Ynetnews.com, (September 8, 2005).

21. James Bennet, "Palestinians' Big Plans for Gaza, With a Bit of Doubt," *New York Times,* (August 27, 2005).

22. Herb Keinon, Matthew Gutman, and JPost staff, "Abbas: Permanent status deal could be reached in 6 months," *Jerusalem Post,* (November 15, 2005); Robin Wright, "Rice Cements Deal on Gaza Borders," *Washington Post,* (November 16, 2005).

23. Audiotape posted August 27, 2005, on the 'Izz Al-Din Al-Qassam Brigades website, translated by MEMRI.

24. Herb Keinon, "PA to get Gush Katif hothouses," *Jerusalem Post,* (August 12, 2005).

25. *New York Times,* (August 27, 2003).

26. NBC News and MSNBC, (May 8, 2001).

27. *Jerusalem Post,* (October 16, 2001).

28. Lee Hockstader, "At Arab, Israeli Schools, Hatred Is Common Bond," *Washington Post,* (September 5, 2001).

29. *Near East Report,* (June 25, 2001); *Jerusalem Post,* (July 20, 2001).

30. *Jerusalem Post,* (May 23, 2001).

31. Quoted in *Jerusalem Post,* (July 20, 2001).

32. *Jerusalem Post,* (May 15, 2005).

33. *Jerusalem Post,* (May 15, 2005).

34. "Germany's Fischer: No Palestinian state if violence goes on," Associated Press, (July 15, 2005).

35. Associated Press, (May 15, 2005).

36. Jerusalem Media & Communication Center, (May 2–7, 2005).

37. Palestinian Authority. Note that the site is often down and the material sometimes moves or is recast as "history," which would only be accurate if Jordan was also included as part of historical Palestine.

38. *Washington Post,* (December 5, 2001).

39. Jitka Maleckova and Alan Kreuger, "Education, Poverty, Political Violence and Terrorism: Is There a Causal Connection?" (July 2002), quoted in the *Daily Star* [Lebanon], (August 6, 2002).

40. "Without distinction—attacks on civilians by Palestinian armed groups," Amnesty International, (July 11, 2002).

41. *Jerusalem Post,* (January 15, 2003).

42. Anthony H. Cordesman, "Escalating to Nowhere: The Israeli-Palestinian War—The Actors in the Conflict: The Palestinian Factions That Challenge Peace and the Palestinian Authority," (DC: CSIS, September 12, 2003), p. 35.
43. International Policy Institute for Counter-Terrorism, "Jordan Closes Hamas Offices in Amman," (August 31, 1999); "Jordan Deports Hamas Leaders to Qatar," (November 22, 1999); "The Jordanian Move against Hamas," (August 31, 1999).
44. Israel Radio, (August 1, 2002).
45. "US Envoy Slams Palestinian Authority over Terror Attacks," Scotsman.com, (July 14, 2004).
46. *Washington Post,* (July 18, 2001), citing an article by Robert Malley and Hussein Agha in the *New York Review of Books* in which they quote the President at the Camp David summit in July 2000.
47. Fox News, (January 8, 2002); *USA Today,* (January 10, 2002).
48. Doron Almog, "Tunnel-Vision in Gaza," *Middle East Quarterly,* (Summer 2004).
49. *Jerusalem Post,* (August 22, September 22, 2005).
50. For example, three officials from a Palestinian faction that claimed responsibility for an attack on Israel were arrested and then released five hours later, *Haaretz,* (February 5, 2005).
51. See, for example, CNN, (January 13, 2001); Associated Press, (July 31, 2001).
52. Islamic Association for Palestine, (June 9, 2001).
53. Neil Livingstone and David Halevy, *Inside the PLO,* (Readers Digest Press, 1990), pp. 276-288.
54. *Chicago Tribune,* (March 5, 1988).
55. *Washington Post,* (August 10, 2001).
56. Hamas Covenant. See Appendix.
57. *Washington Post,* (September 21, 2003).
58. Reuters, (May 27, 1998).
59. Reuters, (July 31, 2001).
60. *USA Today,* (June 26, 2001).
61. Matthew Levitt, "Hamas from Cradle to Grave," *The Middle East Quarterly,* (Winter 2004).
62. *Washington Post,* (April 6, 2002).
63. Morris Abram, "Israel Under Attack: Anti-Semitism in the United Nations," *The Earth Times,* (December 16-31, 1997).
64. Palestinian Authority TV, (March 3, 2003).
65. Palestine News Agency WAFA, (April 28, 2005).
66. Palestinian Authority TV, (March 3, 2003).
67. *Washington Post,* (September 19, 2003).
68. Ze'ev Dasberg, "Society takes precedence over the individual," *Haaretz,* (November 2, 2003).
69. VOA News, (February 12, 2004).
70. Yair Ettinger, "Highway, fence spur growth in Wadi Ara," *Haaretz,* (July 14, 2004).
71. *Haaretz,* (February 13, 2002).
72. Israeli Foreign Ministry.
73. *Wall Street Journal* editorial, (September 26, 2005).
74. United Nations, (May 6, 2004).
75. Speech to AIPAC Policy Conference, (May 23, 1989).
76. Richard Cohen, "Israel's Day of Light," *Washington Post,* (July 3, 2004).
77. *The Jewish Week* (NY), (February 8, 2002); *Jerusalem Post,* (April 5, 2002).
78. *Washington Jewish Week,* (February 14, 2002).
79. Jewish Telegraphic Agency, (December 30, 2002).

80. Jewish Telegraphic Agency, (February 3, 2004).
81. *Maariv,* (November 24, 2004).
82. "PA bulldozers begin razing remaining Gaza synagogues," *Jerusalem Post,* (September 12, 2005).
83. Herb Keinon, "Cabinet votes not to dismantle Gaza synagogues," *Jerusalem Post,* (September 12, 2005).
84. Herb Keinon, "Cabinet votes not to dismantle Gaza synagogues," *Jerusalem Post,* (September 12, 2005).
85. Yoav Stern, "PA to raze synagogues, spokesman says," *Haaretz,* (September 12, 2005).
86. Khaled Abu Toameh, "PA, Hamas defend synagogue razing," *Jerusalem Post,* (September 12, 2005).
87. "PA bulldozers begin razing remaining Gaza synagogues," *Jerusalem Post,* (September 12, 2005).
88. Radio Damascus, (March 8, 1974).
89. *Jerusalem Post,* (July 16, 1994).
90. *Washington Times,* (July 30, 1990).
91. *Yediot Abaronot,* (January 14, 2005).
92. Israeli-Palestinian Joint Water Committee, "Joint Declaration for Keeping the Water Infrastructure out of the Cycle of Violence," (January 31, 2001).
93. *Mideast Mirror,* (October 7, 1991).
94. *Washington Post,* (September 10, 1995).
95. *Washington Post,* (August 6, 2001).
96. *New York Times,* (January 27, 2002).
97. Quoted in *Gulf News,* (December 28, 2002).
98. Kenneth Timmerman, "Hamas' Friends," *Australia/Israel Review,* (June 2002), p. 13.
99. *Washington Post,* (April 2 and 12, 2002).
100. Matthew Levitt, "A Hamas Headquarters in Saudi Arabia?" Washington Institute for Near East Policy, (September 28, 2005).
101. Associated Press, SANA, (April 26, 2004).
102. *Jerusalem Post,* (May 5, 2004); Associated Press, (May 8, 2004).
103. "Saudi Arabia lifts Israel embargo," *Jerusalem Post,* (November 15, 2005).

20. Settlements

MYTH

"Israel has no right to be in the West Bank.
Israeli settlements are illegal."

FACT

Jews have lived in Judea and Samaria—the West Bank—since ancient times. The only time Jews have been prohibited from living in the territories in recent decades was during Jordan's rule from 1948 to 1967. This prohibition was contrary to the Mandate for Palestine adopted by the League of Nations, which provided for the establishment of a Jewish state, and specifically encouraged "close settlement by Jews on the land," which included Judea and Samaria.

Numerous legal authorities dispute the charge that settlements are "illegal." Stephen Schwebel, formerly President of the International Court of Justice, notes that a country acting in self-defense may seize and occupy territory when necessary to protect itself. Schwebel also observes that a state may require, as a condition for its withdrawal, security measures designed to ensure its citizens are not menaced again from that territory.[1]

According to Eugene Rostow, a former Undersecretary of State for Political Affairs in the Johnson Administration, Resolution 242 gives Israel a legal right to be in the West Bank. The resolution, Rostow noted, "allows Israel to administer the territories" it won in 1967 "until 'a just and lasting peace in the Middle East' is achieved."[2]

MYTH

"Settlements are an obstacle to peace."

FACT

Settlements have never been an obstacle to peace.

- From 1949-67, when Jews were forbidden to live on the West Bank, the Arabs refused to make peace with Israel.
- From 1967-77, the Labor Party established only a few strategic settlements in the territories, yet the Arabs were unwilling to negotiate peace with Israel.
- In 1977, months after a Likud government committed to greater settlement activity took power, Egyptian President Sadat went to Jeru-

salem and later signed a peace treaty with Israel. Incidentally, Israeli settlements existed in the Sinai and those were removed as part of the agreement with Egypt.

■ One year later, Israel froze settlement building for three months, hoping the gesture would entice other Arabs to join the Camp David peace process. But none would.

■ In 1994, Jordan signed a peace agreement with Israel and settlements were not an issue; if anything, the number of Jews living in the territories was growing.

■ Between June 1992 and June 1996, under Labor-led governments, the Jewish population in the territories grew by approximately 50 percent. This rapid growth did not prevent the Palestinians from signing the Oslo accords in September 1993 or the Oslo 2 agreement in September 1995.

■ In 2000, Prime Minister Ehud Barak offered to dismantle dozens of settlements, but the Palestinians still would not agree to end the conflict.

■ In August 2005, Israel evacuated all of the settlements in the Gaza Strip and four in Northern Samaria, but terror attacks continued.

Settlement activity may be a *stimulus* to peace because it forced the Palestinians and other Arabs to reconsider the view that time is on their side. References are frequently made in Arabic writings to how long it took to expel the Crusaders and how it might take a similar length of time to do the same to the Zionists. The growth in the Jewish population in the territories forced the Arabs to question this tenet. "The Palestinians now realize," said Bethlehem Mayor Elias Freij, "that time is now on the side of Israel, which can build settlements and create facts, and that the only way out of this dilemma is face-to-face negotiations."[3]

Many Israelis nevertheless have concerns about the expansion of settlements. Some consider them provocative, others worry that the settlers are particularly vulnerable, and note they have been targets of repeated Palestinian terrorist attacks. To defend them, large numbers of soldiers are deployed who would otherwise be training and preparing for a possible future conflict with an Arab army. Some Israelis also object to the amount of money that goes to communities beyond the Green Line, and special subsidies that have been provided to make housing there more affordable. Still others feel the settlers are providing a first line of defense and developing land that rightfully belongs to Israel.

The disposition of settlements is a matter for the final status negotiations. The question of where the final border will be between Israel and a Palestinian entity will likely be influenced by the distribution of these Jewish towns in Judea and Samaria (the border with Gaza was unofficially defined following Israel's withdrawal). Israel wants to incorporate as many settlers as possible within its borders while the Palestinians want to expel all Jews from the territory they control.

If Israel withdraws toward the 1949 armistice line unilaterally, or as part of a political settlement, many settlers will face one or more options: remain in the territories (the disengagement from Gaza suggests this may not be possible), expulsion from their homes, or voluntary resettlement in Israel (with financial compensation).

The impediment to peace is not the existence of Jewish communities in the disputed territories, it is the Palestinians' unwillingness to accept a state next to Israel instead of one replacing Israel.

MYTH

"The Geneva Convention prohibits the construction of Jewish settlements in occupied territories."

FACT

The Fourth Geneva Convention prohibits the *forcible* transfer of people of one state to the territory of another state that it has occupied as a result of a war. The intention was to insure that local populations who came under occupation would not be forced to move. This is in no way relevant to the settlement issue. Jews are not being forced to go to the West Bank; on the contrary, they are voluntarily moving back to places where they, or their ancestors, once lived before being expelled by others.

In addition, those territories never legally belonged to either Jordan or Egypt, and certainly not to the Palestinians, who were never the sovereign authority in any part of Palestine. "The Jewish right of settlement in the area is equivalent in every way to the right of the local population to live there," according to Professor Eugene Rostow, former Undersecretary of State for Political Affairs.[4]

As a matter of policy, moreover, Israel does not requisition private land for the establishment of settlements. Housing construction is allowed on private land only after determining that no private rights will be violated. The settlements also do not displace Arabs living in the territories. The media sometimes gives the impression that for every Jew who moves to the West Bank, several hundred Palestinians are forced to leave. The truth is that the vast majority of settlements have been built in uninhabited areas and even the handful established in or near Arab towns did not force any Palestinians to leave.

MYTH

"Israel is provocatively settling Jews in predominantly Arab towns, and has established so many facts on the ground territorial compromise is no longer possible."

FACT

Altogether, built-up settlement area is less than two percent of the disputed territories. An estimated 70 percent of the settlers live in what are in effect suburbs of major Israeli cities such as Jerusalem. These are areas that virtually the entire Jewish population believes Israel must retain to ensure its security, and even President Clinton indicated in December 2000 that they should remain under permanent Israeli sovereignty.[5]

Strategic concerns have led both Labor and Likud governments to establish settlements. The objective is to secure a Jewish majority in key strategic regions of the West Bank, such as the Tel Aviv-Jerusalem corridor, the scene of heavy fighting in several Arab-Israeli wars. Still, when Arab-Israeli peace talks began in late 1991, more than 80 percent of the West Bank contained no settlements or only sparsely populated ones.[6]

Today, approximately 250,000 Jews live in roughly 150 communities in the West Bank. The overwhelming majority of these settlements have fewer than 1,000 citizens and several have only a few dozen residents. Analysts have noted that 70–80 percent of the Jews could be brought within Israel's borders with minor modifications of the Green Line.

MYTH

"At Camp David, during Jimmy Carter's presidency, Israel agreed to halt the construction of settlements for five years."

FACT

The five-year period agreed to at Camp David was the time allotted to Palestinian self-government in the territories. The Israeli moratorium on West Bank settlements agreed to by Prime Minister Menachem Begin was only for three months. Begin kept this agreement as Egyptian President Anwar Sadat acknowledged, "We agreed to put a freeze on the establishment of settlements for the coming three months, the time necessary in our estimation for signing the peace treaty."[7]

MYTH

"The Mitchell Report said Israeli settlement policy was as much to blame for the breakdown of the peace process as Palestinian violence and that a settlement freeze was a prerequisite to ending the violence."

FACT

In November 2000, former U.S. Senator George Mitchell was appointed to lead a fact-finding committee to investigate the origins of what would become the Palestinian War, and explore how to prevent future violence. The report his committee issued did recommend a settlement freeze—as one of more than 15 different confidence-building measures—but Mitchell and Warren Rudman, another member of the committee, made clear that settlement activity was in no way equated with Palestinian terrorism. They explicitly stated in a letter clarifying their view: "We do not in any way equate Palestinian terrorism with Israeli settlement activity...."

Mitchell and Rudman also disputed the idea that the cessation of settlement construction and terrorism were linked. "The immediate aim must be to end the violence.... Part of the effort to end the violence must include an immediate resumption of security cooperation between the government of Israel and the Palestinian Authority aimed at preventing violence and combating terrorism." They added, "Regarding terrorism, we call upon the Palestinian Authority, as a confidence-building measure, to make clear through concrete action, to Israelis and Palestinians alike, that terror is reprehensible and unacceptable, and the Palestinian Authority is to make a total effort to prevent terrorist operations and to punish perpetrators acting in its jurisdiction."[8]

> *"If settlement-building is now concentrated in areas that the Palestinians themselves acknowledge will remain part of Israel in any future peace agreement, why the obsessive focus on settlements as an 'obstacle to peace?'"*
>
> **—Yossi Klein Halevi**[9]

MYTH

"Israel's plan to link Jerusalem and Ma'aleh Adumim is meant to sabotage the peace process."

FACT

In March 2005, Israel announced the intention to build 3,500 homes on a strip of territory between the community of Ma'aleh Adumim and Jerusalem.[10] The decision immediately caused an uproar as Palestinian officials claimed it was "a kind of terror against the peace process and against the Palestinian people," and Secretary of State Condoleezza Rice said it was at odds with U.S. policy.[11]

This is a good example of the importance of understanding not only the politics of the issue, but the geography.

Map 24 The Future Borders of Israel and Palestine?

Proposed Palestinian State

Israeli Settlement Blocs
Annexed to Israel

1967 "border"

MEDITERRANEAN
SEA

0   15
miles

N

Sea of
Galilee

Haifa

Jenin

Tulkarm

Nablus

Qalqilya

Ariel
(est. bloc pop. 39,000)

Tel Aviv

Modiin Illit
(est. bloc pop. 31,000)

Ramallah

Jordan River

ISRAEL

Jerusalem

Jericho

Ma'aleh
Adumim
(est. bloc pop. 33,000)

Gush Etzion
(est. bloc pop. 42,000)

Bethlehem

Hebron

Gaza

GAZA
STRIP

Dead
Sea

JORDAN

ISRAEL

EGYPT

Ma'aleh Adumim is in the West Bank, so it is called a settlement, but it is actually a suburb of Israel's capital, barely three miles outside the city limits, a ten-minute drive away. Ma'aleh Adumim is not a recently constructed outpost on a hilltop; it is a 30-year-old community that is popular because it is clean, safe, and close to where many residents work. It is also the largest Jewish community in the territories, with a population of 27,300.

Because of its size and location, it is understood by both Israelis and Palestinians that Ma'aleh Adumim will not be dismantled or evacuated; it will be part of Israel after a peace agreement is reached. That is why the plan to link the city to Jerusalem was conceived during Prime Minister Rabin's term. The development was part of his plan to connect all of the large settlement blocs just outside Jerusalem's city limits.

To understand why the plan has the support of Israel's major parties, just look at a map. If Ma'aleh Adumim is not linked to Jerusalem, the city would be an island. We hear a lot about Palestinian concerns about the contiguity of a future Palestinian state, but the same principal applies to the future boundaries of Israel.

Why should it be a problem for Israel to fill in the empty gap between the city and this bedroom community? The corridor is approximately 3,250 acres and does not have any inhabitants, so no Palestinians will be displaced. And why shouldn't Israel be able to build in and around the city that the U.S. Congress said "should be recognized as the capital of the State of Israel" and "should remain an undivided city"?

In his April 14, 2004, letter to Prime Minister Sharon, President Bush acknowledged that Israel would incorporate some settlements inside its borders:

> In light of new realities on the ground, including already existing major Israeli populations centers, it is unrealistic to expect that the outcome of final status negotiations will be a full and complete return to the armistice lines of 1949, and all previous efforts to negotiate a two-state solution have reached the same conclusion.[12]

Given that Ma'aleh Adumim is the largest of these population centers, the decision to develop around the town is consistent with the policy expressed in Bush's letter. It is also consistent, incidentally, with the Clinton plan.

Would the completion of the building project known as E-1 prevent the creation of a contiguous Palestinian state? Again, a look at the map shows that it would not. The security fence is being built roughly along the Green Line, and around the major settlement blocs, such as Ma'aleh Adumim, which are expected to be within the final negotiated borders of the state. The area of the West Bank beyond the fence is contiguous.

MYTH

"Israel must dismantle all the settlements in the West Bank or peace is impossible."

FACT

When serious negotiations begin over the final status of the West Bank, battle lines will be drawn over which settlements should be incorporated into Israel, and which must be evacuated. In August 2005, Prime Minister Ariel Sharon acknowledged that "not all the settlements that are today in Judea and Samaria will remain Israeli."

In Gaza, Israel's intent was to withdraw completely, and no settlements were viewed as vital to Israel for economic, security, or demographic reasons. The situation in the West Bank is completely different because Jews have strong historic and religious connections to the area stretching back centuries. Moreover, the West Bank is an area with strategic significance because of its proximity to Israel's heartland and the fact that roughly one-quarter of Israel's water resources are located there.

> *"Clearly, in the permanent agreement we will have to give up some of the Jewish settlements."*
>
> **—Prime Minister Ariel Sharon**[13]

The disengagement from Gaza involved only 21 settlements and approximately 8,500 Jews; more than 100 settlements with a population of roughly 250,000 are located in Judea and Samaria. Any new evacuation from the West Bank will involve another gut-wrenching decision that most settlers and their supporters will oppose with even greater ferocity than the Gaza disengagement. Most Israelis, however, favor withdrawing from small, isolated communities, and about half of the settlements have fewer than 500 residents.

Approximately two-thirds of the Jews in the West Bank live in five settlement "blocs" that are all near the 1967 border. Most Israelis believe these blocs should become part of Israel when final borders are drawn and Prime Minister Sharon has repeatedly said the large settlement blocs will "remain in our hands."

As the table shows, these are large communities with thousands of residents. Evacuating them would be the equivalent of dismantling major American cities the size of Maryland's capital, Annapolis, Juneau, Alaska, or Augusta, Georgia.

"Consensus" Settlements

Bloc	No. of Communities	Population	Approximate. Area (sq. miles)
Ma'ale Adumim	6	33,000	28
Modiin Illit	4	31,205	2
Ariel	15	38,909	47
Gush Etzion	18	42,322	10
Givat Ze'ev	5	14,603	3
Total	45	160,039	90

Ma'ale Adumim is a suburb of Israel's capital, barely three miles outside Jerusalem's city limits, a ten-minute drive away. Ma'ale Adumim is the largest Jewish city in the territories, with a population of 27,300. Approximately 6,000 people live in surrounding settlements that are included in the Ma'ale bloc. Israel has long planned to fill in the empty gap between Jerusalem and this bedroom community (referred to as the E1 project). The corridor is approximately 3,250 acres and does not have any inhabitants, so no Palestinians would be displaced. According to the Clinton plan, Ma'ale was to be part of Israel.

The Gush Etzion Bloc consists of 18 communities with a population of more than 42,000 just 10 minutes from Jerusalem. Jews lived in this area prior to 1948, but the Jordanian Legion destroyed the settlements and killed 240 women and children during Israel's War of Independence. After Israel recaptured the area in 1967, descendants of those early settlers reestablished the community. The largest of the settlements is the city of Betar Illit with more than 24,000 residents.

The Givat Ze'ev bloc includes five communities just northwest of Jerusalem. Givat Ze'ev, with a population of nearly 11,000, is the largest.

Modiin Illit is a bloc with four communities. The city of Modiin Illit is the largest, with more than 26,000 people situated just over the Green Line, about 23 miles northwest of Jerusalem and the same distance east of Tel Aviv.

Ariel is now the heart of the second most populous bloc of settlements. The city is located just 25 miles east of Tel Aviv and 31 miles north of Jerusalem. Ariel and the surrounding communities expand Israel's narrow waist (which was just 9 miles wide prior to 1967) and ensure that Israel has a land route to the Jordan Valley in case Israel needs to fight a land war to the east. It is more controversial than the other consensus settlements because it is the furthest from the 1949 Armistice Line, extending approximately 12 miles into the West Bank.

Nevertheless, Barak's proposal at Camp David included Ariel among the settlement blocs to be annexed to Israel; the Clinton plan also envisioned incorporating Ariel within the new borders of Israel. Most peace plans assumed that Israel would annex sufficient territory to incorporate 75–80 percent of the Jews currently living in the West Bank. Using the figures in the table above, however, it appears that Israel would fall short of that demographic goal even if these six blocs were annexed. The total population of these communities is approximately 160,000, which is roughly 64 percent of the estimated 250,000 Jews living in Judea and Samaria. The expectation, however, is that roughly one-third of the Jews living in other settlements will move into these blocs, which would bring the total close to 80%, but still require Israel to evacuate another 50,000 people.

In 1995, Prime Minister Yitzhak Rabin said Israel would keep the settlement blocs of Ma'ale Adumim, Givat Ze'ev, and Gush Etzion. Prior to the 2000 Camp David Summit, even Palestinian negotiator Saeb Erekat said the Palestinians could accept Israel holding onto Ma'ale Adumim and Givat Ze'ev.

At Camp David, Israel insisted that 80 percent of the Jewish residents of Judea and Samaria would be in settlement blocs under Israeli sovereignty. President Clinton agreed and proposed that Israel annex 4–6 percent of the West Bank for three settlement blocs to accomplish this demographic objective and swap some territory within Israel in exchange.

Recognizing the demographics of the area, President Bush acknowledged the inevitability of some Israeli towns in the West Bank being annexed to Israel in his 2004 letter to Prime Minister Sharon. In his meeting a year later with Palestinian Authority President Abbas, however, he seemed to hedge his support by saying that any such decision would have to be mutually agreed to by Israelis and Palestinians. Nevertheless, the future border is likely to approximate the route of the security fence, given the Israeli prerequisite (with U.S. approval) of incorporating most settlers within Israel.

Would the incorporation of settlement blocs prevent the creation of a contiguous Palestinian state? A look at Map 24 shows that it would not. The total area of these communities is only about 1.5 percent of the West Bank. A kidney-shaped state linked to the Gaza Strip by a secure passage would be contiguous. Some argue that the E1 project linking Ma'ale Adumim to Jerusalem would cutoff east Jerusalem, but even that is not necessarily true as Israel has proposed constructing a four-lane underpass to guarantee free passage between the West Bank and the Arab sections of Jerusalem.

Ultimately, Israel may decide to unilaterally disengage from the West Bank and determine which settlements it will incorporate within the borders it delineates. Israel would prefer, however, to negotiate a peace treaty with the Palestinians that would specify which Jewish communities will remain intact within the mutually agreed border of Israel, and which will need to be evacuated. Israel will undoubtedly insist that some or all of the "consensus" blocs become part of Israel.

Notes

1. *American Journal of International Law,* (April, 1970), pp. 345-46.
2. *New Republic,* (October 21, 1991), p. 14.
3. *Washington Post,* (November 1, 1991).
4. *American Journal of International Law,* (1990, Vol. 84), p. 72.
5. *Haaretz,* (September 13, 2001).
6. *Jerusalem Post,* (October 22, 1991).
7. Middle East News Agency, (September 20, 1978).
8. Letter from George Mitchell and Warren Rudman to ADL Director Abraham Foxman, (May 11, 2001).
9. *Los Angeles Times,* (June 20, 2001).
10. "Mofaz okays 3,500 housing units in Ma'aleh Adumim," *Jerusalem Post,* (March 20, 2005).
11. Etgar Lefkovits, "Building controversy," *Jerusalem Post,* (March 28, 2005).
12. Letter from George W. Bush to Ariel Sharon, (April 14, 2004).
13. Prime Minister Ariel Sharon, Address to the Likud Central Committee, (January 5, 2004).

21. The Arms Balance

MYTH

"The threat from Israel, and the withdrawal of the United States' offer to build the Aswan Dam, drove Egypt to seek arms from the Soviet Union in 1955. This started the Middle East arms race."

FACT

In 1955, Nasser turned to the Soviet Union in anger because the United States had armed Iraq, Egypt's hated rival, and promoted the Baghdad Pact. Nasser opposed that agreement, as he did any defense alliance with the West.

Egypt began to receive Soviet Bloc arms in 1955. The United States, hoping to maintain a degree of influence in Egypt and to induce Nasser to reduce his arms acquisitions, offered to build the Aswan Dam. But Nasser increased his arms orders and spurned a U.S. peace initiative. Egypt had embarked on a policy of "neutralism," which meant that Nasser intended to get aid from both East and West if he could, while maintaining his freedom to attack the West and assist Soviet efforts to gain influence in the Arab and Afro-Asian worlds. As a result of these actions, and Nasser's increasing hostility to the West, the United States withdrew the Aswan offer. Egypt then nationalized the Suez Canal.

Immediately after Nasser made his 1955 arms deal, Israel appealed to the United States—not for a gift of arms, but for the right to purchase them. The U.S. recognized the need to maintain an arms balance, but it referred Israel to France and other European suppliers. It was not until 1962 that the United States agreed to sell Israel its first significant American system, the HAWK anti-aircraft missile.

MYTH

"The Arab states have had to keep pace with an Israeli-led arms race."

FACT

In most cases, the reverse was true. Egypt received the Soviet IL-28 bomber in 1955. It was not until 1958 that France provided Israel with a squadron of comparable Sud Vautour twin-jet tactical bombers. In 1957, Egypt obtained MiG-17 fighter planes. Israel received the comparable

Super Mystere in 1959. Egypt had submarines in 1957, Israel in 1959. After the Egyptians obtained the MiG-21, the Israelis ordered the Dassault Mirage III supersonic interceptor and fighter-bomber.

Egypt received ground-to-air missiles—the SA-2—two years before Israel obtained HAWK missiles from the United States. Later, Washington reluctantly agreed to sell Israel Patton tanks.

Even when the United States began selling arms to Israel in the 1960s, it maintained a policy of balance whereby similar sales were made to Arab states. In 1965, for example, the first major tank sale to Israel was matched by one to Jordan. A year later, when Israel received Skyhawks, the U.S. provided planes to Morocco and Libya, as well as additional military equipment to Lebanon, Saudi Arabia and Tunisia.[1]

It was not until 1968, when the Johnson Administration sold Israel Phantom jets, that America's arms transfer policy shifted to emphasize maintaining the Jewish State's qualitative advantage. Since then, however, the U.S. has frequently sold sophisticated arms (e.g., F-15s, AWACS and Stinger missiles) to Israel's adversaries, which have eroded the Jewish State's qualitative edge.

MYTH

"Israel is militarily superior to its neighbors in every area and has maintained a qualitative edge over its enemies."

FACT

Israel's qualitative military edge has declined as Arab and Muslim states acquire increasingly sophisticated conventional and unconventional arms. In fact, despite its pledges to the contrary, the United States is allowing Israel's qualitative edge to dissipate. In some cases, U.S. arms transfers to the Arabs are the reason for this erosion.

Israel's standing army is smaller than those of Egypt, Iran and Syria. Even with its reserves, Israel is outmanned by Egypt and Iran. In addition, Israel is likely to have to face a combination of enemies; together, virtually any combination of likely opponents would be superior in manpower, tanks and aircraft. During the 1990's, the Arab states and Iran imported more than $180 billion worth of the most sophisticated weapons and military infrastructure available from both the Western and Eastern blocs. In 2004, Saudi Arabia alone spent $21.6 billion (and the Bush Administration notified Congress in 2005 of its intention to sell the Saudis another $2 billion worth of arms), while Iran spent more than $17 billion. Between 2001 and 2004, Egypt purchased $6.5 billion worth of arms (by comparison, Israel spent $4.4 billion). In 2005, Syria renewed its military purchases from Russia, obtaining SA-18 antiaircraft missiles and the promise of additional weapons. Israel allocates about

$9 billion for defense annually, while Iran and the Arab states, many of which are in a state of war with Israel, spend more than $40 billion a year.[2]

In addition to the quantity of weapons, Israel must also be concerned with the erosion of its qualitative edge as the Arab states acquire increasingly sophisticated systems. In 2005, for example, the United Arab Emirates took delivery of F-16 fighters, which were newer and more advanced that those sold to Israel. This was the first sale of the planes to a non-NATO country.[3]

In addition to the sheer quantity of arms, these states are also buying and producing increasing numbers of nonconventional weapons. The buildup of chemical and biological weapons, combined with the pursuit of a nuclear capability, makes Israel's strategic position more precarious.

Beyond the security threat, this massive arms build-up also requires Israel to spend about 9 percent of its GDP on defense. Even this high level of spending is insufficient, however, to meet the Arab threat, as budgetary restrictions have forced Israel to make substantial cuts in its defense allocations. Arab arms sales have significantly raised the cost to Israel of maintaining its own defense, exacerbating the strain on Israel's economy.

MYTH

"The sale of U.S. arms to Saudi Arabia has reduced the need for American troops to defend the Persian Gulf. These weapons pose no threat to Israel."

FACT

The Saudi armed forces are structurally incapable of defending their country. They were helpless in the face of the Iraqi threat in 1990–91, despite the Saudi acquisition of more than $50 billion in U.S. arms and military services in the decade preceding the Gulf War.[4] If Saddam Hussein had continued his blitzkrieg into Saudi Arabia before American forces arrived in August 1990, much of the weaponry the United States sold to Riyadh over the years might have fallen into Saddam's hands.

The Saudis' small armed forces cannot withstand an assault by a force three to four times its size. Moreover, it makes no sense to say that advanced American weapons can help the Saudis counter external threats but that those same arms pose no danger to Israel.

The U.S. has no way to ensure that the vast quantities of aircraft and missiles it sells to Saudi Arabia will not be used against Israel. The possibility of these weapons falling into the hands of enemies of the United States cannot be ruled out either, given the Saudis' support for terrorists and the possibility that the monarchy could be overthrown by a more hostile regime.

In past Arab-Israeli wars, the Saudis never had a modern arsenal of sufficient size to make their participation in an Arab coalition against Israel a serious concern. The Saudi buildup since the 1973 War changes this equation. The Kingdom could be pressured into offensive action against Israel by other eastern front partners precisely because of this buildup.

"I wish Israel did not need defensive weapons of mass destruction or the region's most powerful defense forces. I wish the world had not driven the Jewish State into allocating its limited resources away from its universities and toward its military, but survival must come first, and Israel's military strength is the key to its survival. Anyone who believes that survival can be assured by moral superiority alone must remember the Warsaw Ghetto and the Treblinka gas chambers."

—Alan Dershowitz[5]

MYTH

"Israel refuses to sign the Nuclear Non-Proliferation Treaty to conceal its nuclear arsenal, and therefore threatens its neighbors."

FACT

Though Israel does not formally acknowledge that it has a nuclear capability, it has been widely reported that Israel has been a member of the nuclear club for a number of years. During that time, Israel has never tested, used or threatened the use of nuclear weapons.

Israel's decision not to be bound by the Non-Proliferation Treaty (NPT) is based largely on the grounds that the treaty has done little to stem nuclear proliferation in the region. Iraq is a signatory to the NPT, and yet was able to amass a large amount of nuclear material without the knowledge of the International Atomic Energy Agency prior to the Israeli attack on its reactor in 1981. More recently, it was discovered that another signatory to the NPT, Iran, has had a secret nuclear weapons program for more than a decade and now may have a bomb within five to ten years.

Israel has called for the creation of a nuclear-free zone in the Middle East and has stated many times that it will not be the first state to introduce nuclear weapons into the region.

MYTH

"Arms control in the Middle East is impossible so long as Israel refuses to give up its nuclear weapons."

FACT

Israel's assumed nuclear deterrent is an option of last resort, needed to offset the threats it faces from the large imbalance in conventional arms, chemical weapons and ballistic missiles possessed by the Arab states. Israel has no incentive to unilaterally attack its neighbors with nuclear weapons whereas the Arabs—as history has shown—have both the capability and motivation to join in a war against Israel.

The desire of Arab and Islamic regimes to obtain weapons of mass destruction also has more to do with notions of national pride and rivalries with other nations than Israel's arsenal. For example, Saddam Hussein used his chemical weapons against a domestic threat, the Kurds, and Iraq's motivation for pursuing nuclear weapons was the threat Hussein felt from Iran.[6] Pakistan developed the first "Islamic bomb" to counter rival India's bomb. And Iranian Foreign Minister Kamal Kharrazi has said, "Iran has a high technical capability and has to be recognized by the international community as a member of the nuclear club. This is an irreversible path."[7]

Arms control must therefore begin with a reduction in Arab military offensive capability. Arab "arms control" proposals in essence have only called for Israel to give up nuclear arms without offering anything substantive in return.

MYTH

"Egypt is no longer a military threat since signing a peace treaty with Israel."

FACT

While Egypt remains formally at peace with Israel and honors its Camp David commitments, Cairo has nevertheless amassed a substantial offensive military capability in recent years. Prudent Israeli military planners have no choice but to carefully monitor Egypt's buildup in case regional events take a dramatic turn for the worse. If the present regime in Cairo were overthrown, for example, the prospect for continued stable relations with Israel would diminish substantially.

Egypt was the third largest purchaser of arms from 2001-2004, trailing only China and India. Despite its status as a U.S. ally, Egypt has purchased Scud missiles from North Korea and is believed to possess chemical weapons.[8] Its army, air force and navy now field a wide range of the most sophisticated Western arms, many identical to Israel's own weapons. In 2003, for example, Egypt requested F-15 jets armed with JDAM (joint direct attack munition) "smart" bombs. These sophisticated weapons were used by U.S. forces in the 2003 war with Iraq. Egypt's military also now has Abrams tanks, F-16 fighter planes and Apache attack helicopters.

These arms transfers are a matter of concern for Israel because the principal threats faced by Egypt today are internal ones. No nation poses any danger to Egypt. So why has Egypt been spending billions of dollars to amass an arsenal that includes 3,000 tanks and more than 500 aircraft, especially when it has serious economic problems caused in large measure by an exponentially growing population that does not have enough food, shelter, or employment? If Egypt's military simulations are any indication of the regime's thinking, Israel has good reason to worry. Egyptian forces have staged large-scale military training exercises that included simulated operations crossing into the Sinai against an unnamed adversary to the east (i.e., Israel). In fact, Israel is the "enemy" in all of Egypt's war games.

In December 2003, Israel protested Egypt's use of unmanned aerial vehicles and drones to spy on Israeli military facilities. Israel reportedly threatened to shoot down the drones, whose flights violate the peace treaty and prompted increased concern over Egypt's military buildup.[9]

Israel is also worried about the looming succession crisis in Egypt. President Hosni Mubarak is now in his late 70s and has been the nation's ruler since Anwar Sadat's assassination in 1981. No one knows who will follow Mubarak. Given the strong Muslim fundamentalist movement in the country, and the antipathy of the military toward Israel, it is by no means certain that Mubarak's successor will maintain the "cold peace" that has prevailed now for more than 30 years.

MYTH

"Iran has no ambition to become a nuclear power and poses no threat to Israel or the United States."

FACT

Iran has made no secret of its antipathy for the United States and Israel—President Mahmoud Ahmadinejad said Israel should be wiped off the map—and, and has become one of the most serious threats to stability in the Middle East. American and Israeli intelligence assessments agree that the Islamic regime in Iran will be able to complete a nuclear weapon within ten years, and possibly much sooner if its current program is not stopped.

In 1990, China signed a 10-year nuclear cooperation agreement that allowed Iranian nuclear engineers to obtain training in China. In addition, China has already built a nuclear research reactor in Iran that became operational in 1994. In 2002, Iran revealed that it had purchased special gas from China that could be used to enrich uranium for the production of nuclear weapons.

Iran is a signatory to the nuclear Non-Proliferation Treaty, which allows the peaceful pursuit of nuclear technology, including uranium mining and enrichment, under oversight by the International Atomic Energy Agency (IAEA). The gas purchase was supposed to be reported to the IAEA, but it was concealed instead. Chinese experts have also been involved in the supervision of the installation of centrifuge equipment that can be used to enrich uranium.

According to the CIA, "Iran continues to use its civilian nuclear energy program to justify its efforts to establish domestically or otherwise acquire the entire nuclear fuel cycle. Iran claims that this fuel cycle would be used to produce fuel for nuclear power reactors, such as the 1,000-megawatt lighter-water reactor that Russia is continuing to build at the southern port city of Bushehr. However, Iran does not need to produce its own fuel for this reactor because Russia has pledged to provide the fuel throughout the operating lifetime of the reactor and is negotiating with Iran to take back the irradiated spent fuel."[10]

In 2002, two previously unknown nuclear facilities were discovered in Iran. One in Arak produces heavy water, which could be used to produce weapons. The other is in Natanz. In February 2003, Iranian President Mohammad Khatami announced the discovery of uranium reserves near the central city of Yazd and said Iran was setting up production facilities "to make use of advanced nuclear technology for peaceful purposes."[11] This was an alarming development because it suggested Iran was attempting to obtain the means to produce and process fuel itself, despite the agreement to receive all the uranium it would need for civilian purposes from Russia.

Further evidence of Iran's pursuit of nuclear weapons was revealed in late 2003 and early 2004 when Pakistan's top nuclear scientist, Abdul Qadeer Khan, admitted he provided nuclear weapons expertise and equipment to Iran. The Iranian government, confronted in February 2004 with new evidence obtained from the secret network of nuclear suppliers surrounding Khan, acknowledged it had a design for a far more advanced high-speed centrifuge to enrich uranium than it previously revealed to the IAEA. This type of centrifuge would allow Iran to produce nuclear fuel far more quickly than the equipment that it reluctantly revealed to the agency in 2003. This revelation proved that Iran lied when it claimed to have turned over all the documents relating to their enrichment program. In July 2004, Iran broke the seals on nuclear equipment monitored by UN inspectors and was again building and testing machines that could make fissile material for nuclear weapons. Teheran's move violated an agreement with European countries under which Iran suspended "all uranium enrichment activity." Defying a key demand set by 35 nations, Iran announced on September 21, 2004, that it had started converting raw uranium into the gas needed for enrichment, a process that can be used to make nuclear weapons. A couple of weeks later, Iran announced it had processed several tons of raw "yellowcake" uranium to prepare it for enrichment—a key step in developing atomic weapons.[12]

Secretary of State Colin Powell said the United States has intelligence indicating Iran is trying to fit missiles to carry nuclear weapons, which he intimated would only make sense if Iran was also developing or planning to develop a nuclear capability. "There is no doubt in my mind—and it's fairly straightforward from what we've been saying for years—that they have been interested in a nuclear weapon that has utility, meaning that it is something they would be able to deliver, not just something that sits there," Powell said.[13]

In February 2005, Ali Agha Mohammadi, spokesman of Iran's Supreme National Security Council, said Iran will never scrap its nuclear program, and talks with the Europeans are aimed at protecting the country's nuclear achievements, not negotiating an end to them. In May, Iran confirmed that it had converted 37 tons of uranium into gas, its first acknowledgment of advances made in the production process for enriched uranium. This means Tehran is in a position to start enriching uranium quickly if negotiations with the Europeans over the future of its nuclear program fail.[14]

On September 2, 2005, the IAEA reported that Iran had produced about seven tons of the gas it needs for uranium enrichment since it restarted the process the previous month. A former UN nuclear inspector said that would be enough for an atomic weapon. In unusually strong language, an IAEA report also said questions remain about key aspects of Iran's 18 years of clandestine nuclear activity and that it still was unable "to conclude that there are no undeclared nuclear materials or activities in Iran."[15]

Iran subsequently threatened to resume uranium enrichment and bar open inspections of its nuclear facilities if the IAEA decides to refer it to the Security Council for possible sanctions. Newly elected Iranian President Mahmoud Ahmadinejad defended his country's right to produce nuclear fuel in a fiery speech to the UN General Assembly and later raised worldwide concern about nuclear proliferation when he said, "Iran is ready to transfer nuclear know-how to the Islamic countries due to their need."[16]

Masud Yazaiari, spokesperson of the Iranian Revolutionary Guards, warned that Iran would respond to any Israeli efforts to stop their nuclear program. "Their threats to attack our nuclear facilities will not succeed," Yazaiari said. "They are aware that Tehran's response would be overwhelming and would wipe Israel off the face of the earth."[17]

Notes

1. Mitchell Bard, *The Water's Edge And Beyond*, (NJ: Transaction Publishers, 1991), p. 194-209.

2. Aluf Benn, "Israel worried about possible new Russia-Syria arms deals," *Haaretz*, (October 26, 2005); Information from the Stockholm International Peace Research Institute (SIPRI).

3. Arieh O'Sullivan, "US Sells world's best F-16s to UAE," *Jerusalem Post*, (May 5, 2005).

4. Arms Control and Disarmament Agency; Defense Security Assistance Agency Report; World Military Expenditures and Arms Transfers.

5. Alan Dershowitz, *Chutzpah*, (MA: Little Brown, and Co., 1991), p. 249.

6. Josef Joffe, "A World Without Israel," *Foreign Policy*, (January/February 2005), pp. 36-42.

7. Associated Press, (June 12, 2004).

8. Aluf Benn, "Israel worried about possible new Russia-Syria arms deals," *Haaretz*, (October 26, 2005); Center for Strategic and International Studies, United Nations (UN) Institute for Disarmament Research.

9. *Jerusalem Post*, (December 21, 2003).

10. Unclassified Report to Congress on the Acquisition of Technology Relating to Weapons of Mass Destruction and Advanced Conventional Munitions, (Langley, VA: CIA, 2004).

11. Associated Press, (February 11, 2003).

12. *Telegraph*, (July 27, 2004); Associated Press, (October 6, 2004).

13. *Washington Post*, (November 18, 2004).

14. Associated Press, (May 9, 2005).

15. *Chicago Tribune*, (September 3, 2005).

16. Associated Press, (September 15 & 20, 2005).

17. *Maariv*, (July 27, 2004).

22. The Media

"Press coverage of Israel is proportional to its importance in world affairs."

FACT

It is hard to justify the amount of news coverage given to Israel based on that nation's importance in world affairs or American national interests. How is it that a country the size of New Jersey routinely merits top billing over seemingly more newsworthy nations such as Russia, China and Great Britain?

Israel probably has the highest per capita fame quotient in the world. Americans know more about Israeli politics than that of any other foreign country. Most of Israel's leaders, for example, are more familiar in the United States than those of America's neighbors in Canada or Mexico. In addition, a high percentage of Americans are conversant on the Arab-Israeli conflict.

One reason Americans are so knowledgeable about Israel is the extent of coverage. American news organizations usually have more correspondents in Israel than in any country except Great Britain.

"Israel receives so much attention because it is the only country in the Middle East that affects U.S. interests."

FACT

The Middle East is important to the United States (and the Western world) primarily because of its oil resources. Events that might threaten the production and supply of oil affect vital U.S. interests. The United States also has an interest in supporting friendly regimes in the region. Attention is warranted because the Middle East is the scene of repeated conflagrations that directly or indirectly affect American interests. Events in countries like Jordan, Lebanon and Iran have required the intervention of U.S. troops, and nothing focuses the attention of the public like American lives being endangered abroad. The United States has been deeply involved in each of the Arab-Israeli wars, but has also had its own independent battles, most notably the Gulf War with Iraq in 1991 and

"Operation Iraqi Freedom" in 2003. The media is now very focused on Iraq because of the continuing U.S. troop deployment there.

On the other hand, Americans are not typically interested in the fratricidal wars of people in distant lands when the fighting does not appear to have any bearing on U.S. interests. This is true in Africa, Latin America and even the Balkans. Similarly, inter-Arab wars have not generated the kind of interest that Israel's problems have. However, the Israeli-Palestinian dispute—two people fighting over one land—is a particularly compelling story. It is made all the more so by the fact that it is centered in the Holy Land.

Another explanation for the disproportionate coverage Israel receives relative to Arab countries is that few correspondents have a background in Middle East history or speak the regional languages. Journalists are more familiar with the largely Western culture in Israel than the more alien Muslim societies.

MYTH

"Media coverage of the Arab world is objective."

FACT

When journalists are allowed to pierce the veil of secrecy, the price of access to dictators and terrorists is often steep. Reporters are sometimes intimidated or blackmailed. In Lebanon during the 1980s, for example, the Palestine Liberation Organization had reporters doing their bidding as the price for obtaining interviews and protection. During the Palestinian War, Israeli journalists were warned against going to the Palestinian Authority and some received telephone threats after publishing articles critical of the PA leadership.[1]

When asked to comment on what many viewers regard as CNN's bias against Israel, Reese Schonfeld, the network's first president, explained, "When I see them on the air I see them being very careful about Arab sensibilities." Schonfeld suggested the coverage is slanted because CNN doesn't want to risk the special access it has in the Arab world.[2]

In Arab countries, journalists are usually escorted to see what the dictator wants them to see or they are followed. Citizens are warned by security agencies, sometimes directly, sometimes more subtly, that they should be careful what they say to visitors.

In the case of coverage of the PA, the Western media relies heavily on Palestinian assistants to escort correspondents in the territories. In addition, Palestinians often provide the news that is sent out around the world. For example, at least two journalists working for Agence France-Presse simultaneously worked for PA media outlets. An Associated Press correspondent also worked for the PA's official newspaper. One veteran journalist said, "It's like employing someone from the [Israeli] Government Press Office or one of the Israeli political parties to work as a journalist."[3]

"By my own estimate," journalist Ehud Ya'ari wrote, "over 95 percent of the TV pictures going out on satellite every evening to the various foreign and Israeli channels are supplied by Palestinian film crews. The two principle agencies in the video news market, APTN and Reuters TV, run a whole network of Palestinian stringers, freelancers and fixers all over the territories to provide instant footage of the events. These crews obviously identify emotionally and politically with the intifada and, in the 'best' case, they simply don't dare film anything that could embarrass the Palestinian Authority. So the cameras are angled to show a tainted view of the Israeli army's actions, never focus on the Palestinian gunmen and diligently produce a very specific kind of close-up of the situation on the ground."[4]

A particularly egregious incident occurred in October 2000 when two non-combatant Israeli reservists were lynched in Ramallah by a Palestinian mob. According to reporters on the scene, the Palestinian police tried to prevent foreign journalists from filming the incident. One Italian television crew managed to film parts of the attack and these shocking images ultimately made headlines around the world. A competing Italian news agency took a different tack, placing an advertisement in the PA's main newspaper, *Al Hayat-Al-Jadidah,* explaining that it had nothing to do with filming the incident:

> My dear friends in Palestine. We congratulate you and think that it is our duty to put you in the picture (of the events) of what happened on October 12 in Ramallah. One of the private television stations which competes with us (and not the official Italian television station RTI) filmed the events; *that* station filmed the events. Afterwards Israeli Television broadcast the pictures, as taken from one of the Italian stations, and thus the public impression was created as if we (RTI) took these pictures.
>
> We emphasize to all of you that the events did not happen this way, because we always respect (will continue to respect) the journalistic procedures with the Palestinian Authority for (journalistic) work in Palestine and we are credible in our precise work.
>
> We thank you for your trust, and you can be sure that this is not our way of acting (note: meaning we do not work like the other television stations). We do not (and will not) do such a thing.
>
> Please accept our blessings.
> Signed
> Ricardo Christiano
> Representative of the official Italian station in Palestine[5]

If a news organization strays from the pro-Palestinian line, it comes under immediate attack. In November 2000, for example, the Palestinian Journalist's Union complained that the Associated Press was presenting a false impression of the Palestinian War. The Union called AP's coverage a conscious crime against the Palestinian people and said it served the Israeli position. The Union threatened to adopt all necessary measures against AP staffers as well as against AP bureaus located in the PA if the agency continued to harm Palestinian interests.[6]

"We were filming the beginning of the demonstration. Suddenly, a van pulled in hurriedly. Inside, there were Fatah militants. They gave their orders and even distributed Molotov cocktails. We were filming. But these images, you will never see. In a few seconds, all those youngsters surrounded us, threatened us, and then took us away to the police station. There, we identified ourselves but we were compelled to delete the controversial pictures. The Palestinian Police calmed the situation but censored our pictures. We now have the proof that those riots are no longer spontaneous. All the orders came from the Palestinian hierarchy."

—Jean Pierre Martin[7]

MYTH

"Journalists covering the Middle East are driven by the search for the truth."

FACT

It will come as no surprise to learn that journalists in the Middle East share an interest in sensationalism with their colleagues covering domestic issues. The most egregious examples come from television reporters whose emphasis on visuals over substance encourages facile treatment of the issues. For example, when NBC's correspondent in Israel was asked why reporters turned up at Palestinian demonstrations in the West Bank they knew were being staged, he said, "We play along because we need the pictures."[8] The networks can't get newsworthy pictures from closed societies such as Syria, Saudi Arabia, Iran or Libya.

Israel often faces an impossible situation of trying to counter images with words. "When a tank goes into Ramallah, it does not look good on TV," explains Gideon Meir of the Israeli Foreign Ministry. "Sure we can explain why we are there, and that's what we do. But it's words. We have to fight pictures with words."[9]

The magnitude of the problem Israel confronts is clear from Tami Allen-Frost, deputy chairman of the Foreign Press Association and a producer for Britain's ITN news, who says "the strongest picture that stays in the mind is of a tank in a city" and that "there are more incidents all together in the West Bank than there are suicide bombings. In the end, it's quantity that stays with you."[10]

MYTH

"Israel gets favorable coverage because American Jews control the media and have disproportionate political influence."

FACT

If Jews controlled the media, it's not likely you'd hear Jews complaining so much about the anti-Israel bias of the press. It is true that the amount of attention Israel receives is related to the fact that the largest Jewish population outside Israel is in the United States, and that Israel greatly concerns American Jews. Large numbers of Jews do hold significant positions in the media (though they by no means "control" the press as anti-Semites maintain), and the Jewish population is concentrated in major media markets such as New York and Los Angeles, so it is not surprising the spotlight would be directed at Israel.

Politically, Jews wield disproportionate power in the United States and use it to advocate policies that strengthen the U.S.-Israel relationship; however, there is no evidence this has translated into favorable press coverage for Israel. It is possible to argue the pro-Arab lobby has as much or more influence on the media and encourage an anti-Israel bias.

MYTH

"Arab officials tell Western journalists the same thing they tell their own people."

FACT

Arab officials often express their views differently in English than they do in Arabic. They express their true feelings and positions to their constituents in their native language. For external consumption, however, Arab officials have learned to speak in moderate tones and often relate very different views when speaking in English to Western audiences. Long ago, Arab propagandists became more sophisticated about how to make their case. They now routinely appear on American television news broadcasts and are quoted in the print media and come across as reasonable people with legitimate grievances. What many of these same people say in Arabic, however, is often far less moderate and reasonable. Since Israelis can readily translate what is said in Arabic they are well aware of the views of their enemies. Americans and other English-speakers, however, can easily be fooled by the slick presentation of an Arab propagandist.

To give just one example, Palestinian peace negotiator Saeb Erekat is frequently quoted by the Western media. After the brutal murder of two Israeli teenagers on May 9, 2001, he was asked for a reaction. The *Washington Post* reported his response:

> Saeb Erekat, a Palestinian official, said in English at a news conference that "killing civilians is a crime, whether on the Palestinian or the Israeli side." The comment was not reported in Arabic-language Palestinian media.[11]

The unusual aspect of this story was that the *Post* reported the fact that Erekat's comment was ignored by the Palestinian press.

Over the years Yasser Arafat was famous for saying one thing in English to the Western media and something completely different to the Arabic press in his native tongue. This is why the Bush Administration insisted that he repeat in Arabic what he said in English, in particular condemnations of terrorist attacks and calls to end violence. It is more difficult for Arab leaders to get away with doubletalk today because their Arabic remarks are now translated by watchdog organizations and disseminated in English.

MYTH

"Journalists are well-versed in Middle East history and therefore can place current events in proper context."

FACT

One cause of misunderstanding about the Middle East and bias in media reporting is the ignorance of journalists about the region. Few reporters speak Hebrew or Arabic, so they have little or no access to primary resources. They frequently regurgitate stories they read in English language publications from the region rather than report independently. When they do attempt to place events in historical context, they often get the facts wrong and create an inaccurate or misleading impression. To cite one example, during a recitation of the history of the holy sites in Jerusalem, CNN's Garrick Utley reported that Jews could pray at the Western Wall during Jordan's rule from 1948 to 1967.[12] In fact, Jews were prevented from visiting their holiest shrine. This is a critical historical point that helps explain Israel's position toward Jerusalem.

Case Study

A *Washington Post* story about the "cycle of death" in the West Bank included an interview with Raed Karmi, an official in Fatah, the dominant faction in Yasser Arafat's Palestine Liberation Organization. The report begins with the observation that Karmi is running out to join a battle against Israeli soldiers and grabs an M-16 assault rifle. What the story fails to mention is that only Palestinian police are supposed to be armed. The report implies that Israeli and Palestinian violence is equivalent in this "cycle" because Karmi said he was acting to avenge the death of a Palestinian who the Israelis assassinated for organizing terrorist attacks. Karmi admits that he participated in the kidnapping and execution-style murder of two Israelis who had been eating lunch in a Tulkarm restaurant. Karmi was jailed by the Palestinian Authority, but he was released after just four months and subsequently killed four more Israelis, including a man buying groceries and a driver who he ambushed. "I will continue attacking Israelis," he told the *Post.*[13]

MYTH

"Israelis cannot deny the truth of pictures showing their abuses."

FACT

A picture may be worth thousand words, but sometimes the picture and the words used to describe it are distorted and misleading. There is no question that photographers and television camera crews seek the most dramatic pictures they can find, most often showing brutal Israeli Goliaths mistreating the suffering Palestinian Davids, but the context is often missing.

In one classic example, the Associated Press circulated a dramatic photo of an angry baton-wielding Israeli soldier standing over a bloody young man. It appeared the soldier had just beaten the youth. The picture appeared in the *New York Times*[14] and spurred international outrage because the caption, supplied by AP, said, "An Israeli policeman and a Palestinian on the Temple Mount." Taken at a time when Palestinians were rioting following Ariel Sharon's controversial visit to the al-Aksa mosque, the picture appeared to be a vivid case of Israeli brutality. It turned out, however, the caption was inaccurate and the photo actually showed an incident that might have conveyed almost the exact opposite impression had it been reported correctly.

In fact, the victim was not a Palestinian beaten by an Israeli soldier, it was a policeman protecting an American Jewish student, Tuvia Grossman, who had been riding in a taxi when it was stoned by Palestinians. Grossman was pulled out of the taxi, beaten and stabbed. He broke free and fled toward the Israeli policeman. At that point a photographer snapped the picture.

Besides getting the victim wrong, AP also inaccurately reported that the photograph was taken on the Temple Mount.

When AP was alerted to the errors, it issued a series of corrections, several of which still did not get the story straight. As is usually the case when the media makes a mistake, the damage was already done. Many outlets that had used the photo did not print clarifications. Others issued corrections that did not receive anywhere near the prominence of the initial story.

Another example of how pictures can be both dramatic and misleading was a Reuters photo showing a young Palestinian being arrested by Israeli police on April 6, 2001. The boy was obviously frightened and wet his pants. Once again the photo attracted worldwide publicity and reinforced the media image of Israelis as brutal occupiers who abuse innocent children. In this instance it is the context that is misleading. Another Reuters photographer snapped another picture just before the first one was taken. It showed the same boy participating in a riot against Israeli soldiers. Few media outlets published this photo.

MYTH

"The press makes no apologies for terrorists."

FACT

The media routinely accepts and repeats the platitudes of terrorists and their spokespersons with regard to their agendas. The press gullibly treats claims that attacks against innocent civilians are acts of "freedom fighters." In recent years some news organizations have developed a resistance to the term "terrorist" and replaced it with euphemisms such as "militant" because they don't want to be seen as taking sides or making judgments about the perpetrators.

For example, after a Palestinian suicide bomber blew up a pizza restaurant in downtown Jerusalem on August 9, 2001, killing 15 people, the attacker was described as a "militant" (*Los Angeles Times, Chicago Tribune,* NBC Nightly News) and "suicide bomber" (*New York Times, USA Today*). ABC News did not use the word "terrorist." When a Palestinian woman walked into a crowded beach restaurant in Haifa and detonated a bomb that killed 21 people, including four children on October 4, 2003, the Reuters account said she had waged an "attack" in retaliation for previous Israeli army actions and that the bombing showed that Palestinian officials had failed to "rein in the militants."[15]

Clifford May of the Middle East Information Network pointed out the absurdity of the media coverage: "No newspaper would write, 'Militants struck the World Trade Center yesterday,' or say, 'They may think of themselves as freedom fighters, and who are we to judge, we're news people.'"[16]

"By any logic, militants engaged in warfare don't blow up little babies."

—Tom Fiedler, Executive Editor, *Miami Herald*[17]

One of the best examples of how the press sometimes distinguishes terrorist attacks against other nations was a list of "recent terror attacks around the world" disseminated in November 2003 by the Associated Press, probably the most influential news service in the world. The list cited 15 terrorist incidents during the five-year period between August 1998 and August 2003. During that period, more than 800 Israelis were murdered in terrorist attacks, but not one of the incidents in Israel made the list.[18] Similarly, when AP released its Year in Photos 2003, six of the 130 photos chosen related to human suffering in the Israeli-Palestinian conflict. All six were of Palestinians.

In a memo to the *New York Times* foreign desk, former Jerusalem bureau chief James Bennet criticized his paper's reluctance to use the word "terrorism." He said, "The calculated bombing of students in a university cafeteria, or of families gathered in an ice cream parlor, cries out to be called what it is. . . . I wanted to avoid the political meaning that comes with 'terrorism,' but I couldn't pretend that the word had no usage at all in plain English." Bennett acknowledged that not using the term was "a political act in itself."[19]

Rather than apologize for terrorists, the media sometimes portrays the victims of terror as equivalent to the terrorists themselves. For example, photos are sometimes shown of Israeli victims on the same page with photos of Israelis capturing terrorists, giving the sense, for example, that the Palestinian held in handcuffs and blindfolded by a soldier is as much a victim as the shocked woman in being helped from the scene of a suicide bombing.

In one of the most egregious examples, after a suicide bombing in Petah Tikva on May 27, 2002, CNN interviewed the mother of the bomber, Jihad Titi. The parents of a 15-month-old girl killed in the attack, Chen and Lior Keinan, were also interviewed. The interviews with the Keinans were not shown on CNN international in Israel or elsewhere around the world until hours after the interview with Titi's mother had been broadcast several times.

This was even too much for CNN, which subsequently announced a policy change whereby it would no longer "report on statements made by suicide bombers or their families unless there seemingly is an extraordinarily compelling reason to do so." [20]

MYTH

"The Palestinian Authority places no restrictions on foreign reporters."

FACT

A case study of the Palestinian Authority's idea of freedom of the press occurred following the September 11 terrorist attacks against the United States. An Associated Press cameraman filmed Palestinians at a rally in Nablus celebrating the terror attacks and was subsequently summoned to a Palestinian Authority security office and told that the material must not be aired. Yasser Arafat's Tanzim also called to threaten his life if he aired the film. An AP still photographer was also at the site of the rally. He was warned not to take pictures and complied.

Several Palestinian Authority officials told AP in Jerusalem not to broadcast the videotape. Ahmed Abdel Rahman, Arafat's Cabinet secretary, said the Palestinian Authority "cannot guarantee the life" of the cameraman if the footage was broadcast. [21] The cameraman requested that the material not be aired and AP caved in to the blackmail and refused to release the footage.

More than a week later, the Palestinian Authority returned a videotape it confiscated from AP showing a Palestinian rally in the Gaza Strip in which some demonstrators carried posters supporting Osama bin Laden. Two separate parts of the six-minute tape involving "key elements" were erased by the Palestinians, according to an AP official. [22]

Israel Radio reported September 14, 2001, that the Palestinian Authority seized the footage filmed that day by photographers from various international (including Arab) news agencies covering Hamas celebrations of the attacks against America held in cities across the West Bank and Gaza. The celebrants waived photographs of wanted terrorist Osama bin Laden. [23] The very same news programs and networks that broadcast the photo opportunities produced by the Palestinian Authority (Arafat donating blood, Palestinian students in a moment of silence, posters supporting America) failed to broadcast the news that the PA is using terror and intimidation to discourage the airing of unfavorable reports.

In October 2001, after the United States launched attacks against Afghanistan, Palestinians supporting bin Laden staged rallies in the Gaza

Strip that were ruthlessly suppressed by Palestinian police. The PA took measures to prevent any media coverage of the rallies or the subsequent riots. The Paris-based Reporters Without Frontiers issued a scathing protest to the PA. "We fear the Palestinian Authority takes advantage of the focus of international media on the American riposte to restrain more and more the right to free information," said Robert Menard, general secretary of the journalists' organization. The group also protested Palestinian orders not to broadcast calls for general strikes, nationalistic activities, demonstrations or other news without permission from the PA. The aim of the press blackout was expressed by an anonymous Palestinian official, "We don't want anything which could undermine our image."[24]

In August 2002, the Palestinian journalists' union banned journalists from photographing Palestinian children carrying weapons or taking part in activities by terrorist organizations because the pictures were hurting the Palestinians' image. The ban came after numerous photographs were published showing children carrying weapons and dressing up like suicide bombers. Shortly before the union acted, six children were photographed carrying M16 rifles and Kalashnikovs during a pro-Iraq rally in the Gaza Strip. Another group, the Palestinian Journalists Syndicate, issued a similar ban that included photographing masked men. The Foreign Press Association expressed "deep concern" over the effort to censor coverage, and the threats of sanctions against journalists who disregarded the ban.[25]

In July 2004, as Gaza became increasingly unstable, and protests were being mounted against corruption in the Palestinian Authority, Palestinian journalists covering the crisis received death threats. They were told, for example, to stay away from a rally in Gaza to protest Arafat's decision to appoint his cousin as the commander of the PA security forces. One reporter who works for an international news organization said journalists were told that anyone who went to the rally would suffer the same fate as a Palestinian legislator who was shot after he called for reforms in the PA in a television interview. The Gaza rally was subsequently either downplayed or ignored by the Palestinian media.[26] In July 2005, the Palestinian Journalists Syndicate in the Gaza Strip called on Palestinian journalists to celebrate Israel's "retreat" from Gaza and to refrain from covering clashes between rival Palestinian groups.[27]

Journalists from Arab nations are also subject to censorship. In January 2003, for example, the PA's General Intelligence Service arrested a correspondent for al-Jazeera television. The journalist was accused of harming the national interests of the Palestinian people by reporting that Fatah had claimed responsibility for a double suicide bombing in Tel Aviv. In January 2004, journalists working for Arab satellite TV stations were told to refer to all Palestinians killed by the IDF as *shahids* (martyrs).

Numerous incidents have also been reported of physical attacks on journalists who offended PA officials. A reporter for a Saudi-owned news channel was wounded by gunfire when he was driving through the Gaza Strip. He was then dragged from his car and beaten because his station had allowed criticism of Yasser Arafat and other officials. A week later, 100 Palestinian journalists went to Arafat's headquarters in Ramallah to pledge allegiance to him.[28]

MYTH

"The media carefully investigates Palestinian claims before publicizing them."

FACT

Palestinians have learned that they can disseminate almost any information to the media and it will be published or broadcast somewhere. Once it is picked up by one media outlet, it is inevitably repeated by others. Quickly, misinformation can take on the appearance of fact, and while Israel can present evidence to correct the inaccuracies being reported, the damage is usually already done. Once an image or impression is in someone's mind, it is often difficult, if not impossible to erase it.

For example, a Palestinian boy was stabbed to death in a village near a Jewish settlement. The media repeated Palestinian claims that the boy was attacked by settlers when in fact it was later revealed that he had been killed in a brawl between rival Palestinian clans.[29] On another occasion, a 10-year-old Palestinian girl was allegedly killed by IDF tank fire. This time it turned out she died as a result of Palestinians shooting in the air to celebrate the return of Muslim worshipers from Mecca.[30]

It is said that there are three types of lies: lies, damn lies, and statistics. One staple of Palestinian propaganda has been to distribute false statistics in an effort to make Israeli actions look monstrous. For example, if an incident involves some death or destruction, they can grossly exaggerate the figures and a gullible media will repeat the fabricated data until they become widely accepted as accurate. This occurred, for example, during the Lebanon War when Yasser Arafat's brother claimed that Israel's operations had left 600,000 Lebanese homeless. He made the number up, but it was repeated by the International Committee of the Red Cross and publicized in the media. By the time the ICRC repudiated the figure, it was too late to change the impression that Israel's military operation to defend itself from terrorist attacks on its northern border had created an unconscionable refugee problem.[31]

This happened again after Israel's operation in Jenin in April 2002 when Palestinian spokesman Saeb Erekat told CNN that at least 500 people were massacred and 1,600 people, including women and children, were missing. It was a fabrication as the Palestinians' own review committee later concluded.[32]

What is perhaps more outrageous than the repetition of Erekat's lie is that media outlets continue to treat him as a legitimate spokesperson, giving him access that allows him to regularly disseminate misinformation. If an American official was ever found to have lied to the press, they would lose all credibility and would have little or no chance of being given a forum to express their views.

Notes

1. *Jerusalem Report,* (May 7, 1991).
2. *New York Jewish Week,* (August 31, 2001).
3. "Where the reporting stops," *Jerusalem Post,* (January 18, 2005).
4. *Jerusalem Report,* (May 7, 1991).
5. *Al Hayat-Al-Jadidah,* (October 16, 2001).
6. *Al Hayat-Al-Jadidah* (November 2, 2001).
7. Report filed by Jean Pierre Martin on October 5, 2000, a day after his Belgian television team from RTL-TV1 was filming in the area of Ramallah.
8. *Near East Report,* (August 5, 1991).
9. *Jerusalem Report,* (April 22, 2002).
10. *Jerusalem Report,* (April 22, 2002).
11. *Washington Post,* (May 10, 2001).
12. CNN, (October 10, 2000).
13. *Washington Post,* (September 7, 2001).
14. *New York Times,* (September 30, 2000).
15. Tom Fiedler, "Handle with care: words like 'conflict,' 'terrorist,' " *Miami Herald,* (January 4, 2004).
16. *Washington Post,* (September 13, 2001).
17. Fiedler, (January 4, 2004).
18. *WorldnetDaily,* (November 24, 2003).
19. Quoted in Daniel Okrent, "The War of the Words: A Dispatch From the Front Lines," *New York Times,* (March 6, 2005).
20. *Forward,* (June 28, 2002).
21. Associated Press, (September 12, 2001).
22. Jewish Telegraphic Agency, (September 20, 2001).
23. Associated Press and *Jerusalem Post,* (September 13, 2001); International Media Review Analysis, http://www.imra.org.il, (September 13-14, 2001); Jewish Telegraphic Agency, (September 20, 2001).
24. *Jerusalem Post,* (October 10, 2001).
25. *Jerusalem Post,* (August 26, 2002).
26. *Jerusalem Post,* (July 24, 2004).
27. Khaled Abu Toameh, "PA to journalists: All slain Palestinians are martyrs," *Jerusalem Post,* (January 12, 2004) and "PA journalists urged to celebrate Gaza 'retreat,' " *Jerusalem Post,* (July 27, 2005).

28. *Jerusalem Post,* (January 12 & 14, 2004).
29. Arnon Regular, "Palestinian boy likely stabbed to death in West Bank clan feud," *Haaretz,* (July 21, 2005).
30. Margot Dudkevitch, "PA arrests suspect in girl's murder," *Jerusalem Post,* (February 1, 2005).
31. *Washington Post,* (June 25, 1982).
32. *New York Post,* (May 3, 2002).

23. Arab/Muslim Attitudes Toward Israel

The desire for peaceful relations between Jews and Arabs sometimes leads people to overlook public comments by Arab officials and media publications that are often incendiary and sometimes outright anti-Semitic. Frequently, more moderate tones are adopted when speaking to Western audiences, but more accurate and heartfelt views are expressed in Arabic to the speaker's constituents. The following is just a tiny sample of some of the remarks that have been made regarding Israel and the Jews. They are included here because they demonstrate the level of hostility and true beliefs of many Arabs and Muslims. Of course, *not all* Arabs and Muslims subscribe to these views, but the examples are not random, they are beliefs held by important officials and disseminated by major media. They are also included because one of the lessons of the Holocaust was that people of good will are often unwilling to believe that people who threaten evil will in fact carry out their malevolent intentions.

Anti-Semitism

"The Jewish nation, it is known, from the dawn of history, from the time Allah created them, lives by scheme and deceit."

—PA Communications Minister, Imud Falouji
Palestinian television, August 8, 2002

"We know that the Jews have manipulated the Sept. 11 incidents and turned American public opinion against Arabs and Muslims.... We still ask ourselves: Who has benefited from Sept. 11 attacks? I think they (the Jews) were the protagonists of such attacks."

—Saudi Interior Minister Prince Nayef in *Assyasah* (Kuwait)
translation from Saudi magazine *'Ain-Al-Yaqin,* November 29, 2002

"They succeeded in gaining control in most of the [world's] most powerful states, and they—a tiny community—became a world power. But 1.3 billion Muslims must not be defeated by a few million Jews. A way must be found.... The Europeans killed six million Jews out of 12 million, but today the Jews are in control of the world via their proxies. They lead oth-

ers to fight and die for them.... If we are weak, no one will support us. The Israelis respect only the strong, and we must therefore all unite."

**—Malaysian Prime Minister Mahatir Mohammad
at the opening of the Organization of Islamic States summit
October 16, 2003**

"O God, strengthen Islam and Muslims, humiliate infidelity and infidels. O God, destroy your enemies, the Jewish and crusader enemies of Islam."

**—Shaykh Jamal Shakir
Sermon from King Abdallah mosque in Amman
Amman Jordan Television Channel 1 in Arabic
March 5, 2004**

"The Prophet said: the Jews will hide behind the rock and tree, and the rock and tree will say: oh servant of Allah, oh Muslim this is a Jew behind me, come and kill him! Why is there this malice? Because there are none who love the Jews on the face of the earth: not man, not rock, and not tree; everything hates them. They destroy everything, they destroy the trees and destroy the houses. Everything wants vengeance on the Jews, on these pigs on the face of the earth, and the day of our victory, Allah willing, will come."

**—Shaykh Ibrahim Mudayris
Palestine Authority TV
September 10, 2004**

"The Zionist attempts to transmit dangerous diseases like AIDS through exports to Arab countries."

**—Al-Manar (Hizballah TV)
November 23, 2004**

"The Jews are the cancer spreading all over the world ... the Jews are a virus like AIDS hitting humankind ... Jews are responsible for all wars and conflicts...."

**—Sermon by Sheik Ibrahim Mudeiris
Palestine Authority TV
May 13, 2005**

Blood Libel

"The Talmud says that if a Jew does not drink every year the blood of a non-Jewish man, he will be damned for eternity."

—Saudi Arabian delegate Marouf al-Dawalibi before the UN Human Rights Commission conference on religious tolerance December 5, 1984

"During this holiday [Purim], the Jew must prepare very special pastries, the filling of which is not only costly and rare—it cannot be found at all on the local and international markets.... For this holiday, the Jewish people must obtain human blood so that their clerics can prepare the holiday pastries.... Before I go into the details, I would like to clarify that the Jews' spilling human blood to prepare pastry for their holidays is a well-established fact, historically and legally, all throughout history. This was one of the main reasons for the persecution and exile that were their lot in Europe and Asia at various times.... during the holiday, the Jews wear carnival-style masks and costumes and overindulge in drinking alcohol, prostitution, and adultery...."

—Dr. Umayma Ahmad Al-Jalahma of King Faysal University Saudi government daily *Al-Riyadh,* March 10, 2002

"Christian Europe showed enmity toward the Jews when it transpired that their rabbis craftily hunt anyone walking alone, [tempting] him to enter their house of worship. Then they take his blood to use for baked goods for their holidays, as part of their ritual."

—Columnist Dr. Muhammad bin S'ad Al-Shwey'ir, Al-Jazirah (Saudi Arabia), September 6, 2002

Peace

"Unless the Palestine problem is settled, we shall have difficulty in protecting and safeguarding the Jews in the Arab world."

—Syrian delegate, Faris el-Khouri, *New York Times,* February 19, 1947

"The Arab world is not in a compromising mood. It's likely, Mr. Horowitz, that your plan is rational and logical, but the fate of nations is not decided by rational logic. Nations never concede; they fight. You won't

get anything by peaceful means or compromise. You can, perhaps, get something, but only by the force of your arms. We shall try to defeat you. I am not sure we'll succeed, but we'll try. We were able to drive out the Crusaders, but on the other hand we lost Spain and Persia. It may be that we shall lose Palestine. But it's too late to talk of peaceful solutions."

—Arab League Secretary Azzam Pasha,
September 16, 1947

"[A]ll our efforts to find a peaceful solution to the Palestine problem have failed. The only way left for us is war. I will have the pleasure and honor to save Palestine."

—Transjordan's King Abdullah,
April 26, 1948

"The representative of the Jewish Agency told us yesterday that they were not the attackers, that the Arabs had begun the fighting. We did not deny this. We told the whole world that we were going to fight."

—Jamal Husseini before the Security Council,
April 16, 1948

"This will be a war of extermination and a momentous massacre which will be spoken of like the Mongolian massacres and the Crusades."

—Azzam Pasha, Secretary-General of the Arab League,
May 15, 1948

"I am not solely fighting against Israel itself. My task is to deliver the Arab world from destruction through Israel's intrigue, which has its roots abroad. Our hatred is very strong. There is no sense in talking about peace with Israel. There is not even the smallest place for negotiations."

—Egyptian President Nasser,
October 14, 1956

"Our forces are now entirely ready not only to repulse the aggression, but to initiate the act of liberation itself, and to explode the Zionist presence in the Arab homeland. The Syrian army, with its finger on the trigger, is united. . . . I, as a military man, believe that the time has come to enter into a battle of annihilation."

—Syrian Defense Minister Hafez Assad,
May 20, 1967

"Arab policy at this stage has but two objectives. The first, the elimination of the traces of the 1967 aggression through an Israeli withdrawal from all the territories it occupied that year. The second objective is the elimination of the traces of the 1948 aggression, by the means of the elimination of the State of Israel itself. This is, however, as yet an abstract, undefined objective, and some of us have erred in commencing the latter step before the former."

—Mohammed Heikal, a Sadat confidant and
editor of the semi-official *Al-Ahram,*
February 25, 1971

"The Arab armies entered Palestine to protect the Palestinians from the Zionist tyranny but, instead, they abandoned them, forced them to emigrate and to leave their homeland, and threw them into prisons similar to the ghettos in which the Jews used to live."

—PLO spokesman Mahmud Abbas ("Abu Mazen"),
***Falastin a-Thaura,* March 1976**

"Saddam, you hero, attack Israel with chemical weapons."

—Palestinians marching in support of Saddam
Hussein's invasion of Kuwait,
Associated Press, August 12, 1990

"We will not arrest the sons of our people in order to appease Israel. Let our people rest assured that this won't happen."

—Chief of the PA Preventive Security in the West Bank, Jebril Rajoub,
Islamic Association for Palestine, June 9, 2001

"... Allah willing, this unjust state ... Israel will be erased; this unjust state, the United States will be erased; this unjust state, Britain will be erased ... Blessings to whoever waged Jihad for the sake of Allah ... Blessings to whoever put a belt of explosives on his body or on his sons' and plunged into the midst of the Jews ..."

—Sermon by Sheikh Ibrahim Madhi
a few days after Yasser Arafat's cease-fire declaration
PA Television, June 8, 2001

"Didn't we throw mud in the face of Bill Clinton, who dared to propose a state with some adjustments? Were we honest about what we did? Were we right in what we did? No, we were not. After two years of violence, we are now calling for what we rejected."

—Nabil Amr, ex-minister in the PA cabinet,
Quoted in the *Jerusalem Report,* October 21, 2002

"Just as Ramallah, Gaza, Nablus, and Jenin are Palestinian cities, so are Haifa, Nazareth, Jaffa, Ramle, Lod, Beersheba, Safed, and others Palestinian cities.... The Zionist Jews are foreigners in this land. They have no right to live or settle in it. They should go somewhere else in the world to establish their state and their false entity... They must leave their homes... We do not believe in so-called 'peace with Israel' because peace cannot be made with Satan. Israel is the greatest Satan."

—Palestinian Christian cleric Father 'Atallah Hanna,
sermon in the Greek Orthodox Cathedral in Jerusalem,
January 19, 2003

"Hamas will keep its weapons in its hands and will defend any part of the homeland.... Our national problem is not related only to the West Bank, Gaza, and al-Quds... but to Palestine, all [the territory of] Palestine."

—Hamas leader Mahmoud al-Zahar
***Al Hayat Al-Jadidah,* July, 5, 2005.**

"Oh Allah, liberate our Al-Aksa Mosque from the defilement of the occupying and brutal Zionists... Oh Allah, punish the occupying Zionists and their supporters from among the corrupt infidels. Oh Allah, scatter and disperse them, and make an example of them for those who take heed."

—Sheikh Abd Al-Rahman Al-Sudayyis,
imam of Islam's most holy mosque, Al-Haram in Mecca
Sermon on Saudi Channel 1, July 15, 2005

"Al-Qassam warriors, rain rockets on the settlers! Don't let any Jew sleep!
The Al-Aqsa Brigades will make you tremble in Haifa and Tel Aviv; they will strike you in Safed and Acre.
Because we do not distinguish between [Jewish] Palestine and [Arab] Palestine.

For [as] Jaffa is the same as Gaza, Tel-al-Zuhour [Tel Aviv] is the same as Rafah, and the Galilee is the same as Hebron.
We make no distinction between the parts of the earth of the homeland."

—Song broadcast on Hamas radio station Sawt Al-Aksa
August 16, 2005

"We will continue our martyrdom operations inside Israel until all our lands are liberated, by God's will.... We won't lay down our weapons as long as Jerusalem and the West Bank are under occupation."

—Muhamemd Hijazi, commander of a Fatah-
affiliated militias in the Gaza Strip
***Jerusalem Post,* September 12, 2005**

"We will not rest and will not abandon the path of Jihad and martyrdom as long as one inch of our land remained in the hands of the Jews."

—Raed Saed, a senior Hamas leader
***Ynet News,* September 19, 2005**

"First of all this Palestinian land, and all the Arabic nation, is all part of the same area. In the past, there was no independent Palestinian state; there was no independent Jordanian state; and so on. There were regions called Iraq or Egypt, but they were all part of one country.... Our main goal is to establish a great Islamic state, be it pan-Arabic or pan-Islamic."

—Hamas leader Mahmoud al-Zahar,
The Media Line, September 22, 2005

Phased Plan & the Destruction of Israel

"If we agree to declare our state over what is now 22 percent of Palestine, meaning the West Bank and Gaza, our ultimate goal is the liberation of all historic Palestine from the River to the Sea...We distinguish the strategic, long-term goals from the political phased goals, which we are compelled to temporarily accept due to international pressure."

—Faisal al-Husseini,
***Al-Arabi,* June 24, 2001**

"Israel is much smaller than Iran in land mass, and therefore far more vulnerable to nuclear attack."

—Former Iranian President Ali Rafsanjani, quoted in *Jerusalem Report,* March 11, 2002

"We defeated the Crusaders 800 years ago and we will defeat the enemies of Islam today."

—Nazareth Deputy Mayor Salman Abu Ahmed, quoted in *Jerusalem Report,* March 4, 2002

". . . we shall return to the 1967 borders, but it does not mean that we have given up on Jerusalem and Haifa, Jaffa, Lod, Ramla, Nayanyah [Al-Zuhour] and Tel Aviv [Tel Al-Rabia]. Never. We shall return to every village we had been expelled from, by Allah's will. . . . Our approval to return to the 1967 borders is not a concession for our other rights. No! . . . this generation might not achieve this stage, but generations will come, and the land of Palestine . . . will demand that the Palestinians return the way Muhammad returned there, as a conqueror."

—Sheikh Ibrahim Mudyris, Friday sermon, February 4, 2005

Hamas would *"definitely not"* be prepared for coexistence with Israel should the IDF retreat to its 1967 borders. *"It can be a temporary solution, for a maximum of 5 to 10 years. But in the end Palestine must return to become Muslim, and in the long term Israel will disappear from the face of the earth."*

—Hamas leader Mahmoud al-Zahar *Yediot Aharonot,* June 24, 2005

Sanctioning Violence

"The ruling to kill the Americans and their allies—civilians and military—is an individual duty for every Muslim who can do it in any country in which it is possible to do it, in order to liberate the al-Aksa Mosque and the holy mosque [Mecca] from their grip, and in order for their armies to move out of all the lands of Islam, defeated and unable to threaten any Muslim."

—The *fatwa* (religious edict) issued by Osama bin Laden in 1998

"The Palestinian people are in a state of emergency against the failure of the Camp David summit. If the situation explodes, the Palestinian people living in the areas controlled by the Palestinian Authority are ready for the next fierce battle against the Israeli occupation. . . . The next Intifada will be more violent than the first one especially since the Palestinian people now possess weapons allowing them to defend themselves in a confrontation with the Israeli army. . . . the Lebanese experience of wiping out the Israeli occupation from southern Lebanon gave the Palestinian people the needed moral strength and added to their spirit of armed struggle."

—A "senior security figure" in the Palestinian Authority,
Kul Al-Arab, July 14, 2000

"We are teaching the children that suicide bombs make Israeli people frightened and we are allowed to do it. . . . We teach them that after a person becomes a suicide bomber he reaches the highest level of paradise."

—Palestinian "Paradise Camp" counselor speaking to BBC interviewer,
quoted in *Jerusalem Post*, July 20, 2001

"If they go from Sheba'a, we will not stop fighting them. Our goal is to liberate the 1948 borders of Palestine . . . [Jews] can go back to Germany or wherever they came from."

—Hizballah spokesperson Hassan Ezzedin
New Yorker, October 14, 2002

"If they [Jews] all gather in Israel, it will save us the trouble of going after them worldwide."

—Hizballah leader Sheikh Sayyed Hassan Nasrallah
Lebanon Daily Star, October 23, 2002

"The jihad and suicide bombings will continue—the Zionist entity will reach its end in the first quarter of the current century. It is therefore up to you [Muslim holy fighters] to be patient—the Hamas takes upon itself the liberation of all Palestinian land from the sea to the river in the Rafah [in the south] and until Rosh Hanikra [in the north]."

—Hamas spiritual leader Sheikh Ahmed Yassin
Al-Ayyam, December 28, 2002

"There is no doubt that the new wave (of attacks) in Palestine will wipe off this stigma (Israel) from the face of the Islamic world.... Anybody who recognizes Israel will burn in the fire of the Islamic nation's fury (while) any (Islamic leader) who recognizes the Zionist regime means he is acknowledging the surrender and defeat of the Islamic world.... As the Imam [Ayatollah Ruhollah Khomeini] said, Israel must be wiped off the map."

—Speech by Mahmoud Ahmadinejad
Associated Press, October 26, 2005

Sources:

Foreign Broadcast Information Service
Haaretz
Israeli Foreign Ministry
Jerusalem Post
MEMRI
Near East Report
Palestinian Media Watch
Intelligence and Terrorism Information Center at the Center for Special Studies
Various news sources

APPENDICES

The Military Balance in the Middle East

Country	Regular Troops	Reserve Troops	Total	Tanks	Aircraft*
Israel	186,500	445,000	631,500	3,930	798
Egypt	450,000	254,000	704,000	~3,000	518
Jordan	100,700	60,000	160,700	970	106
Lebanon	61,400		61,400	350	
Palestinian Authority	~45,000		~45,000		
Iran	518,000	350,000	868,000	~1,700	335
Syria	289,000	132,500	421,500	3,700	510
Saudi Arabia	171,500	20,000	191,500	750	~345

Note: Iraq has been removed. It has approximately 130,000 security forces (most of which are various internal security components). This increases to "anticipated" forces of some 186,335, of which 35,000 will be Iraq's national army. It currently has zero tanks and aircraft in service (although there is talk of giving the new security forces a small number of leftover operational tanks from Saddam's arsenal that are now under U.S. control).

*Refers to total number of combat aircraft.

Sources: Shai Feldman and Yiftah Shapir, Eds., *The Middle East Military Balance*, (Cambridge: MIT Press, 2004); Anthony Cordesman, "Syrian Military Forces and Capabilities," Center for Strategic and International Studies, (April 15, 2003); AIPAC

The Middle East Road Map

(April 30, 2003)

A Performance-Based Roadmap to a Permanent Two-State Solution to the Israeli-Palestinian Conflict

The following is a performance-based and goal-driven roadmap, with clear phases, timelines, target dates, and benchmarks aiming at progress through reciprocal steps by the two parties in the political, security, economic, humanitarian, and institution-building fields, under the auspices of the Quartet [the United States, European Union, United Nations, and Russia]. The destination is a final and comprehensive settlement of the Israel-Palestinian conflict by 2005, as presented in President Bush's speech of 24 June, and welcomed by the EU, Russia and the UN in the 16 July and 17 September Quartet Ministerial statements.

A two-state solution to the Israeli-Palestinian conflict will only be achieved through an end to violence and terrorism, when the Palestinian people have a leadership acting decisively against terror and willing and able to build a practicing democracy based on tolerance and liberty, and through Israel's readiness to do what is necessary for a democratic Palestinian state to be established, and a clear, unambiguous acceptance by both parties of the goal of a negotiated settlement as described below. The Quartet will assist and facilitate implementation of the plan, starting in Phase I, including direct discussions between the parties as required. The plan establishes a realistic timeline for implementation. However, as a performance-based plan, progress will require and depend upon the good faith efforts of the parties, and their compliance with each of the obligations outlined below. Should the parties perform their obligations rapidly, progress within and through the phases may come sooner than indicated in the plan. Non-compliance with obligations will impede progress.

A settlement, negotiated between the parties, will result in the emergence of an independent, democratic, and viable Palestinian state living side by side in peace and security with Israel and its other neighbors. The settlement will resolve the Israel-Palestinian conflict, and end the occupation that began in 1967, based on the foundations of the Madrid Conference, the principle of land for peace, UNSCRs 242, 338 and 1397, agreements previously reached by the parties, and the initiative of Saudi Crown Prince Abdullah—endorsed by the Beirut Arab League Summit—calling for acceptance of Israel as a neighbor living in peace and security, in the context of a comprehensive settlement. This initiative is a vital element of international efforts to promote a comprehensive peace on all tracks, including the Syrian-Israeli and Lebanese-Israeli tracks.

The Quartet will meet regularly at senior levels to evaluate the parties' performance on implementation of the plan. In each phase, the parties are expected to perform their obligations in parallel, unless otherwise indicated.

Phase I: Ending Terror and Violence, Normalizing Palestinian Life, and Building Palestinian Institutions—Present to May 2003

In Phase I, the Palestinians immediately undertake an unconditional cessation of violence according to the steps outlined below; such action should be accompanied by supportive measures undertaken by Israel. Palestinians and Israelis resume security cooperation based on the Tenet work plan to end violence, terrorism, and incitement through restructured and effective Palestinian security services. Palestinians undertake comprehensive political reform in preparation for statehood, including drafting a Palestinian constitution, and free, fair and open elections upon the basis of those measures. Israel takes all necessary steps to help normalize Palestinian life. Israel withdraws from Palestinian areas occupied from September 28, 2000 and the two sides restore the status quo that existed at that time, as security performance and cooperation progress. Israel also freezes all settlement activity, consistent with the Mitchell report.

At the outset of Phase I:

■ Palestinian leadership issues unequivocal statement reiterating Israel's right to exist in peace and security and calling for an immediate and unconditional ceasefire to end armed activity and all acts of violence against Israelis anywhere. All official Palestinian institutions end incitement against Israel.

■ Israeli leadership issues unequivocal statement affirming its commitment to the two-state vision of an independent, viable, sovereign Palestinian state living in peace and security alongside Israel, as expressed by President Bush, and calling for an immediate end to violence against Palestinians everywhere. All official Israeli institutions end incitement against Palestinians.

Security

■ Palestinians declare an unequivocal end to violence and terrorism and undertake visible efforts on the ground to arrest, disrupt, and restrain individuals and groups conducting and planning violent attacks on Israelis anywhere.

■ Rebuilt and refocused Palestinian Authority security apparatus begins sustained, targeted, and effective operations aimed at confronting all those engaged in terror and dismantlement of terrorist capabilities and infrastructure. This includes commencing confiscation of illegal weapons and consolidation of security authority, free of association with terror and corruption.

■ GOI takes no actions undermining trust, including deportations, attacks on civilians; confiscation and/or demolition of Palestinian homes and property, as a punitive measure or to facilitate Israeli construction; destruction of Palestinian institutions and infrastructure; and other measures specified in the Tenet work plan.

■ Relying on existing mechanisms and on-the-ground resources, Quartet representatives begin informal monitoring and consult with the parties on establishment of a formal monitoring mechanism and its implementation.

■ Implementation, as previously agreed, of U.S. rebuilding, training and resumed security cooperation plan in collaboration with outside oversight board (U.S.–Egypt–Jordan). Quartet support for efforts to achieve a lasting, comprehensive cease-fire.

• All Palestinian security organizations are consolidated into three services reporting to an empowered Interior Minister.

• Restructured/retrained Palestinian security forces and IDF counterparts progressively resume security cooperation and other undertakings in implementation of the Tenet work plan, including regular senior-level meetings, with the participation of U.S. security officials.

■ Arab states cut off public and private funding and all other forms of support for groups supporting and engaging in violence and terror.

■ All donors providing budgetary support for the Palestinians channel these funds through the Palestinian Ministry of Finance's Single Treasury Account.

■ As comprehensive security performance moves forward, IDF withdraws progressively from areas occupied since September 28, 2000, and the two sides restore the status quo that existed prior to September 28, 2000. Palestinian security forces redeploy to areas vacated by IDF.

Palestinian Institution-Building

■ Immediate action on credible process to produce draft constitution for Palestinian statehood. As rapidly as possible, constitutional committee circulates draft Palestinian constitution, based on strong parliamentary democracy and cabinet with empowered prime minister, for public comment/debate. Constitutional committee proposes draft document for submission after elections for approval by appropriate Palestinian institutions.

■ Appointment of interim prime minister or cabinet with empowered executive authority/decision-making body.

■ GOI fully facilitates travel of Palestinian officials for PLC and Cabinet sessions, internationally supervised security retraining, electoral and other reform activity, and other supportive measures related to the reform efforts.

■ Continued appointment of Palestinian ministers empowered to undertake fundamental reform. Completion of further steps to achieve genuine separation of powers, including any necessary Palestinian legal reforms for this purpose.

■ Establishment of independent Palestinian election commission. PLC reviews and revises election law.

■ Palestinian performance on judicial, administrative, and economic benchmarks, as established by the International Task Force on Palestinian Reform.

■ As early as possible, and based upon the above measures and in the context of open debate and transparent candidate selection/electoral campaign based on a free, multi-party process, Palestinians hold free, open, and fair elections.

■ GOI facilitates Task Force election assistance, registration of voters, movement of candidates and voting officials. Support for NGOs involved in the election process.

■ GOI reopens Palestinian Chamber of Commerce and other closed Palestinian institutions in East Jerusalem based on a commitment that these institutions operate strictly in accordance with prior agreements between the parties.

Humanitarian Response

■ Israel takes measures to improve the humanitarian situation. Israel and Palestinians implement in full all recommendations of the Bertini report to improve humanitarian conditions, lifting curfews and easing restrictions on movement of persons and goods, and allowing full, safe, and unfettered access of international and humanitarian personnel.

■ AHLC reviews the humanitarian situation and prospects for economic development in the West Bank and Gaza and launches a major donor assistance effort, including to the reform effort.

■ GOI and PA continue revenue clearance process and transfer of funds, including arrears, in accordance with agreed, transparent monitoring mechanism.

Civil Society

■ Continued donor support, including increased funding through PVOs/ NGOs, for people to people programs, private sector development and civil society initiatives.

Settlements

- GOI immediately dismantles settlement outposts erected since March 2001.

- Consistent with the Mitchell Report, GOI freezes all settlement activity (including natural growth of settlements).

Phase II: Transition—June 2003–December 2003

In the second phase, efforts are focused on the option of creating an independent Palestinian state with provisional borders and attributes of sovereignty, based on the new constitution, as a way station to a permanent status settlement. As has been noted, this goal can be achieved when the Palestinian people have a leadership acting decisively against terror, willing and able to build a practicing democracy based on tolerance and liberty. With such a leadership, reformed civil institutions and security structures, the Palestinians will have the active support of the Quartet and the broader international community in establishing an independent, viable, state.

Progress into Phase II will be based upon the consensus judgment of the Quartet of whether conditions are appropriate to proceed, taking into account performance of both parties. Furthering and sustaining efforts to normalize Palestinian lives and build Palestinian institutions, Phase II starts after Palestinian elections and ends with possible creation of an independent Palestinian state with provisional borders in 2003. Its primary goals are continued comprehensive security performance and effective security cooperation, continued normalization of Palestinian life and institution-building, further building on and sustaining of the goals outlined in Phase I, ratification of a democratic Palestinian constitution, formal establishment of office of prime minister, consolidation of political reform, and the creation of a Palestinian state with provisional borders.

- **International Conference:** Convened by the Quartet, in consultation with the parties, immediately after the successful conclusion of Palestinian elections, to support Palestinian economic recovery and launch a process, leading to establishment of an independent Palestinian state with provisional borders.

  - Such a meeting would be inclusive, based on the goal of a comprehensive Middle East peace (including between Israel and Syria, and Israel and Lebanon), and based on the principles described in the preamble to this document.

  - Arab states restore pre-intifada links to Israel (trade offices, etc.).

  - Revival of multilateral engagement on issues including regional water resources, environment, economic development, refugees, and arms control issues.

■ New constitution for democratic, independent Palestinian state is finalized and approved by appropriate Palestinian institutions. Further elections, if required, should follow approval of the new constitution.

■ Empowered reform cabinet with office of prime minister formally established, consistent with draft constitution.

■ Continued comprehensive security performance, including effective security cooperation on the bases laid out in Phase I.

■ Creation of an independent Palestinian state with provisional borders through a process of Israeli-Palestinian engagement, launched by the international conference. As part of this process, implementation of prior agreements, to enhance maximum territorial contiguity, including further action on settlements in conjunction with establishment of a Palestinian state with provisional borders.

■ Enhanced international role in monitoring transition, with the active, sustained, and operational support of the Quartet.

■ Quartet members promote international recognition of Palestinian state, including possible UN membership.

Phase III: Permanent Status Agreement and End of the Israeli-Palestinian Conflict—2004–2005

Progress into Phase III, based on consensus judgment of Quartet, and taking into account actions of both parties and Quartet monitoring. Phase III objectives are consolidation of reform and stabilization of Palestinian institutions, sustained, effective Palestinian security performance, and Israeli-Palestinian negotiations aimed at a permanent status agreement in 2005.

■ **Second International Conference:** Convened by Quartet, in consultation with the parties, at beginning of 2004 to endorse agreement reached on an independent Palestinian state with provisional borders and formally to launch a process with the active, sustained, and operational support of the Quartet, leading to a final, permanent status resolution in 2005, including on borders, Jerusalem, refugees, settlements; and, to support progress toward a comprehensive Middle East settlement between Israel and Lebanon and Israel and Syria, to be achieved as soon as possible.

■ Continued comprehensive, effective progress on the reform agenda laid out by the Task Force in preparation for final status agreement.

■ Continued sustained and effective security performance, and sustained, effective security cooperation on the bases laid out in Phase I.

■ International efforts to facilitate reform and stabilize Palestinian institutions and the Palestinian economy, in preparation for final status agreement.

■ Parties reach final and comprehensive permanent status agreement that ends the Israel-Palestinian conflict in 2005, through a settlement negotiated between the parties based on UNSCR 242, 338, and 1397, that ends the occupation that began in 1967, and includes an agreed, just, fair, and realistic solution to the refugee issue, and a negotiated resolution on the status of Jerusalem that takes into account the political and religious concerns of both sides, and protects the religious interests of Jews, Christians, and Muslims worldwide, and fulfills the vision of two states, Israel and sovereign, independent, democratic and viable Palestine, living side-by-side in peace and security.

■ Arab state acceptance of full normal relations with Israel and security for all the states of the region in the context of a comprehensive Arab-Israeli peace.

The Covenant of the Islamic
Resistance Movement (HAMAS)

The following is excerpted from the covenant of the Islamic Resistance Movement (HAMAS). The full text is available in the Jewish Virtual Library (http://www.jewishvirtuallibrary.org/jsource/Terrorism/Hamas_covenant_complete.html).

Our struggle against the Jews is very great and very serious. It needs all sincere efforts. The Islamic Resistance Movement is but one squadron that should be supported...until the enemy is vanquished and Allah's victory is realized. It strives to raise the banner of Allah over every inch of Palestine...It is one of the links in the chain of the struggle against the Zionist invaders ...

The Prophet, Allah bless him and grant him salvation, has said: "The Day of Judgement will not come about until Moslems fight the Jews (killing the Jews), when the Jew will hide behind stones and trees. The stones and trees will say 'there is a Jew behind me, come and kill him' ".... There is no solution for the Palestine question except through Jihad. Initiatives, proposals and international conferences are all a waste of time and vain endeavors. Palestine is an Islamic land.

Zionist organizations under various names and shapes, such as Freemasons, Rotary Clubs, espionage groups and others...are all nothing more than cells of subversion and saboteurs. The Islamic peoples should perform their role in confronting the conspiracies of these saboteurs.

Moslem society confronts a vicious enemy which acts in a way similar to Nazism. He has deprived people of their homeland. In their Nazi treatment, the Jews made no exception for women or children.

Our enemies took control of the world media. They were behind the French Revolution and the Communist Revolution.... They were behind World War I, when they were able to destroy the Islamic Caliphate, making financial gains and controlling resources. They obtained the Balfour Declaration, formed the League of Nations through which they could rule the world. They were behind World War II, through which they made huge financial gains by trading in armaments, and paved the way for the establishment of their state. It was they that instigated the replacement of the League of Nations with the United Nations and the Security Council to enable them to rule the world through them. There is no war going on any where, without [them] having their finger in it.

The Palestinian Liberation Organization adopted the idea of the secular state, which completely contradicts the idea of religious ideology. The day the PLO adopts Islam as its way of life, we will become its soldiers, and fuel for its fire that will burn the enemies. Until that day, the Islamic Resistance Movement's stand towards the PLO is that of the son towards his father, the brother towards his brother and the relative to relative, who suffers his pain and supports him in confronting the enemies, wishing him to be wise and well-guided. . . .

The Zionist invasion is a vicious invasion. It does not refrain from resorting to all methods, using all evil and contemptible ways to achieve its end. It relies greatly on the secret organizations it gave rise to, such as the Freemasons, the Rotary and Lions Club, other sabotage groups. All these organizations work in the interest of Zionism...They aim at undermining societies, destroying values, corrupting consciences, deteriorating character and annihilating Islam. It is behind the drug trade and alcoholism in all its kinds so as to facilitate its control and expansion.

Writers, intellectuals, media people, orators, educators and teachers, and all the various sectors in the Arab and Islamic world—all of them are called upon to perform their role, and to fulfill their duty, because of the ferocity of the Zionist offensive and the Zionist influence in many countries exercised through financial and media control.

The Zionist plan is limitless. After Palestine, the Zionists aspire to expand from the Nile to the Euphrates. When they will have digested the region they overtook they will aspire to further expansion, and so on. Their plan is embodied in the *Protocols of the Elders of Zion,* and their present conduct is the best proof of what we are saying. Leaving the circle of struggle with Zionism is high treason, and cursed be he who does that.

United Nations Security Council Resolution 242

(November 22, 1967)

The Security Council,

Expressing its continuing concern with the grave situation in the Middle East,

Emphasizing the inadmissibility of the acquisition of territory by war and the need to work for a just and lasting peace in which every State in the area can live in security,

Emphasizing further that all Member States in their acceptance of the Charter of the United Nations have undertaken a commitment to act in accordance with Article 2 of the Charter.

1. *Affirms* that the fulfillment of Charter principles requires the establishment of a just and lasting peace in the Middle East which should include the application of both the following principles:

(i) Withdrawal of Israeli armed forces from territories occupied in the recent conflict;

(ii) Termination of all claims or states of belligerency and respect for an acknowledgement of the sovereignty, territorial integrity and political independence of every State in the area and their right to live in peace within secure and recognized boundaries free from threats or acts of force;

2. *Affirms further* the necessity:

(a) For guaranteeing freedom of navigation-through international waterways in the area;

(b) For achieving a just settlement of the refugee problem;

(c) For guaranteeing the territorial inviolability and political independence of every State in the area, through measures including the establishment of demilitarized zones;

3. *Requests* the Secretary General to designate a Special Representative to proceed to the Middle East to establish and maintain contacts with the States concerned in order to promote agreement and assist efforts to achieve a peaceful and accepted settlement in accordance with the provisions and principles in this resolution;

4. *Requests* the Secretary General to report to the Security Council on the progress of the efforts of the Special Representative as soon as possible.

Recommended Internet Resources

*For the most comprehensive coverage of topics related to this book, as well as a regularly updated version of **Myths & Facts**, visit our Jewish Virtual Library (**http://www.JewishVirtualLibrary.org**). The Library contains an extensive bibliography of more than 1,000 web sites. The following are selected from that list:*

About Israel
http://alisrael.co.il

American Israel Public Affairs Committee (AIPAC)
http://www.aipac.org

American Jewish Committee
http://www.ajc.org

Anti-Defamation League (ADL)
http://www.adl.org

Arutz Sheva Israel National Radio
http://www.a7.org

Begin-Sadat Center for Strategic Studies
http://www.biu.ac.il/SOC/besa/

CAMERA
http://www.camera.org

Central Zionist Archives
http://www.wzo.org.il/cza/index.htm

The David Project
http://www.davidproject.org/

Dinur Center for the Study of Jewish History
http://www.hum.huji.ac.il/dinur

Embassy of Israel (US)
http://www.israelemb.org

Golan Heights Information Server
http://english.golan.org.il

Ha'aretz
http://www.haaretz.co.il

Hasbara Fellowships
http://www.israelactivism.com/

Hillel
http://www.hillel.org

HonestReporting.com
http://www.honestreporting.com

The Interdisciplinary Center
https://www.idc.ac.il/eng/default.asp

International Christian Embassy Jerusalem
http://www.icej.org/

International Policy Institute for Counter-Terrorism
http://www.ict.org.il

Internet Jewish History Sourcebook
http://www.fordham.edu/halsall/jewish/jewishsbook.html

Institute for Advanced Strategic and Political Studies
http://www.iasps.org/index.php

Israel Defense Forces (IDF)
http://www.idf.il

Israel on Campus Coalition
http://israeloncampuscoalition.org/

Israel Radio
http://www.israelradio.org

Israeli Central Bureau of Statistics
http://www.cbs.gov.il/engindex.htm

Israeli Ministry of Foreign Affairs
http://www.israel-mfa.gov.il/mfa/home.asp

Israeli Prime Minister's Office
http://www.pmo.gov.il/english

Jaffee Center for Strategic Studies
http://www.tau.ac.il/jcss

Jerusalem Capital of Israel
http://www.jerusalem-archives.org

Jerusalem Post
http://www.jpost.com

Jerusalem Report
http://www.jrep.com

Jewish Telegraphic Agency (JTA)
http://www.jta.org

Knesset—The Israeli Parliament
http://www.knesset.gov.il

Maps of the Middle East
http:// http://www.lib.utexas.edu/maps/middle_east.html

Middle East Media & Research Institute (MEMRI)
http://www.memri.org

Middle East Review of International Affairs
http://www.biu.ac.il/SOC/besa/meria/index.html

Palestinian Media Watch
http://www.pmw.org.il

Peace Now
http://www.peacenow.org.il/English.asp

Pedagogic Center, The Department for Jewish Zionist Education, The Jewish Agency for Israel
http://www.jajz-ed.org.il

Stand With Us
http://www.standwithus.com/

Terrorism Research Center
http://www.terrorism.com

The Israel Project
http://theisraelproject.org/

U.S. State Department
http://www.state.gov

United Jewish Communities
UJC http://www.ujc.org

Virtual Jerusalem
http://www.virtualjerusalem.com

Washington Institute for Near East Policy
http://www.washingtoninstitute.org

World Zionist Organization Student and Academics Department
http://www.wzo.org.il

Suggested Reading

Aumann Moshe. *Land Ownership in Palestine 1880–1948.* Jerusalem: Academic Committee on the Middle East, 1976.

Avineri Shlomo. *The Making of Modern Zionism: Intellectual Origins of the Jewish State.* NY Basic Books, 1981.

Avneri Arieh. *The Claim of Dispossession.* NJ: Transaction Books, 1984.

Bard, Mitchell G. and Moshe Schwartz. *1001 Facts Everyone Should Know About Israel.* MD: Rowman and Littlefield, 2005.

Bard, Mitchell G. *From Tragedy to Triumph: The Politics behind the Rescue of Ethiopian Jewry.* CT: Greenwood, 2002.

Bard, Mitchell G. *The Complete Idiot's Guide to Middle East Conflict,* Third Edition. NY: Alpha Books, 2005.

Bard, Mitchell. *The Water's Edge And Beyond.* NJ: Transaction Publishers, 1991.

Becker, Jillian. *The PLO.* NY: St. Martin's Press, 1985.

Begin, Menachem. *The Revolt.* NY: EP Dutton, 1978.

Bell, J. Bowyer. *Terror Out Of Zion.* NJ: Transaction, 1996.

Ben-Gurion, David. *Rebirth and Destiny of Israel.* NY: Philosophical Library, 1954.

Collins, Larry and Dominique Lapierre. *O Jerusalem!.* NY: Simon and Schuster, 1972.

Dershowitz, Alan. *The Case for Israel.* NJ: John Wiley & Sons, Inc., 2003.

Eban, Abba. *Heritage: Civilization and the Jews.* NY: Summit Books, 1984.

Eban Abba. *My Country: The Story of Modern Israel.* NY: Random House, 1972.

Gilbert, Martin. *Israel: A History.* NY: William Morrow & Co., 1998.

Hazony, Yoram. *The Jewish State: The Struggle for Israel's Soul.* NY: Basic Books, 2001.

Hertzberg Arthur. *The Zionist Idea.* PA: Jewish Publications Society, 1997.

Herzl, Theodor. *The Diaries of Theodore Herzl.* NY: Peter Smith Publishers, 1987.

Herzl, Theodor. *The Jewish State.* Dover Publications, 1989.

Herzog, Chaim. *The Arab-Israeli Wars.* NY: Random House, 1984.

Johnson, Paul. *A History of the Jews.* NY: HarperCollins, 1988.

Katz, Samuel. *Battleground-Fact and Fantasy in Palestine.* SPI Books, 1986.

Kollek, Teddy. *Jerusalem.* Washington, D.C.: Washington Institute For Near East Policy, 1990.

Lacquer, Walter and Barry Rubin. *The Israel-Arab Reader.* NY: Penguin, 2001.

Lewis, Bernard. *The Jews of Islam.* NJ: Princeton University Press, 1984.

Lewis, Bernard. *The Middle East: A Brief History of the Last 2000 Years.* NY: Touchstone Books, 1997.

Livingstone, Neil C., and David Halevy. *Inside the PLO.* NY: William Morrow and Co., 1990.

Lorch Netanel. *One Long War.* NY: Herzl Press, 1976.

Meir, Golda. *My Life.* NY: Dell, 1975.

Netanyahu, Benjamin. *A Place Among Nations: Israel and the World.* NY: Warner Books, 1998.

Oren, Michael. *Six Days of War: June 1967 and the Making of the Modern Middle East.* NY: Oxford University Press, 2002.

Pipes, Daniel. *The Hidden Hand: Middle East Fears of Conspiracy.* Griffin Trade Paperback, 1998.

Pipes, Daniel. *The Long Shadow: Culture and Politics in the Middle East.* NJ: Transaction Publishers, 1990.

Porath Yehoshua. *The Emergence of the Palestinian-Arab National Movement, 1918–1929.* London: Frank Cass, 1996.

Porath Yehoshua. *In Search of Arab Unity 1930–1945.* London: Frank Cass and Co., Ltd., 1986.

Porath Yehoshua. *Palestinian Arab National Movement: From Riots to Rebellion: 1929–1939. vol. 2.* London: Frank Cass and Co., Ltd., 1977.

Rabin, Yitzhak. *The Rabin Memoirs.* CA: University of California Press, 1996.

Ross, Dennis. *The Missing Peace: The Inside Story of the Fight for Middle East Peace.* NY: Farrar, Strauss and Giroux, 2004.

Sachar Howard. *A History of Israel: From the Rise of Zionism to Our Time.* NY: Alfred A. Knopf, 1998.

Safran Nadav. Israel *The Embattled Ally.* MA: Harvard University Press, 1981.

Sanjuan, Pedro. *The UN Gang: A Memoir of Incompetence, Corruption, Espionage, Anti-Semitism, and Islamic Extremism at the UN Secretariat.* NY: Doubleday, 2005.

Schiff Ze'ev and Ehud Ya'ari. *Intifada.* NY: Simon & Schuster, 1990.

Schiff Zeev and Ehud Yaari. *Israel's Lebanon War.* NY: Simon and Schuster, 1984.

Schoenberg, Harris. *Mandate For Terror: The United Nations and the PLO.* NY: Shapolsky 1989.

Stillman Norman. *The Jews of Arab Lands.* PA: The Jewish Publication Society of America 1989.

Stillman Norman. *The Jews of Arab Lands in Modern Times.* NY: Jewish Publication Society, 1991.

Weizmann Chaim. *Trial and Error.* NY: Greenwood Press, 1972.

Wigoder, Geoffrey, ed. *New Encyclopedia of Zionism and Israel.* NJ: Fairleigh Dickinson University Press, 1994.

Ye'or, Bat. *The Dhimmi.* NJ: Associated University Press, 1985.

Index of Myths

Alphabetical Index

American-Israeli Cooperative Enterprise (AICE)

The AMERICAN-ISRAELI COOPERATIVE ENTERPRISE (AICE) was established in 1993 as a nonprofit 501(c)(3), nonpartisan organization to strengthen the U.S.-Israel relationship by emphasizing the fundamentals of the alliance and the values our nations share. Tangibly, this means developing social and educational programs in the U.S. based on innovative, successful Israeli models that address similar domestic problems, and bringing novel U.S. programs to Israel. These cooperative activities, which stem from our common values, are called *Shared Value Initiatives*.

The objectives and purposes of AICE include:

- To provide a vehicle for the research, study, discussion and exchange of views concerning nonmilitary cooperation (*Shared Value Initiatives*) between the peoples and governments of the United States and Israel.
- To facilitate the formation of partnerships between Israelis and Americans.
- To publicize joint activities, and the benefits accruing to America and Israel from them.
- To explore issues of common historical interest to the peoples and governments of the United States and Israel.
- To sponsor research, conferences and documentaries.
- To serve as a clearinghouse on joint U.S.-Israeli activities.
- To provide educational materials on Jewish history and culture.
- To promote scholarship in the field of Israel studies.

AICE also runs the Jewish Virtual Library, a comprehensive online Jewish encyclopedia covering everything from anti-Semitism to Zionism (www.JewishVirtual Library.org).

BOARD OF DIRECTORS
Howard Rosenbloom President/Treasurer
Dr. Arthur Bard Vice President/Secretary
Mitchell G. Bard Executive Director

ADVISORY BOARD

Dorothy Bard	Stephen J. Lovell
Newton Becker	Bernice Manocherian
Martin Block	J. George Mitnick
Renee Comet	Sy Opper
Henry Everett z"l	Terry M. Rubinstein
Howard Friedman	Sholom Shefferman
Jerry Gottesman	Irving Shuman
Paula Gottesman	Alan Slifka
Eugene M. Grant	Louis S. Sorell
Andy Lappin	Arnold Wagner
Dr. Brad Levinson	Jane Weitzman

About the Author

Mitchell Bard is the Executive Director of the nonprofit American-Israeli Cooperative Enterprise (AICE) and a foreign policy analyst who lectures frequently on U.S.-Middle East policy. Dr. Bard is also the director of the Jewish Virtual Library. Dr. Bard has appeared on local and national television and radio outlets. His work has been published in academic journals, magazines and major newspapers. He is the author/editor of:

- *The Water's Edge And Beyond: Defining the Limits to Domestic Influence on U.S. Middle East Policy*
- *Partners for Change: How U.S.-Israel Cooperation Can Benefit America*
- *U.S.-Israel Relations: Looking to the Year 2000*
- *Building Bridges: Lessons For America From Novel Israeli Approaches To Promote Coexistence*
- *Forgotten Victims: The Abandonment of Americans in Hitler's Camps*
- *The Complete Idiot's Guide to World War II*
- *The Complete Idiot's Guide to Middle East Conflict*
- *The Complete History of the Holocaust*
- *The Holocaust (Turning Points in World History)*
- *The Nuremberg Trials (At Issue in History)*
- *The Nuremberg Trials (Eyewitness to History)*
- *From Tragedy to Triumph: The Politics behind the Rescue of Ethiopian Jewry*
- *The Complete Idiot's Guide to Understanding the Brain*
- *On One Foot: A Middle East Guide for the Perplexed or How to Respond on Your Way to Class When Your Best Friend Joins an Anti-Israel Protest*
- *The Founding of the State of Israel*
- *1001 Facts Everyone Should Know About Israel* (co-author Moshe Schwartz)

Dr. Bard is also the author/editor of six studies published by AICE:

- *Learning Together: Israeli Innovations in Education that Could Benefit Americans*
- *Experience Counts: Innovative Programs For The Elderly In Israel That Can Benefit Americans*
- *Good Medicine: Israeli Innovations In Health Care That Could Benefit Americans*
- *Breakthrough Dividend: Israeli Innovations In Biotechnology That Could Benefit Americans.*
- *Rewriting History in Textbooks*
- *TENURED OR TENUOUS: Defining the Role of Faculty in Supporting Israel on Campus*

Bard holds a Ph.D. in political science from UCLA and a master's degree in public policy from Berkeley. He received his B.A. in economics from the University of California at Santa Barbara.